DATE DUE

			PRINTED IN U.S.A.

Authors
& Artists
for Young
Adults

ISSN 1040-5682

R

Authors & Artists for Young Adults

VOLUME 26

Thomas McMahon
Editor

GALE

DETROIT · LONDON

Thomas McMahon, *Editor*

Joyce Nakamura, *Managing Editor*
Hal May, *Publisher*

Diane Andreassi, Joanna Brod, Ken Cuthbertson, R. Garcia-Johnson, J. Sydney Jones,
Jon Saari, Gerard J. Senick, Pamela L. Shelton, Tracy J. Sukraw,
Sketchwriters/Contributing Editors

Victoria B. Cariappa, *Research Manager*
Cheryl L. Warnock, *Project Coordinator*
Michael P. LaMeau, Andrew Guy Malonis, Barbara McNeil, *Research Specialists*
Jeffrey D. Daniels, Norma Sawaya, *Research Associates*
Phyllis Blackman, Talitha A. Jean, Corrine A. Stocker, *Research Assistants*

Susan M. Trosky, *Permissions Manager*
Maria L. Franklin, *Permissions Specialist*
Edna Hedblad, Michele Lonoconus, *Permissions Associate*

Mary Beth Trimper, *Production Director*
Carolyn Fischer, *Production Assistant*

Randy Bassett, *Image Database Supervisor*
Gary Leach, *Graphic Artist*
Robert Duncan, Michael Logusz, *Imaging Specialists*
Pamela A. Reed, *Photography Coordinator*

Library of Congress Catalog Card Number 89-641100
ISBN 0-7876-1973-6
ISSN 1040-5682

10 9 8 7 6 5 4 3 2 1

Printed in the United States of America

Authors and Artists for Young Adults

TEEN BOARD

The staff of *Authors and Artists for Young Adults* wishes to thank the following young adult readers for their teen board participation:

Contents

Introduction

Authors and Artists for Young Adults is a reference series designed to serve the needs of middle school, junior high, and high school students interested in creative artists. Originally inspired by the need to bridge the gap between Gale's *Something about the Author,* created for children, and *Contemporary Authors,* intended for older students and adults, *Authors and Artists for Young Adults* has been expanded to cover not only an international scope of authors, but also a wide variety of other artists.

Although the emphasis of the series remains on the writer for young adults, we recognize that these readers have diverse interests covering a wide range of reading levels. The series therefore contains not only those creative artists who are of high interest to young adults, including cartoonists, photographers, music composers, bestselling authors of adult novels, media directors, producers, and performers, but also literary and artistic figures studied in academic curricula, such as influential novelists, playwrights, poets, and painters. The goal of *Authors and Artists for Young Adults* is to present this great diversity of creative artists in a format that is entertaining, informative, and understandable to the young adult reader.

Entry Format

Each volume of *Authors and Artists for Young Adults* will furnish in-depth coverage of twenty to twenty-five authors and artists. The typical entry consists of:

—A detailed biographical section that includes date of birth, marriage, children, education, and addresses.

—A comprehensive bibliography or filmography including publishers, producers, and years.

—Adaptations into other media forms.

—Works in progress.

—A distinctive essay featuring comments on an artist's life, career, artistic intentions, world views, and controversies.

—References for further reading.

—Extensive illustrations, photographs, movie stills, cartoons, book covers, and other relevant visual material.

A cumulative index to featured authors and artists appears in each volume.

Compilation Methods

The editors of *Authors and Artists for Young Adults* make every effort to secure information directly from the authors and artists through personal correspondence and interviews. Sketches on living authors and artists are sent to the biographee for review prior to publication. Any sketches not personally reviewed by biographees or their representatives are marked with an asterisk (*).

Highlights of Forthcoming Volumes

Among the authors and artists planned for future volumes are:

Nathan Aaseng	Victor Hugo	Garth Nix
Scott Adams	Paul Jennings	Naomi Shihab Nye
Lloyd Alexander	Julie Johnston	Robert B. Parker
Sherman Alexie	Sebastian Junger	Trey Parker and Matt Stone
Lillian Jackson Braun	Annette Curtis Klause	Marsha Qualey
Melvin Burgess	Susan Kuklin	Erich Maria Remarque
James Cameron	Jonathan Larson	Elizabeth Ann Scarborough
Daniel Defoe	Ursula Le Guin	Shelley Stoehr
Loren D. Estleman	Sharyn McCrumb	Paul Theroux
Michael Thomas Ford	James A. Michener	Joan D. Vinge
Terry Goodkind	Lensey Namioka	Michael Whelan
Karen Hesse	Larry Niven	Margaret Willey

Contact the Editor

We encourage our readers to examine the entire *AAYA* series. Please write and tell us if we can make AAYA even more helpful to you. Give your comments and suggestions to the editor:

BY MAIL: The Editor, *Authors and Artists for Young Adults*, 27500 Drake Rd., Farmington Hills, MI 48331-3535.

BY TELEPHONE: (800) 347-GALE

Authors & Artists for Young Adults

James W. Bennett

■ Personal

Born in 1942; married, wife's name, Judith; children: Jason. *Education:* Wesleyan University, B.A., 1964; attended graduate school at Illinois State University, 1966. *Hobbies and other interests:* Mythology, photography.

■ Addresses

Home—729 Dale, Normal, IL 61761.

■ Career

Writer. Worked as a teacher of creative writing at a community college until 1976; aide to high school-aged mentally handicapped students, Bloomington, IL, 1983-95. Currently writer-in-residence for Illinois secondary schools.

■ Awards, Honors

"1995's Finest YA Novel," *Voice of Youth Advocates,* 1996, for *The Squared Circle.*

■ Writings

FOR YOUNG ADULTS

I Can Hear the Mourning Dove, Houghton Mifflin, 1990.
Dakota Dream, Scholastic, 1994.
The Squared Circle, Scholastic, 1995.
Blue Star Rapture, Simon & Schuster, 1998.

OTHER

A Quiet Desperation, Nelson (Nashville, TN), 1983.
The Flex of the Thumb, Pin Oak Press (Springfield, IL), 1996.

■ Work in Progress

A novel entitled *Faith Wish.*

■ Sidelights

The broad appeal of the fiction of young adult novelist James W. Bennett comes from a common experience everybody shares: how individuals navigate through institutions. For Bennett, sometimes discomfort can result from the impact institutions have on individual self-definition. All of us, Bennett believes, have had feelings of rebellion against institutional wounds. "I think any book that I have written would take any reader on a trip to answer these questions: 'Who am I within this framework? How do I define myself? How do I establish integrity but know the difference between just rebelling for its own sake and rebelling based on some imperative?',” Bennett explained to Jon Saari in an interview for *Authors and Artists for Young Adults* (*AAYA*).

Of special interest to Bennett are stories of teenagers who have, in his words, “slipped through the cracks.” These marginalized youth often have found themselves hurt by the institutions—schools, hospitals, foster homes—designed to protect them. This irony is a constant in Bennett's books, and his task is, as he said of Grace, the protagonist of *I Can Hear the Mourning Dove*, to “discover the human being inside.” “I would like my readers to recognize that the handicapped are not throwaway people,” Bennett told *Publishers Weekly* interviewer Lynda Brill Comerford. “Within them lies enormous courage and a strong nourishing drive.”

Early Interest in Literature

Bennett recalls from his own high school days that he enjoyed getting a pass from study hall to the library where he would find a work of fiction to read rather than doing homework. There he would spend his time reading works by John R. Tunis, Jack London, Jackson Schultz, and the “Little House on the Prairie” books. He describes himself as both “a very average student” and “not a very average student.” Today, he visits secondary schools regularly under the auspices of a program he designed. Funded by the Illinois state board of education, the writer-in-residence program gives Bennett the chance to talk about his books and writing career. “I like to tell the students I was an underachiever. There are always kids who need to hear that,” Bennett told Saari, continuing, “I do like to be up front with them with the fact that I was not an outstanding student when I was young. I did not achieve a lot as a teenager. I did not mature until later. Teachers like to hear that too. I like to work with basic kids as well as honors kids.”

Bennett's ideas of being a writer date from his undergraduate days in Illinois when he served as an intern at a daily newspaper. Graduate studies in English at Illinois State University led Bennett to a community college teaching job. His career as a writer stems from a profound crisis in his life. “I had been a teacher. . . . In 1974 I went through a severe mental breakdown, was hospitalized, and lost my job. So my whole life is B.B. and A.B.—before the breakdown and after the breakdown.” He continued, “I was just moving around from job to job, from situation to situation. All the while I kept writing and writing and writing. It's a good question what kept me going: perversion or determination. One of the two. In any case I was off the track. I wasn't a teacher anymore; I really didn't have a career,” he explained to Saari.

While hospitalized, Bennett began writing to understand better his own emotions and the feelings of others in similar situations. Acquainted with a nineteen-year-old female patient, Bennett studied her closely to learn all that he could. “She was difficult to approach, but I realized that it was worth the effort to get through her shy exterior,” Bennett told Comerford. What he could not learn through observation, Bennett investigated by such methods as interviewing teenage sales clerks at the local mall. There he gained the knowledge of teen fashion and cosmetic preferences he lacked, heightening the authenticity of his story. Bennett filled notebooks with his research and ideas, letting the novel take shape over a three-year period.

The result of Bennett's efforts was *I Can Hear the Mourning Dove*, published in 1990, the story of Grace Braun, a sixteen-year-old who is confined to a hospital psychiatric unit after a failed suicide attempt. Grace has a history of mental depression, and the recent death of her father has hurt her deeply. While hospitalized, Grace keeps a diary of her thoughts that reveals the depths of her depression. She also meets Luke Wolf, a rebellious teenager, who admits to “pulling the plug” on his paralyzed friend and does not understand the criminality of his act.

Grace copes with life by being overly polite and withdrawing from social situations. Released from the hospital and facing life at a new school, Grace tries to fit in, but when a gang of toughs assaults her, she lands back in the hospital. Through the help of her psychiatrist, her mother, a friend, and Luke, Grace takes the necessary steps to heal herself. “With tenderness and remarkable insight, Bennett identifies the causes and effects of Grace's suffering and reveals her intricate system of defenses,” wrote Diane Roback in *Publishers Weekly*. Stephanie Zvirin added in *Booklist*: “Few novels written for teenagers have dared to probe as deeply into mental illness as this one."

Bennett maneuvered his way through the land mines of the publishing industry with great difficulty. One problem was how to categorize his novels. As he explained in his *AAYA* interview, "I never started out to write books for young adults. That just happened in spite of itself. They are extremely mature books. They are only in the young adult grouping by the skin of their teeth and that primarily because the main characters are young."

Bennett kept writing over a ten-year time span before breaking into the YA market. His first novel

Following the death of her father, a mentally disturbed girl finds friendship with an angry, rebellious boy in Bennett's first novel for young adults.

was rejected by three publishers before Houghton Mifflin decided to buy it. "I did not know people that I sent books. My first editor at Houghton Mifflin was Matilda Welter. I just liked the name Matilda so I picked her out," Bennett admitted to *AAYA*. "Finally Houghton Mifflin published that book as a YA. Pretty much I have been on that same track ever since. This has never gotten easy. I never had the skids greased. I have never had a successful relationship with an agent. I have grinded it out on my own. It is dumb on the one hand to try to bring the market to you; on the other hand, I have never gotten any pleasure from writing material that doesn't really challenge or interest me. So I just kind of swing there back and forth."

In his second YA novel, *Dakota Dream*, Bennett examines the confusion of Floyd Rayfield, whose life since the death of his parents has been a series of foster families and group homes. Fifteen-year-old Floyd is on a quest for his roots, which he is convinced can be found in the Dakota Indian culture. In fact, Ray believes he is a Dakota Indian and learns all he can about Dakota culture and customs. After a dream, Floyd renames himself Charley Black Crow, Dakota Warrior. When he sees himself being pinned in by his group home, Floyd steals a motorcycle and travels 800 miles to the Pine Ridge Reservation. There a Dakota chief takes Ray on a vision quest, accepting him as a Dakota. From Chief Bear-in-cave Floyd learns that he must have courage to face his life and trust for those trying to help him. "Floyd is finely drawn and comes painfully alive for the reader. He no doubt expresses the frustration of countless children caught in our social services system," opined Shirley Carmony in *Voice of Youth Advocates*. According to Deborah Stevenson in *Bulletin of the Center for Children's Books*, "Readers puzzling out their own identities will empathize with self-possessed Floyd, fighting to define himself in a difficult world."

Bennett's Prize Winner

The Squared Circle uses basketball as the means by which Sonny Youngblood learns how the adult world exploits talented athletes. Bennett's novel, like Spike Lee's film *He Got Game*, shows the pressures on a gifted athlete who is manipulated by those who want to benefit from his extraordinary talent. Youngblood, an eighteen-year-old high school senior, uses basketball to escape from his mother's mental breakdown and father's abandonment. Through flashbacks, Bennett fills in the story of Sonny's life—a sadistic high school coach, a girl friend who leaves him, and a mother who ends up catatonic. A high school All-American and prolific point scorer, Sonny, through the influence of his Uncle Seth who receives illegal payments from alumni, chooses to attend Southern Illinois University on an athletic scholarship.

Sonny's presence has an immediate impact on the team's success, as it moves up in the national rankings while Sonny himself emerges as a media celebrity. But not all is right with this picture; Sonny learns that there are strings attached to big-time college sports. He has already realized that campus fraternity life makes some unpleasant social demands through its ingrained hazing and racism, and his game has been affected by lethargy. In a dramatic scene that shows Sonny's emerging understanding of previously invisible forces, he challenges his uncle about the under-the-table payoffs. Then, in what appears to be a deliberate act, Sonny cuts the fingers off his right hand while chopping wood for an art class.

"Bennett pulls no punches. His story is fiction, but his sobering indictment of Division One college athletics is right out of the daily sports pages," wrote Tom S. Hurlburt in *School Library Journal*. In a similar vein, Susan Dove Lempke in *Booklist* concluded: "Bennett can certainly not be accused of romanticizing Sonny's life, and high-school-age readers may be impressed by his tough writing style and openness about sexuality, even as they are intrigued by the moral complexities he presents." "It is difficult to adequately describe the power of this book," exclaimed Dorothy M. Broderick in *Voice of Youth Advocates*. "It is a masterpiece." *The Squared Circle* was named "America's finest YA novel" for 1995 by *Voice of Youth Advocates*.

Blue Star Rapture, Bennett's second book on the corruption of college sports, takes place at a basketball camp, where Tyrone, a six-foot, nine-inch high schooler, is attracting the attention of the college scouts. The novel's narrator, T. J., is Tyrone's best friend, and the street agents (men who receive illegal payments for influencing high school players to sign with college teams) reason one way to Tyrone is through T. J. Meanwhile T. J. has befriended a girl at a nearby bible camp

Caught up in a college recruitment scandal, a star basketball player must come to terms with painful memories in this 1995 work.

who commits suicide, a plot development that permits Bennett to draw a parallel between religious fanaticism and college recruiting methods, as both use undue pressure tactics.

Bennett's next novel, the yet-to-be-published *Faith Wish*, has a character who first appeared in *Blue Star Rapture*. In *Faith Wish*, a teenage girl who is attractive and popular finds herself facing a dilemma right before graduation when she discovers she is pregnant. Her father is an itinerant preacher who heads a bible camp Bennett describes as "so fringe it is nearly a cult." "Sometimes," Bennett commented to *AAYA*, "things will grow wings on their own that you weren't really sure was significant until later. That happened to the girl in this story."

Quality Comes First

Bennett sets high standards for students who read his books, commenting to *AAYA*, "They challenge teenagers who like to read to go to the next level." He sees students taking the books to their English teachers and saying, "'I would like to write an essay about the symbol of the cave in *Dakota Dream*, I would like to write an essay about the symbol of the beauty and the beast in *I Can Hear the Morning Dove.*' They are really books meant to be functional in the classroom. They are very hybrid kinds of books. They are very adult and yet they have teenage characters. They are also young adult. That is part of their problem. They are highly regarded by critics, but they are very difficult to classify."

The creative process cannot be rushed by Bennett, who can take from two to two and a half years to write a novel, which he describes as unusually high for a YA book. "I write slowly. I am a slow painstaking worker. Focus does not come to me easily. I have to reshuffle the outline deck time and time again until I get it the way I like it," he told *AAYA*. "There is a lot of research always. Some of it is library research; some of it is hands-on. Or I go to the place itself. When I wrote *The Squared Circle* I spent several weeks just traveling to small communities in southern Illinois, where the book was set. There is a whole system of Egyptian mythology working its way through the story. The extreme southern tip of Illinois is usually called little Egypt, and there are a lot of Egyptian place names down there, so I wanted that for the setting. I had to do a lot of coffee drinking in local coffee shops, and talking with local editors of these little county newspapers just so I could know that area inside out."

This meticulous approach to writing Bennett combines with an emphasis on literary quality. He wants his readers to experience his novels as works of fiction that succeed or fail on their literary merits. Recent trends in YA literature has left Bennett questioning an emphasis he finds troubling. "I see too many books out there that I would essentially call agenda books. Those are stories that use fiction to deliver a point of view that is either political or socio-political or what have you. I don't think that is what good fiction is. I think good fiction is always character based, puts you in the company of compelling individuals whose story is a journey you want to take. I

If you enjoy the works of James W. Bennett, you may also want to check out the following books and films:

A. E. Cannon, *The Shadow Brothers,* 1990.
Robert Cormier, *The Chocolate War,* 1974.
Kristen D. Randle, *The Only Alien on the Planet,* 1995.
He Got Game, a film by Spike Lee, 1998.

would think that would be one good reason to have a fiction for that age group that is challenging quality fiction and not a vehicle for a point of view."

■ Works Cited

Bennett, James W., interview with Jon Saari for *Authors and Artists for Young Adults,* June 29, 1998.

Brill Comerford, Lynda, interview with James W. Bennett, *Publishers Weekly,* December 21, 1990, p. 15.

Broderick, Dorothy M., review of *The Squared Circle, Voice of Youth Advocates,* February, 1996, p. 379.

Carmony, Shirley, review of *Dakota Dream, Voice of Youth Advocates,* April, 1994, pp. 22-23.

Dove Lempke, Susan, review of *The Squared Circle, Booklist,* December 15, 1995, p. 697.

Hurlburt, Tom S., review of *The Squared Circle, School Library Journal,* December, 1995, p. 128.

Roback, Diane, review of *I Can Hear the Mourning Dove, Publishers Weekly,* July 13, 1990, p. 57.

Stevenson, Deborah, review of *Dakota Dream, Bulletin of the Center for Children's Books,* February, 1994, p. 182.

Zvirin, Stephanie, review of *I Can Hear the Mourning Dove, Booklist,* January 15, 1991, p. 1052.

■ For More Information See

PERIODICALS

Booklist, January 15, 1994, p. 918.
Kirkus Reviews, February 1, 1994, p. 138; March 1, 1998, p. 334.
Publishers Weekly, November 20, 1995, p. 79; March 30, 1998, pp. 83-84.

Voice of Youth Advocates, October, 1990, p. 213.
Wilson Library Bulletin Supplement, September, 1991,
   p. S7.

—Sketch by Jon Saari

Judy Blume

Censorship (council of advisors), PEN, Society of Children's Book Writers and Illustrators (member of board).

■ Awards, Honors

Selection, Best Books for Children list, *New York Times*, 1970, Nene Award, Hawaii Association of School Librarians and the Hawaii Library Association, 1975, Young Hoosier Book Award, Association for Indiana Media Educators, 1976, and North Dakota Children's Choice Award, Children's Round Table of the North Dakota Library Association, 1979, all for *Are You There God? It's Me, Margaret;* Charlie May Swann Children's Book Award, Arkansas Elementary School Council, 1972; Young Readers Choice Award, Pacific Northwest Library Association, and Sequoyah Children's Book Award, Oklahoma Library Association, both 1975; Arizona Young Readers Award, Arizona State University and University of Arizona-Tempe, Massachusetts Children's Book Award, Education Department of Salem State College, Georgia Children's Book Award, College of Education of the University of Georgia, and South Carolina Children's Book Award, South Carolina Association of School Librarians, all 1977, Rhode Island Library Association Award, 1978, North Dakota Children's Choice Award, Children's Round Table of the North Dakota Library Association, and West Australian Young Readers' Book Award, Library Association of Australia, both 1980, United States Army in Europe Kinderbuch Award and Great

■ Personal

Born February 12, 1938, in Elizabeth, NJ; daughter of Rudolph (a dentist) and Esther (Rosenfeld) Sussman; married John M. Blume (an attorney), August 15, 1959 (divorced, 1975); married Thomas Kitchens (a physicist), 1976 (divorced, 1979); married George Cooper (a law professor and writer), June 6, 1987; children: (first marriage) Randy Lee, Lawrence Andrew; stepchildren: Amanda. *Education:* New York University, B.A., 1960. *Religion:* Jewish.

■ Addresses

Home—New York, NY. *Agent*—Harold Ober Associates, Inc., 425 Madison Ave., New York, NY 10017.

■ Career

Writer. Founder of KIDS Fund, 1981. *Member:* Authors Guild (member of council), Authors League of America, National Coalition Against

Stone Face Award, New Hampshire Library Council, both 1981, all for *Tales of a Fourth Grade Nothing;* Selection, Outstanding Books of the Year list, *New York Times,* 1974, Arizona Young Readers Award, Arizona State University and University of Arizona-Tempe, and Young Readers Choice Award, Pacific Northwest Library Association, both 1977, and North Dakota Children's Choice Award, 1983, all for *Blubber;* South Carolina Children's Book Award, South Carolina Association of School Librarians, 1978, for *Otherwise Known as Sheila the Great;* Michigan Young Reader's Award, Michigan Council of Teachers, 1980, for *Freckle Juice.*

Texas Bluebonnet list, 1980, CRABery Award, Michigan Young Reader's Award, Michigan Council of Teachers, and International Reading Association Children's Choice Award, all 1981, First Buckeye Children's Book Award, State Library of Ohio, Nene Award, Hawaii Association of School Librarians and Hawaii Library Association, Sue Hefley Book Award, Louisiana Association of School Libraries, United States Army in Europe Kinderbuch Award, West Australian Young Readers' Book Award, North Dakota Children's Choice Award, Children's Round Table of the North Dakota Library Association, Colorado Children's Book Award, University of Colorado, Georgia Children's Book Award, Tennessee Children's Choice Book Award, Texas Bluebonnet Award, Texas Association of School Librarians and the Children's Round Table, and Utah Children's Book Award, Children's Literature Association of Utah, all 1982, Northern Territory Young Readers' Book Award, Young Readers Choice Award, Pacific Northwest Library Association, Garden State Children's Book Award, New Jersey Library Association, Iowa Children's Choice Award, Iowa Educational Media Association, Arizona Young Readers' Award, Arizona State University and University of Arizona-Tempe, Young Reader Medal, California Reading Association, and Young Hoosier Book Award, all 1983, Land of Enchantment Book Award, New Mexico Library Association and New Mexico State International Reading Association, 1984, Sunshine State Young Reader's Award, Florida Association for Media in Education, 1985, and Children's Choice Award, Mesa, AZ Public Library, 1987, all for *Superfudge.*

Honor Book, 1982, for *Starring Sally J. Freedman as Herself;* CRABery Award, 1982, American Book Award nomination, Dorothy Canfield Fisher Children's Book Award, Vermont Department of Libraries and the Vermont Congress of Parents and Teachers, Buckeye Children's Book Award, Young Reader Medal, California Reading Association, and finalist, American Book Award, Association of American Publishers, all 1983, Blue Spruce Colorado Young Adult Book Award, Colorado Library Association, and Iowa Children's Choice Award, Iowa Educational Media Association, both 1985, all for *Tiger Eyes;* selection, Children's Books of the Year, Child Study Association of America, 1985, for *The Pain and the Great One;* selection, Best Books for Young Adults, American Library Association, 1986, for *Letters to Judy;* California Young Reader Medal, Iowa Children's Choice Award, Nene Award from the Children of Hawaii, Nevada Young Readers Award, Sunshine State Young Reader's Choice Award, Pennsylvania Young Reader's Award, Michigan Readers Choice Award, all 1993, for *Fudge-a-Mania;* Parent's Choice Award, 1993, for *Here's to You, Rachel Robinson.*

Golden Archer Award, 1974; Today's Woman Award, Council of Cerebral Palsy Auxiliary, Nassau County, 1981; Outstanding Mother Award, 1982; Eleanor Roosevelt Humanitarian Award, Favorite Author—Children's Choice Award, Milner Award, Friends of the Atlanta Public Library, for children's favorite living author, and Jeremiah Ludington Memorial Award, all 1983; Carl Sandburg Freedom to Read Award, Chicago Public Library, 1984; Civil Liberties Award, Atlanta American Civil Liberties Union, and John Rock Award, Center for Population Options, Los Angeles, both 1986; D.H.L., Kean College, 1987; Excellence in the Field of Literature Award, New Jersey Education Association, 1987; South Australian Youth Media Award for Best Author, South Australian Association for Media Education, 1988; Most Admired Author, Heroes of Young America Poll, 1989; National Hero Award, Big Brothers/Big Sisters, 1992; Dean's Award, Columbian University College of Physicians and Surgeons, 1993; Margaret A. Edwards Award for Outstanding Literature for Young Adults, American Library Association, 1996, for lifetime achievement writing for teens.

■ Writings

JUVENILE FICTION

The One in the Middle Is The Green Kangaroo (picture book), illustrated by Lois Axeman, Reilly & Lee, 1969, revised edition, Bradbury, 1981, new revised edition with new illustrations, 1991, illustrated by Irene Trivas, Bantam Doubleday Dell, 1992.

Iggie's House, Bradbury, 1970.

Are You There God? It's Me Margaret, Bradbury, 1970.

Then Again, Maybe I Won't, Bradbury, 1971.

Freckle Juice, illustrated by Sonia O. Lisker, Four Winds, 1971.

Tales of a Fourth Grade Nothing, Dutton, 1972.

Otherwise Known as Sheila the Great, Dutton, 1972.

It's Not the End of the World, Bradbury, 1972.

Deenie, Bradbury, 1973.

Blubber, Bradbury, 1974.

Starring Sally J. Freedman as Herself, Bradbury, 1977.

Superfudge, Dutton, 1980.

Tiger Eyes, Bradbury, 1981.

The Pain and the Great One (picture book), illustrated by Irene Trivas, Bradbury, 1984.

Just as Long as We're Together, Orchard, 1987.

Fudge-a-Mania, Dutton, 1990.

Here's to You, Rachel Robinson, Orchard, 1993, Bantam Doubleday Dell, 1995.

OTHER

Forever . . . (young adult novel), Bradbury, 1975.

Wifey (adult novel), Putnam, 1977.

The Judy Blume Diary: The Place to Put Your Own Feelings, Dell, 1981.

Smart Women (adult novel), Putnam, 1984.

Letters to Judy: What Your Kids Wish They Could Tell You (nonfiction), Putnam, 1986.

The Judy Blume Memory Book, Dell, 1988.

(And producer with Lawrence Blume) *Otherwise Known as Sheila the Great* (screenplay adapted from her novel), Barr Films, 1989.

Summer Sisters (adult novel), Delacorte, 1998.

Contributor to *Free to Be . . . You and Me*, 1974, and *Once Upon a Time . . .*, Putnam, 1986. Blume's works have been translated into fourteen languages, including German, Scandinavian, French, Dutch, Hebrew, Spanish, and Japanese. Some of Blume's works are held in the Kerlan Collection, University of Minnesota.

■ Adaptations

Forever . . . was adapted as a television film broadcast by CBS-TV, February 6, 1978; *Blubber, Freckle Juice,* and *Superfudge,* filmstrips with cassettes and teachers' guides, were produced by Pied Piper in 1984; *Freckle Juice* was adapted as an animated film by Barr Films in 1987; *Fudge,* a children's television series, was broadcast on ABC-TV, 1994-96, and on CBS-TV, 1997; *Tales of a Fourth Grade Nothing* was adapted as a play. *Wifey* was produced by Audio Book in 1979. Listening Library produced various Blume books for audio with teachers' guides entitled: *Freckle Juice,* 1982; *Blubber,* 1983; *The One in the Middle Is the Green Kangaroo,* 1983; *Deenie,* 1983. Listening Library adapted Blume books for audio entitled: *Are You There God? It's Me, Margaret,* 1985; *It's Not the End of the World,* 1985; *The Pain and the Great One,* 1985. Blume books adapted for audio by Ingram include: *Superfudge,* 1992; *Fudge-A-Mania,* 1993; *Tales of a 4th Grade Nothing,* 1996; *Are You There God? It's Me, Margaret,* 1997; *Sheila the Great,* 1997.

■ Overview

Whether they find them in the library and read them with their parents, or borrow them from friends and secretly read them alone, young people love Judy Blume books. Millions and millions of sales, television and film adaptations, and numerous awards from organizations across the United States demonstrate her popularity. Some critics argue that the success of Blume's work is due to the discussion of sex and sexuality in her books for young adults. A few of these contain explicit sex scenes, discuss the physical changes that take place during adolescence, or feature language that would not be allowed in classrooms. Such behavior—thinking about sex, having sexual relations, using profane language—happens in Blume's world. Instead of punishing her characters for their actions in her books, Blume communicates that many of these thoughts and behaviors are normal. At the same time, Blume provides information that can help readers evaluate their own beliefs and actions.

Various individuals and organizations have condemned Blume's work for its treatment of sexuality and language. Many of them have fought to keep some of her books out of reach of children, off the shelves of public and school libraries. Rather than sitting silently by as her books and others are censored, Blume has lent her voice to the work of civil liberties organizations. A number of critics have also come to her defense. Since the mid-1980s, they have pointed out that her books are funny, her narrators often speak directly to the reader, her characters communicate with one another realistically, and she leaves solutions up to her characters. Blume's books, some say, are about growing up and learning to make choices. "Sex is the least of her concerns," observed Mark Oppenheimer in the *New York Times Book Review*. Although the debate about Blume's appeal and appropriateness continues, one thing is certain. As Alice Phoebe Naylor and Carol Wintercorn, writing in the *Dictionary of Literary Biography (DLB)*, put it, Blume "revolutionized realistic fiction for children." In the words of Oppenheimer, Blume "opened" the flood gates in children's fiction to candid discussions of the many problems children face today.

Blume was born in New Jersey in 1938. Her mother loved to read and spent her afternoons with books. Her father, a dentist, built a special relationship with Blume. As a child, Blume read books, listened to the radio, danced, and enjoyed a comfortable family setting. Still, by the time she was a teenager, Blume began to feel as though she could not tell her parents everything about her life, and she had many unanswered questions. Blume was an excellent student, and when she reached high school, she was busy in extracurricular efforts from chorus to the school newspaper. She was accepted to Boston University, but became ill and transferred to New York University.

Family Life Blossoms

During her sophomore year in college, Blume fell in love with a lawyer, John Blume, and they were married in 1959. Blume was pregnant with her first child when she graduated from college, and her daughter Randy Lee was born in 1961. A son, Lawrence Andrew, followed two years later. Blume stayed at home to care for her husband and children, but she was not satisfied with this domestic role. She attempted to exercise her creativity in various ways. As John Neary explained in *People*, Blume tried to become a songwriter, and then she made banners for children's bedrooms. Next, she began to write. The first stories and books Blume submitted to publishers were rejected, but Blume persisted.

When she found a brochure from New York University offering a course on writing for children and teenagers, Blume enrolled. As part of her coursework, she wrote what would become her

first published work, *The One in the Middle Is the Green Kangaroo*, a picture book which features a second-grade child who laments his position between his older and younger siblings. Blume took the course the next semester as well, and wrote the draft for *Iggie's House*, a story that addresses racial prejudice that became Blume's second book. Around the same time, Blume was notified that *The One in the Middle is the Green Kangaroo* had been accepted for publication. After more than two years of rejections, Blume was ecstatic.

Blume's first two books were relatively well received. Zena Sutherland, in *Bulletin of the Center for Children's Books*, commented that *The One in the Middle is the Green Kangaroo* "does treat a real

When her family moves, eleven-year-old Margaret makes new discoveries about growing up, friendship, and religion in Blume's award-winning 1970 novel.

problem in a believable way, and as a story it is satisfying." Blume's third book, however, received mixed reviews before it went on to become a favorite of pre-adolescent girls. *Are You There God? It's Me, Margaret*, published in 1970, is based on Blume's own experiences as an adolescent. The novel begins as Margaret Simon's family moves to suburban New Jersey; Margaret must make new friends, and she begins to worry about getting her period and wearing a bra. Margaret is also concerned about religion. Born to a non-practicing Christian mother and Jewish father, Margaret is not sure how she wants to worship. She talks to God, makes bargains with him, and visits houses of worship.

Although some of those who read and reviewed Blume's first novel for young adults praised its humor and realistic dialogue, the treatment of menstruation in the book was criticized for various reasons. George W. Arthur, writing in *Book Window,* commented that the "very funny book" is marred by the "excessive, almost obsessive, concern with a girl's period." Ann Evans, writing in the *Times Literary Supplement*, did not find the book funny. The work, according to her, focuses too much on the body, and "Margaret's private talks with God are insufferably self-conscious and arch." A *Kirkus Reviews* critic remarked, "there's danger in the preoccupation with the physical signs of puberty. . . ."

Blume's next book, *Then Again, Maybe I Won't*, published in 1971, features a male protagonist, Vic. Like Margaret, Vic has just moved to a new town and is worried about the changes taking place in his body. His problems center around the way his family has changed since his father became wealthy, and his own uncontrollable erections. Vic also worries about wet dreams. Although it did not prove to be as popular as *Are You There God? It's Me, Margaret, Then Again, Maybe I Won't* received similar criticism for its explicit treatment of sexuality.

Books Take New Slant

Blume's next two books, for younger readers, are realistic but contain no mention of the adolescent concerns taken up in *Are You There God? It's Me, Margaret* and *Then Again, Maybe I Won't*. *Freckle Juice* (1971) features Andrew, a second grader envious of a classmate's freckles. Another classmate

In this 1973 work, Deenie's biggest concern is whether to become a model . . . until she is diagnosed with scoliosis.

sells him a formula for freckle juice that does not give him freckles, so he makes do with a magic marker. According to Alice Adkins in *School Library Journal*, the characters in the book "are amusingly depicted." *Tales of a Fourth Grade Nothing* (1972) introduces Manhattanite Peter Warren Hatcher and his little brother Fudge. In the book's most memorable scene, Peter learns that his brother Fudge has swallowed his pet turtle. This book won numerous awards from organizations throughout the United States and continues to be a favorite with children. As Mark Oppenheimer noted in the *New York Times Book Review*, by 1996, it "had sold over six million copies."

Two of Blume's books for older readers, both published in 1972, followed. In *Otherwise Known as Sheila the Great,* an insecure girl at summer camp will not allow people to view her as ordinary, or to learn that she is afraid of swimming and dogs. By the end of the book, however, Sheila Tubman begins to reveal her true self. According to Naylor and Wintercorn in *DLB,* Blume wrote *It's Not the End of the World* after her children asked her if she and her husband would ever divorce. Karen Newman, the book's twelve-year-old protagonist, learns to cope with her parents' separation and impending divorce.

With *Deenie* (1973) and *Blubber* (1974), Blume once again stirred critics; *Deenie* contained a frank discussion of masturbation, and *Blubber,* a tale about cruelty, includes some profanity. In *Deenie,* a beautiful thirteen-year-old girl whose mother wants her to become a model is shocked when she is diagnosed with scoliosis. She fears that her habit of touching herself at night is the cause, until she learns that her habit is called masturbation, and it has nothing to do with her disease. As Naylor and Wintercorn explained in *DLB,* Blume wrote this book "after meeting a child with scoliosis" and after conducting research on the disease. *School Library Journal* critic Melinda Schroeder found *Deenie* "compelling."

Blubber, based on actual events that occurred in Blume's daughter's classroom, is presented from the perspective of a fifth-grade girl, Jill, who takes part in the humiliation of Linda, a classmate derisively nicknamed "Blubber." At first, Jill taunts the overweight Linda, but by the end of the book, Jill finds herself ostracized. A critic for *Booklist* believed that Jill does not really learn a lesson from her behavior; "she simply finds out that when the tables are turned, it hurts. . . ." Zena Sutherland of *Bulletin of the Center for Children's Books* noted the work's "good characterization and dialogue."

Forever . . ., the story of a young woman's first sexual relationship, alarmed some readers. As she explained to Linda Bird Francke and Lisa Whitman in *Newsweek,* Blume wrote the book at the request of her daughter, who wanted to read about a young woman who had sex but was not punished because of it. Katherine, the narrator and protagonist of *Forever . . .,* meets Michael at a New Year's Eve party and falls in love. The couple's relationship progresses through various stages, and they have intercourse. Although Katherine believes that she and Michael will be together forever, when her parents send her away to camp she is attracted to another man and decides to end her relationship with Michael.

Some critics expressed concern that *Forever . . .* would lead impressionable young readers to think and act promiscuously. "The young tend to follow the life-style of their peers: will Katherine and Michael's affair help to impose yet another imprimatur on casual sex?" wondered G. Bott in *Junior Bookshelf.* In 1980, in *The Marble in the Water,* David Rees wrote, "What sort of picture would a being from another planet form of teenage and pre-teenage America were he able to read *Are You There, God? It's Me, Margaret* and *Forever?* He would imagine that youth was obsessed with bras, period pains, deodorants, orgasms, and family planning. . . . Adolescents do of course have period pains and worry about the size of their breasts or penises; they fall in love and some of them sleep together. There should obviously be a place for all these concerns in teenage novels; but to write about them, as Judy Blume does, to the exclusion of everything else is doing youth a great disservice."

John Gough re-evaluated *Forever . . .* in 1985 in *The Use of English.* Asserting that "popularity infuriates critics," he decided to "reconsider the case against Blume by looking at . . . the book that has attracted the most violent criticism." He stated, "It is a major achievement that Blume presents the heroine as the one who takes the initiative, the one whose heart changes." He argued that the characters "are not cut-out stereotypes. They are changeable, ambivalent and at times self-contradictory. They are human." He added, "Simple words and sentences, real-sounding dialogue, can be very effective, and at times very funny." Gough concluded that if "critical adults remember in their hearts the joy, pain, hope and anguish of teenage years, their view of *Forever . . .* might be less jaundiced. They might then be able to see the real literary qualities" of the book.

In the late 1970s the author's body of work came under scrutiny. Writing in *The Lion and the Unicorn,* R. A. Siegal explained that Blume's works provide "easy, rapid reading," adding that Blume "is a careful observer" and her "most characteristic technique and the key to her success is the first person narrative." Still, commented Siegal,

Blume's "books are impoverished because she fails to establish a vital relationship between place and character . . . the quest turns inward. . . . This may be good training for life in narcissistic, self-absorbed, suburban America but, in the long run, it is poor nourishment for the imagination of children." Similarly, Naomi Decter remarked in *Commentary:* "The consistent and overriding message of her books . . . is that the proper focus of one's curiosity and concern is oneself. Everywhere Miss Blume garners high praise for her 'respectful,' 'realistic,' and 'accurate' depiction of children's preoccupation with themselves."

A young woman's first sexual experience is the subject of Blume's groundbreaking, controversial 1975 novel.

Still other reviewers found fault with Blume's books for being too traditional. A critic for *Interracial Books for Children Bulletin* remarked that Blume demonstrated a lack of feminism. "With the exception of *Deenie,* her perspective seems to be virtually untouched by the women's movement . . . not one [of her girl characters] fights the feminist fight. . . . Sex roles are rarely questioned." The critic noted that the "class setting of Blume's books is usually middle and mostly suburban" and that "Blume's treatment of ethnic and racial issues is equally wanting and limited in scope."

Blume's marriage to her first husband ended in 1975. She met a physicist, Thomas Kitchen, and married him in 1976. Along with Blume's children, they lived in London, England, and then Santa Fe, New Mexico. Blume's most autobiographical book, *Starring Sally J. Freedman as Herself,* appeared in 1977, as did her first novel for adults, *Wifey.* *Starring Sally J. Freedman as Herself* is set in Florida in the 1940s. Ten-year-old Sally is convinced that Adolf Hitler is hiding in her apartment building. Critics commented on a dearth of plot, and as Brigitte Weeks wrote in the *Washington Post Book World,* Sally is not brought "close to the reader." Still, wrote M. Hobbs in *Junior Bookshelf,* the "story moves at a good pace with lively humour." Although it was written for a mature audience, *Wifey* troubled those who feared that young people would read anything written by Blume. *Wifey,* the story of a woman who is unhappy in her marriage and indulges in extramarital affairs, contains explicit sexual scenes.

Sales Climb Despite Critics

Despite the opinions of critics, teachers, librarians, and parents, young readers were enchanted with Blume and her work. "While the storm rages around them, Blume and her fans enjoy the quiet warmth of good communication," Judith M. Goldberger observed in *Newsletter on Intellectual Freedom.* "Many of today's children have found a source of learning in Judy Blume. . . . Her voice is clear to them. She tells them there is a time at which each person must decide things for him or herself. In that sense, she carries an ageless message about the sanctity of individual rights."

Blume herself was pleased that she had made young readers happy. "I knew intuitively what kids wanted to know," Blume told Neary in *People*

In this finalist for the 1983 American Book Award, a fifteen-year-old must learn to cope when her father is killed in a robbery.

Blume continued the story begun in *Tales of a Fourth Grade Nothing* with *Superfudge*. In this book, the Hatcher family has moved to Princeton, New Jersey, and Fudge is ready to enter kindergarten. Fudge is still a problem for Peter: he keeps Peter out of the bathroom, sticks stamps all over the baby, and kicks his kindergarten teacher. "No one knows the byways of the under-twelves better than Blume," commented Pamela D. Pollack in *School Library Journal.* Brigitte Weeks of the *Washington Post Book World* remarked that the book demonstrates Blume's ability to create "good clean fun," adding, "Blume's books for younger readers are funny . . . important to children is the clear knowledge that Blume is on their team."

Tiger Eyes, a young adult novel, appeared the following year. In a departure from Blume's other works, *Tiger Eyes* takes up issues of violence, grief, growth, and renewal. Davey's father is killed in his convenience store by robbers, and he dies in her arms. Gradually Davey comes to terms with her father's death and helps her mother cope as well. She also meets a young Hispanic college student, Wolf, and they slowly develop a nurturing relationship. Margaret Mason of the *Washington Post Book World* praised Blume's insight and character development: "even if your father hasn't been murdered, even if you're no longer 15, and even if you'd rather think about something else, she puts you inside that girl . . . at once achingly vulnerable, funny and tough." According to Jean Fritz in the *New York Times Book Review,* the novel is "masterly" and "not to be dismissed as simply another treatment of death and violence." Robert Lipsyte wrote in the *Nation* that *Tiger Eyes* is Blume's "finest book—ambitious, absorbing, smoothly written, emotionally engaging and subtly political. It is also a lesson on how the conventions of a genre can best be put to use."

in 1978, "because I remembered what I wanted to know. I think I write most about sexuality because it was uppermost in my mind when I was a kid: the need to know, and not knowing how to find out." "I have this gift, this memory," she explained to Sybil Steinberg in a *Publishers Weekly* interview. "I write about what I know is true of kids going through those same stages." She stated, "My responsibility to be honest with my readers is my strongest motivation." Blume was also proud of her independence. "I do very well," she told *Newsweek.* "I support myself. I support my children."

After the publication of *Tiger Eyes*, Blume revealed that she had taken out a paragraph discussing masturbation, and that she rewrote scenes using "inflammatory" language to prevent censorship. "I am finding more editorial resistance today to language and sexuality in books for young people than I did when I began to publish, eleven years ago," she told Norma Klein in *Top of the News.* Blume lamented the situation. "This climate of fear is contagious and dangerous." Blume served as a member of civil liberties organizations, and she won awards for her contribution to the civil liberties movement.

If you enjoy the works of Judy Blume, you may also want to check out the following books and films:

James W. Bennett, *I Can Hear the Mourning Dove*, 1990.
Caroline B. Cooney, *Don't Blame the Music*, 1986.
Mary Downing Hahn, *The Wind Blows Backward*, 1993.
The Man in the Moon, starring Reese Witherspoon, Miramax, 1991.

Since she began her career in the early 1970s, thousands of children have written to Blume to ask her questions or to discuss feelings when they felt they could not communicate with their parents. *Letters to Judy: What Your Kids Wish They Could Tell You* is a presentation of some of these heartfelt letters arranged by subject, from sex and drugs to mental illness and divorce. Blume comments on the letters, sometimes addressing her remarks to children and other times to adult parents or teachers. Phyllis Theroux remarked in *Washington Post Book World*, "the children Blume introduces are such radiantly candid and innocent human beings that we cannot help but look at our own children with a deeper understanding and compassion." Elizabeth McCardell, in *Reading Time*, found that she could not put the book down; she called it "disturbing, moving" and "sometimes funny." Blume contributed all the proceeds gained from this book to The Kids Fund.

Blume remarried in 1987 (she had divorced her second husband in 1979) to a law professor and writer. That same year, she also introduced three girls, Stephanie, Alison, and Rachel, in *Just As Long As We're Together*. The focus in this book is on seventh-grader Stephanie, her family, and her friends. Stephanie's father and mother are separated, but she thinks her father is just away on business. When she learns the truth, she begins to gain weight. At the same time, she and her best friend Rachel are having trouble getting along as Stephanie develops a relationship with another girl, Alison. According to Josephine Humphreys in the *New York Times Book Review*, the novel seems "like a Blume medley, with strains of earlier stories wound together."

■ Update

During the 1980s, with her appeal to young people as strong as ever, some critics pointed out that skill and empathy, not just discussions of sex, had won Blume fans. John Gough asserted in the *School Librarian* that Blume "is an under-rated writer, critically abused or neglected, who deserves close attention and stands up to critical scrutiny very well." He continued, "Judy Blume is concerned to describe characters surviving, finding themselves, growing in understanding, coming to terms with life." Faith McNulty wrote in the *New Yorker* that Blume "won her audience through honest work, superior craftsmanship, and a talent for recreating an evanescent period of life—the years from nine to thirteen. . . . I find much in Blume to be thankful for."

To the delight of her many fans, Blume wrote two sequels in the early 1990s. *Fudge-a-Mania* furthers the adventures of Peter Hatcher and his little brother. *Here's To You, Rachel Robinson*, published in 1993, is the sequel to *Just As Long As We're Together*. Rachel is a perfect student, obsessed with being the best. Rachel's seventh-grade year is difficult now that her brother Charles, expelled from a boarding school, is home. According to a *Publishers Weekly* critic, Blume's characters are "multidimensional," "believable," and "complex." "Blume remains one of the best practitioners of the genre—thoughtful . . . funny, and empathetic," commented Roger Sutton in *Bulletin of the Center for Children's Books*.

In the late 1990s, many of Blume's first young fans, along with her own children, were adults. (Randy Lee, her daughter, had begun a career as a commercial airline pilot, and her son was a filmmaker—he and Blume collaborated to write and produce a screenplay, *Otherwise Known as Sheila the Great*.) Living in New York, Blume wrote another novel for adults: *Summer Sisters* (1998) takes a pair of best friends from sixth grade to high school, college, and life as young adults. Some of Blume's older works, however, were still selling well. Indeed, books like *Tales of a Fourth-Grade Nothing* had become popular classics, read by the children of earlier Blume fans.

In 1996, the Young Adult Library Services Association of the American Library Association gave Blume the Margaret A. Edwards Award for Outstanding Literature for Young Adults, awarded to an author for lifetime achievement in writing for teenagers. While "Judy Blume's willingness to recognize children's serious thoughts about sex, religion and class made her a figure of controversy 25 years ago," as Mark Oppenheimer commented in the *New York Times Book Review,* "Blume has become an icon, as famous for those who tried to cleanse libraries of her books as for the books themselves."

■ Works Cited

Adkins, Alice, review of *Freckle Juice, School Library Journal,* January, 1972, p. 50.

Review of *Are You There, God? It's Me, Margaret, Kirkus Reviews,* October 1, 1970, p. 1093.

Arthur, George W., review of *Are You There, God? It's Me, Margaret, Book Window,* Summer, 1978.

Review of *Blubber, Booklist,* January 1, 1975.

Bott, G., review of *Forever . . ., Junior Bookshelf,* February, 1977, p. 49.

Decter, Naomi, "Judy Blume's Children," *Commentary,* March, 1980, pp. 65-67.

Evans, Ann, review of *Are You There, God? It's Me, Margaret, Times Literary Supplement,* April 7, 1978.

Francke, Linda Bird, with Lisa Whitman, "Growing Up With Judy," *Newsweek,* October 8, 1978, pp. 99-102.

Fritz, Jean, "The Heroine Finds a Way," *New York Times Book Review,* November 15, 1981, pp. 56, 58.

Goldberger, Judith M., "Judy Blume: Target of the Censor," *Newsletter on Intellectual Freedom,* May, 1981, pp. 57, 61.

Gough, John, "Reconsidering Judy Blume's Young Adult Novel 'Forever . . .'," *The Use of English,* Spring, 1985, pp. 29-36.

Gough, John, "Growth, Survival and Style in the Novels of Judy Blume," *School Librarian,* May, 1987, pp. 100-106.

Review of *Here's To You, Rachel Robinson, Publishers Weekly,* August 16, 1993, p. 105.

Hobbs, M., review of *Starring Sally J. Freedman as Herself, Junior Bookshelf,* August, 1983, pp. 169-70.

Humphreys, Josephine, "Fat, 13 and Basically O.K.," *New York Times Book Review,* November 8, 1987, p. 33.

Klein, Norma, "Some Thoughts on Censorship: An Author Symposium," *Top of the News,* Winter, 1983, pp. 137-53.

Lipsyte, Robert, "A Bridge of Words," *Nation,* November 21, 1981, pp. 551-53.

Mason, Margaret, "Judy Blume: Growing Up with Grief," *Washington Post Book World,* September 13, 1981, pp. 9-10.

McCardell, Elizabeth, review of *Letters to Judy, Reading Time,* Number 3, 1987, pp. 68-69.

McNulty, Faith, "Children's Books for Christmas," *New Yorker,* December 5, 1983, pp. 198, 201.

Naylor, Alice Phoebe, and Carol Wintercorn, "Judy Blume," *Dictionary of Literary Biography,* Volume 52: *American Writers for Children Since 1960: Fiction,* Gale, 1986, pp. 30-38.

Neary, John, "The 'Jacqueline Susann of Kids' Books,' Judy Blume, Grows Up With an Adult Novel," *People,* October 16, 1978, pp. 47-54.

"Old Values Surface in Blume Country," *Interracial Books for Children Bulletin,* Number 5, 1977.

Oppenheimer, Mark, "Why Judy Blume Endures," *New York Times Book Review,* November 16, 1997.

Pollack, Pamela D., review of *Superfudge, School Library Journal,* August, 1980, pp. 60-61.

Rees, David, "Not Even for a One-Night Stand," *The Marble in the Water: Essays on Contemporary Writers of Fiction for Children and Young Adults,* 1980, pp. 173-84.

Schroeder, Melinda, review of *Deenie, School Library Journal,* May, 1974, p. 53.

Siegal, R. A., "Are You There, God? It's Me, Me, Me!: Judy Blume's Self-Absorbed Narrators," *The Lion and the Unicorn,* Fall, 1978, pp. 72-77.

Steinberg, Sybil, "Judy Blume," *Publishers Weekly,* April 17, 1978, pp. 6-7.

Sutherland, Zena, review of *The One in the Middle Is the Green Kangaroo, Bulletin of the Center for Children's Books,* April, 1970, p. 125.

Sutherland, Zena, review of *Blubber, Bulletin of the Center for Children's Books,* May, 1975, p. 142.

Sutton, Roger, review of *Here's To You, Rachel Robinson, Bulletin of the Center for Children's Books,* October, 1993, p. 39.

Theroux, Phyllis, "Judy Blume Listens to Her Young Readers," *Washington Post Book World,* April 27, 1986, pp. 3-4.

Weeks, Brigitte, review of *Starring Sally J. Freedman as Herself, Washington Post Book World,* August 14, 1977, p. F4.

Weeks, Brigitte, "The Return of Peter Hatcher," *Washington Post Book World,* November 9, 1980.

■ For More Information See

BOOKS

Lee, Betsy, *Judy Blume's Story,* Dillon, 1981.

Weidt, Maryann, *Presenting Judy Blume*, Twayne, 1989.
Wheeler, Jill C., *Judy Blume*, Abdo & Daughters, 1996.

PERIODICALS

Harper's Bazaar, July, 1984, p. 44.
Horn Book, January-February, 1985, p. 85.
Kirkus Reviews, September 1, 1973, p. 965; March 15, 1998.
NEA Today, October, 1984, p. 10.
New York Times Book Review, July 19, 1998, p. 18.
New York Times Magazine, December 3, 1978.
People Weekly, March 19, 1984, p. 38.
Psychology Today, October, 1986, p. 80.
Teen Magazine, October, 1982, p. 30.
Time, August 23, 1982, pp. 65-66.
Voice of Youth Advocates, December, 1993, p. 287.
Writer's Digest, January 1, 1980, pp. 18-24.*

—Sketch by R. Garcia-Johnson

Jorge Luis Borges

numerous universities in the United States and throughout the world, including University of Texas, 1961-62, University of Oklahoma, 1969; University of New Hampshire, 1972, and Dickinson College, 1983; Harvard University, Cambridge, MA, Charles Eliot Norton Professor of Poetry, 1967-68. Editor at various Argentine journals and magazines.

■ Personal

Also wrote under pseudonym Francisco Bustos and joint pseudonyms Honorio Bustos Domecq, B. Lynch Davis, and B. Suarez Lynch; born August 24, 1899, in Buenos Aires, Argentina; died of liver cancer, June 14, 1986, in Geneva, Switzerland; buried in Plainpalais, Geneva, Switzerland; son of Jorge Guillermo Borges (a lawyer, teacher, and writer) and Leonor Suarez (a translator; maiden name, Acevedo); married Elsa Astete Millan, September 21, 1967 (divorced, 1970); married Maria Kodama, April 26, 1986. *Education:* Collége Calvin, Geneva, Switzerland, 1918; Cambridge University.

■ Career

Writer. Miguel Cane branch library, Buenos Aires, Argentina, municipal librarian, 1937-46; National Library, Buenos Aires, director, 1955-73. Teacher of English literature at several private institutions and lecturer in Argentina and Uruguay, 1946-55; University of Buenos Aires, Buenos Aires, professor of English and North American literature, beginning 1956. Visiting professor or guest lecturer at

■ Awards, Honors

Buenos Aires Municipal Literary Prize, 1928, for *El idioma de los argentinos;* Gran Premio de Honor, Argentine Writers Society, 1945, for *Ficciones, 1935-44;* Gran Premio Nacional de la Literatura (Argentina), 1957, for *El Aleph;* Prix Formentor (shared with Samuel Beckett), International Congress of Publishers, 1961; named as an honorary fellow, Modern Language Association of America, 1961; Commandeur de l'Ordre des Lettres et des Arts (France), 1962; named as an honorary fellow, American Association of Teachers of Spanish and Portuguese, 1965; Ingram Merrill Foundation Award, 1966; Matarazzo Sobrinho Inter-American Literary Prize, Bienal Foundation, 1970; nominated for Neustadt International Prize for Literature, *World Literature Today* and University of Oklahoma, 1970, 1984, and 1986; Jerusalem Prize, 1971; named an honorary member, American Academy of Arts and Letters and National Institute of Arts and Letters, 1971; Alfonso Reyes Prize (Mexico), 1973; Gran Cruz del Orden al merito Bernardo O'Higgins from Government of Chile, 1976, Gold Medal From French Academy, Order of Merit, Federal Republic of Germany, and Icelandic Falcon Cross, all 1979; Miguel de Cervantes Award (Spain) and Balzan Prize (Italy), both 1980; Ollin Yoliztli Prize (Mexico), 1981; T.S. Eliot Award for Creative Writing, Ingersoll Foundation and Rockford Institute, 1983; Gold Medal of Menendez Pelayo University (Spain), La Gran Cruz de la Orden Alfonso X, el Sabio (Spain), and Legion d'Honneur (France), all 1983; Knight of the British Empire. Recipient of honorary degrees from numerous colleges and universities, including University of Cuyo (Argentina), 1956, University of the Andes (Colombia), 1963, Oxford University, 1970, University of Jerusalem, 1971, Columbia University, 1971, Michigan State University, 1972, and Harvard University, 1981.

■ Writings

SHORT STORIES

Historia universal de la infamia, Tor (Buenos Aires), 1935, revised edition published as *Obras completas*, Volume 3, Emecé, 1964, translation by di Giovanni published as *A Universal History of Infamy*, Dutton, 1972.

El jardín de senderos que se bifurcan (also see below; titled means "Garden of the Forking Paths"), Sur, 1941.

(With Adolofo Bioy Casares, under joint pseudonym H. Bustos Domecq) *Seis problemas para Isidro Parodi*, Sur, 1942, translation by di Giovanni published under authors' real names as *Six Problems for Don Isidro Parodi*, Dutton, 1983.

Ficciones, 1935-44 (includes *El jardin de senderos que se bifurcan*), Sur, 1944, revised edition published as *Obras completas*, Volume 5, Emecé, 1956, reprinted, with English introduction and notes by Grodon Brotherson and Peter Humle, Harrap, 1976, translation by Anthony Kerrigan and others published as *Ficciones*, edited and with an introduction by Kerrigan, Grove, 1962 (published in England as *Fictions*, John Calder, 1965), reprinted, Limited Editions Club (New York), 1984.

(With Bioy Casares, under joint pseudonym H. Bustos Domecq) *Dos fantasías memorables*, Oportet & Haereses, 1946, reprinted under authors' real names with notes and bibliography by Horacio Jorge Becco, Edicom (Buenos Aires), 1971.

El Aleph, Losada, 1949, revised edition, 1952, published as *Obras completas*, Volume 7, Emecé, 1956, translation and revision by di Giovanni in collaboration with Borges published as *The Aleph and Other Stories, 1933-1969*, Dutton, 1970.

(With Luisa Mercedes Levinson) *La hermana de Eloísa* (title means "Eloisa's Sister"), Ene (Buenos Aires), 1955.

(With Bioy Casares) *Crónicas de Bustos Domecq*, Losada, 1967, translation by di Giovanni published as *Chronicles of Bustos Domecq*, Dutton, 1976.

El informe de Brodie, Emecé, 1970, translation by di Giovanni in collaboration with Borges published as *Dr. Brodie's Report*, Dutton, 1971.

El matrero, Edicom, 1970.

El congreso, El Archibrazo, 1971, translation by di Giovanni in collaboration with Borges published as *The Congress* (also see below), Enitharmon Press, 1974, translation by Alberto Manguel published as *The Congress of the World*, F.M. Ricci (Milan), 1981.

El libro de arena, Emecé, 1975, translation by di Giovanni published with *The Congress* as *The Book of Sand*, Dutton, 1977.

(With Bioy Casares) *Nuevos cuentos de Bustos Domecq*, Libreria de la Ciudad, 1977.

Rosa y azul (contains "La rosa de Paraceleso" and "Tigres azules") Sedmay (Madrid), 1977.

Veinticinco agosto 1983 y otros cuentos de Jorges Luis Borges (includes interview with Borges), Siruela, 1983.

POETRY

Fervor de Buenos Aires (title means "Passion for Buenos Aires"), Serantes (Buenos Aires), 1923, revised edition, Emecé, 1969.

Luna de enfrente (title means "Moon across the Way") Proa (Buenos Aires), 1925.

Cuaderno San Martín (title means "San Martin Copybook"), Proa, 1929.

Poemas, 1923-1943, Losada, 1943, 3rd enlarged edition published as *Obra poética, 1923-1964*, Emecé, 1964, translation published as *Selected Poems, 1923-1967* (bilingual edition; also includes prose), edited, with an introduction and notes, by Norman Thomas di Giovanni, Delacorte, 1972.

El hacedor (prose and poetry; Volume 9 of *Obras completas*; title means "The Maker"), Emecé, 1960, translation by Mildred Boyer and Harold Morland published as *Dreamtigers*, University of Texas Press, 1964, reprinted, 1985.

Seis poemas escandinavos (title means "Six Scandinavian Poems"), privately printed, 1966.

Siete poemas (title means "Seven Poems"), privately printed, 1967.

El otro, el mismo (title means "The Other, the Same"), Emecé, 1969.

Elogio de la sombra, Emecé, 1969, translation by di Giovanni published as *In Praise of Darkness* (bilingual edition), Dutton, 1974.

El oro de los tigres (also see below; title means "The Gold of Tigers"), Emecé, 1972.

Siete poemas sajones/Sevon Saxon Poems, Plain Wrapper Press, 1974.

La rosa profunda (also see below; title means "The Unending Rose"), Emecé, 1975.

La moneda de hierro (title means "The Iron Coin") Emecé, 1976.

Adrogue (prose and poetry), privately printed, 1977.

Historia de la noche (title means "History of the Night"), Emecé, 1977.

The Gold of Tigers: Selected Later Poems (contains translations of *El oro de los tigres* and *La rosa profunda*), translated by Alastair Reid, Dutton, 1977.

La cifra, Emecé, 1981.

(With Kodama) *Atlas* (prose and poetry), Sudamericana, 1984, translation by Kerrigan published as *Atlas,* Dutton, 1985.

Les conjures (originally published as *Los conjurados* in 1985), translated by Silvia Baron Supervielle (Geneva), Jacques T. Quentin, 1990.

ESSAYS, LITERARY CRITICISM, AND LECTURES

Inquisiciónes (title means "Inquisitions"), Proa, 1925.

El tamaño de mi esperanza (title means "The Measure of My Hope"), Proa, 1926.

El idioma de los argentinos (title means "The Language of the Argentines"), M. Gleizer (Buenos Aires), 1928, 3rd edition (includes three essays by Borges and three by Jose Edmundo Clemente), Emecé, 1968.

Figari, privately printed, 1930.

Las Kennigar, Colombo (Buenos Aires), 1933.

Historia de la eternidad (title means "History of Eternity"), Viau y Zona (Buenos Aires), 1936, revised edition published as *Obras completas,* Volume 1, Emecé, 1953, reprinted, 1978.

Nueva refutacion del tiempo (title means "New Refutation of Time"), Oportet y Haereses, 1947.

Aspectos de la literature gauchesca, Numero (Montevideo), 1950.

(With Delia Ingenieros) *Antiguas literaturas germanicas,* Fondo de Cultura Economica (Mexico), 1951, revised edition with Maria Esther Vazquez published as *Literaturas germánicas medievales,* Falbo, 1966, reprinted, Emecé, 1978.

Otras inquisiciónes, Sur (Buenos Aires), 1952, published as *Obras completas,* Volume 8, Emecé, 1960, translation by Ruth L. C. Simms published as *Other Inquisitions, 1937-1952,* University of Texas Press, 1964.

(With Margarita Guerrero) *El Martín Fierro,* Columba, 1953, reprinted, Emecé, 1979.

(With Bettina Edelberg) *Leopoldo Lugones,* Troquel, (Buenos Aires), 1955.

(With Guerrero) *Manual de zoología fantástica,* Fondo de Cultura Economica, 1957, translation published as *The Imaginary Zoo,* University of California Press, 1969, revised Spanish edition with Guerrero published as *El libro de los seres imaginarios,* Kier (Buenos Aires), 1967, translation and revision by di Giovanni and Borges published as *The Book of Imaginary Beings,* Dutton, 1969.

La poesia gauchesca (title means "Gaucho Poetry"), Centro de Estudios Brasileiros, 1960.

(With Vasquez) *Introducción a la literatura inglesa,* Columba, 1965, translation by L. Clark Keating and Robert O. Evans published as *An Introduction to English Literature,* University Press of Kentucky, 1974.

(With Esther Zemborain de Torres) *Introducción a la literatura norteamericana,* Columba, 1967, translation by Keating and Evans published as *An Introduction to American Literature,* University Press of Kentucky, 1971.

Borges on Writing (lectures), edited by Norman Thomas di Giovanni, Daniel Halpern, and Frank MacShane, Dutton, 1973, Ecco, 1994.

(With Alicia Jurado) *Qué es el budismo?* (title means, "What Is Buddhism?"), Columba, 1976, Emecé, 1991.

Borges oral (lectures), edited by Martin Mueller, Emecé, 1979.

Siete noches (lectures), Fondo de Cultura Economica, 1980, translation by Weinberger published as *Seven Nights,* New Directions, 1984.

Nuevos ensayos dantescos (title means "New Dante Essays") Espasa-Calpe, 1982.

Textos cautivos: Ensayos y resenas en "El Hogar" (1935-39) (title means "Captured Texts: Essays and Reviews in 'El Hogar' [1936-39]"), edited by Rodriguez Monegal and Enrique Sacerio-Gari, Tusquets, 1986.

El aleph borgiano (chiefly book reviews which appeared in journals, 1922-84), edited by Juan Gustavo Cobo Borda and Martha Kovasics de Cubides, Biblioteca Luis-Angel Arango (Bogota), 1987.

Testimony to the Invisible & Other Essays on Swedenborg, Swedenborg Foundation, 1995.

TRANSLATIONS

Virginia Woolf, *Orlando,* Sur, 1937.

(Also author of prologue) Franz Kafka, *La metamorfosis,* [Buenos Aires], 1938, reprinted, Losada, 1976.

Henri Michaux, *Un barbaro en Asia,* Sur, 1941.

(Also author of prologue) Herman Melville, *Bartleby, el escribiente,* Emecé, 1943, reprinted, Marymar (Buenos Aires), 1976.

William Faulkner, *Las palmeras salvajes,* Sudamericana, 1956.

(Also editor and author of prologue) Walt Whitman, *Hojas de hierba,* Juarez (Buenos Aires), 1969.

OMNIBUS VOLUMES

La muerte y la brújula (stories; title means "Death and the Compass"), Emecé, 1951.

Obras completas, nine volumes, Emecé, 1953-1960, revised edition edited by Carlos V. Frías, published as one volume, 1974.

Cuentos (title means "Stories"), Monticello College Press, 1958.

Antología personal (prose and poetry), Sur, 1961, translation published as *A Personal Anthology,* edited and with foreword by Kerrigan, Grove Press, 1967.

Labyrinths: Selected Stories and Other Writings, edited by Donald A. Yates and James E. Irby, preface by Andre Maurois, New Directions, 1962, augmented edition, 1964, reprinted, Modern Library, 1983.

Nueva antología personal, Emecé, 1968.

Prologos, con un prólogo de prólogos (title means "Prologues, with a prolougue of prologues"), Torres Aguero (Buenos Aires), 1975.

(With others) *Obras completas en colaboracion* (title means "Complete Works in Collaboration"), Emecé, 1979.

Narraciones (stories), edited by Marcos Ricardo Bamatan, Catedra, 1980.

Borges: A Reader (prose and poetry), edited by Emir Rodriguez Monegal and Reid, Dutton, 1981.

Ficcionario: Una antologia de sus textos, edited by Rodriguez Monegal, Fondo de Cultura Economica, 1985.

Biblioteca personal: Prólogos (Alianza, 1988).

OTHER

(Author of afterword) Ildefonso Pereda Valdes, *Antología de la moderna poesia uruguaya,* El Ateneo (Buenos Aires), 1927.

Evaristo Carriego (biography), M. Gleizer, 1930, revised edition published as *Obras completas,* Volume 4, Emecé (Buenos Aires), 1955, translation by di Giovanni published as *Evaristo Carrigo: A Book about Old Time Buenos Aires,* Dutton, 1984.

Discusión, Gleizer (Buenos Aires), 1932, revised edition, Alianza (Madrid), Emecé, 1976.

(Editor with Pedro Henriquez Urena) *Antología clasica de la literatura Argentina,* Kapelusz (Buenos Aires), 1937.

(Editor with Bioy Casares and Silvina Ocampo) *Antología de la literatura fantastica,* with foreword by Bioy Casares, Sudamericana, 1940, enlarged edition with postscript by Bioy Casares, 1965, translation of revised version published as *The Book of Fantasy,* with introduction by Ursula K. Le Guin, Viking, 1988.

(Author of prologue) Bioy Casares, *La invencion de Morel,* Losada, 1940, reprinted, Alianza, 1981, translation by Simms published as *The Invention of Moral and Other Stories,* University of Texas Press, 1964, reprinted, 1985.

(Editor with Bioy Casares and Ocampo and author of prologue), *Antología poetica argentina,* Sudamericana, 1941.

(Compiler and translator with Bioy Casares) *Los mejores cuentos policiales* (title means "The Best Detective Stories"), Emecé, 1943, reprinted, Alianza, 1972.

(Editor with Silvina Bullrich) *El compadrito: Su destino, sus barrios, su música* (title means "The Buenos Aires Hoodlum: His Destiny, His Neighborhoods, His Music"), Emecé, 1945, 2nd edition, Fabril, 1968.

(With Bioy Casares, under joint pseudonym B. Suarez Lynch) *Un modelo para la muerte* (novel; title means "A Model for Death"), Oportet & Haereses, 1946.

(Compiler and translator with Bioy Casares) *Los mejores cuentos policiales: Segunda serie,* Emecé, 1951.

(Editor and translator with Bioy Casares) *Cuentos breves y extraordinarios: Antología,* Raigal (Buenos

Aires), 1955, revised and enlarged edition, Losada, 1973, translation by Kerrigan published as *Extraordinary Tales*, Souvenir Press, 1973.

(With Bioy Casares) *Los orilleros* [and] *El paraiso de los creyentes* (screenplays; titles mean "The Hoodlums" and "The Believers' Paradise"; "Los orilleros" produced by Argentine director Ricardo Luna, 1975), Losada, 1955, reprinted, 1975.

(Editor and author of prologue, notes, and glossary with Bioy Casares) *Poesia gauchesca* (title means "Gaucho Poetry"), two volumes, Fondo de Cultura Economica, 1955.

(Editor with Bioy Casares) *Libro del cielo y del infierno* (anthology; title means "Book of Heaven and Hell"), Sur, 1960, reprinted, 1975.

(Editor and author of prologue) *Macedonio Fernandez*, Culturales Argentinas, Ministerio de Educacion y Justicia, 1961.

Para las seis cuerdas: Milongas (song lyrics: title means "For the Six Strings: Milongas"), Emecé, 1965.

Dialogo con Borges, edited by Victoria Ocampo, Sur, 1969.

(Compiler and author of prologue) Evaristo Carriego, *Versos*, Universitaria de Buenos Aires, 1972.

(With Bioy Casares and Hugo Santiago) *Les Autres: Escenario original* (screenplay; produced in France and directed by Santiago, 1974), C. Bourgois (Pairs), 1974.

(Author of prologue) Carlos Zubillaga, *Carlos Gardel*, Jucar (Madrid), 1976.

Cosmogonias, Libreria de la Ciudad, 1976.

Libro de suenos (Transcripts of Borges's and others' dreams; title means "Book of Dreams"), Torres Aguero, 1976.

(Author of prologue) Santiago Daove, *La muerte y su traje*, Calicanto, 1976.

Borges—Imagenes, memorias, dialogos, edited by Vazquez, Monte Aviula, 1977.

Borges para millones, Corregidor (Buenos Aires), 1978.

(Editor with Maria Kodama) *Breve antologia anglosajona*, Emecé, 1979.

(Compiler) Paul Groussac, *Jorge Luis Borges selecciona lo mejor de Paul Groussac*, Fraterna (Buenos Aires), 1981.

(Compiler and author of prologue) Francisco de Quevedo, *Antología poetica*, Alianza, 1982.

(Compiler and author of introduction) Leopoldo Lugones, *Antología poetica*, Alianza, 1982.

(Compiler and author of prologue) Pedro Antonio de Alarcon, *El amigo de la muerte*, Siruela (Madrid), 1984.

En voz de Borges (interviews), Offset, 1986.

Dialogos (interviews), edited by Osvaldo Ferrari, Sudamericana, 1986, Seix Barral, 1992, published as *Dialogos ultimos*, Sudamericana, 1987.

A/Z, Siruela (Madrid), 1988.

Borges, el otro: diccionario arbitrario (philosophy), compiled by Napoleon de Armas, Cordillera (Venezuela), 1991.

Borges: un dialogo sobre cine y los venidos a menos, prologo de Roberto Alifano, Camilo Cappelletto (Buenos Aires), 1992.

(With Thiago de Mello) *Borges na luz de Borges* (interviews), Pontes, 1992.

Borges en la Escuela Freudiana de Buenos Aires, Agalma (Buenos Aires), 1993.

(Author of introduction) Rene Burri, *Gauchos*, Takarajima, 1993.

Collected Fictions, translated by Andrew Hurley, Viking, 1998.

Also founding editor of *Prisma* magazine, 1921, and *Proa* magazine, 1921, 1924-25, and a publisher of *Martín Fierro*. Editor at *Crítica*, weekly arts supplement section, beginning 1933; *El Hogar*, "Foreign Books and authors," 1936-39; (with Bioy Casares) *Destiempo* magazine, 1936; *Los Anales de Buenos Aires* journal, 1946-48.

■ Sidelights

Although Ireneo Funes, a Uruguayan teenager, was paralyzed and confined to his chair, he "knew by heart the forms of the southern clouds at dawn on the 30th of April, 1882, and could compare them in his memory with the mottled streaks on a book in Spanish binding he had only seen once." Funes remembered every moment of his life, and he had spent entire days recreating his past with his memory. His remarkable memory also allowed him to master English, French, Portuguese, and Latin.

Funes's amazing memory was accompanied by fantastic perception. "We, at one glance, can perceive three glasses on a table; Funes, all the leaves and tendrils and fruit that make up a grape vine." While Funes's gifts intensified or enriched his sedentary existence, they also troubled him at times. Funes found it difficult "to comprehend that the generic symbol *dog* embraces so many unlike individuals of diverse size and form; it bothered him that the dog at three fourteen (seen from the side) should have the same name as the dog at three fifteen (seen from the front)." Funes distracted himself by giving names like *"meat blanket"* and *"sulphur"* to numbers from one beyond twenty-four thousand ("In place of five hundred, he would say *nine*"). When Funes wanted to go to sleep, he had to struggle to ignore his perceptions and memories.

Ireneo Funes, and his millions of memories, existed only in the mind of Jose Luis Borges, who wrote a fabricated memoir describing this fictional character as if he'd really known him. Because of his talent for writing innovative, thought-provoking narrative fiction like that found in the short story "Funes the Memorious," Borges is widely recognized as one of the most influential intellectuals of the twentieth century. A master of metaphors, Borges artfully addressed ancient questions about time, memory, history, and mortality. As Octavio Paz, the great Mexican writer, observed in the *New Republic*, Borges "ceaselessly explored" a "single theme" in his work: "man lost in the labyrinth of a time made of changes that are repetitions, man preening before the mirror of unbroken eternity, man who has found immortality and has conquered death but neither time nor old age."

In addition to gem-like short stories which indulged the fantastic, mystic, and metaphysic in strict literary form, Borges wrote insightful essays and symbolist poetry. He was known for transcending the borders of traditional genres; some of his short stories feature scholarly footnotes and references to imaginary books and fictional people, and many of his essays and stories seem poetic in composition and style. In the *New Republic*, Paz explained that, for Borges, the "division" between genres was "arbitrary. His essays read like stories; his stories are poems; and his poems make us think, as though they were essays. The bridge connecting them is thought."

While Borges demonstrated his unique talent in his essays and poetry, many critics agree that, in the words of John Updike in his book *Picked-Up Pieces*, the "great achievement" of Borges's "art is his short stories." Julio Cortázar, an Argentine writer known for his own fantastic short stories, described the intrigue created by Borges's work in *Books Abroad*: "What some literary critics admire above all in Borges is a genius of geometrical invention, a maker of literary crystals whose condensation responds to exact mathematical laws

This 1972 work collects more than 100 of Borges's poems, chosen by the author himself and translated by such writers as Alastair Reid, W. S. Merwin, John Updike, and Robert Fitzgerald.

of logic. Borges has been the first to insist on that rigorous construction of things which tend to appear, on the surface, as absurd and aleatory. The fantastic, as it appears in Borges's stories, makes one think of a relentless geometrical theorem." Borges, as James Gardner explained in the *New Criterion*, "never attempted a novel." He "was always a miniaturist. None of his works extends beyond roughly six thousand words. . . . Perhaps he realized that his stories were primarily the treatment of a single imaginative impulse; perhaps he felt (no doubt rightly) that their jewel-like concision could not fill out a larger form."

Although he was born in Argentina on the eve of the twentieth century, Borges incorporated American, English, German, French, and Spanish nineteenth-century literature and esoteric philosphy in his own writing. He counted Edgar Allan Poe, Samuel Taylor Coleridge, Edmund Spenser, Rudyard Kipling, G. K. Chesterton, Paul Valery, Walt Whitman, Franz Kafka, and Arthur Schopenhauer among his precursors and engaged the work of these authors in an intertextual dialogue. According to James E. Irby in the introduction to *Labyrinths*, "Borges is always quick to confess his sources and borrowings, because for him no one has claim to originality in literature; all writers are more or less faithful amanuenses of the spirit, translators and annotators of pre-existing archetypes."

The English translation of Borges's *Ficciones* brought him international exposure in the early 1960s, and he began to serve as a precursor to younger writers around the world. Borges won numerous international prizes and distinctions for his contribution to literature (with the exception of the coveted Nobel prize). He was presented with honorary degrees from some of the world's most prestigious universities and soon became known as one of literature's most charming and distinguished personalities.

Despite his international appeal and impact, some literary critics argue that Borges was, at heart, Latin American. As Octavio Paz asserted, "Europeans were amazed by the universality of Borges," but "none of them observed that his cosmopolitanism was not, and could not have been, anything but the point of view of a Latin American. . . . The Latin American can regard the West as a totality, and not with the fatally provincial vision of a Frenchman, a German, an Englishman, or an Italian."

Others suggest that Borges's essential contribution was to Latin American literature, which "boomed" in the 1960s and 70s with the "magical realism" found in the work of Colombian Gabriel García Márquez and Julio Cortázar. According to James Neilson in *Encounter*, "Borges is the genius who stripped away ornate Hispanic rhetoric from their [Latin American writers] written language . . . and who freed them from the obligation to compile 'realistic' committed novels about their own societies. Since Borges showed them that fantasy was respectable, few serious Latin American writers have looked back: for the last twenty years fantasy has been the predominant mode and it is the principal characteristic of most translated Latin American works."

Borges Is Born to Write

Jorge Luis Borges was born in Buenos Aires on August 24, 1899, to a family that cherished literature. His father, Jorge Guillermo Borges, was a lawyer, professor, and amatuer writer who regretted the fact that he had not devoted his life to writing. His mother, Leonor Acevedo de Borges, was a translator. Borges' paternal grandmother, an Englishwoman, taught Borges to read English before he could read Spanish. The family expected Borges to become a writer, and he was encouraged to explore his father's library. He was still a child when he read some of the great works of the Americans Mark Twain, Henry Wadsworth Longfellow, and Poe. Borges also began to write as a child; when he was just nine years old his Spanish translation of "The Happy Prince," by Oscar Wilde, was published in a local newspaper. He was thirteen years old when his first original story, "El rey de la selva," was published.

If Borges's intellect was shaped by his family's rapacious appetite for literature, it was also influenced by the people and culture of Buenos Aires. When Borges was a young boy, Argentina was still a young nation; its first years were bloody and highly politicized. Borges came to know his country's political history intimately. Through his maternal grandmother, Borges was related to Colonel Isidoro Suárez, a figure in the Argentine war of independence, and the patriot Francisco Narciso de Laprida. Borges's father's grandfather, Colonel Francisco Borges, was killed during the Argentine civil wars. There was violence to be found in tales about *gauchos* (the cowboys of the Argentine pampas immortalized in the Argentine classic *Martin Fierro*), and in stories of urban knife-fights.

As critics have suggested, these two themes that animated Borges's childhood, intellectual contemplation and physical violence, were expressed in his writings as an adult. Recalling that Borges "suffered from an attraction to the darkness and the violence of America," Octavio Paz asserted in the *New Republic* that the "law of spiritual gravity governs Borges's work: the macho Latin faces the metaphysical poet. The contradiction that informs his intellectual speculations and his fictions— the struggle between the metaphysical and the skeptical—reappears violently in the field of feelings. . . . It appears again and again in his writings. It was perhaps a vital and instinctive response to his skepticism, his civilized tolerance."

Borges left Argentina and his childhood in 1914, when his family began a tour of Europe and got stuck in Geneva, Switzerland. As Borges once recalled for *New York Times Book Review* contributor Amelia Barili, "We were so ignorant that we did not know that was the year of the First World War." Jorge and his sister, Norah, were sent to study at the Collége Calvin in Geneva, where Borges was expected to learn his lessons in French and study Latin. He eagerly learned both languages and familiarized himself with French and German literature and philosophy. Borges's time in Geneva not only gave him the opportunity to experience and imbibe European culture, it made him forever loyal to Switzerland. As he told Barili, "I am Swiss."

When Borges graduated from college in 1918 and the war ended, he traveled to Spain. There, the young man joined a group of avant-garde poets known as the *ultraístas*. Led by writers like Rafael Cansinos Assens, Guillermo de Torre, and Gerardo Diego, and influenced by Dadaism, Imagism, and German Expressionism, the *ultraístas* attempted to construct abstract poetry with emphasis on the use of the metaphor.

Constructing A Cosmopolitan Literature in Buenos Aires

When the Borges family returned to Argentina in 1921, Borges brought the modern expressionism he had learned in Spain from the *ultraístas* with him and led the Argentine *ultraísmo* movement. He began collaborative relationships with writers Silvina Ocampo and Adolfo Bioy-Cesares that lasted for decades. With such writers, Borges published *Prisma*, a literary magazine which made its debut in 1921, and continued the publication of two other literary journals, *Proa* and *Martín Fierro*.

These publications, and the essays Borges wrote for them, were marked by a cosmopolitan intellectual discourse and by attempts to construct bridges linking Argentine and European literature. As James Gardner noted in the *New Criterion*, "the Argentine writers of Borges's youth were conscious of their standing apart from the distant wellsprings of European literature," but there was "a general sense among them of trying to keep up with developments abroad, consciously cultivating a cosmopolitan environment through allusions to the most recent European writers and painters,

and delighting to fill their pages with quotations in French, German, and English." The contribution to Argentine literature that Borges made with his essays was one of style as well as content. According to Paz in the *New Republic*, Borges's essays are still "memorable, mainly for their orginality, their diversity, and their style. Humor, sobriety, acuity—and suddenly, an unusual twist. Nobody else had written that way in Spanish."

Borges published three collections of poetry during these early years, *Fervor de Buenos Aires* (1923), *Luna de enfrente* (1925), and *Cuarderno San Martin* (1929). In *Fervor de Buenos Aires*, urban themes, colorful descriptions of Buenos Aires, and praise for Borges's native city dominate. In *The New Criterion*, Gardner noted that the poems in this collection "usually alternate between the traditional eleven-syllable line of Spanish verse and lines of arbitrary length." According to Gardner, the poems in *Luna de enfrente* and *Cuaderno San Martín* were largely inspired by the works of Walt Whitman and the French Symbolists. Gardner asserts that, as early as "1923 we can hear the soft-spoken clarity of voice and the tenacious sense of place that would characterize" Borges's "poetry for sixty years to come."

Borges increasingly began to devote his time to short, narrative fiction, and the first of these pieces were collected in *Historia universal de la infamia* (1935). Each of these realistic stories portrays a fictional or historical character—a knife fighter, rogue, or criminal—with imaginary facts and fabricated details. Although Borges would later write other detective pieces, like "Death and the Compass" (published in *Ficciones*) and more realistic stories, like "Emma Zunz" (in *El Aleph*), by the late 1930s Borges's stories were increasingly embedded in the realm of the philosophical or fantastic.

Borges was working at a branch of the Buenos Aires municipal library in 1938 when he suffered emotional and physical trauma. First, his father, who had been blind for some time, died. Then, while walking up a dark staircase, Borges hit his head on a window pane and suffered septicemia. Worried that he would not be able to write as he once had, Borges attempted to write an unusual story that would not reveal any mental defects he may have suffered. The story, about a man who sets out to write, word for word, Cervantes's classic novel *Don Quixote* three hundred years after

Cervantes, was published in *El Sur,* Argentina's foremost literary journal. "Pierre Menard, Author of the *Quixote,*" became one of Borges' well-known pieces, sent Borges' work in a new direction and eventually influenced the course of Latin American and western literature. This story, along with others, was published in *El jardín de senderos que se bifurcan* (1942) and later in *Ficciones, 1935-44* (1944).

Borges's Transcendent Short Stories

"From a formal point of view," wrote Alberto Julián Pérez in the *Dictionary of Literary Biography,* "it is the fantastic story, as conceived by Poe, that

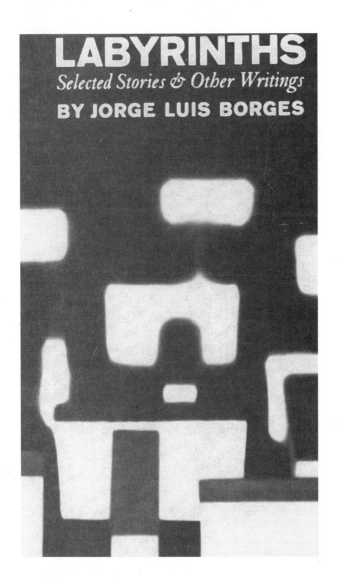

Short stories, essays, and poems are gathered in this 1964 work.

is the generic source most evident in Borges's stories. But . . . [fantastic literature] is for him (as it is for other writers and thinkers, such as Voltaire, Jonathan Swift, and Franz Kafka) not an end but rather a means to an end . . . to create a literature of ideas, capable of commenting on the questions and broodings of the cultural world." Borges addressed such "questions and broodings" with a surprisingly small number of literary devices used alone or in combinations. According to James E. Irby in an introduction to *Labyrinths,* "Borges once claimed that the basic devices of all fantastic literature are only four in number: the work within the work, the contamination of reality by dream, the voyage in time, and the double."

Like a jeweler transforming a coarse rock into a brilliant, multifaceted gem with just a few cuts, Borges created stories that suggest a myriad of meanings. "Pierre Menard, autor del *Quijote,*" to cite one example, is just a few pages long, but scholars have written countless papers and pages offering different interpretations of it. David I. Grossvogel explained in his book *Mystery and Its Fictions: From Oedipus to Agatha Christie* that, because the only difference between Cervantes's *Don Quixote* and Menard's *Don Quixote* is "the way in which Borges's reader reads them," the reader is forced to "become a fictional character." "Within the infinite recession of the dream dreaming the dreamer dreaming . . . the reader is thrust through the fiction into a confrontation with the unknowable that creates the existential sense that the fiction is investigating."

In the *Dictionary of Literary Biography,* Pérez offered the idea that Borges "succeeds in satirizing the intellectual habit of the symbolist writers and their conception of the writer as an aesthete and scholar," as well as in laughing "at himself" in "Pierre Menard, autor del *Quijote.*" According to John Stark in his book, *The Literature of Exhaustion,* Borges's "bias against historical literature appears under the surface of 'Pierre Menard, Author of the *Quixote.*' This fiction implies that if a man living in a later century can exactly reproduce *Don Quixote,* the original version cannot have been linked in any way with its historical era."

Some of the most discussed and analyzed stories among Borges's works appear in *Ficciones, 1935-1944.* In "Tlön, Uqbar, Orbis Tertius," a story that reads like an essay and cites imagined works supposedly written by actual scholars and writers, a narrator mentions an imaginary world, Tlön; readers gradually find that Tlön, a "labyrinth" created by men, is not only "real," it is gradually replacing the dimensions of the present and past world. The narrator realizes that "English and French and mere Spanish will disappear from the globe. The world will be Tlön. I pay no attention to all this and go on revising, in the still days at the Androgué hotel, an uncertain Quevedian translation (which I do not intend to publish) of Browne's *Urn Burial.*"

The narrator in the short story "La lotería en Babilonia" explains how a company conducting a lottery restructured the Babylonians' existence with a completely controlled system of randomness and uncertainty. "La muerte y la brújula," a detective

story set in Buenos Aires, features the literary devices of the double and the labyrinth. In "The Garden of Forking Paths," a spy must solve a riddle of a book with that title in order to complete his mission.

Other well-known stories by Borges were collected in *El Aleph,* published in 1949. "El Aleph" reports the existence of a stone which encompasses and represents the potential of the infinite universe. "El Zahir" is the story of a coin that moves its possessors to dwell on its image and to perceive it as an object that will help them systematically understand and comprehend that space. In "La Espera," a man dreams his assassins are coming to get him. As he was able to kill his assassins in a recurring dream, he thought perhaps that he could kill his "real" ones as well. But he could not be sure that he was not already dead and dreaming of waiting to kill or be killed. "Emma Zunz" follows a woman as she finds out that her father, who had been betrayed by her boss, has taken his own life. In order to get revenge, Emma has to arrange her own violation.

In its numerous permutations, Borges's "literature basically is about literature," as John Stark explained in his book, *The Literature of Exhaustion.* According to Stark, this idea is emphasized in "The Library of Babel." "The library described in the story oppresses a viewer because of its regularity: made of hexagonal cubicles, and having five shelves on each wall, thirty-two books on each shelf, 410 pages in each book, forty lines on each page, eight letters in each line. . . . In this story the universe is a library, and the books, both individually and collectively, mean nothing substantive. The only meaning in the universe derives from its relentless order or, in other words, its artifice."

Ficciones Brings Borges International Acclaim

Although Borges lived through some turbulent political times that affected his personal life, as Joseph Epstein explained in *Commentary,* "there was his politics and there was his writing and, insofar as he could control them, never did the twain meet. . . . Borges's stories do appear drained of all political content: questions of good and evil do not arise in his stories and neither can he ever be said to seek to persuade his readers to any conclusions. He wished to entertain and

The title work of this 1978 collection describes a stone which encompasses infinite power.

move them, but to move them in a particular direction—toward wonder and wonderment over life's mysteries." As a result of his approach to politics in his work, James E. Irby observed in the introduction to *Labyrinths,* "save for the admiration of a relatively small group," Borges was "criticized as non-Argentine, as an abstruse dweller in an ivory tower."

When Borges finally did receive "belated recognition as a major writer of our time," according to Irby in his introduction to *Labyrinths,* it came "more from Europe" than from Borges's "native America." International and domestic politics, Borges's English heritage, and his disdain for totalitarianism further precluded his potential popularity at home and abroad during World War II and the decade following it. In the early 1940s, while many Argentines sympathized with the Germans, Borges's loyalty was with the Allies. Borges disliked the mass-supported Colonel Juan Domingo Perón, a populist leader who came to power as a dictator in Argentina in 1946 and who put Borges' mother in jail. After Borges signed an anti-Perón document, Perón attempted to humiliate Borges by designating him as the national poultry inspector of market chicken and rabbits. Borges did not accept the insulting appointment, and he left his job at the municipal library. He began to work as a teacher at the Instituto Superior de Cultura Inglesa and the Colegio Libre de Estudios Superiores and moved into a downtown Buenos Aires apartment with his mother.

After the fall of Perón in 1955, the new government appointed Borges as the director of the Biblioteca Nacional. Borges became a professor of English literature at the Facultad de Filosofia y Letras. *Ficciones, 1935-44* was finally translated into English in the early 1960s, and Borges won the Prix Formentor (the International Publishers Prize) in 1961, with Samuel Beckett. That year, Borges finally acquired international fame: in the words of James Neilson, writing in *Encounters,* Borges's "reputation overflowed Buenos Aires and penetrated into every city in the Western world."

Borges was invited to teach and lecture around the world. In addition, according to Neilson, "inevitably, imitators soon began to appear, busying themselves with turning out enigmatic tales concerning labyrinths, mirrors, tigers, resumés of nonexistent treatises, and all the other features of the Borgesian universe," while Borges "abandoned" his "private world" and "took refuge in Argentina's past or in Anglo-Saxon verse and Icelandic sagas."

This change in Borges's status as a writer at home and abroad coincided with the descent of darkness, or at least a yellow hue, over Borges's perception of the world. (He told Robert Alifano in *Twenty-Four Conversations with Borges* that yellow was the only color he could see). By 1956, the man who lived to read and write could no longer see. But Borges did not let blindness stop his work. He enlisted his mother, who served as his secretary, to read to him, and he dictated his writing to her. He also called upon friends to read to him, listen to him recite poetry, converse with him, and guide him on walks around Buenos Aires and tours around the world.

Until his very last years, Borges was surrounded by people who were happy to visit with him. Alfred J. MacAdam, the editor of *Review,* recalled that Borges was polite ("a nineteenth-century man adrift in the late twentieth century"), and that his wit was sharp and clever. Christopher Hitchens wrote in the *Spectator* that Borges "was always searching for a mutually agreeable topic" during conversations," and "seemed at times to fear that it was he, lonely, sightless and claustrated, who might be the dull partner in chat. When he found a subject that would please, he began to bubble and grin, and even to tease."

Blindness and Alienation

At a time when readers around the world were just gaining exposure to Borges stories, Borges began to invest more time in his poetry, which appeared in *El hacedor* (1960, translated as *Dreamtigers),* and *Antología personal* (1961). Stuart Evans, writing in *Dictionary of Literary Biography Yearbook 1986,* reminded critics that Borges thought of himself as a poet and quoted Borges in the foreword to his *Selected Poems, 1923-67:* "In the long run, perhaps, I shall stand or fall by my poems."

According to Miguel Enguídanos in the introduction to *Dreamtigers,* this collection demonstrates Borges's devotion to poetry because, as a collection, it is a poem. *Dreamtigers,* then, is not just an assortment of "odd poems, stories, parables, sketches, fragments, and apocryphal quotations. . . . Actually this juxtaposing of fragments, bits, and snippets corresponds to a poetic criterion of an extremely high order: that of creating a book—*the* book—which is the mirror of life."

Evan's brief survey of Borges's poetry recalls its most frequent themes: otherness, oblivion, and death. Evans explained that Borges's poems about death "became increasingly involved with his perplexities concerning time and a sort of Nietzschean sense of continuity, somewhat at odds with his brooding over loss of identity and his growing sense of oblivion." Despite his preoccupation with such themes, wrote Evans, Borges was not a "gloomy poet." Instead, he was a "'literalist of the imagination,' who is, if sometimes melancholy, never morbid. Throughout his work there is a powerful element of delight in his discoveries: his exploration of Buenos Aires, his study of other languages and literature's, his interest in philosphy and metaphysic . . . , his discovery of himself through ancestors, loves, his poetry and fiction, and eventually in his blindness." Evans cited the "Poem of the Gifts" as an example of Borges's "surpassing courage and goodwill."

Borges also demonstrated his courage and goodwill during the 1960s by continuing to take advantage of offers to teach and lecture abroad despite his increasing age and his blindness. According to a *New Yorker* story, "Many who had read him came to hear him, and carried away, as a talisman, an image of him that added affection to awe: frail, soft-spoken in both English and Spanish, his hands clasping a walking stick in front of him, he mesmerized his listeners with his careful phrasing, his modesty, his wit, the warm and often mischievous humor of his spoken asides."

This 1981 work is the first collaboration between Borges and his long-time friend, Adolfo Bioy-Casares.

Borges married Elsa Astete Millán in September, 1967, and they lived together while Borges taught at Harvard. In 1970, the couple divorced, and Borges took up residence with his elderly mother once more. That same year, *El informe de Brodie* appeared and received mixed reviews. "In this book he recovers many of the favorite themes of his youth (the adventures of hoodlums and knife duels)," wrote Pérez in *Dictionary of Literary Biography,* "but the author who mastered so well the poetics of the fantastic tale could not apply to his work the poetics of realism with equal success." Thomas O. Bente assured readers in *Américas* that "although the subject matter and thrust of many of the stories are modified, their essence is still very much within the Borges vein, and the reader should not be alarmed with the new configurations the stories take." *El libro de arena* (1975) marked a return to the fantastic for Borges, who was in his seventies when it was published. According to Pérez, this collection is "equal to his best works of the 1940s."

Borges was teaching abroad when, in 1973, Perón returned from exile to serve as an elected president in Argentina. When Perón died, his inexperienced widow came to power. When the country seemed threatened by the onset of chaos, the military decided to take control of the government. Intent on destroying the Peronist movement and left-wing organizations, it clandestinely kidnapped, imprisoned, and killed countless Argentine citizens.

Unlike some of Latin America's most famous writers, Borges was not passionately involved in contemporary politics. Nevertheless, as a public figure who commanded respect from people around the world, Borges was expected to take a stand and to decry the military and its methods. But, as Jaime Alazraki explained in the *Dictionary of Literary Biography Yearbook 1986*, Borges identified the generals with the fathers of Argentine Independence and believed that the military were "the only gentlemen left capable of saving the country." Borges "believed that the military should intervene in the nation's political life and seize power by force."

As Alazraki wrote, because Borges sided "with the torturers and assassins of his own nation," he lost contact with many of his friends, family members, and beloved writers. The military government, on the other hand, seemed to favor Borges. Writing in 1982 in *Encounter*, Neilson noted that a general described Borges as a "national monument," and Borges was "regularly raised aloft like a martial trophy by Argentines who rarely read any books but who are infuriated by the Swedish Academy's refusal to give their man the Nobel Prize." Ultimately, Borges published a poem expressing his discontent with the Falklands war Argentina's military government had provoked with England in the newspaper *Clarin*.

It was around this time that Borges grew very ill. He was diagnosed with cancer of the liver and was told that he was going to die. Borges was noted for saying that, instead of fearing death, he welcomed it. William D. Montalbano quoted Borges in the *Los Angeles Times*, "I believe that if they told me that I would die tonight, I would feel relieved, but one knows so little of oneself

that perhaps I would be terrified. I don't know, but I feel rather impatient. I have lived too long."

Borges kept his terminal prognosis a secret and began to plan his final months. If, as Alazraki explained in the *Dictionary of Literary Biography Yearbook 1986,* Borges felt as though Argentina "had been lost to him, he believed that Switzerland offered him a peace he could not find in his native land." According to Alazraki, Borges decided to "die in the country of his adolescence, in that 'tower of reason' where life is as private as its aloof citizens and runs as serene as the Rhone waters. That environment was much closer to his intellectual constructs and labyrinthian artifices." Borges traveled to Geneva with María Kodama, his former student, secretary, and collaborator. There they were married. Kodama stayed by Borges's side as he endured medical tests, took walks, suffered the failure of his body, recited his last poems, and finally died on June 14, 1986. He was eighty-seven years old.

Catholic and Protestant eulogies for Borges were held at the Saint Pierre Cathedral in Geneva, and his body was buried in Plainpalais, an exclusive cemetery. Alazraki remembered that the writer's best friends, family members, and writers were not present at the funeral. Nevertheless, in Argentina, President Raul Alfonsin announced a formal decree of mourning, and writers and readers of great literature around the world lamented Borges' passing.

While Borges may have been ready to pass on, his friends and admirers were not ready to lose him. Alfred J. MacAdam, for one, wrote in *Review,* "For most of us Borges had always been there, and we simply assumed he always would be. He was immortal." Some would say that the great writer *is* immortal—he lives on, like his character Ireneo Funes, in his works. Borges was well aware of this potential for his literal recreation. According to the *New Yorker,* he once remarked: "When writers die, they become books, which is, after all, not too bad an incarnation."

■ Works Cited

Alazraki, Jaime, "Jorge Luis Borges," *Dictionary of Literary Biography Yearbook 1986*, Gale Research, 1987, pp. 206-209.

Bente, Thomas O., "Borges Revisited," in *Américas*, November-December, 1973, pp. 36-40.

Borges, Jorge Luis, "Borges on Life and Death," in an interview with Amelia Barili, in *New York Times Book Review*, July 13, 1986, pp. 1, 27-9.

Borges, "Funes the Memorious," translated by James E. Irby, in *Labyrinths*, edited by Donald A. Yates & James E. Irby, Modern Library, 1983, pp. 59-66.

Borges, "Tlön, Uqbar, Orbis Tertius," translated by James E. Irby, in *Labyrinths*, edited by Donald A. Yates & James E. Irby, Modern Library, 1983, pp. 3-18.

Borges, Jorge Luis, and Roberto Alifano, *Twenty-Four Conversations with Borges, Including a Selection of Poems: Interivews by Roberto Alifano, 1981-83*, Lascaux, 1984.

Cortázar, Julio, "The Present State of Fiction in Latin America," translated by Margery A. Safir, *Books Abroad*, Summer, 1976, pp. 533-40.

Enguídanos, Miguel, introduction to *Dreamtigers* by Jorge Luis Borges, translated by Mildred Boyer and Harold Morland, University of Texas Press, 1985.

Epstein, Joseph, "Señor Borges's Portico," *Commentary*, April, 1987, pp. 55-62.

Evans, Stuart, "The Poetry of Jorge Luis Borges," *Dictionary of Literary Biography Yearbook 1986*, Gale Research, 1987, pp. 209-213.

Gardner, James, "Jorge Luis Borges, 1899-1986," *New Criterion*, October, 1986, pp. 16-24.

Grossvogel, David I., "Borges: The Dream Dreaming the Dreamer," *Mystery and Its Fictions: From Oedipus to Agatha Christie*, The Johns Hopkins University Press, 1979, pp. 127-46.

Hitchens, Christopher, "Jorge Luis Borges," *Spectator*, June 21, 1986, pp. 12-13.

Irby, James E., introduction to *Labyrinths: Selected Stores & Other Writings* by Jorge Luis Borges, edited by Donald A. Yates and James E. Irby, New Directions, 1964, pp. xv-xxiii.

MacAdam, Alfred J., "Jorge Luis Borges: 1899-1986," in *Review*, January-June, 1986, p. 4.

Montalbano, William D., "Borges, Dean of Latin American Writers, Dies," *Los Angeles Times*, June 15, 1986.

Neilson, James, "In the Labyrinth: The Borges Phenomenon," *Encounter*, June-July, 1982, pp. 47-58.

Paz, Octavio, "In Time's Labyrinth," translated by Charles Lane, *The New Republic*, November 3, 1986, pp. 30-4.

Pérez, Alberto Julián, "Jorge Luis Borges," translated by Virginia Lawreck, *Dictionary of Literary Biography*, Volume 113, Gale Research, 1992, pp. 67-81.

Stark, John, "Jorge Luis Borges," *The Literature of Exhaustion*, Duke University Press, 1974, pp. 20-2.

"The Talk of the Town," *New Yorker*, July 7, 1986, pp. 19-20.

Updike, John, *Picked-Up Pieces*, Alfred A. Knopf, 1975, p. 183.

■ For More Information See

BOOKS

Agheana, Ion Tudro, *Reasoned thematic dictionary of the prose of Jorge Luis Borges*, Ediciones del Norte, 1990.

Aizenberg, Edna (editor), *Borges and His Successors: the Borgesian Impact on Literature and the Arts*, University of Missouri Press, 1990.

Alazraki, Jaime, *Jorge Luis Borges*, Taurus, 1976,

Alazraki, *Critical Essays on Jorge Luis Borges*, G. K. Hall, 1987.

Alazraki, *España en Borges*, Ediciones El Arquero (Madrid), 1990.

Balderston, Daniel, *Out of Context: Historical Reference and the Representation of Reality in Borges*, Duke University Press, 1993.

Bell-Villada, Gene H., *Borges and His Fiction: A Guide to His Mind and Art*, The University of North Carolina Press, 1981.

Bugin, Richard, *Conversations with Jorge Luis Borges*, Holt, Rinehart & Winston, 1969.

Canto, Estela, *Borges: An Intimate Portrait*, translated by Elaine Kerrigan, Chronicle, 1992.

Carrizo, Antonio, *Borges, el memorioso: Conversaciones de Jorge Luis Borges con Antonio Carrizo*, Fondo de Cultura Económica, 1982.

Cheselka, Paul, *The Poetry and Poetics of Jorge Luis Borges*, Peter Lang, 1987.

Chiappini, Julio, *Borges y Kafka*, Editorial Zeus (Argentina), 1991.

Cozarinsky, Edgardo, *Borges In/and/on Film*, translated by Gloria Waldman and Ronald Christ, Lumen Books, 1988.

Fishburn, Evelyn, and Psiche Hughes, *A Dictionary of Borges*, forewords by Mario Vargas Llosa and Anthony Burgess, Duckworth, 1990.

Foster, David William, *Jorge Luis Borges: An Annotated Primary and Secondary Bibliography*, Garland, 1984.

Henriksen, Zheyla, *Tiempo sagrado y tiempo profano en Borges y Cortazar*, Editorial Pliegos (Madrid), 1992.

Hernandez, B., Manuel, *Borges, de la ciudad al mito*, Ediciones Uniandes (Colombia), Universidad de los Andes, 1991.

Hernandez Martin, Jorge, *Readers and Labyrinths: Detective Fiction in Borges, Bustos Domecq, and Eco*, Garland, 1995.

Jaen, Didier Tisdel, *Borges' Esoteric Library: Metaphysics to Metafiction*, University Press of America, 1992.

Lennon, Adrian, *Jorge Luis Borges*, Chelsea House, 1992.

Lindstrom, Naomi, *Jorge Luis Borges: A Study of the Short Fiction*, Twayne, 1990.

Maier, Linda S., *Borges and the European Avant-Guarde*, P. Lang, 1992.

Malloy, Sylvia, *Signs of Borges*, translated and adapted by Oscar Montero in collaboration with the author, Duke University Press, 1994.

Merrell, Floyd, *Unthinking Thinking: Jorges Luis Borges, Mathematics, and the New Physics*, Purdue University Press, 1991.

Monegal, Emir Rodriguez, *Jorge Luis Borges: A Literary Biography*, E.P. Dutton, 1978.

Sarlo Sabajanes, Beatriz, *Jorge Luis Borges: A Writer on the Edge*, edited by John King, Verso, 1993.

Stabb, Martin S., *Jorge Luis Borges*, Frederick Ungar, 1980.

Stabb, *Borges Revisited*, Twayne, 1991.

Sucre, Guillermo, *Borges el poeta*, U.N.A.M., 1967.

Wheelock, Carter, *The Mythmaker: A Study of Motif and Symbol in the Short Stories of Jorge Luis Borges*, University of Texas Press, 1969.

PERIODICALS

Booklist, January 1, 1987, p. 689; December 15, 1988, p. 681.
Book World, August 9, 1992, p. 9.
Los Angeles Times Book Review, January 20, 1985, p. 8.
Modern Fiction Studies, Summer, 1990, pp. 149-66.
New York Times Book Review, November 3, 1985, p. 46.
Publishers Weekly, September 13, 1985, p. 122; July 27, 1998, pp. 51-52.
World Literature Today, Winter, 1992, pp. 21-26.

■ Obituaries

PERIODICALS

London Review of Books, August 7, 1986, pp. 6-7.
National Review, July 18, 1986, pp. 20-21.
New York Review of Books, August 14, 1986, p. 11.
North American Review, September, 1986, pp. 75-78.
Washington Post, June 15, 1986.*

—*Sketch by Ronie-Richele Garcia-Johnson*

Bebe Moore Campbell

National Endowment for the Arts grant, 1980; Golden Reel Award, Midwestern Radio Theatre Workshop Competition, for *Sugar on the Floor; New York Times* Notable Book selection, for *Your Blues Ain't Like Mine;* Mayor's Certificate of Appreciation, Los Angeles, CA; NAACP Image Awards, 1994, for outstanding literary work.

■ Personal

Born in 1950, in Philadelphia, PA; daughter of George Linwood Peter and Doris (a social worker; maiden name, Carter) Moore; married Tiko F. Campbell (divorced); married Ellis Gordon, Jr. (a banker); children: Maia, one stepson. *Education:* University of Pittsburgh, B.A. (summa cum laude), 1968.

■ Career

Freelance writer. National Public Radio commentator, *Morning Edition.* Guest on television talk shows, including *Donahue, Oprah, Sonya Live,* and *Today,* and numerous radio shows. Public school teacher in Atlanta, GA, Washington, DC, and Pittsburgh, PA, 1970-76. *Member:* Alpha Kappa Alpha, Delta Sigma Theta.

■ Awards, Honors

Body of Work Award, National Association of Negro Business and Professional Women, 1978;

■ Writings

Successful Women, Angry Men: Backlash in the Two-Career Marriage (nonfiction), Random House, 1986.
Sweet Summer: Growing Up With and Without My Dad, Putnam, 1989.
Your Blues Ain't Like Mine, Putnam, 1992.
Brothers and Sisters, Putnam, 1994.
Singing in the Comeback Choir, Putnam, 1998.

Also author of nonfiction short story, "Old Lady Shoes" and a radio play based on it. Contributor to periodicals including *Adweek, Black Enterprise, Ebony, Lear's, Ms., New York Times Book Review, New York Times Magazine, Publishers Weekly, Savvy, Seventeen, Washington Post,* and *Working Mother.* Contributing editor of *Essence.*

■ Adaptations

Motown Productions bought an option to the film rights to *Sweet Summer* in 1989; the option is held by Aunt Jack Productions. *Brothers and Sisters* and

Your Blues Ain't Like Mine were produced for audio cassette by Ingram, 1994. Disney's Touchstone Pictures optioned the rights to *Brothers and Sisters* in 1995.

■ Sidelights

"He looked up when he heard the truck. Stood up when he heard the motor stop. The headlights revealed three men, one sort of short, the other two tall and strong-looking, their expressions fixed and hard. For a moment he sat in dazed uncertainty. Then fear, as primal as the first scream, flooded his body. 'Turn them damn lights out!' he heard one of the men say. They're coming for me, he thought. He didn't realize that he'd bitten his tongue until he tasted blood in his mouth as he called, `Mama.'" Fifteen-year-old Armstrong Todd, the protagonist of Bebe Moore Campbell's first novel, *Your Blues Ain't Like Mine*, was right to be scared: he was about to be killed, to become a victim of ignorance and racism.

In *Your Blues Ain't Like Mine* and her other novels, however, Campbell does not just communicate the feelings of African American characters, or relate the injustices they suffer. Instead, she treats all her characters as complex individuals and does not render them in stereotypical fashion. Noted for her thoughtful treatment of racial issues, her portrayal of black fatherhood, and her discussions of the problems of middle-class, well-educated blacks, Campbell has won praise from critics. As her books are well-written and engrossing, and address and explore contemporary social issues, Campbell is a popular author, in demand in bookstores and on talk shows. For her memoir, *Sweet Summer*, and novels, *Your Blues Ain't Like Mine*, *Brothers and Sisters*, and *Singing in the Comeback Choir*, Campbell is increasingly regarded as an important African American writer of the twentieth century.

Campbell's parents divorced when she was an infant. While her father was a willing participant in her life, writing letters and sending her mother money, she lived with him only during the summers. Campbell looked forward to those summers with her father. She wrote in *Sweet Summer*, "it became an end-of-June ritual, an annual event, something I could set my clock by, set my heart on. . . . It wasn't my ritual alone, of course. I was like a lot of northern black children making

the annual trek down south to the Carolinas, to Georgia, Alabama, or Mississippi. Across Philly in the summer of 1957, hundreds, maybe thousands of black kids were packed and waiting to be driven to wide open spaces, barefoot living, outhouses, watermelon patches, swimming holes, Grandma, Daddy."

As Campbell explained in *Sweet Summer*, due to an automobile accident that occurred after Campbell was born, Campbell's father could not walk. When she was with him, she pushed him in his wheelchair, assisted him during the day, and went for fast car rides. She played with her cousins, watched her grandmother kill and skin chickens, and admired her father for his strength, his smile, and his laugh. She secretly imagined that he would learn to walk again. At the end of the summer, she would pick out an entire wardrobe of school clothes that her father would pay for, then return home to her mother, grandmother, and cousin Michael.

Campbell describes life with her mother and grandmother, or "the Bosoms," as she called them, as somewhat stifling. Her mother, a social worker who had won a scholarship to earn a college education, insisted that Campbell speak properly, with crisp enunciation and perfect grammar. She pushed her daughter to recite poems in church, to excel at school, and to exhibit excellent, cultured behavior, especially in public. Campbell occasionally longed for her more relaxed life with her father. "It was during the week that I needed men the most. Especially the week leading up to the church program, the week my mother went officially berserk. Crazy. Demented. She stalked me from the time she got in from work until I lay my weary head on my pillow. Woman was getting on my nerves. My very last little nine-year-old nerve."

Campbell graduated from the Philadelphia High School for Girls, and went on to the University of Pittsburgh, where she received a degree in early childhood education. Campbell spent the years after college working as a teacher in Atlanta, Washington, D.C., and Philadelphia. In 1976 she enrolled in a writing course taught by the notable African American author Toni Cade Bambara. Campbell then began a successful career as a freelance writer, and contributed articles to several national publications including *Ebony*, *Essence*, the *New York Times*, and the *Washington Post*.

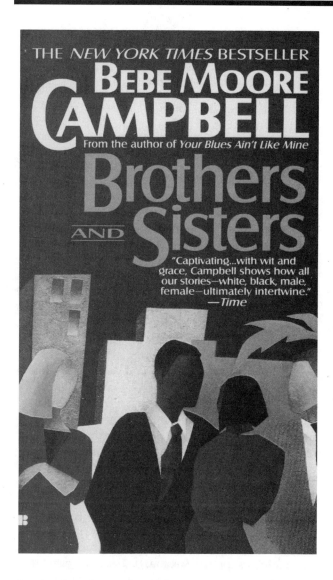

THE *NEW YORK TIMES* BESTSELLER
BEBE MOORE
CAMPBELL
From the author of *Your Blues Ain't Like Mine*
Brothers
AND Sisters
"Captivating...with wit and grace, Campbell shows how all our stories—white, black, male, female—ultimately intertwine."
—*Time*

Set in the aftermath of the 1992 Los Angeles riots, this bestselling work concerns two female coworkers—one black and one white—and a man who comes between them.

The following year, after Campbell's daughter was born, her father was killed in a car accident. Campbell wrote in *Sweet Summer* about her grief upon learning of her father's death from her Uncle Norman: "'He was coming to see you, Bebe. . . . You know your daddy, he just hopped in the car and got on the road. He was bringing a camera to take pictures of the baby.' When Uncle Norman said that, I remembered the pictures I'd promised to send Daddy weeks before and felt the first flicker of pain course through my body. Something swept through me, hot as lightning. All at once I was shaking and crying."

While "the fat insurance checks" her father left her "transformed" her "lifestyle," Campbell wrote, "I could feel his death reshaping my life, or at least the life I thought I was entitled to. There are gifts that only a father can give a daughter. . . . I was prepared to receive a daily ration of such gifts, albeit belatedly, but it was not to be." Campbell mourned not just the loss of her father, but the loss of the men in her life. "Those men who used to entice me with their storytelling, yank my plaits, throw me quarters and tell me what a pretty girl I was are mostly beyond my reach now," Campbell wrote in *Sweet Summer*. She divorced, remarried, and moved to Los Angeles.

Campbell continued her career as a writer and took up pressing social issues in various articles. She also conducted research and wrote a nonfiction book, *Successful Women, Angry Men: Backlash in the Two-Career Marriage*. Although, to some extent, Campbell drew from her own experiences to write *Successful Women*, her second book was completely autobiographical.

Sweet Summer and *Your Blues Ain't Like Mine*

In *Sweet Summer*, which opens as Campbell recalls the death of her father, she describes her relationship with him. Campbell tells of her life in the fall and winter with her mother, grandmother, and aunt, and in the summer with her father. In Philadelphia, with the women in her family, Campbell is exhorted, as Bharati Mukherjee noted in the *New York Times Book Review*, to "*do* something, to *be* someone." Life in North Carolina is much different—Campbell could relax, play, and enjoy the company of her father. "This material is potent, and some of the characters unforgettable," commented Mukherjee. According to Veronica Chambers of the *Los Angeles Times Book Review*, "many of Campbell's readers mistook" the book "for fiction." In addition to noting the power of the book, some critics praised its positive portrayal of a black father, and of father-daughter relationships in the African American community.

Campbell began to write novels in the early 1990s. The first of these won her increased critical attention. Based on the actual murder of a young African American, Emmett Till, in 1955, *Your Blues Ain't Like Mine* was also born of Campbell's memories of the discussion following the event. Campbell's first novel introduces a light skinned, fifteen-year-old African American who leaves Chicago to visit Mississippi in 1955. One night, as the teen is relaxing in a pool hall, he remembers a French phrase his father brought back from Europe after World War II, and uses it as he flirts with a white woman. The woman is married to the owner of the pool hall, and her husband and his friends determine to punish Armstrong for speaking so boldly to a white woman. Armstrong is brutally murdered in a powerful scene. Campbell relates the activities, thoughts, and feelings of the murderers as they attempt to escape justice.

As the murder is investigated by the authorities, the two families involved must confront a seemingly unending parade of difficulties. After one young white man secretly calls reporters from the north, newspapers around the country become interested in the story. In one scene, white reporters from New York visit Armstrong's family: "We heard about what happened to your grandson. It was a terrible thing. We know things are unstable down here between whites and colored, and well, ma'am, if we can write about what happened, it might be a chance to see justice done." Armstrong's mother, Delotha, "was struck by the word 'justice'; she thought that finding that for Armstrong would be the last thing she could do for him." Delotha "knew that she was waking up, reclaiming her vitality, her will, and all the power that Armstrong's death had drained from her. She looked the men straight in their eyes. 'He was my son,' she said. . . . 'We'll both talk to you.'"

Critics praised *Your Blues Ain't Like Mine* for its presentation of diverse characters. "Campbell presents us with a medley of individuals as complicated as our country's racial history," remarked Chambers in the *Los Angeles Times Book Review*. "Much of the power of this novel results from Ms. Campbell's subtle and seamless shifting of point of view," wrote Clyde Edgerton in the *New York Times Book Review*. Edgerton also commented that the story "enables a railing against the abuses of power" and "an understanding of the seeds of such abuse by way of an understanding of our own hearts, our capabilities for love, fear, hate, and finally, self-respect."

Getting Along in *Brothers and Sisters*

Campbell's next book, *Brothers and Sisters*, was published after the 1992 Rodney King riots in Los

If you enjoy the works of Bebe Moore Campbell, you may also want to check out the following books and films:

Maya Angelou, *I Know Why the Caged Bird Sings*, 1974.
Christopher Paul Curtis, *The Watsons Go to Birmingham—1963*, 1995.
Lorraine Hansberry, *A Raisin in the Sun*, 1959.
Do the Right Thing, a film by Spike Lee, 1989.

Angeles, and, as DeNeen L. Brown pointed out in a live *Washington Post* chat with Campbell, an attempt to answer King's anguished question, "Can't we all just get along?" Campbell elaborated, "I thought about the question, and I decided to explore it through a workplace and a friendship that was rooted in that workplace. . . . You never finish dealing with race in this society, so I wanted that friendship to deal with race, to reflect that. I wanted to show how difficult it was for two people who had a lot in common to overcome race."

Brothers and Sisters, set in Los Angeles, features an African American protagonist, a professional woman who is working hard to advance her career as a banker. Ester Jackson's progress seems to be determined, to some degree, on race relations inside and outside her office. She develops a friendship with a white woman, Mallory, which is jeopardized especially when an African American man in the office is attracted to Mallory instead of Ester. To make matters worse, another black employee may be stealing from accounts. Black and white characters alike are torn by the memory of the Rodney King trial, verdict, and riots. Their attempts to reach some understanding of the events which traumatized Los Angeles are emphasized in the novel. The book also takes up, as Brown noted in the *Washington Post*, affirmative action, sexual harassment, "welfare reform, black-on-black racism, white-on-black racism, and black-on-white racism. . . ."

Critics once again noted Campbell's fictional discussion of race. A *Publishers Weekly* critic remarked that Campbell demonstrated an "authoritative grasp of racial issues." Christopher John Farley of

Time wrote that Campbell "shows how all our stories—white, black, male, female—ultimately intertwine." Some critics commented on the suspense of the novel. "Readers won't want to put this book down until the injustices are resolved," wrote Ginny Ryder in *School Library Journal*. Vanessa V. Friedman stated in *Entertainment Weekly*, "Campbell can certainly tell a story."

Not all critics enjoyed *Brothers and Sisters*. Elizabeth Gleick of the *New York Times Book Review* asserted that Campbell's "genuine attempt to address the complexities of race in the modern age" meets with "uneven success." Erin J. Aubry, writing in the *Los Angeles Times Book Review*, noted that the characters in *Brothers and Sisters* "are all eminently forgettable mouthpieces for a variety of sociological ills that crowd out any possibility for engaging, believable characters." Both Aubry and Gleick concluded that *Your Blues Ain't Like Mine* was written with more heart and emotion than *Brothers and Sisters*. Despite such criticism, *Brothers and Sisters* became a best-seller.

Campbell's Voice Sings in Her Third Novel

The heroine in Campbell's third novel, *Singing in the Comeback Choir*, is the executive producer of a television talk show. Born and raised in Philadelphia by her jazz-singer grandmother, Maxine McCoy is alarmed when her grandmother suffers a stroke. Despite the fact that her job is demanding, that she is pregnant, and that she is still dealing with her husband's recent, brief affair, Maxine flies off to care for her grandmother, Lindy; Lindy had given up her career as a singer to work as a nurse and care for Maxine when her mother died. When Maxine arrives home in North Philly, she finds that Lindy is ill and bitter and unwilling to consider living in a nursing home. Maxine's old neighborhood, once respectable, is run-down and crime-ridden. Maxine works to convince her to sing once more. In the process of finding a way to help her grandmother recover spiritually and physically, Maxine contributes to the well-being of her childhood community.

The novel, according to Cassandra Spratling in the *Detroit Free Press*, "is about knowing what you're meant to do in life and doing it." Barbranda Lumpkins of *USA Today* wrote that "Campbell does make you think about where you come from and how you got where you are." In *Booklist*,

Donna Seaman praised Campbell's creation of "enveloping scenes of supple humor, expansive spirit, and extraordinary warmth." According to Seaman, Campbell's "voice is soft and caressing, but it packs quite a punch." Betsy Groban wrote in the *New York Times Book Review* that at the novel's conclusion, "we have come to care deeply about Maxine and Lindy, which makes the novel's inventive resolution even more gratifying."

In an interview with Jody Benjamin published in the *Detroit Free Press*, Campbell explained that she "wanted to focus on forgiveness as a way to renew and resurrect the soul" in *Singing in the Comeback Choir*. She also wanted to discuss the problem of contemporary black communities and the dislocation of those who have left the inner city. "I think a lot of African-American people—particularly those who are middle class—have those same feelings of anger, despair and hope when they go back to their old neighborhoods. Never before has there been such a gap between the [black] middle class and the urban poor."

The success of Campbell's books has transformed her into an authority on race relations, and she is called upon to provide opinions in discussions of such issues. She has appeared on various talk shows, including *Oprah* and *Today*. (Bebe Moore Campbell is not the only member of her family to appear on television—her daughter, Maia Campbell, is an actress who starred in the television series, *In the House*.) Campbell, who continues to write at home in Los Angeles, may also be heard occasionally on National Public Radio's *Morning Edition*.

■ Works Cited

Aubry, Erin J., review of *Brothers and Sisters, Los Angeles Times Book Review*, September 4, 1994.

Review of *Brothers and Sisters, Publishers Weekly*, July 4, 1994, p. 51.

Brown, DeNeen L., "A Book to Bind Prince George's," *Washington Post*, November 13, 1997, p. A1.

Campbell, Bebe Moore, *Your Blues Ain't Like Mine*, Ballantine, 1995.

Campbell, Bebe Moore, *Sweet Summer*, Fawcett, 1996.

Campbell, Bebe Moore, live chat with DeNeen L. Brown, *Washington Post* guest forum at http://www.washingtonpost.com, November 25, 1997.

Campbell, Bebe Moore, interview with Jody A. Benjamin of the *Sun-Sentinel* (South Florida), "Campbell Tells a Tale of Faith, Resurrection," reprinted in *Detroit Free Press*, March 22, 1998, p. 3G.

Chambers, Veronica, "No Better Blues," review of *Your Blues Ain't Like Mine, Los Angeles Times Book Review*, September 6, 1992, pp. 3, 8.

Edgerton, Clyde, "Medicine for Broken Souls," review of *Your Blues Ain't Like Mine, New York Times Book Review*, September 20, 1992, p. 13.

Farley, Christopher John, "Wary Friends," review of *Brothers and Sisters, Time*, October 17, 1994, p. 81.

Friedman, Vanessa V., review of *Brothers and Sisters, Entertainment Weekly*, September 9. 1994, p. 78.

Gleick, Elizabeth, "To Live and Die and Do Your Banking in L.A.," review of *Brothers and Sisters, New York Times Book Review*, October 16, 1994, p. 18.

Groban, Betsy, review of *Singing in the Comeback Choir, New York Times Book Review*, April 12, 1998, p. 17.

Lumpkins, Barbranda, review of *Singing in the Comeback Choir, USA Today*, March 24, 1998.

Mukherjee, Bharati, "The South Had All the Laughter," review of *Sweet Summer, New York Times Book Review*, June 11, 1989, p. 47.

Ryder, Ginny, review of *Brothers and Sisters, School Library Journal*, February, 1995, p. 134.

Seaman, Donna, review of *Singing in the Comeback Choir, Booklist*, December 15, 1997.

Spratling, Cassandra, review of *Singing in the Comeback Choir, Detroit Free Press*, March 1, 1998, p. 7E.

■ For More Information See

PERIODICALS

African American Review, Summer, 1997, p. 369.
Black Enterprise, February, 1995, p. 224.
Boston Globe, October 26, 1992, p. 32.
Chicago Tribune, October 25, 1992, p. 5.
Essence, July, 1992, p. 42.
Glamour, August, 1989, p. 170.
Kirkus Reviews, June 15, 1992, p. 733.
San Francisco Chronicle, September 20, 1992, p. 7.
School Library Journal, January, 1993, p. 142.
Village Voice, July 4, 1989, p. 63.

—Sketch by R. Garcia-Johnson

Joseph Conrad

■ Personal

Birth-given name Jozef Teodor Konrad Nalecz Korzeniowski; name legally changed; born December 3, 1857, in Berdiczew, Podolia, Russia (now Poland); naturalized British citizen, 1886; died of a heart attack, August 3, 1924, in Bishopsbourne, Kent, England; buried in Canterbury, England; son of Apollo Nalecz (a poet, writer, and political activist) and Ewa (Bobrowski) Korzeniowski; married Jessie George, March 24, 1896; children: Alfred Borys, John Alexander. *Education:* Studied at schools in Poland and under tutors in Europe. *Religion:* Roman Catholic.

■ Career

Joined French Merchant Marine, 1874, sailed to Martinique and to West Indies as apprentice and then steward, 1875; British Merchant Service, 1878-94, traveled to Africa, Australia, India, Indonesia, and the Orient; full-time writer, 1894-1924. *Member:* Athenaeum Club.

■ Writings

FICTION

Almayer's Folly: A Story of an Eastern River (novel), Macmillan, 1895, published as *Almayer's Folly*, Doubleday, Page, 1921, reprinted, Penguin, 1976.

An Outcast of the Islands (novel), D. Appleton, 1896, reprinted, Penguin, 1975.

The Children of the Sea: A Tale of the Forecastle (novel), Dodd, Mead, 1897 (published in England as *The Nigger of the "Narcissus": A Tale of the Sea*, Heinemann, 1898), published with new preface by Conrad as *The Nigger of the "Narcissus": A Tale of the Forecastle*, Doubleday, Page, 1914, published under English title, Doubleday, Page, 1926, reprinted under title *The Nigger of the "Narcissus,"* Doubleday, Doran, 1938, recent edition, Norton, 1979.

Tales of Unrest (stories; includes "The Idiots," "An Outpost of Progress," and "The Lagoon"), Scribner, 1898, reprinted, Penguin, 1977.

Lord Jim: A Romance (novel), Doubleday, McClure, 1900 (published in England as *Lord Jim: A Tale*, W. Blackwood, 1900), published under English title, Doubleday, Page, 1927, published as *Lord Jim*, introduction by J. Donald Adams, Modern Library, 1931, enlarged edition, F. Watts, 1966, recent edition, Oxford University Press, 1983.

(With Ford Madox Heuffer [later Ford Madox Ford]) *The Inheritors: An Extravagant Story* (novel), McClure, Phillips, 1901, reprinted with introduction by Elaine L. Kleiner, Gregg Press, 1976.

"Youth: A Narrative," and *Two Other Stories* (contains "Youth, A Narrative," "Heart of Darkness" [also see below], and "The End of the Tether"), W. Blackwood, 1902, published as *"Youth" and Two Other Stories*, McClure, Phillips, 1903, reprinted with introduction by Morton Dauwen Zabel, Doubleday, 1959, recent edition published as *"Youth," "Heart of Darkness," and "The End of the Tether,"* Oxford University Press, 1984.

Typhoon, illustrations by Maurice Grieffenhagen, Putnam, 1902 (also see below).

Typhoon, and Other Stories (includes "To-Morrow" [also see below] and "Falk"), Heinemann, 1903, Doubleday, Page, 1926.

(With Ford) *Romance* (novel), Smith, Elder, 1903, McClure, Phillips, 1904, reprinted with afterword by Arthur Mizener, New American Library, 1968.

Nostromo: A Tale of the Seaboard (novel), Harper & Brothers, 1904, recent edition, Oxford University Press, 1984.

The Secret Agent: A Simple Tale (novel), Harper & Brothers, 1907, recent edition, Viking, 1985 (also see below).

The Point of Honor: A Military Tale, illustrations by Dan Sayre Broesbeck, McClure, 1908.

"Falk," "Amy Foster," "To-Morrow": Three Stories by Joseph Conrad, McClure, Phillips, 1908.

A Set of Six (stories), Methuen, 1908, Doubleday, Page, 1915.

Under Western Eyes (novel), Harper & Brothers, 1911, recent edition, Viking, 1985.

'Twixt Land and Sea (stories; includes "The Secret Sharer" [also see below], "A Smile of Fortune," and "Freya of the Seven Isles"), Hodder & Stoughton, 1912, reprinted, Penguin, 1978.

Chance: A Tale in Two Parts (novel), Doubleday, Page, 1913, reprinted, 1957, recent edition, Hogarth Press, 1984.

Victory: An Island Tale (novel), Doubleday, Page, 1915, reprinted, Penguin, 1966.

Within the Tides: Tales (includes "Because of the Dollars" [also see below] and "The Planter of Malata"), Dent, 1915, Doubleday, Page, 1916, reprinted, Penguin, 1978.

The Shadow Line: A Confession (novel), Doubleday, Page, 1917, recent edition, Oxford University Press, 1985.

The Arrow of Gold: A Story Between Two Notes (novel), Doubleday, Page, 1919, reprinted, Norton, 1968.

The Rescue: A Romance of the Shallows (novel), Doubleday, Page, 1920, reprinted, Norton, 1968.

The Rover (novella), Doubleday, Page, 1923, reprinted, T. Nelson, 1964.

(With Heuffer) *The Nature of a Crime*, Doubleday, Page, 1924.

Suspense: A Napoleonic Novel (unfinished), Doubleday, Page, 1925.

Tales of Hearsay, preface by R. B. Cunninghame Graham, Doubleday, Page, 1925.

The Sisters (unfinished), introduction by Ford, C. Gaige, 1928.

"Heart of Darkness" and "The Secret Sharer," introduction by Albert J. Guerard, New American Library, 1950.

Stories and novels also in other multi-titled volumes.

PLAYS

One Day More: A Play in One Act (adaptation of Conrad's story "To-Morrow"; first performed June 25, 1905), Clement Shorter, 1917, Doubleday, Page, 1920 (also see below).

The Secret Agent: A Drama in Four Acts (adaptation of Conrad's novel of the same title), H. J. Goulden, 1921 (also see below).

Laughing Anne: A Play (adaptation of Conrad's story "Because of the Dollars"), Morland Press, 1923 (also see below).

Laughing Anne [and] *One Day More*, introduction by John Galsworthy, J. Castle, 1924, Doubleday, Page, 1925.

Three Plays: Laughing Anne, One Day More, [and] *The Secret Agent*, Methuen, 1934.

CORRESPONDENCE

Lettres Francaises, introduction and notes by Georges Jean-Aubry, Gallimard, 1920.

Joseph Conrad's Letters to His Wife, Bookman's Journal, 1927.

Letters From Joseph Conrad, 1895-1924, edited with introduction and notes by Edward Garnett, Bobbs-Merrill, 1928.

Conrad to a Friend: One Hundred Fifty Selected Letters From Joseph Conrad to Richard Curle, edited with introduction and notes by Richard Curle, Bobbs-Merrill, 1928.

Letters of Joseph Conrad to Marguerite Poradowska, 1890-1920, translated from the French and edited with introduction and notes by John A. Gee and Paul J. Sturm, Yale University Press, 1940.

Joseph Conrad: Letters to William Blackwood and David S. Meldrum, edited by William Blackburn, Duke University Press, 1958.

Conrad's Polish Background: Letters to and From Polish Friends, translated by Halina Carroll, edited by Zdzislaw Najder, Oxford University Press, 1964.

Joseph Conrad and Warrington Dawson: The Record of a Friendship, edited by Dale B. J. Randall, Duke University Press, 1968.

Joseph Conrad's Letters to Cunninghame Graham, edited by C. T. Watts, Cambridge University Press, 1969.

The Collected Letters of Joseph Conrad, edited by Frederick R. Karl and Laurence Davies, Cambridge University Press, Volume I: *1861-1897,* 1983, Volume II: *1898-1902,* 1988.

OTHER

The Mirror of the Sea: Memories and Impressions (autobiographical essays), Harper & Brothers, 1906, reprinted, Marlboro Press, 1988 (also see below).

A Personal Record (autobiography), Harper & Brothers, 1912, reprinted, Marlboro Press, 1988 (published in England as *Some Reminiscences,* Eveleigh Nash, 1912; also see below).

Notes on Life and Letters (essays), Doubleday, Page, 1921, reprinted, Books for Libraries Press, 1972.

Notes on My Books, Doubleday, Page, 1921.

(Contributor) *Hugh Walpole: Appreciations,* Doran, 1923.

(Contributor) Charles Kenneth Scott-Moncrief, editor, *Marcel Proust: An English Tribute,* Chatto & Windus, 1923.

Last Essays (includes "Geography and Some Explorers"), introduction by Richard Curle, Doubleday, Page, 1926, reprinted, Books for Libraries Press, 1970.

Joseph Conrad's Diary of His Journey up the Valley of the Congo in 1890, Strangeways, 1926 (also see below).

Joseph Conrad's Prefaces to His Works, introduction by Edward Garnett, Dent, 1937.

Joseph Conrad on Fiction, edited by Walter F. Wright, University of Nebraska Press, 1964.

Congo Diary and Other Uncollected Pieces, edited by Najder, Doubleday, 1978.

The Mirror of the Sea [and] *A Personal Record,* Oxford University Press, 1988.

Contributor to periodicals, including *Oxford and Cambridge Review,* London *Times, Fortnightly Review,* and the *Daily Mail.*

OMNIBUS VOLUMES

Wisdom and Beauty From Conrad, selected and arranged by M. Harriet M. Capes, Melrose, 1915, Doubleday, 1922, reprinted, Haskell House, 1976.

The Shorter Tales of Joseph Conrad, Doubleday, 1924, reprinted, Books for Libraries Press, 1970.

The Complete Short Stories of Joseph Conrad, Hutchinson, 1933.

The Famous Stories of Joseph Conrad, Doubleday, 1938.

A Conrad Argosy, Doubleday, 1942.

The Portable Conrad, edited with introduction and notes by Zabel, Viking, 1947, reprinted, Penguin, 1976.

Tales of Land and Sea, illustrated by Richard M. Powers, introduction by William McFee, Hanover House, 1953.

Tales of the East and West, edited with introduction by Zabel, Doubleday, 1958.

Tales of Heroes and History, edited by Zabel, Doubleday, 1960.

Tales of the East, edited with introduction by Zabel, Doubleday, 1961.

Great Short Works of Joseph Conrad, Harper, 1967.

Stories and Tales of Joseph Conrad, Funk & Wagnalls, 1968.

Sea Stories, Granada, 1984.

Stories and novels also published together in other collections; works widely represented in anthologies.

COLLECTED WORKS

The Works of Joseph Conrad, twenty-one volumes, Dent, 1923-38, reprinted and enlarged, twenty-six volumes, 1946-55.

The Collected Works of Joseph Conrad, twenty-one volumes, Doubleday, 1925.

Collections of Conrad's papers are located at the Beinecke Library, Yale University; New York Public Library; British Library; Cornell University; Dartmouth University; and the Houghton Library at Harvard University, among other locations.

■ Adaptations

Lord Jim was released as a movie starring Peter O'Toole by Columbia in 1965; Conrad's short story

"The Secret Sharer" was adapted into a one-act play of the same title by C. R. Wobbe in 1969; the award-winning 1979 United Artists film *Apocalypse Now,* starring Marlon Brando and Martin Sheen, is an adaptation of Conrad's "Heart of Darkness," as is the 1994 Turner television movie, *Heart of Darkness,* starring Tim Roth and John Malkovich.

■ Sidelights

Writing in his *The Great Tradition,* the respected critic F. R. Leavis noted that Joseph Conrad "is among the greatest novelists in the language—in any language." Indeed, language is at the very heart of Conrad country. That he is widely regarded as one of the foremost prose stylists of English literature is no small achievement for a man who did not learn the language until he was twenty. English was, in fact, his fourth language, after Polish, German, and French. An outsider himself—born Polish and naturalized as a British citizen—Conrad explores the penumbral world of the alienated, the disillusioned, the isolated, and morally devastated. He was, according to Kingsley Widmer in *Concise Dictionary of British Literary Biography* (*CDBLB*), "a major figure in the transition from Victorian fiction to the more perplexed forms and values of twentieth-century literature. . . . Though writing in a time and culture often characterized as optimistic and affirmative, Conrad displays senses of defeat shading into a cosmic malignancy and an anxiously heavy ideological conservatism." In novels, novellas, and short stories such as *The Nigger of the "Narcissus," Lord Jim, Typhoon,* "Youth," "Heart of Darkness," and "The Secret Sharer," he explores the clash of cultures between modern and primitive, minutely describes the seagoing life as few other writers have been able to, and engages the reader in romanticized, symbolic adventure yarns. In later works such as *Nostromo, The Secret Agent,* and *Under Western Eyes,* Conrad turned from novels of the sea to political and societal tales, pioneering, especially in *The Secret Agent,* the oft-times bumbling world of espionage and terrorism upon which the writers Graham Greene and John Le Carre later expanded. With his 1913 novel, *Chance,* Conrad finally achieved not only celebrity but also financial security, and with the invention of his character Captain Marlow, Conrad also broke new ground in fiction technique, establishing the distancing effect of reported narration.

"In many ways, Conrad is our representative modern man and artist," wrote Frederick R. Karl in his biography, *Joseph Conrad: The Three Lives.* "An exile, a drifter, a marginal man until well into his thirties, he exemplifies many aspects of the modern sensibility. . . . In probing exile, dislocation of time and place, language disorientation, and shifting loyalties, he extended our view of the shadows of existence. Indeed, he suggested that the shadows were to be the main area of existence in the twentieth century." Karl goes on to compare Conrad to Freud, "his exact contemporary," both of whom explored the unmapped territories of irrationality and the abnormal. "And [Conrad] returned from this primitive, discontinuous world not with solutions but with ways of better understanding that savage Congo and primigenial heart of darkness that dwells under the most bland exteriors."

Just as critics traditionally divide Conrad's work into three distinct phases—the early sea tales, the middle political novels, and the later, less cohesive and artistic novels—so too can Conrad's entire life be divided into three periods: his youth in Poland and France, the years at sea, and his life as a writer. As Widmer noted in *CDBLB,* Conrad's life is "distinctive for its drastic fracturing. Several times exiled, with major changes of scene, nationality, and language, he seems to have suffered from a powerful sense of loss and alienation."

The Polish Years

Joseph Conrad was born Jozef Teodor Konrad Nalecz Korzeniowski, on December 3, 1857, in a part of Russia that is now Poland. He was the only child of Apollo and Ewa Korzeniowski, both active in the Polish nationalist movement of the mid-nineteenth century, and both former members of the Polish landed gentry, reduced in means by the time of Conrad's birth. Apollo squandered his wife's dowry, and thereafter threw himself into literary activity, a pattern somewhat duplicated by Conrad himself when he suddenly had a family of his own to support in 1896. In addition to his poetry, dramas, and translations, Apollo managed other people's estates.

Soon, Apollo had also become involved in Polish nationalism, leading a revolutionary cadre which protested Russian occupation of their land. Both parents were arrested by the authorities for their involvement in the nationalist cause, and in May 1862, the family was exiled to Volgoda, Russia. This exile was the breeding ground for a family tragedy, with the young Conrad almost dying of pneumonia on the way to Volgoda, and his mother, Ewa, dying of tuberculosis not long after their arrival in a second place of exile, Chernikhov in the Ukraine. Thereafter, Conrad was shuttled between his father and family relations, setting up a pattern of rootlessness and illness—he was prone to nervous attacks and headaches perhaps epileptic in origin—that would remain with him for the rest of his days.

Conrad was largely tutored at home in French and Polish. Apollo was allowed to leave exile, and moved several more times, finally settling in Cracow where he died in 1869 when the young Conrad was only eleven. An orphan now, he was supported and raised by various relations, primarily his mother's brother, Tadeusz Bobrowski, a successful lawyer. A sickly, introverted child suffering from the psychological scar of abandonment, Conrad reverted to books for much of his emotional sustenance. He was a voracious reader of romances and adventure stories. The physical exile he experienced with his parents was extended in adolescence to a psychological exile, a repressing of his emotions and connections with the outside world. But from his reading, particularly travel accounts and the sea stories of James Fenimore Cooper, he began to form a romantic plan of going to sea himself. After several years of cajoling, he finally talked his uncle into allowing him to attend a maritime school in Marseille. In October 1874, Conrad set off for France and a new life.

The Years at Sea

According to Karl, Conrad's three-and-a-half years in France "were momentous, an interlude or an interim that served several functions." Karl went on to explain that "these years cannot be dismissed as lighthearted or fun-filled, in which the young man simply sowed his wild oats or exorcised his Polish romanticism. They were a period of desperation as well as a time of high adventure." Half the time was spent actually aboard ship, gaining sailing experience on voyages to the West Indies as an apprentice seaman and steward. He may also have been involved in smug-

gling operations, running contraband arms for right-wing rebels in Colombia. In the course of these early adventures, Conrad met many of the men who would later populate the pages of his fiction.

Supported by his Uncle Tadeusz with an annual allowance of 2,000 francs, Conrad regularly exceeded this allowance, losing money at the gambling tables in Monte Carlo and then writing often to his uncle for extra funds. There was, in addition, much time spent on shore where Conrad studied at a maritime school to become a mate, and during this period he also continued his reading and began early attempts at writing. It is speculated that Conrad may also have been involved in smuggling operations into Spain in support of the right-wing Carlists who were attempting to re-establish the monarchy there. Some biographers have also written of a possible romantic liaison between Conrad and an older woman involved in the Carlist cause, a romance that ended unhappily. Whether such an unsuccessful romance or the pressure of his gambling debts was responsible, the fact is that Conrad attempted suicide in 1878, shooting himself in the chest.

Recovering from his wound, Conrad signed on the English ship *Mavis*, bound for Constantinople, and began a fifteen-year career as a sailor in the English fleet. As Karl noted, "Thus began the young man's formal sea career. It was unromantic and exceptionally hard work, unsanitary, unglamorous." In the next fifteen years, Conrad "was involved in several near wrecks, lived amid men who had been shipwrecked, assimilated their harrowing stories as well as his own hazardous experiences." His sailing posts took him to the South Pacific and the South China Sea, to exotic locales such as Java and Borneo, scenes of many of his later works. He also read widely of the sailing life, learned English—though always with a strong accent—and began to pass various maritime officer's examinations which would eventually lead to a Master's Certificate in the British Merchant Service. Known as "Polish Joe" aboard ship, Conrad became a naturalized British citizen in 1886 and changed his name to Joseph Conrad.

As Widmer pointed out in *CDBLB*, Conrad may have attained the rank of captain, but "was not really very successful in the merchant marine." He spent long periods on land without a berth and had only one small command in 1888. He continued to be in part supported by his uncle until he was in his mid-thirties. During the years Conrad was at sea, sailing ships were in their last days, and thus his settled occupation was far from secure. In 1890 he accepted a job as commander of a Congo River steamboat, a posting which took him to Africa under the auspices of a Belgium firm. His time in Africa introduced him to the ravages of imperialism on that continent and a trip upriver to rescue an agent of the company, one Georges Antoine Klein, later served as material for one of his most famous works, "Heart of Darkness." Klein died on the return trip and Conrad was laid up in Kinshasa, formerly Leopoldville, fighting both fever and dysentery. Returning to Europe, his health was greatly impaired. For the next five years of his sailing life, Conrad spent increasingly less time at sea and more time creating a new persona for himself: that of an English writer.

The Sea Novels

Conrad's Uncle Tadeusz died in 1894, and a year later Conrad published his first novel, *Almayer's Folly*. Like his father before him, Conrad turned to writing as an occupation, as a source of income. From the first, he viewed the writer's life not as bohemian, but "as a settled and orderly way of life, in contrast to his maritime career," according to Widmer. "He married Jessie George, a pleasantly dull and submissive younger woman, in 1896 and settled into conventional British middle-class family life." Conrad would eventually have two children: Borys in 1898 and John in 1906.

Not surprisingly, in his early novels Conrad turned to his own sea-going experiences aboard the trading vessel *Vidar* throughout the Malay Archipelago and to the tales he had heard while at sea. Exotic romances were a popular genre in the late nineteenth century, and Conrad soon established a reputation for such works. *Almayer's Folly* is the first of a trilogy of works including *An Outcast of the Islands* and *The Rescue*, which are set in Malaya and have as their theme, as Widmer noted, "the destructiveness of debased romantic idealism in weak colonialist characters in an alien environment." Much of the action of the three interconnected novels is set in motion by the romantic plans of the European trader, Thomas Lindgard, to restore a native kingdom while at the same time garnering colonial wealth.

Chronologically late in the series, *Almayer's Folly* deals with the Dutch trader, Kaspar Almayer, a protege of Lindgard's who is an incompetent dreamer, ambitious but corrupt, and whose overweening romanticism ultimately proves his undoing. Melodramatic in tone, *Almayer's Folly* is interesting not only for its theme but also for technical devices with which Conrad experimented. The failed European idealist is a recurrent theme in Conrad's fiction, and his use of flashback, flashforward, and juxtaposition of various points of view also foreshadow much of his later work. This initial novel, however, also presents a certain "oddity of style," according to Widmer, a lush

The author's first book, the start of a trilogy dealing with colonialist characters, was begun while he was still at sea.

and "high-flown rhetoric" that is in no small part the result of interference with Polish and French syntax. But as Widmer went on to observe, this very oddity and redundancy created a "persisting tone of ominousness, mysteriousness, and ironic reflectiveness, which partly distinguishes some of Conrad's fiction from simpler commercial exoticism." Begun in the 1880s while Conrad was still at sea, *Almayer's Folly* was well received by critics, including the novelist H. G. Wells. Its publication initiated a friendship between Conrad and the editor, Edward Garnett, who greatly helped to further Conrad's writing career and set the former sailor on a new course in life.

An Outcast of the Islands continued the Malayan story, and the third novel in the series was also started in 1896 though not finished until 1920. Several short stories next appeared, collected in *Tales of Unrest*. Important among these is "Karain: A Memory," in which Conrad first employs the technique of a distancing narrative frame in which the story is told at one or more removes from the actual action. To achieve this effect, Conrad employs a character within the story who relates the action after the fact. Such a technique helped Conrad to "avoid what would otherwise be painfully intense subjectivity," according to Widmer, as well as "to provide ambivalent moral separation from the action." Another important early short story is "An Outpost of Progress," Conrad's first use of the material he gathered while in the Belgian Congo, a harsh and ironic look at the supposedly civilizing influences of European imperialism on primitive societies.

Then in 1897 Conrad's first major work, *The Nigger of the "Narcissus"* was published, initially under the title *The Children of the Sea*. If Conrad's earlier work was derivative of sea stories of Cooper, Frederick Marryat, Richard Henry Dana, and Herman Melville, this third novel "transcends and transforms the sea tale," according to Dwight H. Purdy in *Contemporary Authors*. For this work, Conrad drew on his own experiences as second mate on the British ship *Narcissus* in 1884. As Adam Gillon described the novel in his *Joseph Conrad*, it is on one level a simple sea yarn about a violent storm, a ship in danger, the crew's struggle for survival, and the docking of the ship in port. "But fortunately," Gillon wrote, "there is much more in the book. It is a tale of a ship called the *Narcissus* but also of a man called James Wait, and of the strange relationship between him

EVERYMAN

THE HEART OF DARKNESS

JOSEPH CONRAD

Conrad's first-hand experiences with European imperialism in Africa informed his celebrated 1902 work.

and the crew; it is a story about the ship as a microcosm, in which man's destiny, his goodness and evil, are symbolically revealed; about Conrad's love and hate of the sea; above all, it is about the problem of an outcast's conflict with a social group."

Wait is a black man, the "nigger" of the title, who is a malingerer, feigning an illness to avoid work. He is confined to a cabin for his shamming by the chief mate. The other crewmen side with Wait and a mutinous situation ensues. But Conrad also inserts a note of ambiguity, for the mate and captain are actually acting out of kindness, seeing that Wait truly has become ill. A sudden storm restores a sense of order to the ship, for the crew and officers must pull together to save themselves and the ship. But with Wait's death, the narrator of the tale, an unnamed crew member, sees that the unity the crew has felt is as artificial as Wait's earlier feigned illness.

The Nigger of the "Narcissus" is not a tale of racial discrimination, though reviewers and critics have pointed out Conrad's use of the black man, Wait, as a symbol of loneliness, otherness, darkness, and the subconscious. Early reviewers praised the novel for its realism and attention to detail. An anonymous reviewer in the *Spectator* wrote that Conrad "has given us an extraordinarily vivid picture of life on board of a sailing-vessel in the merchant marine," while Harold Frederic noted in the *Saturday Review* that Conrad "gives us the sea as no other story-teller of our generation has been able to render it." Later critics plumbed the symbolic and psychological depths of the novel, praising Conrad for the new direction of his writing. Widmer contended, however, that the novel "is hardly the 'masterpiece' that some later critics have called it, marred as it is by a confused narration and irascible bigotries."

Conrad in part solved his problems of narration by introducing in his next novella, "Youth," the garrulous narrator, Captain Marlow. This novella relates a gripping and rather humorous situation that took place on the ship *Judea*. But soon Conrad was employing Marlow for much larger ends: as narrator of the novella, "Heart of Darkness," considered by many to be—along with *Lord Jim*—one of the author's greatest works.

The *Roi des Belges* served as Conrad's model for the boat in "Heart of Darkness."

"Heart of Darkness" and *Lord Jim*

"Heart of Darkness" is a fictionalized account of Conrad's own trip to the Congo in 1890. On one level, the novella is a story of the search for Kurtz, one of Belgium's most profitable ivory traders. On another symbolic level, the tale is a voyage into the heart of darkness within each of us. Marlow again is employed as the narrator and chief protagonist of the story, which he relates to four companions on board a boat on the Thames River near London. A young man in his tale, fresh from Europe, Marlow is sent on a journey up the Congo River to relieve the ivory trader, Kurtz. Marlow knows of Kurtz prior to his journey—the trader is thought to be a great civilizing influence in darkest Africa, a noble representative of the white man's burden.

But Marlow is confronted at many points on his journey with the evil and dehumanizing effects of colonialism: a French man-of-war which fires indiscriminately at natives in the bush; black workers are left to die by their white masters. The colonization of Africa by Europeans is a far cry from ennobling, and Marlow's ultimate disillusionment comes when he finally encounters Kurtz, who has himself become a power-hungry exploiter of the native population, running a cruel feudal kingdom upriver. This journey forces Marlow to confront both the degeneracy and corruption of Kurtz, as well as those same impulses which linger in his own heart.

Kurtz' famous line at his death—"The horror, the horror!"—have been taken to indicate both a level of understanding in the trader of the debased regime he has created, as well as an echoing regret that his kingdom is coming to a premature end. Marlow's subsequent lie to Kurtz's fiancee—telling her that the dying man's words were a repetition of her name—has likewise been interpreted by critics as a simple white lie or as an acceptance by Marlow that Kurtz was indeed an apostle of truth. Such ambiguities and varied levels of reading have made "Heart of Darkness" one of the greatest short novels in the English language.

Contemporary reviewers praised Conrad for his insight and vivid use of language. "The art of Mr. Conrad is exquisite and very subtle," observed a reviewer for the *Athenaeum*, who went on to note that "Heart of Darkness" cannot be read carelessly "as evening newspapers and railway novels are perused—with one mental eye closed and the other roving. Mr Conrad himself spares no pains, and from his readers he demands thoughtful attention." A reviewer in the *Times Literary Supplement* felt that the concluding scene of the novella was "crisp and brief enough for Flaubert." Conrad's novella quickly entered the canon, eliciting response from critics on both sides of the Atlantic. In an essay originally published in 1917, the American critic H. L. Mencken focussed on the character of Kurtz, concluding that he was "at once the most abominable of rogues and the most fantastic of dreamers."

As morally corrupt as Kurtz is, the story is not so much about him as about Marlow and his discovery of good and evil in each individual; his quest is not so much for Kurtz, but for the truth within himself. As such, the novella has also been compared to Virgil's *Aeneid* as well as Dante's *Inferno* and Goethe's *Faust*. As Lillian Feder noted in *Nineteenth-Century Fiction*, the novella has "three levels of meaning: on one level it is the story of man's adventures; on another, of his discovery of certain political and social injustices; and on a third, it is a study of his initiation into the mysteries of his own mind." Critics still debate to what degree Marlow finds his evil double in Kurtz and how far, in fact, he identifies with him. Conrad would employ this theme of doubling in later works, as well, most notably in *Lord Jim* and "The Secret Sharer."

Other critics have remarked upon the psychological aspects of the work as well as its tone. The American novelist and critic, Albert J. Guerard, in his *Conrad the Novelist*, noted not only Conrad's "dramatized psychological intuitions," but also the "impressionist method" and the "random movement of the nightmare" which works on the "controlled level of a poem." Guerard pointed to the contrasting use of dark and light by Conrad as a conscious symbol, and to his vegetative images which grow to menacing proportions. "'Heart of Darkness' . . . remains one of the great dark meditations in literature," Guerard wrote, "and one of the purest expressions of a melancholy temperament." As Frederick R. Karl noted in his *A Reader's Guide to Joseph Conrad*, "Heart of Darkness" is one of the world's greatest novellas: "It asks troublesome questions, disturbs preconceptions, forces curious confrontations, and possibly changes us." Conrad's novella is where, according to Karl, "the nineteenth century becomes the twentieth."

Published in 1900, *Lord Jim* literally announced the new century and its ambiguous, anti-heroic depths. Though published in book form two years before "Heart of Darkness," *Lord Jim* appeared serially after magazine publication of that novella. In *Lord Jim*, Conrad continued his pursuit of exposing romantic idealism in what became his first successful long novel. Once again narrated by Marlow, who makes a somewhat delayed appearance in the novel, *Lord Jim* has what Widmer characterized in *CDBLB* as a "somewhat bifurcated narrative," the result of Conrad fleshing out a magazine story into a full-length novel. The first part of the novel takes place aboard the *Patna*, a ship ferrying a load of Muslim pilgrims. Struck by the floating wreckage of another ship, the *Patna* begins to sink. The officers and crew on board panic, including Jim, a pastor's son who has a romanticized view of himself based largely on the adventure yarns he read as a child. They abandon ship, leaving the pilgrims to their fate. But the ship does not sink, and when it is towed into port, Jim and the officers stand trial for their cowardice.

Marlow makes his entrance at the trial, intrigued by the young Jim and feeling compassion for him in his disgrace. Marlow helps the youth, arranging through a trader friend of his, Stein, to send Jim to Patusan in the Malay Archipelago as his representative. Jim proves himself there, leading the native people against local rivals and helping to defend them from raiders. He earns the title of "Tuan Jim," or Lord Jim, marries a local woman, and becomes a leader of these people. At this point, Gentleman Brown, an English pirate, makes his appearance, threatening Patusan society. Jim captures the pirate, but feeling an odd connection to the man and his debased condition—another example of Conrad's doubling—he lets Brown and his band go on their promise to leave the archipelago. The locals cannot believe Jim's folly: he even allows Brown to leave fully armed. But Jim promises to forfeit his life should any further harm come from Brown. Breaking his word, Brown makes a second attempt to invade the Patusan village, and the son of the headman is killed in the process. Lord Jim is executed as a result.

Conrad advanced in his technical mastery with *Lord Jim*, employing chronological juxtapositions, sudden jumps in time, and the framing technique of Marlow's narration which makes ambivalent any reading of Jim's character. Conrad also dealt with themes ranging from the meaning of heroism and courage to self-understanding and the subjugation of native peoples by European civilization. But most critics view *Lord Jim* as a consummate exploration of romantic idealism and the conflict between such idealism and pragmatic action. Thus, some critics have found a Hamlet-like quality to the novel, and the trader Stein, in one of the most famous snippets of dialogue from the novel, at one point even poses the question of "how to be." Conrad seems to be saying that any of us, faced with difficult circumstances, might fail a moral test, might come short of one's ideal vision of oneself. Guerard, in his *Conrad the Novelist*, observed that the universal appeal of *Lord Jim* derives from this very fact of moral ambiguity: "Nearly everyone has jumped off some *Patna* and most of us have been compelled to live on, desperately or quietly engaged in reconciling what we are with what we would like to be."

From the earliest reviews, *Lord Jim* has been considered perhaps Conrad's greatest novel, and has been favorably compared to the best that Western literature contains. A reviewer in the *Spectator* noted that *Lord Jim* was "the most original, remarkable, and engrossing novel of a season by no means unfruitful of excellent fiction," while an *Academy* critic pronounced that "*Lord Jim* is a searching study—prosecuted with patience and understanding—of a cowardice of a man who was not a coward." A *Bookman* contributor acknowledged that the novel "may find various criticism."

However, the anonymous reviewer concluded that, "Judged as a document, it must be acknowledged a masterpiece."

And that is largely the judgement that has followed. Though Conrad's work was forgotten for a time after his death, *Lord Jim*, along with a handful of his other works, made a comeback in the mid-twentieth century. Like others of his novellas, short stories, and novels, *Lord Jim* has also come under criticism as being racist in content, for Conrad's continual identification of people of color with the darker forces of chaos. Yet many critics contend also that Conrad was no more susceptible to racist thought than others of his time, and was in fact ahead of his time in calling attention to the ravages caused by colonialism.

Political and social issues apart, *Lord Jim* becomes a fascinating case study of a romantic idealist. Some scholars also take a more biographical approach to the novel, and in this reading, Jim is a representative of Conrad himself who jumped the Polish ship of state at its most difficult moment to settle in England. The Polish Nobel poet, Czeslaw Milosz, in *Atlantic Monthly*, made the point that the name of Jim's ship, *Patna*, is intended to resonate with the Latin *patria* or "fatherland." Other, more psychoanalytically-minded reviewers note the fact that *Lord Jim* was published the same year as Freud's *Interpretation of Dreams*, both books heralding a new century of unconscious forces at work. Still others, including Ira Sadoff in the *Dalhousie Review*, credit Jim with being a proto-existential hero. "Camus' greatest novel, *The Stranger*, written forty-two years after *Lord Jim*, is the epitome of the existential novel," Sadoff noted. "Yet Meursault, the hero of the book, is not so different from Jim." But beyond all these interpretations and readings is the simple fact that the book presents a great yarn. As G. S. Fraser commented in *Critical Quarterly*, "It is, in fact, part of the interest and range of Conrad that he appeals not only to the sort of reader who enjoys, say George Eliot or Henry James but to the sort who enjoys Robert Louis Stevenson, Rider Haggard, or Conan Doyle."

Conrad's Middle Period

Though Conrad had achieved a critical reputation by the early 1900s, his financial situation was not to be envied. Forever in debt to friends and his agent, James Pinker, he and his family moved to Pent Farm in Kent in 1898, renting a brick cottage from a young writer named Hueffer, later known as Ford Madox Ford. While living in Kent, Conrad and Ford collaborated on two novels, *The Inheritors* and *Romance,* and Conrad came into contact with other writers nearby, including Stephen Crane, H. G. Wells, and Henry James, whom Conrad greatly revered. Other literary friends, including John Galsworthy and George Bernard Shaw, helped with the occasional loan as well as the word in the ear of publishers and critics to further his literary career. The birth of a second son in 1906 made straitened circumstances even more difficult. Ford and Conrad fell out over rent owed, and in 1907 the Conrad family moved to Bedfordshire, and from there in 1909 to Aldington, where they occupied four rooms over a butcher shop. By 1910, Conrad's debt had grown to over $100,000 in late-twentieth-century values.

Yet all the while, Conrad managed to keep writing. During these difficult years, he turned out some of his finest novels, including *Nostromo, The Secret Agent,* and *Under Western Eyes,* as well as his short story masterpiece, "The Secret Sharer." While the novels leave the sea behind for more political and social issues—a critique of materialism in *Nostromo,* an anarchist bombing in *The Secret Agent,* and the world of a double agent in *Under Western Eyes*—the sea is once again the setting for "The Secret Sharer."

Nostromo is set in an imaginary South American Country, Costaguanda, and illustrates, as Purdy observed in *Contemporary Authors,* "the impact of material interests on individuals and communities." Charles Gould and Nostromo are the central characters, both foreigners to Costaguanda and its major town, Sulaco. While Gould has come to reopen the local silver mines that once ruined his

**Marlon Brando (left) and Martin Sheen star in Francis Ford Coppola's acclaimed 1979 film *Apocalypse Now,*
inspired by Conrad's "Heart of Darkness."**

father, Nostromo is an Italian sailor come ashore to try his luck. He rises from a laborer to foreman of the dock workers, and he and Gould are largely responsible for putting down a revolution led by a native Indian. The work has been highly praised for its Dickensian wealth of character, though it was received poorly upon publication.

The Secret Agent is set in London and deals with an attempted anarchist bombing. Verloc, a triple agent, working at once for the police, the anarchists, and an unnamed European power, is commanded by the latter to commit a bombing incident so as to raise the wrath of the British and thereby destroy the political haven anarchists enjoy in England. To this end, he employs his wife's brother, Stevie, who is not quite right in the head. Stevie blows himself up on his way to the mission, and learning of this duplicity, Verloc's wife stabs her husband and then commits suicide. Praised for its ironic tone and "the ferocity of its plot," according to Purdy, *The Secret Agent* is generally considered one of the finer novels of Conrad's middle period.

The final novel of this political phase is *Under Western Eyes,* set both in Russia and Geneva, with echoes to the political foment found in *The Secret Agent.* Razumov is a Russian student of uncertain origins who is implicated in an assassination, but turns in a revolutionary involved in the plot, the romantic idealist Haldin, to save himself. Filled with remorse and feeling himself a moral outcast (not unlike Lord Jim), he is sent to Geneva as a double agent, falls in love with Haldin's sister, and ultimately confesses his sin to other revolutionaries. He ends up badly, first deafened by a revolver shot, and then run over and maimed for life. In this novel, Conrad once again uses his narrative framing device, employing an English professor of languages residing in Geneva as his narrator.

But by far the most widely read piece from Conrad's middle period is the short story, "The Secret Sharer." Widely praised for its rich use of symbol and allusion, this short story once again deals with the theme of doubling. In this case, the central character is a young captain, not unlike Conrad himself on his first command, anxious and unsure of himself. On the first night of the voyage, the young captain discovers a man named Leggatt in the water by the ship. Leggatt confesses to being an accused murderer on the

---

If you enjoy the works of Joseph Conrad, you may also want to check out the following books and films:

Graham Greene, *The Heart of the Matter,* 1948.
Herman Melville, *Billy Budd and Other Prose Pieces*, 1924.
The Sheltering Sky, a film based on the story by Paul Bowles, starring John Malkovich and Debra Winger, 1990.

---

run, but the captain helps him hide away and avoid capture. The two men build a close relationship, and the captain becomes convinced that Leggatt was justified in his crime. He drops Leggatt off on a secluded island, out of reach of the authorities, and feels a sense of self-confidence as a result of helping the fugitive.

Simple in structure and directly narrated by the young captain, the short story is more complicated in theme and modality. Most critical interpretation concludes that the basic theme of the story deals with the captain's coming to terms with himself and his new role. Leggatt serves as a catalyst in this struggle. But critics disagree whether Leggatt is simply a foil for the captain's essential good-heartedness, or if he is a deeper, more malignant agent with whom the captain on an unconscious level identifies. Guerard called "The Secret Sharer" the "most frankly psychological of Conrad's shorter works," and other critics followed suit, linking Conrad himself to the character of the young captain. Yet Jocelyn Baines, in his respected *Joseph Conrad: A Critical Biography,* felt this was overstating the case. "It is intensely dramatic," Baines wrote, "but on the psychological and moral level, rather slight." Tracing the story to an actual incident that took place at sea, Baines concluded that Leggatt was not the ambiguous moral character that many critics make out, but in fact had killed out of provocation and even with cause. According to Baines, Conrad had not intended his story "to be interpreted symbolically."

The battle, however, continues between critics as to the symbolic baggage of the short story, with numerous interpretations of the captain's action and of Leggatt's crime—bashing an unruly and threatening seaman over the head. Reviewers have noted the biblical references in the story and even called Leggatt an existentialist hero, yet perhaps the last word goes to the author himself who in a letter to his friend Edward Garnett noted of his story that "Every word fits and there's not a single uncertain note."

The Final Years

Conrad achieved fame and a stable financial position with his 1913 novel *Chance,* another novel narrated by Marlow which tells the story of Flora DeBaral, the daughter of a bankrupt speculative financier, and her lover, the oversensitive merchant marine master, Captain Anthony, who marries Flora more out of pity than love. As Widmer pointed out, one of the themes the novel deals with is sexual repression, though Widmer also complained that the novel was "melodramatic" in tone. After *Chance* came *Victory,* another novel about a pair of lovers. "After years of financial anxiety and commercial hackery, [Conrad] made considerable money from his writing," Widmer observed in *CDBLB,* "generally in inverse proportion to the quality of the fiction." It is generally agreed that after "The Secret Sharer," the artistic quality of Conrad's writings did decline, and this was in no small part a result of continued ill-health on the part of Conrad and his wife. However, no less a writer than Ernest Hemingway disagreed with the critics. Hemingway once noted that "from nothing else that I have ever read have I gotten what every book of Conrad has given me." He also recounted how, as a young man, he saved four Conrad novels "until I needed them badly." Then he quickly used these up "like a drunkard," feeling like "a young man who has blown his patrimony." *Chance* became a near best-seller on both sides of the Atlantic, and Conrad was now able to sit back and enjoy the fruits of his labors.

In 1914 Conrad and his family made a trip to Poland, a country the writer had not seen since his youth. The visit ended badly, however, when the family was caught in the mobilization for World War One and barely escaped internment. Back in England, Conrad observed the insanity of trench warfare with interest: his oldest son, Borys, went to the front in 1915. In 1916 he met a young American writer, Jane Anderson, who was working as a war correspondent in England, and

promptly fell in love with her, though the affair did not ultimately threaten his stable marriage with Jessie. Conrad was too practical a man to let such a situation get out of hand. Anderson did live in the Conrad home, Capel House, for a time while recuperating from a nervous breakdown, and many scholars and critics speculate on how much influence she had on Conrad's later work. Such work included semi-autobiographical collections and novels such as *Within the Tides, The Shadow Line,* and *The Arrow of Gold,* about Conrad's experiences in Marseilles as a young sailor. He also tried his hand at plays and even a movie script, though like Henry James, he never had much luck in the theater. The Napoleonic Wars interested him in the latter part of his career, and he set two works, the novella *The Rover* and the unfinished work *Suspense,* during that period.

Conrad continued to carry on a lively social life, increasing his circle to include French writers such as Andre Gide. Conrad, who had been such a roamer in his youth, traveled little in his later years, though he did visit the United States in late 1922 at the behest of his American publisher, Doubleday. Back in England he learned of the secret marriage of his son during his absence; he became a grandfather in 1924. Never a man for awards, he refused a knighthood in May of 1924, but incongruously longed until his final days for a Nobel Prize. He was destined never to receive one, and died of a heart attack, still at work on his novel *Suspense,* on August 3, 1924. He was buried four days later in Canterbury. The epigraph from Spenser's *The Faerie Queene,* which Conrad had used for the title page of *The Rover,* was cut into his stone:

"Sleep after toyle, port after stormie seas, Ease after warre, death after life, does greatly please."

■ Works Cited

Baines, Jocelyn, *Joseph Conrad: A Critical Biography,* Weidenfeld and Nicolson, 1960, pp. 346-78.

Conrad, Joseph, *Letters from Joseph Conrad,* edited with an introduction and notes by Edward Garnett, Bobbs-Merrill, 1928.

Conrad, Joseph, *Lord Jim,* Modern Library, 1931.

Conrad, Joseph, "Heart of Darkness" and "The Secret Sharer," New American Library, 1950.

Feder, Lillian, "Marlow's Descent into Hell," Nine-teenth-Century Fiction, March, 1955, pp. 280-92.

Fraser, G. S., "Lord Jim: The Romance of Irony," Critical Quarterly, Autumn, 1966, pp. 231-41.

Frederic, Harold, review of The Nigger of the "Narcissus," Saturday Review, February 12, 1898.

Gillon, Adam, Joseph Conrad, Twayne, 1982, pp. 37, 40.

Guerard, Albert J., Conrad the Novelist, Harvard University Press, 1966, pp. 41-44, 48.

Hemingway, Ernest, By-Line, Scribner, 1967, pp. 132-36.

Karl, Frederick R., A Reader's Guide to Joseph Conrad, Farrar, Straus and Giroux, 1969, pp. 91-144.

Karl, Frederick R., Joseph Conrad: The Three Lives, Farrar, Straus, 1979, pp. xiv-xv, 125.

Leavis, F. R., The Great Tradition, George W. Stewart, 1948.

Review of Lord Jim, Academy, November 19, 1900, p. 443.

Review of Lord Jim, Bookman, February, 1901, p. 161.

Review of Lord Jim, Spectator, November 24, 1900, p. 753.

Mencken, H. L., A Book of Prefaces, Knopf, 1920, pp. 11-66.

Milosz, Czeslaw, "Joseph Conrad in Polish Eyes," Atlantic Monthly, November, 1957, pp. 219-26.

Review of The Nigger of the "Narcissus," Spectator, December 25, 1897.

Purdy, Dwight H., "Joseph Conrad," Contemporary Authors, Volume 131, Gale, 1991, pp. 123-28.

Sadoff, Ira, "Sartre and Conrad: Lord Jim as Existential Hero," Dalhousie Review, Winter, 1969-70, pp. 518-25.

Widmer, Kingsley, "Joseph Conrad," Concise Dictionary of British Literary Biography, Volume 5: Late Victorian and Edwardian Writers, 1890-1914, Gale, 1991, pp. 83-122.

Review of Youth, Athenaeum, December 20, 1902, p. 824.

Review of Youth, Times Literary Supplement, December 12, 1902, p. 372.

■ For More Information See

BOOKS

Bennett, Carl D., Joseph Conrad, Continuum, 1991.

Dictionary of Literary Biography, Gale, Volume 10: Modern British Dramatists, 1940-1945, 1982, Volume 34: British Novelists, 1890-1920: Traditionalists, 1985.

Ford, Ford Madox, Joseph Conrad: A Personal Remembrance, Little, Brown, 1924.

Meyers, Jeffrey, Joseph Conrad: A Biography, Scribner, 1991.

Moser, Thomas C., Joseph Conrad: Achievement and Decline, Harvard University Press, 1958.

Murfin, Ross C., editor, Conrad Revisited: Essays for the Eighties, University of Alabama Press, 1985.

Najder, Zdzislaw, editor, Conrad's Polish Background: Letters to and From Polish Friends, translated by Halina Carroll, Oxford University Press, 1964.

Najder, Zdzislaw, Joseph Conrad: A Chronicle, Rutgers University Press, 1983.

Palmer, John, Joseph Conrad's Fiction: A Study in Literary Growth, Cornell University Press, 1968.

Sherry, Norman, Conrad: The Critical Heritage, Routledge and Kegan Paul, 1973.

Twentieth-Century Literary Criticism, Gale, Volume 1, 1978, Volume 6, 1982, Volume 13, 1984, Volume 25, 1988, Volume 43, 1992, Volume 57, 1995.

PERIODICALS

Bookman, June, 1926, pp. 429-35.

College English, October, 1965, pp. 55-61; December, 1965, pp. 240-43; October, 1967, pp. 628-40.

Critical Quarterly, Spring, 1973, pp. 9-31; Autumn, 1975, pp. 268-79.

Modern Fiction Studies, Spring, 1964, pp. 27-30; Winter, 1966-67, pp. 427-38.

Nineteenth-Century Fiction, June, 1961, pp. 75-80; March, 1967, pp. 369-80; June, 1982, pp. 75-96.

Studies in the Novel, Summer, 1973, pp. 229-47.

Times Literary Supplement, March 15, 1918.

Yale Review, January, 1926, pp. 254-66.*

—Sketch by J. Sydney Jones

Carl Deuker

Personal

Born October 26, 1950, in San Francisco, CA; son of John and Marie (a county clerk; maiden name, Milligan) Deuker; married Anne Mitchell (a teacher), 1978; children: Marian. *Education:* University of California at Berkeley, B.A., 1972; University of Washington, M.A., 1974; University of California at Los Angeles, teaching certificate, 1976. *Religion:* "Fallen away Catholic. Seriously, none." *Politics:* Democrat. *Hobbies and other interests:* Golf, tennis, gardening, "anything with a ball that bounces."

Addresses

Home—2827 Northwest 62nd St., Seattle, WA 98107. *E-mail*—carl_deuker@norshore.wednet.edu.

Career

Saint Luke School, Seattle, WA, teacher, 1977-90; Northshore School District, Bothell, WA, teacher, 1991—. *Seattle Sun* (weekly newspaper), film and book critic, 1980-85. *Member:* Authors Guild, Authors League of America, Phi Beta Kappa.

Awards, Honors

South Carolina Young Adult Book Award, 1992, and American Library Association (ALA) Best Book for Reluctant Readers list, both for *On the Devil's Court;* Nebraska Golden Sower Award, 1996, Pennsylvania Young Reader's Choice Award, 1997, and ALA Best Book for Reluctant Readers list, all for *Heart of a Champion;* New York Library Book for the Teen Age, and nominee, Young Adult Book of the Year in both Tennessee and Texas, both 1997, all for *Painting the Black;* Best Books for Young Adults list, ALA, for *On the Devil's Court, Heart of a Champion,* and *Painting the Black.*

Writings

On the Devil's Court, Little, Brown, 1988.
Heart of a Champion, Little, Brown, 1993.
Painting the Black, Houghton Mifflin, 1997.

Deuker's short story, "If You Can't Be Lucky," was anthologized in *Ultimate Sports,* edited by Donald Gallo.

Work in Progress

A basketball book, expected 1999.

■ Sidelights

Carl Deuker writes sports novels for young readers. He is emphatic about that. "As a child I frequently read sports novels," Deuker told *Authors and Artists for Young Adults* (*AAYA*) in an interview, "or at least I started novels that seemed to be about sports. Pretty soon into the book, I'd find that sports was really way on the back-burner. Often I'd put the book down and turn to something else, usually historical fiction with a lot of war in it. Those books delivered what they promised. As a writer of sports fiction, I decided early on to make sure I delivered on the promise—that sports be front and center. But I also wanted to make sure that each book gave a little bit more."

It is that "little bit more" that has won critical praise, awards, and a loyal readership for Deuker. With three novels to his credit—*On the Devil's Court, Heart of a Champion,* and *Painting the Black*—Deuker has already found a place for himself in the canon of young adult sports writers. Elizabeth Bush, in *Bulletin of the Center for Children's Books,* noted that Deuker "offers a trio of novels that span the calendar with explosive plays, rich characterizations, and incisive scrutiny of the particular power of truly gifted athletes to ignite—and sometimes incinerate—their teams." Bush went on to conclude in her omnibus review of Deuker's work that the author "undeniably drags the seamier aspects of high school athletics into the light . . . but he never sours on the game itself or its power to transform good boys into better men. Bats crack, helmets clash, nets swish, and the rivalries are rabid and infectious." Or as Deuker would say, sports stories with that "little bit more."

Deuker focusses on basketball and baseball in his novels, and on boys like Joe Faust in his first novel, *On the Devil's Court,* who want to succeed so badly that they might sell their very soul for the opportunity; or on great athletes like Jimmy in *Heart of a Champion* or Josh in *Painting the Black* who squander their gifts with alcohol abuse or self-conceit that leads to uncontrolled behavior. Such characters are balanced by other teens such as Seth in *Heart of a Champion* and Ryan in *Painting the Black* who, though not hugely gifted, persevere and succeed through dint of hard work and determination. Thus for Deuker, athletics becomes a microcosm for the world in general—not a backdrop for a story, but a pressure cooker in which youths are tested, in which issues from father-son relations to sexual assault are confronted head-on. Deuker's "little bit more" goes a long way.

A California Youth

Born in San Francisco on October 26, 1950, Deuker grew up in the Bay area. The death of his father when Deuker was three created a sense of loss in him that plays out through much of his work, making father-son relations a major theme. As

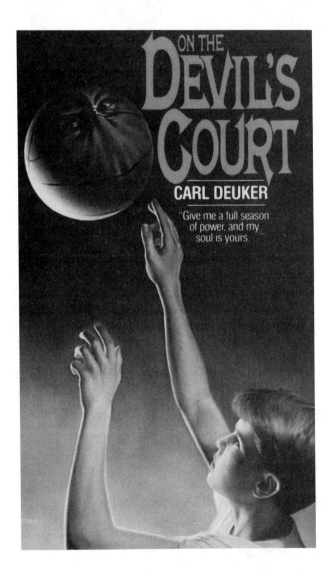

Joe believes his success at home, in school, and on the basketball court is due to a bargain he made with the devil in this 1988 novel.

Deuker noted in his *AAYA* interview, he was frequently alone as a child. "I had an understanding mother who encouraged and allowed elaborate play with tinker toys. I'd set them up all around the house, then have a great time pretending to be the master of the universe. I think writing is, in some very basic way, an adult version of playing tinker toys." At an early age, sports also became a focal point for Deuker. Never an outstanding athlete, Deuker recalled that he spent more time sitting on the bench in high school than playing. He also played on intramural teams in college, but it wasn't so much "official" athletics that mattered most. "Sports has always been a passion," Deuker told *AAYA*. "Again, I was a bit on the solitary side. I played on teams, but I also often played imaginary games in my mind. I'd hit clothespins with a broom handle, pretending to be Willie Mays. I'd shoot walnuts at a pillow in the front room pretending to be Wilt Chamberlain. I'd throw darts in the garage, all the while defeating the Yankees in the seventh game of the World Series. Often I'd actually write down the results of these games, filling notebooks with statistics and records."

In high school he began writing poetry and short stories. "Like most of my generation," Deuker explained, "I was strongly influenced by Bob Dylan, the Beatles, and the Rolling Stones. Dylan and the Beatles in particular drew my attention to the power of words. I frequently had no clue what Dylan's songs were about (I wonder if he did!) but I was mesmerized nonetheless. I had a classmate with whom I started to collaborate. We would write (secretly) during English class, exchanging poems and short stories, risking detention if we were caught writing." An English teacher himself now, the irony of this does not escape Deuker.

In college at the University of California at Berkeley, Deuker continued writing, publishing some early efforts in campus and underground magazines. "I was an English major," Deuker told *AAYA*, "took lots of writing classes, was never the best writer in class, but persisted with writing anyway." Graduating from Berkeley, Deuker went on for an M.A. at the University of Washington, his introduction to the Pacific Northwest. "I did no creative writing at the University of Washington," Deuker recalled. "By that time I had discovered that I did not want to write criticism for a living. After getting my Masters, I went to Los

Angeles and got a job of sorts at the Los Angeles *Daily Journal.* I never did figure out what they hired me for. After a year there, I attended UCLA and got a teaching certificate." Certificate in hand, Deuker returned to the Seattle area where he has taught middle grade and junior high students since 1977. In 1978 he married fellow teacher, Anne Mitchell, and a decade later had a daughter, Marian, "a future shortstop for the Mariners," Deuker promises.

"When I first moved to Washington state, I worked as a freelance movie and book reviewer for the *Seattle Sun,*" Deuker told *AAYA*. "It somewhat satisfied my writing urge, but when the newspaper went bankrupt it was a blessing as it removed an easy outlet. Rather than pursue more freelance work, I decided to try my hand at a YA novel."

On the Devil's Court

Deuker quickly settled on a theme for his novel. "I've always liked Marlowe's *Dr. Faustus,* always enjoyed *Damn Yankees,* and decided to put the two together, change the sport and the audience. The result was *On the Devil's Court.* It took about six months to write, and then went through six full rewrites (one and a half years) before it was published." Luck entered into things also. Deuker initially submitted the novel to the publishing arm of *Atlantic Monthly,* but while his manuscript was in the mail, that publishing division was sold to Little, Brown. No matter; the new publishers liked his manuscript well enough to take it on, beginning a three-book connection between Deuker and editor Ann Rider.

On the Devil's Court tells the story of Joe Faust, only son of a well-known geneticist and a sculptress. He is a high school student passionately in love with basketball; the court is the one place he feels really at home. As Bush noted in her compilation reviews in *Bulletin of the Center for Children's Books,* Deuker sets up a "scenario he revisits in ensuing works" with *On the Devil's Court:* a high school team that badly needs some new talent to get them past a rival and into the finals. In this debut novel, Joe Faust moves from the East Coast to Washington state where he talks his parents into letting him go to a large public school because of its excellent athletics program. But Joe soon runs into trouble: attending a party

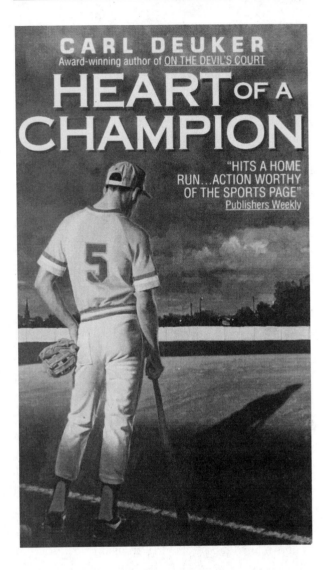

Two friends, one a gifted natural athlete, the other a gutty, hard-working player, take different paths while leading their baseball team to the state playoffs.

where alcohol is present, he falls into a confrontation with the police. Joe's parents thereafter send him to a smaller private school which has a surprisingly good basketball team. Joe wants badly to not just fit in with this team, but to be its main man. Demoted to junior varsity for a time, Joe—inspired by a recent reading of *Dr. Faustus*—offers to cut a deal with the devil, promising himself in exchange for one perfect season: "Give me a full season, give me twenty-four games of this power, and my soul is yours," Joe says.

Joe quickly gets his wish. Back on varsity, he leads his team to the state finals. But soon Joe grows

wary. Did he really make a deal with the devil? Is that what is responsible for his father's heart attack? As Bush pointed out, "Deuker cunningly shrouds the veracity of this deal in ambiguity." Doris Losey, writing in *Voice of Youth Advocates*, commented that "Lots of basketball action mixed with psychological musing result in an unusual novel that may appeal to older teens, but especially to basketball fans." Writing in *School Library Journal*, Gerry Larson, remarking upon the "clever blend" of family conflict, sports action, and superstition, noted that "Adolescent readers will empathize with the mind games that Joe plays as he struggles for self-identity and independence; teachers will delight in the literary references and analogies; and librarians will praise this fine addition to sports fiction." A critic in *Publishers Weekly* observed that "Deuker skillfully blends gritty basketball action with well-rounded characters to create a vivid contemporary morality tale," while *Horn Book*'s Nancy Vasilakis concluded that the "Freudian foundations of the story never detract from the novel's fast-moving plot, and at the end when Joe can tell his father honestly what his own choices for his future are, young readers will rejoice, whether or not they fully comprehend what developmental steps were taken to achieve this measure of independence."

Heart of a Champion

Deuker turned to what he thought was a "clever, funny little animal book" for his next work. "But no publisher agreed," he told *AAYA*. So he went back to sports, writing his "most autobiographical book," taken from two separate parts of his own life. "One character, Seth, mirrors my own background—early death of father, struggling with that fact and with trying to find my place as person and an athlete," Deuker explained. "The other character [Jimmy Winter] is drawn from a student I had who also died tragically in an alcohol-related accident."

In his second novel, Deuker employed baseball as the central sport around which he examines the friendship of two adolescent boys. Seth is just coming to terms with his father's death when he meets the young baseball star, Jimmy, whose own father acts as his coach. But Jimmy's father is also an alcoholic, a fact which ultimately leads to a major conflict in the book. The two boys eat and breathe baseball, playing through Little League and Babe Ruth teams together. Jimmy is forced to leave the area for a time when his father abuses his mother, but returns for his freshman year and becomes the team's leading hitter. The friendship takes a hard knock when, in their sophomore year, Jimmy makes the varsity team while Seth stays behind on the junior varsity. Jimmy and another varsity star, Todd Franks, soon set the team on a path to the playoffs, but Jimmy's drinking and class-cutting earn him a suspension and ruin the squad's hopes for a championship.

Meanwhile, competent, hard-working Seth has worked his way up through the ranks to a spot on the varsity, but his admiration for Jimmy is tempered by his disgust at Jimmy's off-field be-

High school senior Ryan Ward is both inspired by and ashamed of his friend Josh Daniels, the school's star athlete, in this 1997 work.

havior. Another winning season is in the offing until Jimmy is killed in a car accident, drunk at the wheel. The varsity go all the way to the state playoffs, where they ultimately lose. But Seth has learned a lesson from it all, one that is intended for the reader, as well. Not only is Deuker dealing with an anti-drinking message in the book, but also with the proclivity of fans and often other teammates to forgive bad behavior in star athletes. "They were both going to be major-league stars—famous millionaires," Deuker writes in the novel. "Nobody blamed them for blowing the chance for the playoffs. Drinking was part of the package—like Jose Canseco and his fast cars."

One of Deuker's most popular novels, *Heat of a Champion* earned critical praise. "The compelling coming-of-age novel offers a sensitive, moving portrait of adolescence combined with dramatic sports action," noted a contributor in *Horn Book*, a sentiment echoed by a reviewer for *Kirkus Reviews* who wrote that "the baseball action is believable and the contrasts between several sets of characters are thoughtfully explored." Betsy Hearne, writing in *Bulletin of the Center for Children's Books,* praised especially Deuker's examination of the "balance between talent and discipline," and *School Library Journal* reviewer Jack Forman felt that this "well-paced novel will involve many readers." A *Publishers Weekly* critic declared that *Heart of a Champion* "hits a home run" with "action worthy of the sports page."

Painting the Black

Baseball is once again front and center for Deuker's third novel, *Painting the Black,* which also looks at the destructive behavior of a star high school athlete. Josh Daniels is a senior transfer who dazzles his new school with his exploits at quarterback. His teammates idolize, but Josh has a nasty streak towards women. He humiliates another student, Celeste Honor, but everyone, including the administration, seems content to look the other way. Josh's friend, Ryan Ward, is a bit unsettled by this aggressive behavior, but he, too, is of a forgiving nature for this star athlete. Josh, who is also a top pitcher, has inspired Ryan to try out for catcher on the varsity baseball team. For Ryan, Josh is a breath of fresh air, convincing him that he can overcome an earlier accident in which he broke his legs and an arm, and inspiring him to get back on the diamond once again.

If you enjoy the works of Carl Deuker, you may also want to check out the following books and films:

Bruce Brooks, *The Moves Make the Man*, 1984.
Tabitha King, *One on One*, 1993.
Adam Rapp, *Missing the Piano*, 1994.
Hoosiers, a film starring Gene Hackman, 1986.

When baseball season finally rolls around, Ryan and Josh do form a great duo, and Ryan begins to blossom as a result of newfound respect from his classmates. But Josh grows more arrogant as the team looks set to clinch a championship season. However, Josh's aggressive behavior spills over into sexual assault when he attacks Monica Robey, an academic star who has embarrassed him. Ryan interrupts the assault and recognizes Josh, disguised in a wolf's mask. Ryan agonizes over whether or not to turn in his friend. He knows that this will result in a suspension and loss of the championship for his team. Susan Dunn in *Voice of Youth Advocates* observed that "Ryan is forced to take a stand about something for the first time in his life, he finds it no longer easy to escape to the small, safe world he has created for himself." A contributor in *Kirkus Reviews* noted that "Deuker, adept at capturing the thrills during the game, also proves talented at dramatizing Ryan's torment in the face of his friend's deeds; the depiction of a boy coming into his own is resonant and inspiring." Todd Morning wrote in *School Library Journal* that *Painting the Black* was a "well-crafted sports novel that delivers without becoming didactic or boring," while a *Booklist* critic remarked that the "well-written sports scenes—baseball and football—will draw reluctant readers, but it is Ryan's moral courage that will linger when the reading is done." Dunn concluded in *Voice of Youth Advocates* that "Deuker hits the nail on the head. This is an excellent sports story, with a lot more to it than just the game of baseball."

"This novel was inspired by school events," Deuker told *AAYA*. "I was at a school where a girl was 'pantsed' by a hotshot athlete. It was extremely interesting to see the wide variation in reactions among both adults and students. Some thought it was nothing at all; others thought the boy should be expelled from school. What struck me in going through the whole process was that adults decided everything. I wanted to write a book in which a teenager has to decide whether such an assault is a big deal or not."

Writing as a Balancing Act

Deuker's drive to write well can be compared to the athletic aspirations of some of his book characters. "For years I thought I would sit down and write every day until I'd finished the great American novel," Deuker told *AAYA*. "And every once in a while I actually did sit down and write for four hours. But most of the time the task was too intimidating. If you want to write, write. But ten or twenty minutes a day is a good goal for young aspiring writers."

Deuker himself snatches writing time from his teaching and parenting. "Right now I teach full time. I write every morning from five to six and again most evenings, revising mostly then as I do not feel too creative at the end of the day. I try to do the plotting and character development in summers. I write short chapters because I have short writing periods." He is at work on a fourth novel concerning "a neglected 'loser' kid who also is a good athlete trying to see if there is any place in the world for him." Though Deuker sets his books in high school, he senses that many of his readers are actually middle grade and junior high school students, such as those he teaches. "My books are ways for them to peek ahead in their lives and perhaps be a little prepared for what might be coming." For Deuker, one of the most important things an adolescent can do is find a private meaning for his or her life. "We were not put on this earth just to go to work for some company. Every one of us has an artistic impulse of some kind. Find yours—whether it be art, writing, drama, dance, story-telling—it doesn't matter. But whatever it is, nurture it."

Deuker is also humble about his achievements, not unlike Seth or Ryan in his books. "I'll continue to write sports novels as long as ideas come to me," he told *AAYA*. "I have no plans to go full time; I don't think I would have enough ideas, and I don't think I could handle the pressure of writing for a livelihood. Actually, I'm delighted to have published three books and hope to write more. But if I don't, I won't be crushed."

■ Works Cited

Bush, Elizabeth, "Carl Deuker," *Bulletin of the Center for Children's Books*, September, 1997.

Deuker, Carl, *On the Devil's Court*, Little, Brown, 1988.

Deuker, Carl, *Heart of a Champion*, Little, Brown, 1993.

Deuker, Carl, interview with J. Sydney Jones for *Authors and Artists for Young Adults*, conducted April 1998.

Dunn, Susan, review of *Painting the Black, Voice of Youth Advocates*, August, 1977, p. 182.

Forman, Jack, review of *Heart of a Champion, School Library Journal*, June, 1993, p. 126.

Hearne, Betsy, review of *Heart of a Champion, Bulletin of the Center for Children's Books*, September, 1993, p. 7.

Review of *Heart of a Champion, Horn Book*, May-June, 1993, p. 337.

Review of *Heart of a Champion, Kirkus Reviews*, May 15, 1993.

Review of *Heart of a Champion, Publishers Weekly*, May 9, 1994, p. 74.

Larson, Gerry, review of *On the Devil's Court, School Library Journal*, January, 1989, p. 92.

Losey, Doris, review of *On the Devil's Court, Voice of Youth Advocates*, April, 1989, p. 27.

Morning, Todd, review of *Painting the Black, School Library Journal*, May, 1997.

Review of *On the Devil's Court, Publishers Weekly*, November 11, 1988, p. 60.

Review of *Painting the Black, Booklist*, June 15, 1997.

Review of *Painting the Black, Kirkus Reviews*, April 1, 1997, p. 553.

Vasilakis, Nancy, review of *On the Devil's Court, Horn Book*, March, 1988, p. 216.

■ For More Information See

BOOKS

Contemporary Authors, Volume 149, Gale, 1996.
Something about the Author, Volume 82, Gale, 1995.

PERIODICALS

Booklist, December 15, 1988, p. 703; November 1, 1993, p. 534; October 15, 1994, p. 413.

Emergency Librarian, May, 1989, p. 46; January, 1995, p. 56.

Horn Book, May-June, 1997, p. 317.

Voice of Youth Advocates, June, 1994, p. 71.

Wilson Library Bulletin, September, 1989, p. 11; November, 1993, p. 78.

—Sketch by J. Sydney Jones

Nancy Farmer

■ Personal

Born July 9, 1941, in Phoenix, AZ; daughter of Elmon Frank (a hotel keeper) and Sarah (a grade school teacher, maiden name, Marimon) Coe; married Harold Farmer (a literature teacher and poet), 1976; children: Daniel. *Education:* Phoenix College, Arizona, A.A., 1961; Reed College, B.A., 1963; attended Merrit College and University of California at Berkeley, 1969-71. *Politics:* "None whatsoever." *Religion:* Animism. *Hobbies and other interests:* Ethology, criminology, marine biology, African culture and history.

■ Addresses

c/o Orchard Books, 95 Madison Avenue, New York, NY 10016.

■ Career

Worked in the Peace Corps in India, 1963-65; University of California at Berkeley, Berkeley, lab technician, 1969-72; Loxton, Hunting and Associ-ates, Songo, Mozambique, chemist and entomolo-gist, 1972-74; University of Zimbabwe, Rukomeche, Zimbabwe, lab technician and entomologist, 1975-78; freelance scientist and writer in Harare, Zim-babwe, 1978-88; Stanford University Medical School, Palo Alto, CA, lab technician, 1991-92. Freelance writer, 1992—. *Member:* Society of Children's Book Writers and Illustrators, Science Fiction and Fantasy Writers of America.

■ Awards, Honors

Writers of the Future Gold Award, Bridge Publi-cations, 1988; National Endowment for the Arts grant, 1992; Newbery Honor Book, 1995, Notable Children's Book, American Library Association, 1995, and Golden Kite Honor, all for *The Ear, the Eye, and the Arm;* Best Children's Book, Zimbabwe International Book Fair, 1996, for *The Warm Place;* National Book Award finalist for Children's Lit-erature, 1996, Silver medal, Commonwealth Club of California, 1996, Best Book for Young Adults, American Library Association, 1997, and Newbery Honor Book, 1997, all for *A Girl Named Disaster.*

■ Writings

JUVENILE FICTION

Lorelei, College Press (Zimbabwe), 1988.
Tsitsi's Skirt (picture book), College Press, 1988.

The Ear, the Eye, and the Arm, College Press, 1989, Orchard Books, 1994.
Tapiwa's Uncle, College Press, 1992.
Do You Know Me, Orchard Books, 1993.
The Warm Place, Orchard Books, 1995.
Runnery Granary, Greenwillow, 1996.
A Girl Named Disaster, Orchard Books, 1996.

OTHER

Also contributor to *Writers of the Future Anthology, #4,* Bridge Publications, 1988, and *Best Horror and Fantasy of 1992,* St. Martin's Press, 1993.

The Ear, the Eye, and the Arm has been published in German and Italian; *A Girl Named Disaster* has been published in Dutch.

■ Adaptations

"Tapiwa's Uncle," adapted by Aaron Shepard, appears in *Stories on Stage,* H. W. Wilson Company, 1993.

■ Work in Progress

Sim Webb, Casey Jones's Fireman, for Dial Books; an adult science fiction novel titled *VaiDoSol.*

■ Sidelights

Author Nancy Farmer spent from 1972 to 1988 living in the African nations of Mozambique and Zimbabwe. She has drawn upon her varied experiences there for the inspiration for several critically acclaimed story books and a picture book for young people. "I'm a story teller," Farmer explained in a 1998 interview with *Authors and Artists for Young Adults (AAYA).* Readers and reviewers alike evidently agree with her self-assessment, for Farmer's books have enjoyed considerable success. A *Publishers Weekly* critic hailed her as "one of the best and brightest authors for the YA [young adult] audience," and two of Farmer's books have been singled out for special praise: her novels *The Ear, the Eye, and the Arm* and *A Girl Named Disaster* were chosen as Newbery Honor Books.

Farmer was born in Phoenix, Arizona, but she grew up in a hotel in Yuma, 180 miles southwest,

on the U.S.-Mexican border. In her *AAYA* interview, Farmer described her father as being "at various times in his life, a cowboy, a sergeant in the army, a lawyer, and a manager, in successive jobs, of a tuberculosis sanitorium, a tavern, and a hotel [in Yuma]." Elmon Coe took on the latter job after suffering a heart attack, in the vain hope that running a hotel would be "a piece of cake," Farmer stated. Nancy was the youngest of the family's three children by several years, and so she grew up largely on her own. It was during the years that she and her family lived in the hotel that Farmer developed a fascination with storytelling. She recalled to *Something about the Author (SATA),* "Every night until past midnight I listened to stories from truck drivers, cowboys, and railroad workers. My father took me to the American legion hall on bingo nights, and I heard a lot more stories there. People were able to spin tales back then, and they taught me a lot."

Farmer was not interested in school, and she told *AAYA* that she played hooky a lot, "once for an entire year." However, when Farmer attended classes and applied herself, she proved to be a bright, capable student. In fact, she eventually earned a Bachelor of Arts degree from Reed College in Portland, Oregon, and in 1963 she joined the Peace Corps, a U.S. government agency established by President John F. Kennedy to send idealistic young Americans overseas to help meet the needs of developing countries for trained manpower. "I became a Peace Corps volunteer because I wanted to go to India and meet a rich Maharajah," Farmer quipped. "Of course, I didn't tell the Peace Corps that."

Farmer was posted to India from 1963 to 1965 and then traveled for two years prior to returning home in 1967 to work and study at Merrit College and the University of California at Berkeley. When her wanderlust returned in 1971, Farmer and a friend decided to work their way around the world. "We arranged passage on a yacht that was actually in the process of being stolen. We didn't know this. The coast guard arrested the 'captain' as he sailed out under the Golden Gate. We were upset, but they probably saved us from being dumped overboard somewhere," Farmer told *SATA.* When next she sailed, it was aboard a freighter bound for Africa, where Farmer hoped to work as a "freelance scientist." She did so, finding a job as a chemist and entomologist in the former Portuguese colony of

Mozambique in east Africa. After two years there, Farmer moved on to Zimbabwe (formerly known as Rhodesia), where she remained for the next thirteen years, from 1975 to 1988. It was in Zimbabwe that Farmer met and fell in love with Harold Farmer, a public prosecutor and an English instructor at the University of Zimbabwe. Theirs was a whirlwind courtship; as Farmer told *SATA,* the couple had only known each other "about a week" when Harold proposed. They married, and Farmer gave birth in 1978 to a son, whom she and her husband named Daniel.

Literary Beginnings

Farmer has said that her experiences in central Africa had a profound influence on her life and her writing. It was while she was living in Zimbabwe that she decided to become a writer. "One day when my son Daniel was about four years old, I was suddenly inspired to write. I had been reading a novel by Margaret Forster and thought: *I could do that,*" she told *SATA.* "Three hours later I emerged with a complete story. The experience was so surprising and pleasant I did it again the next day. That is how my writing career began." The Shona, the African tribe among whom the Farmers were living, explained Farmer's sudden urge to write as being the result of a visit from a *shave* (pronounced shah-vay), or wandering spirit: "*Shaves* come from people who haven't received proper burial rites. They drift around until they find a likely host, possess whomever it is, and teach him or her a skill. In my case, I got a traditional storyteller."

Even with the *shave*'s guidance, it was four years before Farmer finished her first book. She spent the intervening time honing her literary skills, reading, and studying the writings of such authors as Roald Dahl, J. R. R. Tolkien, C. S. Lewis, P. D. James, Ruth Rendell, and Stephen King. "It takes *at least* four years to learn to write," Farmer explained to *AAYA.* "The horrible truth is that one's first efforts are amateurish. It takes time, practice, and objectivity to correct this problem. I have never understood why people think they can write well without effort. No one expects a first-year medical student to transplant a kidney."

Farmer's first book, a children's story about a young native girl called *Lorelei,* was published in Zimbabwe in 1988. African reviewers were "gen-

erous about it, because it isn't a very good book," Farmer told *AAYA.* Her next three efforts, a picture book called *Tsitsi's Skirt* and two works for juveniles titled *The Ear, the Eye, and the Arm* and *Tapiwa's Uncle,* were all published by the same Zimbabwean publisher, College Press. By the time the latter appeared, Farmer and her family had emigrated to the U.S., primarily for Daniel's benefit. At first, the transition was difficult and Farmer found it impossible to write. "We were so poor we couldn't even afford heat in winter, let alone frills like beds," she recalled. "We bundled up together on the floor under a heap of yard-sale blankets. I read Harold and Daniel all the "Tarzan" and "Conan the Barbarian" books at night."

Farmer's next book—the first by her to be published in the U.S.—was a 1993 juvenile novel called *Do You Know Me.* That book recounts the adventures of a Zimbabwean schoolgirl named Tapiwa, a character whom Farmer had introduced a year earlier in her book *Tapiwa's Uncle. Do You Know Me* tells what happens when Tapiwa's uncle, whose village in Mozambique has been destroyed by bandits, comes to the city to live with Tapiwa's middle-class family. Uncle Zeka involves Tapiwa in wild schemes to make money, usually with disastrous results. A critic in *Kirkus Reviews* described *Do You Know Me* as "an exaggerated, splendidly comical tale enriched by profound undertones." A *Horn Book* reviewer wrote that the book was "very funny" and pointed out that the "contrast between city life in modern Zimbabwe and traditional living in the bush is clearly illustrated."

Fantastic Adventures

On the heels of the publication of *Do You Know Me,* Farmer's American publisher printed her rewritten 1989 book *The Ear, the Eye, and the Arm,* a science fiction adventure story. The work is set in the Zimbabwe of the twenty-third century and tells what happens when the children of the military ruler—a sheltered thirteen-year-old boy named Tendai, his younger sister Rita, and their preschool-age brother Kuda—set out to explore the city so Tendai can earn his merit scouting badge. As the children go from one predicament to the next, they are pursued by a bumbling trio of mutant detectives—the Ear, the Eye, and the Arm of the title—who have been hired by the children's father to rescue them. "Throughout the story it's the thrilling adventure that will grab readers, who will also like the comic, tender characterizations, not only of the brave defiant trio and absurd detectives, but also of nearly every one the kids meet, from street gangsters and spiritual healers to the English tribespeople with their weird customs," reviewer Hazel Rochman stated in *Booklist.* "Demanding and intricate," reviewer Patricia Manning commented in *School Library Journal,* "but often convoluted, it will be rewarding to readers willing to travel beyond everyday places and to work to untangle its many strands."

In her next book, Farmer continued to draw upon the inspiration of her African experiences. *The Warm Place* is about a young giraffe named Ruva, who struggles to get back home to Africa after being captured by a family of demons and sent to a zoo in San Francisco. Ruva is helped in her journey by an assortment of magical animal friends. "The author has created highly original events and characters. . . . Readers will find getting home again with Ruva to be an entertaining and rewarding experience," remarked Sarah Guille in *Horn Book.* "With witty, crisp dialog, this novel will be a fine read," agreed Mary Harris Veeder, writing in *Booklist.*

Farmer's *Runnery Granary* is a picture story book for young readers in the five-to-seven age group. Unlike any of Farmer's other books, *Runnery Granary* is set in the past, in medieval times. The story describes how Mrs. Runnery battles some mischievous gnomes who are gobbling her grain. Reviewer Kathy East of *School Library Journal* praised the book as "A charming tale that story-hour crowds are sure to eat up."

The award-winning *A Girl Named Disaster* was originally meant to be a textbook for African Studies. "I was a lousy student and would be a worse educator," Farmer explained in her *AAYA* interview. Instead, she turned the material into a novel about an eleven-year-old Shona girl named Nhamo, who flees her home village in Mozambique to escape a *ngozi* (angry spirit), a cholera epidemic, and an enforced marriage to an evil man. Nhamo journeys to her father's family in nearby Zimbabwe. Owing to misfortune, what should have been a two-day journey turns into a year-long odyssey that's an educational experience both for the heroine and the young readers who follow her trials and tribulations. Martha Par-

If you enjoy the works of Nancy Farmer, you may also want to check out the following books and films:

Chinua Achebe, *Girls at War, and Other Stories,* 1973.
Ann McCaffrey, *Pegasus in Flight,* 1990.
Joan D. Vinge, *Psion,* 1982.
Sarafina!, a film set in Soweto, South Africa, 1992.

ravano, writing in *Horn Book,* described *A Girl Named Disaster* as "an extraordinarily rich novel." In *School Library Journal* Susan Pine wrote, "This story is humorous and heartwrenching, complex and multilayered. . . ." Norma A. Sisson in *Voice of Youth Advocates* praised *A Girl Named Disaster* as "an excellent example of young adult fiction which draws the teenager into the story to learn about other cultures." A *Publishers Weekly* contributor declared that "Nhamo herself is a stunning creation—while she serves as a fictional ambassador from a foreign culture, she is supremely human. An unforgettable work."

Farmer has completed the yet-to-be-published *Sim Webb, Casey Jones's Fireman,* a retelling of the Casey Jones railroad legend. Another of Farmer's books promises to be a something of a departure for her, although she has occasionally written in the genre; Farmer told *AAYA* that she is working on an adult science fiction novel that is tentatively titled *VaiDoSol.* After that, she said she intends to return to more familiar territory with "three shortish juvenile novels."

■ Works Cited

Review of *Do You Know Me, Horn Book,* June, 1993.
Review of *Do You Know Me, Kirkus Reviews,* May 1, 1993.
Review of *The Ear, the Eye, and the Arm, Publishers Weekly,* September 25, 1996.
East, Kathy, review of *Runnery Granary, School Library Journal,* August, 1996, p. 122.
Farmer, Nancy, comments in *Something about the Author,* Volume 75, Gale, 1993.
Farmer, Nancy, interview with Ken Cuthbertson for *Authors and Artists for Young Adults,* May, 1998.

Review of *A Girl Named Disaster, Publishers Weekly,* October 28, 1996.

Guille, Sarah, review of *The Warm Place, Horn Book,* October, 1995, pp. 597-98.

Manning, Patricia, review of *The Ear, the Eye, and the Arm, School Library Journal,* June, 1994, p. 147.

Parravano, Martha, review of *A Girl Named Disaster, Horn Book,* November-December, 1996, pp. 734-35.

Pine, Susan, review of *A Girl Named Disaster, School Library Journal,* October, 1996, p. 144.

Rochman, Hazel, review of *The Ear, the Eye, and the Arm, Booklist,* April 1, 1994, p. 1436.

Sisson, Norma A., review of *A Girl Named Disaster, Voice of Youth Advocates,* December, 1996, p. 268.

Veeder, Mary Harris, review of *The Warm Place, Booklist,* April 1, 1995, p. 1391.

■ For More Information See

PERIODICALS

Booklist, June 1, 1996, p. 1731.
Bulletin of the Center for Children's Books, March, 1994.
Kirkus Reviews, April 15, 1994.
Publishers Weekly, March 15, 1993; April 11, 1994, p. 66.

—Sketch by Ken Cuthbertson

Ian Fleming

publisher of the *Book Collector*, 1949-64. *Military Service:* Royal Naval Volunteer Reserve, 1939-45; lieutenant; did secret service work as a personal assistant to the director of Naval Intelligence, 1939-45. *Member:* Turf Club, Broodle's Club, Portland Club.

■ Personal

Born May 28, 1908, in London, England; died August 12, 1964; son of Valentine (a major in the armed forces and a Conservative member of the British Parliament) and Evelyn Beatrice (Ste. Crois Rose) Fleming; younger brother of Peter Fleming, also an author; married Anne Geraldine Charteris (formerly Lady Rothermere), March 24, 1952; children: Caspar. *Education:* Attended Eton, Royal Military Academy at Sandhurst, University of Munich, and University of Geneva. *Hobbies and other interests:* Swimming, gambling, golf, book collecting.

■ Career

Moscow correspondent for Reuters Ltd., London, England, 1929-33; associated with Cull & Co. (merchant bankers), London, England, 1933-35; stockbroker with Rowe & Pitman, London, England, 1935-39; returned to Moscow, 1939, officially as a reporter for the *Times,* London, unofficially as a representative of the Foreign Office; Kemsley (later Thomson) Newspapers, foreign manager, 1945-59;

■ Awards, Honors

Order of the Dannebrog, 1945; Young Reader's Choice Award, 1967, for *Chitty-Chitty-Bang-Bang.*

■ Writings

FICTION, UNLESS OTHERWISE NOTED

Casino Royale, J. Cape (London), 1953, Macmillan (New York), 1954, published in paperback as *You Asked for It,* Popular Library, 1955.

Live and Let Die, J. Cape (London), 1954, Macmillan (New York), 1955.

Moonraker, J. Cape (London), and Macmillan (New York), 1955, published as *Too Hot to Handle,* Perma Books, 1957.

Diamonds Are Forever, J. Cape (London), and Macmillan (New York), 1956.

The Diamond Smugglers, J. Cape (London), 1957, Macmillan (New York), 1958.

From Russia, with Love, J. Cape (London), and Macmillan (New York), 1957.

Dr. No, J. Cape (London), and Macmillan (New York), 1958.

Goldfinger, J. Cape (London), and Macmillan (New York), 1959.

For Your Eyes Only: Five Secret Exploits of James Bond, Viking (New York), 1960, published in England as *For Your Eyes Only: Five Secret Occasions in the Life of James Bond,* J. Cape (London), 1960.

Gilt-Edged Bonds: "Casino Royale," "From Russia, with Love," "Doctor No," introduction by Paul Gallico, Macmillan (New York), 1961.

Thunderball, J. Cape (London), and Viking (New York), 1961.

The Spy Who Loved Me, J. Cape (London), and Viking (New York), 1962.

On Her Majesty's Secret Service, J. Cape (London), and New American Library (New York), 1963.

Thrilling Cities (travel essays), J. Cape (London), 1963, New American Library (New York), 1964.

You Only Live Twice, J. Cape (London), and New American Library (New York), 1964.

Chitty-Chitty-Bang-Bang: The Magical Car (juvenile), illustrations by John Burningham, J. Cape (London), 3 volumes, 1964-65, Random House (New York), 1 volume, 1964, collected edition, J. Cape, 1971.

Bonded Fleming: A James Bond Omnibus (contains *Thunderball, For Your Eyes Only,* and *The Spy Who Loved Me*), Viking (New York), 1965.

The Man with the Golden Gun, J. Cape (London), and New American Library (New York), 1965.

More Gilt-Edged Bonds (contains *Live and Let Die, Moonraker,* and *Diamonds Are Forever*), Macmillan (New York), 1965.

Fleming Introduces Jamaica (nonfiction), edited by Morris Cargill, Hawthorn, 1966.

Octopussy (includes the story *The Living Daylights*), New American Library (New York), 1965, published in England as *Octopussy, and The Living Daylights,* J. Cape (London), 1966.

A James Bond Quartet (includes *Casino Royale, Live and Let Die, Moonraker,* and *From Russia, with Love*), J. Cape (London), 1992.

A James Bond Quintet (includes *Diamonds Are Forever, Doctor No, Goldfinger, For Your Eyes Only,* and *The Spy Who Loved Me*). J. Cape (London), 1993.

The Essential James Bond (includes *Thunderball, On Her Majesty's Secret Service, You Only Live Twice, The Man with the Golden Gun, Octopussy,* and *The Living Daylights*), J. Cape (London), 1994.

Ian Fleming's James Bond (includes *Moonraker, From Russia, with Love, Doctor No, Goldfinger, Thunderball,* and *On Her Majesty's Secret Service*), Chancellor Press (London), 1994.

Columnist, under pseudonym Atticus, for the *Sunday Times,* London, during the 1950s. Contributor to *Horizon, Spectator,* and other magazines.

A collection of Fleming's letters, manuscripts, and other papers and memorabilia is housed at Lilly Library, Indiana University, and additional material is owned by Glidrose Productions.

■ **Adaptations**

Films adapted from Fleming's works and/or based on his characters include *Dr. No,* 1962, *From Russia, with Love,* 1963, *Goldfinger,* 1964, *Thunderball,* 1965, *The Poppy Is Also a Flower,* 1966, *Casino Royale,* 1967, *You Only Live Twice,* 1967, *Chitty-Chitty-Bang-Bang,* 1968, *On Her Majesty's Secret Service,* 1969, *Diamonds Are Forever,* 1971, *Live and Let Die,* 1973, *The Man with the Golden Gun,* 1974, *The Spy Who Loved Me,* 1977, *Moonraker,* 1979, *For Your Eyes Only,* 1981, *Never Say Never Again,* 1983, *Octopussy,* 1983, *A View to a Kill,* 1985, *The Living Daylights,* 1987, *License to Kill,* 1989, and *Goldeneye,* 1995.

After Fleming's death, Kingsley Amis continued the James Bond novels (under the pseudonym Robert Markham), as did John Gardner. *The Book of Bond; or, Every Man His Own 007,* by Lt. Col. William (Bill) Tanner, is a guide for gentlemen who would like to be as glamorous as Fleming's hero.

■ **Sidelights**

The name is Bond, James Bond, that highbrow agent of the British secret service, as suave and stalwart as he is sex-charged, a cold-hearted holder of his government's license to kill. Since his creation some five decades ago, Bond has lured readers and movie audiences on improbable but thrilling adventures as he seeks to save society from evildoers of epic proportions.

His creator was Fleming, Ian Fleming, a British blueblood who had to work for a living, a onetime banker and now and again journalist. Out of his own self-embellished experiences as a wartime lieutenant in naval intelligence, Fleming crafted, from 1954 until his death ten years later, fourteen books featuring Bond, to whom he lent his high-society tastes and hard-drinking, woman-

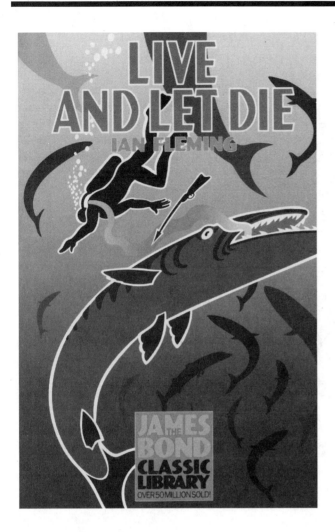

Braving sharks and barracuda, time bombs, and other dangers, James Bond exposes a gangster operation led by the formidable Mr. Big that may be financing the Soviet Union's KGB spy agency in this 1954 novel.

izing ways. "James Bond is simply Ian Fleming day-dreaming in the third person," assessed biographer John Pearson, quoted in a *Forbes* retrospective by Anthony Weller.

Named plainly for the author of Fleming's favorite bird book, James Bond enjoys high-stakes gambling, drives fast cars, drinks vodka martinis (shaken, not stirred), and smokes custom-made cigarettes. He travels to exotic locales, where he suffers violent tortures at the hands of bad-guy foreigners—Le Chiffre, Goldfinger, Scaramanga, Drax, Dr. No—but prevails in the end, enjoying and exploiting along the way the favors of beautiful women with silly names. He has been called a mythical hero for a mythless age.

Critics' opinions about Fleming's body of popular fiction vary widely. Kingsley Amis wrote in *New Statesman* that Fleming "was a good writer, occasionally a brilliant one" with "gifts for sustaining and varying action, and for holding down the wildest fantasies with cleverly synthesised pseudo-facts." Others, however, take the view of Leroy L. Panek, who wrote in his book *The Special Branch: The British Spy Novel, 1890-1980* that Bond is "a muddled hero created by a third-rate hack." Fleming himself held no literary pretensions. He aimed at entertaining his readers and making money, saying that his was simply "the business of getting intelligent, uninhibited adolescents of all ages, in trains, aeroplanes and beds, to turn over the page," according to Joan DelFattore in the *Dictionary of Literary Biography.*

As popular as Fleming's Bond novels were in their day, they have been supplanted over time by Hollywood's Bond movies. Mention "Agent 007" and the shared imagination of contemporary popular culture conjures up Sean Connery, Roger Moore, Timothy Dalton, or Pierce Brosnan, actors who have portrayed the secret agent over the years. Yet some critics make the case that in a *mano a mano* the book-Bond wins out. "Film-Bond turned into a secret agent version of Superman, wearing a tux instead of a cape and destroying his enemies with quips and gadgetry," Weller observed in *Forbes,* adding, "Sean Connery's finesse aside, book-Bond—the archetype—remains a more complex character, and his exploits human and attainable. What amazes the most, going back to the Fleming canon, is the books' hypnotic power—a sheer drive and compelling readability that overcome the dull patches, Bond's total lack of humor and many implausibilities."

A Man for His Time

Fleming created just the kind of hero that readers were looking for in post-World War II Britain. Bond offered them a stylishly modern escape into a dangerous and impossible world that still looked and sounded a lot like their own. And while Bond, with his unexceptional traits and accountability to the establishment, seemed an ordinary enough fellow, he was also unbeatable, free to use any means to achieve his government's desired end. Against the Cold War backdrop of the 1950s and 1960s, Bond came across as a patriot, prevailing on Britain's behalf over foreign enemies.

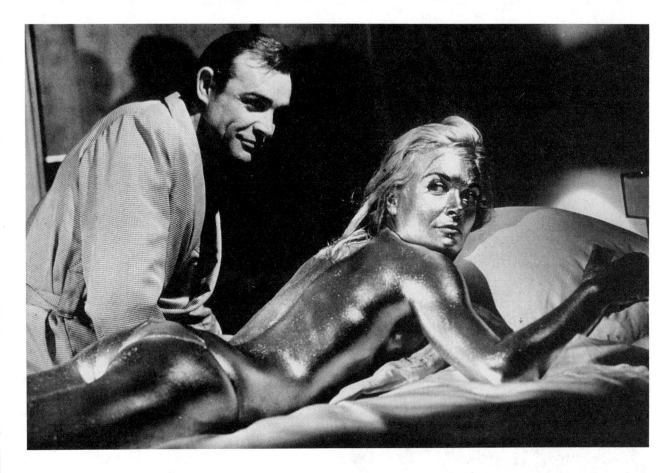

The hit 1964 movie *Goldfinger*, with Sean Connery and Shirley Eaton, launched a Bond film cult following.

Fleming is said to have called Bond "a cardboard dummy" and his adventures "trivial piffle." Yet the self-image Fleming vigorously sought to live out had its Bond-like dimensions, filled as it was with social ambitions, illicit love affairs, heavy drinking, a taste for intrigue, and a regular need for exotic escape. Some critics note that he drew heavily on the expertise of others in order to sound knowledgeable about any number of subjects. Fleming also set out to have experiences that could be translated into exciting stories; when episodes in his own life story lacked drama, he simply altered details in their retelling.

Ian Lancaster Fleming was born into affluence in London in 1908. Fleming's father came from a British banking fortune; his mother was a descendent of the royal house of Lancaster. Fleming was just a boy when his father was killed in France during World War I. His mother controlled the family fortune thereafter, and Fleming never inherited independent means.

Undisciplined and disinterested in academics, the young Fleming devoted himself to sports and romance, and as a result, was in and out of exclusive schools, including Eton and Sandhurst's military academy. He studied and skied for a year in Austria before taking up the study of German, Russian, and French languages at universities in Munich and Geneva. He hoped to join the Foreign Office but failed the exam, so in 1931 he took a job with the Reuters Ltd. news agency. His work there was not without excitement—he was sent to Moscow to cover an espionage trial—but the entry-level pay meant he had to live with his mother. He endured that arrangement for two years, then left the news business for a more lucrative career in banking and stock brokerage.

The Building of Bond

Fleming got his first sample of secret service work in 1939 when his business contacts and foreign language and journalism skills landed him an undercover assignment, of sorts, for the British Foreign Office. He was sent along on a trade mission to Russia and Poland as a member of the press; his real job was to make observations on Russia's suitability as an ally in the brewing war. The experience helped get Fleming into intelligence work after World War II began. Fleming's service as the personal assistant to the director of Naval Intelligence is said to have been largely administrative, but he did travel abroad and make contacts with secret agents, underwent training maneuvers, and even took part in a secret mission involving a Japanese cipher expert. At one point he monitored a successful unit which accompanied troops into newly captured territories in order to confiscate intelligence materials. Fleming would later draw on—and doctor up—these experiences for use in his fiction.

After the war Fleming became the foreign news service manager for a newspaper group. The job allowed him to spend two months out of every winter at Goldeneye, the house he had built in Oracabessa, Jamaica. It was there that he entertained his future wife, Anne, while she waited for a divorce from Fleming's friend, Viscount Esmond Rothermere. And it was at Goldeneye that Fleming wrote his first James Bond novel, *Casino Royale*, and those that would follow, all at a quick pace of one per year. As Weller quotes Fleming: "Would these books have been born if I had not been living in the gorgeous vacuum of a Jamaican holiday? I doubt it."

". . . it was toughness that had landed Jimmy his job with the Secret Service—the job of smashing the ruthless Le Chiffre and his spy network— no matter how many women tried to stop him . . .," read the back-cover blurb of the twenty-five cent American paperback edition of *Casino Royale*. Opening in a resort in the south of France, it is "an extremely engaging affair" whose "especial charm" is "the high poetry with which

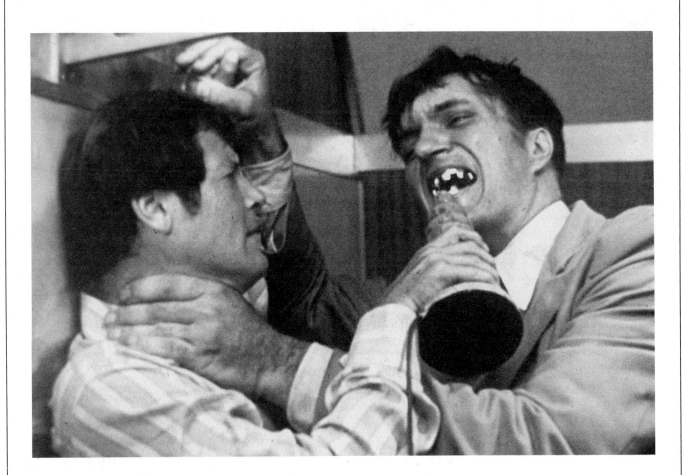

In 1977 Roger Moore played Bond and Richard Kiel costarred as Jaws in *The Spy Who Loved Me*.

[Fleming] invests the green baize lagoons of the casino tables," according to a contributor in the *Times Literary Supplement*.

Bond bests his enemy, the Soviet agent Le Chiffre, in a high-tension game of baccarat; later, captured by Le Chiffre, a naked Bond gets tied to a chair and whacked about the genitals with a carpet beater. ("In the course of the novels he is hurt so repeatedly it's a wonder he can manage to please women at all, much less those as demanding as Pussy Galore, Solitaire Latrelle, Tiffany Case, Honeychile Rider and Tatiana Romanova," Weller wrote of Bond.) These memorable scenes are the first examples of what would become hallmark Bond-isms: his high-stakes gaming with enemies

When the engineer who is building Britain's Moonraker missile is caught cheating at an exclusive Bridge club, Bond is called in to investigate.

(at cards, racing, and golf) and his endurance of unimaginable tortures.

Live and Let Die, Moonraker, Diamonds Are Forever, From Russia, with Love, and *Dr. No* followed in yearly succession, building a following of Bond fans who came to expect imaginative variations on Fleming's adventure formula. The novels were written quickly—"they often seem less planned than vividly dreamt," according to Weller—and Fleming did not concern himself too much with careful plot structure, often splicing action scenes together with irrelevant narrative detours.

Some critics believe that Fleming's early work was his best, citing in particular *From Russia, with Love*. With fewer structural problems and stronger characterization than in other Bond novels, it garnered a good share of favorable reviews. It is said to have been one of President John F. Kennedy's favorite books, an announcement that boosted already steady book sales.

Sex, Snobbery, and Sadism?

Dr. No, set on a Caribbean island from which the metal-handed title character is able to counteract U.S. missile launches, contained a violent scene in which Bond must make a bloody escape through a torture tunnel. It set off a heated debate among critics over what came to be characterized as Fleming's authorial sins of "sex, snobbery and sadism," after an article of that title by Paul Johnson in *New Statesman*. Johnson wrote that *Dr. No* was "without doubt, the nastiest book I have ever read." Writing in *Twentieth Century*, Bernard Bergonzi, another principal in the anti-Bond argument, stated that Fleming "rarely rises above the glossy prose of the advertising copywriter," and that "the erotic fantasies in which Bond is continually involved are decidedly sinister. . . . Mr. Fleming describes scenes of violence with uncommon relish, and it is these that really bring his books down to the horror-comic level. The sadomasochistic note is unmistakable throughout."

Others countered that, as entertainment, the books should not be taken so seriously. "Although, as Mr. Bergonzi noted, irony is quite lacking in the narration, there is an irony of situations; the comedy lies in telling a story of glaring implausibility with an absolutely straight face," wrote Martin Dodsworth in *Twentieth Century*. Added Simon

In this 1956 novel, Agent 007 travels from Africa to New York City and finally to Los Vegas in his search for the source of a diamond smugglers' organization.

Raven in the *Spectator,* "Since when has it been remarkable in a work of entertainment that it should lack a specific 'ethical frame of reference'?"

According to Anthony Lejeune in *National Review,* Fleming took the criticism to heart more than he let on: "Consciously or unconsciously, he subdued the flavor of his narrative, which was a mistake. It weakened the books without appeasing his enemies." *Goldfinger*—whose villain seeks to infiltrate Fort Knox—came out the following year. It contains a famous scene in which Bond outsmarts Goldfinger in a round of golf; it also earned Fleming the worst reviews he had gotten to date. DelFattore wrote that "it lacks plausibility, even by the undemanding standards of Fleming's usual style." By this time Fleming, still a heavy drinker

and smoker, had grown tired and was suffering from ill health. He was finding it hard to come up with new ideas that he could sustain through novel-length adventures. So in 1960 he published five short stories featuring Bond, titled *For Your Eyes Only.* He then set his sights on making a Bond movie.

Fleming developed a story with the help of a group of producers and a scriptwriter, but ended the work there. Later, when he proceeded to publish the story (featuring SPECTRE, an international crime organization, and the hijacking of a NATO bomber carrying nuclear weapons) as *Thunderball,* his former movie collaborators sued. The court permitted the novel's publication, but the movie rights were later granted to one of the collabora-

Timothy Dalton starred as Bond in the 1989 adaptation of *License to Kill.*

If you enjoy the works of Ian Fleming, you may also want to check out the following books and films:

Frederick Forsyth, *The Fist of God*, 1994.
John Le Carre, *The Russia House*, 1999.
David Morrell, *Assumed Identity*, 1993.
The Saint, starring Val Kilmer and Elisabeth Shue, 1997.

tors. Not long after, Fleming suffered a heart attack. During his recuperation, he wrote *Chitty-Chitty-Bang-Bang: The Magical Car*, a children's book about the Pott family and their magic car which he crafted out of stories he had told his son Caspar. It was published in 1964, and made into a popular movie-musical in 1969.

Bond finally hit the big screen in 1962, when Harry Salzman teamed up with another producer, Albert Broccoli, to form Eon Productions. Holding the film rights to all but two of the Bond books (*Thunderball* and *Casino Royale*, which was filmed as a Bond spoof featuring Woody Allen), they first produced *Dr. No*, followed by *From Russia, with Love* and the highly successful *Goldfinger*. A Bond movie-cult following emerged thereafter.

Through lawsuit and illness and movie business, Fleming continued to turn out his annual Bond novels. *The Spy Who Loved Me* was a notable departure from his usual formula, with the story told from the point of view of Bond's love interest, Vivienne Michel, a vulnerable young woman whom Bond saves from two thugs in a motel. It did not deliver the usual adventure fare that Bond fans had come to expect, and was not popular. It was followed by the well-received *On Her Majesty's Secret Service* (in which Bond, allied with a criminal, treks into the Alps after SPECTRE's head honcho) and *You Only Live Twice* (featuring Dr. Shatterhand, a villain who takes pleasure in others' use of his suicide garden). Fleming then completed what he felt was an unsatisfactory manuscript for *The Man with the Golden Gun* in 1964. He intended to revise it, but suffered a hemorrhage that summer and died. The book was published posthumously—flaws and all—as were two short stories, paired under the title *Octopussy, and The Living Daylights*.

Weller has estimated that over sixty million copies of Fleming's novels have been sold over the years, and that more than half the world's population has seen at least one Bond movie. And, since Fleming's death, at least a dozen writers have tried their hand at crafting new Bond adventures (notable among them Kingsley Amis, writing *Colonel Sun* in 1968 under the pseudonym Robert Markham). Clearly Bond did not die with his creator. "Fleming has gone, having given more pleasure to mankind than most of us can ever hope to do," wrote Lejeune, "but Bond survives, with a life of his own, Bond and pseudo-Bond merging into a single epic figure. With his Walther PPK nestling in its Berns Martin Triple-draw holster, and a full-throated roar from twin exhausts of his super-charged Bentley, James Bond has passed triumphantly into the Valhalla of immortal heroes."

■ Works Cited

Amis, Kingsley, "M Is for Murder," *New Statesman*, April 2, 1965, pp. 540-41.

Bergonzi, Bernard, "The Case of Mr. Fleming," *Twentieth Century*, March, 1958.

DelFattore, Joan, "Ian Fleming," *Dictionary of Literary Biography*, Volume 87: *British Mystery and Thriller Writers since 1940, First Series*, Gale, 1989, pp. 86-110.

Dodsworth, Martin, *Twentieth Century*, May, 1958.

Johnson, Paul, "Sex, Snobbery and Sadism," *New Statesman*, April 5, 1958, p. 430.

Lejeune, Anthony, "To Valhalla with Twin Exhausts," *National Review*, September 7, 1965, p. 777.

Panek, Leroy L., *The Special Branch: The British Spy Novel, 1890-1980*, Bowling Green University Popular Press, 1981.

Raven, Simon, "Gilt-Edged Bond," *Spectator*, April 4, 1958, p. 438.

"Spices and Charlatans," *Times Literary Supplement*, April 17, 1953, p. 249.

Weller, Anthony, "Bond at 40," *Forbes*, November 22, 1993.

■ For More Information See

BOOKS

Amis, Kingsley, *The James Bond Dossier*, New American Library, 1965.

Benson, Raymond, *The James Bond Bedside Companion*, Dodd, 1984.

Bond, Mary Wickham, *How 007 Got His Name*, Collins, 1966.

Boyd, Ann S., *The Devil with James Bond!*, John Knox, 1966.

Bryce, Ivar, *You Only Live Once: Memories of Ian Fleming*, Weidenfeld & Nicolson, 1975.

Concise Dictionary of British Literary Biography, Volume 7: *Writers after World War II, 1945-1960*, Gale, 1991.

Contemporary Literary Criticism, Gale, Volume 3, 1975, Volume 30, 1984.

del Buono, Oreste, and Umberto Eco, editors, *The Bond Affair*, translation by R. A. Downie, MacDonald, 1966.

Gant, Richard, *Ian Fleming: The Man with the Golden Pen*, Mayflower, 1966.

Gardner, John E., *Ian Fleming's James Bond*, Avenet, 1987.

Haining, Peter, *James Bond: A Celebration*, W. H. Allen, 1987.

Lane, Sheldon, editor, *For Bond Lovers Only*, Panther, 1965.

Lycett, Andrew, *Ian Fleming: The Man behind James Bond*, 1996.

Pearson, John, *The Life of Ian Fleming*, McGraw, 1966.

Pearson, John, *007 James Bond*, Morrow, 1973.

Pearson, John, *James Bond: The Authorised Biography of 007*, Granada, 1985.

Pelrine, Eleanor, and Dennis Pelrine, *Ian Fleming: Man with the Golden Pen*, Swan, 1966.

Playboy Interviews, Playboy Press, 1967.

Reference Guide to English Literature, second edition, St. James Press, 1991.

Rosenberg, Bruce A., and Ann Steward, *Ian Fleming*, Twayne, 1989.

Rubin, Steven Jay, *The James Bond Films*, Arlington, 1982.

Sauerberg, Lars Ole, *Secret Agents in Fiction: Ian Fleming, John le Carre and Len Deighton*, St. Martin's, 1984.

Snelling, O. F., *007 James Bond: A Report*, Holland, 1964.

Starkey, Lycurgus M., *James Bond: His World of Values*, Abingdon, 1966.

Twentieth-Century Crime and Mystery Writers, St. James Press, 1994.

Van Dover, J. Kenneth, *Murder in the Millions: Earle Stanley Gardner, Mickey Spillane, Ian Fleming*, Ungar, 1984.

Zeiger, Henry A., *Ian Fleming: The Spy Who Came in with the Gold*, Duell, Sloan & Pearce, 1965.

PERIODICALS

Commentary, July, 1968.

Critic, October-November, 1965.

Encounter, January, 1965.

Kirkus Reviews, December 1, 1997.

Life, August 10, 1962.

New Yorker, April 21, 1962.

New York Times, February 16, 1967; April 25, 1967.

New York Times Book Review, July 4, 1961; November 5, 1961; April 1, 1962; December 11, 1966.

Publishers Weekly, August 24, 1964.

Reporter, July 13, 1967.

Times Literary Supplement, October 27, 1966.*

—*Sketch by Tracy J. Sukraw*

Stephen Jay Gould

■ Personal

Born September 10, 1941, in New York, NY; son of Leonard (a court reporter) and Eleanor (an artist; maiden name, Rosenberg) Gould; married Deborah Lee (an artist and writer), October 3, 1965; children: Jesse, Ethan. *Education:* Antioch College, A.B., 1963; Columbia University, Ph.D., 1967.

■ Addresses

Office—Museum of Comparative Zoology, Harvard University, Cambridge, MA 02138.

■ Career

Antioch College, Yellow Springs, OH, instructor in geology, 1966; Harvard University, Cambridge, MA, assistant professor and assistant curator, 1967-71, associate professor and associate curator, 1971-73, professor of geology and curator of invertebrate paleontology at Museum of Comparative Zoology, 1973—, Alexander Agassiz Professor of

Zoology, 1982—. Member of advisory board, Children's Television Workshop, 1978-81, and *Nova*, 1980-92. *Member:* American Association for the Advancement of Science, American Academy of Arts and Sciences, American Society of Naturalists (president, 1979-80), National Academy of Sciences, Paleontological Society (president, 1985-86), Society for the Study of Evolution (vice-president, 1975, president, 1990), Society of Systematic Zoology, Society of Vertebrate Paleontology, History of Science Society, European Union of Geosciences (honorary foreign fellow), Society for the Study of Sports History, Royal Society of Edinburgh, Linnaean Society of London (foreign member), Sigma Xi.

■ Awards, Honors

National Science Foundation, Woodrow Wilson, and Columbia University fellowships, 1963-67; Schuchert Award, Paleontological Society, 1975; National Magazine Award, 1980, for "This View of Life"; Notable Book citation, American Library Association, 1980, and National Book Award in science, 1981, both for *The Panda's Thumb: More Reflections in Natural History;* Scientist of the Year citation, *Discover,* 1981; National Book Critics Circle Award, 1982, American Book Award nomination in science, 1982, and outstanding book award, American Educational Research Association, 1983, all for *The Mismeasure of Man;* MacArthur Foundation Prize fellowship, 1981-86; medal of excellence, Columbia University, 1982; F. V. Haydn Medal, Philadelphia Academy of Natural Sciences, 1982; Joseph Priestley Award and Medal, Dickinson College, 1983; Neil Miner Award, National Association of Geology Teachers, 1983; silver medal, Zoological Society of London, 1984; Bradford Washburn Award and gold medal, Museum of Science (Boston), 1984; distinguished service award, American Humanists Association, 1984; Tanner Lectures, Cambridge University, 1984, and Stanford University, 1989; meritorious service award, American Association of Systematics Collections, 1984; Founders Council Award of Merit, Field Museum of Natural History, 1984; John and Samuel Bard Award, Bard College, 1984; Phi Beta Kappa Book Award in science, 1984, for *Hen's Teeth and Horse's Toes: Further Reflections in Natural History*; Sarah Josepha Hale Medal, 1986; creative arts award for nonfiction, Brandeis University, 1986; Terry Lectures, Yale University, 1986; distinguished service award, American Geological Institute, 1986; Glenn T. Seaborg Award, International Platform Association, 1986; In Praise of Reason Award, Committee for the Scientific Investigation of Claims of the Paranormal, 1986; H. D. Vursell Award, American Academy and Institute of Arts and Letters, 1987; National Book Critics Circle Award nomination, 1987, for *Time's Arrow, Time's Cycle: Myth and Metaphor in the Discovery of Geological Time*; Anthropology in Media Award, American Anthropological Association, 1987; History of Geology Award, Geological Society of America, 1988; T. N. George Medal, University of Glasgow, 1989; Sue T. Friedman Medal, Geological Society of London, 1989; Distinguished Service Award, American Institute of Professional Geologists, 1989; Associe du Museum National D'Historie Naturelle, Paris, 1989; fellow, Royal Society of Edinburgh, 1990; City of Edinburgh Medal, 1990; Britannica Award and Gold Medal, 1990, for dissemination of public knowledge; Forkosch Award, Council on Democratic Humanism, and Phi Beta Kappa Book Award in Science, both 1990, and Pulitzer Prize finalist and Rhone-Poulenc Prize, both 1991, all for *Wonderful Life: The Burgess Shale and the Nature of History*; Iglesias Prize, 1991, for Italian translation of *The Mismeasure of Man*; Distinguished Service Award, National Association of Biology Teachers, 1991; Golden Trilobite Award, Paleontological Society, 1992; Homer Smith Medal, New York University School of Medicine, 1992; UCLA medal, 1992; James T. Shea Award, National Association of Geology Teachers, 1992; Commonwealth Award in Interpretive Science, State of Massachusetts,

1993; J. P. McGovern Award and Medal in Science, Cosmos Club, 1993; St Louis Libraries Literary Award, University of St. Louis, 1994; Gold Medal for Service to Zoology, Linnaean Society of London; Distinguished Service Medal, Teachers College, Columbia University. Recipient of numerous honorary degrees from colleges and universities.

■ Writings

NONFICTION

Ontogeny and Phylogeny, Belknap Press (Cambridge, MA), 1977.

Ever since Darwin: Reflections in Natural History (essays), Norton (New York City), 1977.

The Panda's Thumb: More Reflections in Natural History (essays), Norton, 1980.

(With Salvador Edward Juria and Sam Singer) *A View of Life*, Benjamin-Cummings (Menlo Park, CA), 1981.

The Mismeasure of Man, Norton, 1981, revised and expanded edition, 1996.

Hen's Teeth and Horse's Toes: Further Reflections in Natural History (essays), Norton, 1983.

The Flamingo's Smile: Reflections in Natural History (essays), Norton, 1985.

(With Rosamund Wolff Purcell) *Illuminations: A Bestiary*, Norton, 1986.

Time's Arrow, Time's Cycle: Myth and Metaphor in the Discovery of Geological Time, Harvard University Press (Cambridge, MA), 1987.

An Urchin in the Storm: Essays about Books and Ideas, Norton, 1987.

Wonderful Life: The Burgess Shale and the Nature of History, Norton, 1989.

The Individual in Darwin's World: The Second Edinburgh Medal Address, Edinburgh University Press (Edinburgh), 1990.

Bully for Brontosaurus: Reflections in Natural History, Norton, 1991.

(With Rosamund Wolff Purcell) *Finders, Keepers: Eight Collectors*, Norton, 1992.

Eight Little Piggies: Reflections in Natural History, Norton, 1993.

Dinosaur in a Haystack: Reflections in Natural History, Harmony (New York City), 1995.

Full House: The Spread of Excellence from Plato to Darwin, Harmony, 1996.

Questioning the Millennium: A Rationalist's Guide to a Precisely Arbitrary Countdown, Harmony, 1997.

Leonardo's Mountain of Clams and the Diet of Worms: Essays on Natural History, Harmony, 1998.

Author of *An Evolutionary Microcosm: Pleistocene and Recent History of the Land Snail P. (Poecilozonites) in Bermuda* (Cambridge, MA), 1969. Also author, with Eric Lewin Altschuler, of *Bachanalia: The Essential Listener's Guide to Bach's 'Well-Tempered Clavier.'* Contributor to anthologies, including T. J. M. Schopf, editor, *Models in Paleobiology*, Freeman, Cooper (San Francisco), 1972; Ernst Mayr, editor, *The Evolutionary Synthesis: Perspectives on the Unification of Biology*, Harvard University Press, 1980; Charles L. Hamrum, editor, *Darwin's Legacy: Nobel Conference XVIII, Gustavus Adolphus College, St. Peter, Minnesota*, Harper (New York City), 1983; Gary Larson, *The Far Side Gallery 3*, Andrews & McMeel (Fairway, KS), 1988; *Between Home and Heaven: Contemporary American Landscape Photography*, National Museum of American Art (Washington, DC), 1992; *Understanding Scientific Prose*, edited by Jack Selzer, University of Wisconsin Press (Madison), 1993; (author of afterword) George Gaylord Simpson, *The Dechronization of Sam Magruder*, St. Martin's Press, 1996; and A. C. Fabian, editor, *Evolution*, Cambridge University Press, 1998. Contributor to proceedings of International Congress of Systematic and Evolutionary Biology Symposium, 1973; contributor to *Bulletin of the Museum of Comparative Zoology*, Harvard University. Contributor of numerous articles to scientific journals. Author of monthly column, "This View of Life," in *Natural History*.

OTHER

(Editor, with Niles Eldredge) Mayr, *Systematics and the Origin of Species*, Columbia University Press (New York City), 1982.

(Editor, with Niles Eldredge) Theodosius Dobzhansky, *Genetics and the Origin of Species*, Columbia University Press, 1982.

(Editor) *The Book of Life: An Illustrated History of the Evolution of Life on Earth*, Norton, 1993.

General editor, *The History of Paleontology*, twenty volumes, Ayer, 1980. Associate editor, *Evolution*, 1970-72; member of editorial board, *Systematic Zoology*, 1970-72, *Paleobiology*, 1974-76, and *American Naturalist*, 1977-80; member of board of editors, *Science*, 1986-91.

■ Sidelights

Harvard University professor and paleontologist Stephen Jay Gould has become well known within the scientific community for refining the theories of Charles Darwin within the field of evolutionary biology. He has also become a celebrity among the general reading public due to his efforts to translate the complex work of scientists into language that lay readers can understand. In books such as the award-winning *The Panda's Thumb: Reflections in Natural History* and *Hen's Teeth and Horse's Toes: Further Reflections in Natural History*, Gould communicates his enthusiasm and fascination for the changes that evolution has wrought upon the species that inhabit Earth. As *Los Angeles Times* critic Lee Dembart remarked, Gould is "a man of extraordinary intellect and knowledge and an uncanny ability to blend the two. He sees familiar things in fresh ways, and his original thoughts are textured with meaning and powerfully honed. . . . The publication of a new book by Gould is a cause for celebration." Frederic Golden was equally laudatory in *Time*, praising Gould's ability to "turn a musty, bone-littered, backbiting discipline into the most exciting of sciences. . . . Few writers, in or out of science, shape a better written line."

Gould was born September 10, 1941, in New York City. His father, Leonard Gould, worked as a stenographer at the trial court in the borough of Queens. Self-educated and a Marxist socialist, Leonard Gould was also deeply interested in nature; during a trip to the American Museum of Natural History with his five-year-old son, Leonard's enthusiasm was contagious. Standing before the giant reconstruction of *Tyrannosaurs rex* in the museum's hall of dinosaurs, Stephen knew that he wanted to change his career plans. Instead of being a New York City garbage collector, he wanted to study fossils and bones and geologic periods. By age eleven he had started reading about paleontology, particularly books by George Gaylord Simpson, an advocate of the theory of evolution by natural selection first advanced by nineteenth-century British scientist Charles Darwin. Frustrated that evolution got scant mention in his high school biology textbooks, Gould began to do outside reading on the subject, even tackling Darwin's *The Origin of Species*.

In 1963, Gould enrolled at Antioch College in Yellow Springs, Ohio, where he studied philosophy, geology, and biology. He also actively promoted the leftist political ideals and quest for social justice he had inherited from his father. Graduating with a bachelor's degree in 1963,

Gould then moved back to New York City to begin doctoral studies at Columbia University. He researched snail fossils discovered in Bermuda as part of his doctoral thesis and earned his Ph.D. in paleontology in 1967. Gould had returned to Antioch as a geology instructor in 1966; when he had his advanced degree in hand, he moved to Harvard University, where he began as assistant professor of geology in 1967.

Since beginning his teaching career at Harvard, Gould has advanced up the ranks, from assistant professor to associate professor in 1971, and to full professor two years later. He was appointed curator of invertebrate paleontology at the university's Museum of Comparative Zoology, and the subjects he teaches at Harvard include geology, paleontology, and the philosophy of science. In addition to his academic and museum duties, Gould has also continued his study of land snails, traveling to the West Indies and other places around the globe in search of new fossil evidence.

Revises Darwin's Classic Theory of Evolution

While in agreement with the central theory of evolution advanced by Darwin, Gould still found some contradictions when attempting to corroborate it with fossil evidence. The commonly held theory, which is called "phyletic gradualism," states that evolution occurs in long, slow, gradual waves. However, through his research into the fossil record, Gould could find no evidence of "transitional" creatures—members of a particular species that exhibited alterations in their biological structure, such as members of a species of monkey that grow longer tails over a span of several generations. While gradualism continues to have its adherents, in 1972 Gould and paleontologist Niles Eldredge pioneered an evolutionary theory they called "punctuated equilibrium." In a paper entitled "Punctuated Equilibria: An Alternative to Phyletic Gradualism," which was published in *Models in Paleobiology*, the two scientists postulated that evolution does not occur in waves, as Darwin had theorized in his *Origin of Species*, but rather as distinct, rapid changes within small populations of a species over a single generation. These moments of rapid change in a species' biological makeup are interspersed between long periods of stability. As R. Z. Sheppard restated the central question in *Time*: "given world enough and time, accidents take on aspects of a plan. But does

nature 'know' this, or is a grand design the projection of the human brain?" Gould and Eldredge contended that gradualism was the result of Darwin's own cultural expectations rather than physical evidence. Continuing to develop the theory of punctuated equilibrium in further papers and studies, Gould was honored in 1975 by the Paleontological Society with its Schuchert Award for excellence in research by a paleontologist under forty years of age.

In 1974 Gould was invited to begin writing a column in the monthly magazine *Natural History*. Under the heading "This View of Life," his intent was—and still is—to clarify, for readers possessing a basic understanding of evolutionary theory, the more sophisticated aspects of its study, as well as to report on new findings and theories in the study of evolutionary biology. As a model, he has used the nineteenth-century tradition of scientific writing geared at both lay and scholarly readers utilized by such writers as geologist Charles Lyell and Darwin himself. Gould's essays quickly showed him to be an eloquent, talented writer, on par with his predecessors and with a respect for the intelligence of his reader. "The problem is that in this country the notion of writing for the public got somehow assimilated in the notion of cheapening, simplifying, adulterating," the paleontologist told John Tierney in a 1987 interview for *Rolling Stone*. "There's no reason why it should." Gould's columns helped strengthen his reputation as an expert on evolutionary biology and gained him a wide following among non-scientists interested in the history of life on earth.

Begins Series of Essay Collections

In 1977 Gould compiled a selection of his *Natural History* essays into a book, which he called *Ever since Darwin: Reflections in Natural History*. Featuring essays ranging in subject from continental drift to the theories concerning planetary collision postulated by Immanuel Velikovsky, the book has been praised by *New York Times Book Review* contributor James Gorman as "the best sort of popularization. Gould never mystifies science," but rather, "he shows both its power and its weaknesses." *Ever Since Darwin* would be the first of several "Reflections in Natural History" essay collections Gould has published in book form; others include *The Panda's Thumb, Hen's Teeth and Horse's Toes, The Flamingo's Smile, Bully for Bronto-*

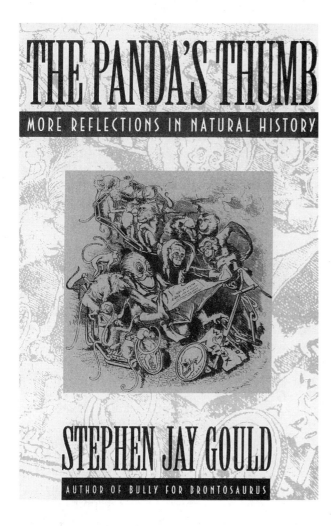

THE PANDA'S THUMB
MORE REFLECTIONS IN NATURAL HISTORY

STEPHEN JAY GOULD
AUTHOR OF BULLY FOR BRONTOSAURUS

Gould explains odd phenomena relating to evolutionary biology in this collection of essays, the winner of the 1981 National Book Award.

saurus, Eight Little Piggies, and *Dinosaur in a Haystack.* Characteristic of each of these intriguingly titled books has been Gould's ability to shed light on complex scientific principles through the use of interesting, quirky examples from nature.

This focus on the quirks or imperfections of nature underlies Gould's central contention, expressed through his theory of punctuated equilibrium: that the evolutionary process has been fueled by a series of sporadic mutations or alterations to a species population that have ultimately served some use to that species. For example, in *The Panda's Thumb,* Gould describes the animal's extra "thumb," which is not actually a thumb at all. It is an enlarged wrist bone, the result of a mutation, that resulted in a genetic change en-

abling formerly carnivorous, pawed bears possessing it to strip leaves from bamboo shoots efficiently enough to allow them to consume sufficient vegetation to sustain them; the species eventually became herbivorous and the enlarged wrist bone became a dominant trait.

In *Bully for Brontosaurus,* published in 1991, Gould continues his reflections on both the advances in his profession and his personal experiences. From describing the reaction of *Bounty* captain William Bligh to being served an echidna (a kind of anteater) for dinner, Gould embarks on a discussion of the uses and misuses of statistics, using his own bout with asbestos-related cancer—in 1982 he was diagnosed with a deadly form called mesothelioma, but was cured—as an example of the uses of statistics within science. Further along, the reader encounters President Andrew Jackson, the Brothers Grimm, the purported inventor of baseball, Abner Doubleday, and Siamese twins Eng and Chang. In the book's preface Gould explains his writing style as "beginning with something small and curious and then working outward and onward by a network of lateral connections." "In the hands of a lesser writer or thinker, this discursive technique might seem arch and strained, even infuriatingly confusing," contended John Noble Wilford in his *New York Times Book Review* appraisal of *Bully for Brontosaurus.* "But Mr. Gould has the agility to get away with it." *Dinosaur in a Haystack* continues Gould's characteristic musings as he frames his discussion of evolutionary biology within the terms of a discussion of the lives of Edgar Allan Poe, King Lear, Adolf Hitler, and Linnaeus.

Expert Witness on Behalf of Evolution

In 1981 Gould was called as an expert witness in a trial in Arkansas that echoed the famous Scopes trial of 1925, popularly known as the "Monkey Trial" and the subject of the 1960 film *Inherit the Wind.* The Arkansas legislature had passed a law requiring that public schools teach as literal fact the Judeo-Christian account of creation: the story outlined in the Bible in the book of Genesis whereby God created the world and all creatures in it in six days. State legislators decided to label the proposed class "Creation Science." Someone challenged the legislature's move on the basis that the law was unconstitutional. During the ensuing court case, Gould was called to testify for the

If you enjoy the works of Stephen Jay Gould, you may also want to check out the following books:

Edmund Blair (editor), *Galileo's Commandment: An Anthology of Great Science Writing*, 1997.

Richard Dawkins, *River Out of Eden: A Darwinian View of Life*, 1996.

Niles Eldredge, *Life in the Balance: Humanity and the Biodiversity Crisis*, 1998.

plaintiff and help the court establish that because the tenets of the legislature's so-called "creation science" went against all scientific evidence yet uncovered, it could not properly be called "scientific" at all.

While Gould viewed the court battle personally, as an attempt to debunk his profession, the case also ultimately served as an important legal precedent and has since been used to defeat similar efforts to introduce "Creationism" into public schools. "Of course I believe in the First Amendment and of course I don't want to see nonsense taught as science in schools," Gould explained to interviewer Jean Ross of *Contemporary Authors.* "But the reaction of evolutionists to creation is very personal. We are a small profession. Some three thousand people in this country spend their professional lifetimes studying evolution, and creationism is a direct threat to one of the most exciting things scientists have ever learned. Of course we had to fight [this law]." For his efforts in this trial, Gould was named *Discover* magazine's Scientist of the Year in 1981.

Surviving Cancer

Gould's diagnosis with a deadly form of cancer in 1982 transformed his work. Not only did he write about the experience in several of his *Natural History* columns, but his work since the early 1980s has also carried with it a heightened sense of urgency. His range of topics has become far wider: from black widow spiders to the horrors of nuclear winter. He has also entertained a long-term academic debate with fellow biologist E. O. Wilson, also of Harvard and the author of the controversial book *Sociobiology*, regarding biologi-

cal determinism. Wilson, also highly lauded for his published writings, supports the central tenet of biological determinism: that the economic and social differences between individuals of differing genders, races, and ethnic groups are the result of basic inherited genetic differences, that one's lot in life is ultimately determined by biology. "Gould's view of the biological determinists is that they are doubly blinded," noted R. C. Lewontin in the *New York Review of Books,* both by "antique" racial and ethnic prejudices and by the assumption that the statistics generated by their studies result in "a real object, or at least a number that characterizes one."

Perhaps because of his brush with mortality, Gould has written extensively on time. *Full House: The Spread of Excellence from Plato to Darwin*, which Gould published in 1996, uses a discussion of baseball to delve into the development of the world and its inhabitants over time. Ted Williams was the last major league player to bat .400, which he did in 1941. Why has no one been able to duplicate this feat for almost a half century? Gould contends it is not because players were better then, bats more finely crafted, or any other such reason. Rather, it is because the skill of the batter has been balanced out by the skill of every other player on both teams: because most all players are better than they were fifty years ago, fewer players now stand out as exceptional. Gould carries this point into the realm of evolutionary biology, showing by analogy that evolution has exhibited "progress" through creating increasing degrees of complexity within species, and that it is bacteria, not humankind, that exhibits the full potential of evolution. Another book by Gould that expands in detail upon time-related topics is *Time's Arrow, Time's Cycle: Myth and Metaphor in the Discovery of Geological Time*, which discusses the two differing concepts of geological time: linear time and circular time. In *Questioning the Millennium: A Rationalist's Guide to a Precisely Arbitrary Countdown*, published in 1997, Gould reviews the history of human reaction to millennia and other apocalyptic events throughout known history, including a discussion of why our current time chronology began with year one rather than year zero (the chronology was prepared by a monk in the sixth century, before the mathematical concept of "zero" had been derived).

The Mismeasure of Man, which won the National Book Critics' Circle Award for Essays in 1982, takes up the debate with Wilson by dealing with intelligence testing. Gould argues that testing specific cultural or ethnic groups with regard to their intelligence quota, or IQ, comparing them to other groups, and labelling them intellectually inferior or superior as a result, is a violation of the scientific process. *The Mismeasure of Man,* in setting forth Gould's major arguments against biological determinism, accomplishes three things, according to *New York Times Book Review* contributor Jean Goodfield: "He demonstrates the strengths and limits of quantitative measure in the sciences. . . . He shows that while science can never be wholly detached and objective, nevertheless . . . [it] provides us both with a method for challenging the status quo and for revealing firm knowledge about the world. And . . . he reaffirms that most things are humanly possible, and that attempts to confine human beings to limited categories are both downright wicked and bound to be self-defeating."

In 1989 Gould published *Wonderful Life: The Burgess Shale and the Nature of History.* The first part of the book chronicles the results of his 1987 investigation of a fossil bed in Yoho National Park, located in the Rocky Mountains of the Canadian province of British Columbia, and considered by scientists to be the most unusual fossil depository yet discovered on Earth. A permanent record created by a catastrophic mud-slide half a billion years in the past, in the Cambrian period, the Burgess Shale contains fossil records of twenty-five distinct types of soft-bodied invertebrates, twenty-one of which have never before been encountered by scientists. The central question addressed by Gould is why some forms survived and others disappeared, and could a biologist have been able to predict the survivors?

The second part of *Wonderful Life* discusses the reevaluation of the Burgess Shale—originally discovered and classified in 1909 by Smithsonian Institution president Charles Dolittle Walcott—in the 1970s by three British paleontologists. Cambridge University professor Harry Wittington, along with graduate students Derek Briggs and Simon Conway Morris, are the characters in the five-act drama that Gould plays out in the second half of his book, as they discover that the fossils were actually three-dimensional rather than flat representations of invertebrates and then recreate many of the animals revealed in the shale. "Gould may be the last great apologist for a style of intellectual work that has mostly fallen from favor: the business of classifying, categorizing and pigeonholing," contended James Gleick in the *New York Times Book Review.*

Gould continues to teach at Harvard and lives near the Cambridge, Massachusetts, campus where he and his wife, Deborah Lee, have raised the couple's two sons. When not teaching, writing, or researching, Gould sings in local choral groups and has a passion for Gilbert and Sullivan operettas.

This 1982 National Book Critics' Circle Award recipient deals with the issue of IQ testing as a means of labeling an ethnic or cultural group.

■ Works Cited

Dembart, Lee, review of *An Urchin in the Storm: Essays about Books and Ideas, Los Angeles Times,* June 2, 1987.

Gleick, James, "Survival of the Luckiest," *New York Times Book Review,* October 22, 1989, pp. 1, 40.

Golden, Frederic, "Bones, Baseball and Evolution," *Time,* May 30, 1983, p. 41.

Goodfield, Jean, "A Mind is Not Described by Numbers," *New York Times Book Review,* November 1, 1981, pp. 11-12.

Gorman, James, "The History of a Theory," *New York Times Book Review,* November 20, 1977.

Gould, Stephen Jay, in an interview with Jean Ross for *Contemporary Authors New Revision Series,* Volume 27, Gale, 1989.

Gould, Stephen Jay, *Bully for Brontosaurus: Reflections in Natural History,* Norton, 1991.

Lewontin, R. C., "The Inferiority Complex," *New York Review of Books,* October 22, 1981, pp. 12-16.

Sheppard, R. Z., "Antidotes," *Time,* September 30, 1985, p. 76.

Tierney, John, interview with Stephen Jay Gould in *Rolling Stone,* January 15, 1987, pp. 38-41, 58-61.

Wilford, John Noble, "The Stan Musial of Essay Writing," *New York Times Book Review,* May 12, 1991, p. 11.

■ For More Information See

BOOKS

Pearlman, Dale Ann, editor, *Stephen J. Gould and Immanuel Velikovsky: Essays in the Continuing Velikovsky Affair,* Ivy Press (Forest Hills, NY), 1996.

PERIODICALS

American Spectator, August, 1991, pp. 9-11.

Booklist, October 15, 1992, p. 378.

Kirkus Reviews, July 1, 1998, p. 946.

Los Angeles Times Book Review, November 27, 1988, p. 14; October 29, 1989, pp. 10, 14; April 19, 1992, p. 10; October 20, 1996, p. 10.

New York Review of Books, September 14, 1980, p. 7; February 19, 1981, pp. 34-36; May 8, 1983, pp. 3, 22-23; September 22, 1985, p. 24; May 14, 1992, p. 34; January 3, 1993, pp. 5-6; January 21, 1996, pp. 9, 11.

New York Times Book Review, June 14, 1987, p. 35; September 22, 1996, pp. 9, 11.

People, June 2, 1986, pp. 109-14.

Publishers Weekly, August 22, 1977, p. 56; August 8, 1980, p. 68; September 11, 1981, p. 66; March 4, 1983, p. 93; August 9, 1985, p. 68; December 4, 1995, p. 48; June 24, 1996, p. 36; July 28, 1997, p. 59.

School Library Journal, March, 1981, p. 163; December, 1993, pp. 32-33.

Science News, August 23, 1986, p. 121.

U.S. News & World Report, February 9, 1988, p. 64.

OTHER

"Stephen Jay Gould: This View of Life," *Nova* (television series), Public Broadcasting System, 1984.*

—*Sketch by Pamela L. Shelton*

Alex Haley

Roots: The Next Generations, and *Palmerstown, U.S.A.;* lectured extensively and appeared frequently on radio and television; adviser to African American Heritage Association, Detroit, MI. *Member:* Authors Guild, Society of Magazine Writers.

■ Personal

Born August 11, 1921, in Ithaca, NY; died of cardiac arrest, February 10, 1992, in Seattle, WA; buried on the grounds of the Alex Haley Museum at the site of his childhood home in Henning, TN; son of Simon Alexander (a professor) and Bertha George (a teacher; maiden name, Palmer) Haley; married Nannie Branch, 1941 (divorced, 1964); married Juliette Collins, 1964 (divorced, 1972); married Myra Lewis; children: (first marriage) Lydia Ann, William Alexander; (second marriage) Cynthia Gertrude. *Education:* Attended Alcorn Agricultural & Mechanical College (now Alcorn State University); attended Elizabeth City Teachers College, 1937-39.

■ Career

U.S. Coast Guard, 1939-59, retiring as chief journalist; freelance writer, 1959-92. Founder and president of Kinte Corporation, Los Angeles, CA, 1972-92. Board member of New College of California, 1974; member of King Hassan's Royal Academy. Script consultant for television miniseries *Roots*,

■ Awards, Honors

Litt.D. from Simpson College, 1971, Howard University, 1974, Williams College, 1975, and Capitol University, 1975; honorary doctorate from Seton Hall University, 1974; special citation from National Book Award committee, 1977, for *Roots: The Saga of an American Family;* special citation from Pulitzer Prize committee, 1977, for *Roots: The Saga of an American Family;* Spingarn Medal from NAACP, 1977; *Roots: The Saga of an American Family* received numerous other awards and honors; nominated to Black Filmmakers Hall of Fame, 1981, for producing *Palmerstown, U.S.A.*, 1981.

■ Writings

(With Malcolm X) *The Autobiography of Malcolm X*, Grove, 1965.

Roots: The Saga of an American Family, Doubleday, 1976.

Alex Haley Speaks (recording), Kinte Corporation, 1980.

A Different Kind of Christmas, Doubleday, 1988, abridged edition, Literacy Volunteers of New York City, 1991.

(With David Stevens) *Queen* (screenplay adapted from dictation tapes), Columbia Broadcasting System (CBS-TV), 1993.

Author of forewords, *Somerset Homecoming,* by Dorothy Redford and Michael D'Orso, Anchor/Doubleday, 1988; *Marva Collins' Way: Returning to Excellence in Education,* by Marva Collins, J. P. Tarcher, 1990; and *They That Go Down to the Sea: A Bicentennial Pictorial History of the United States Coast Guard,* by Paul A. Powers, United States Coast Guard Chief Petty Officers Association, 1990. Initiated "Playboy Interviews" feature for *Playboy,* 1962. Contributor to periodicals, including *Reader's Digest, New York Times Magazine, Smithsonian, Harper's,* and *Atlantic.*

■ Work in Progress

Haley was working on two projects at the time of his death: *My Search for Roots,* an account of how *Roots: The Saga of an American Family* was researched and written; and a study of the town of Henning, Tennessee, where Haley was raised.

■ Adaptations

Roots: The Saga of an American Family was adapted by American Broadcasting Company (ABC), as the television miniseries *Roots,* 1977, and *Roots: The Next Generations* (also known as *Roots II*), 1979; Haley served as script consultant for both productions. Filmmaker Spike Lee used *The Autobiography of Malcolm X* as the source for his 1992 film biography *Malcolm X. Queen,* a novel based on an outline and research left by Haley, was published by Morrow in 1993.

■ Sidelights

Alex Haley was a journalist, essayist, and historical novelist, but he is best known for writing the benchmark 1976 novel *Roots: The Saga of an American Family,* which was celebrated as an affirmation of African American heritage and as a universal story of humankind's search for identity. The fictionalized account of seven generations of his own family from their ancestral home in Africa to their days as slaves in America was made into a television movie that aired for one week on consecutive nights in 1977, drawing millions

of American viewers. Lance Morrow of *Time* said, "Along the way, Americans of both races discovered that they share a common heritage, however, brutal; that the ties that link them to their ancestors also bind them to each other." Eleven years before *Roots,* Haley also gained recognition for writing an "as-told-to" autobiography of Malcolm X that was released shortly after the leader was gunned down.

Born in 1921 in Ithaca, New York, Alexander Murray Palmer Haley was the eldest of three sons born to Bertha George Palmer and Simon Alexander Haley. Both his parents were in their first year of graduate school when Haley was born. His mother was studying at the Ithaca Conserva-

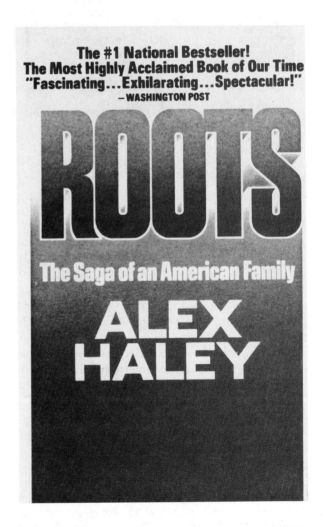

The result of twelve years of research and travel in Africa, Haley's account of seven generations of his family sold millions of copies worldwide and earned more than 270 awards.

tory of Music and his father at Cornell University. Both went on to become teachers, Bertha at the local elementary school and Simon at black colleges in the South. When Alex was a boy the family moved to Henning, Tennessee, where Alex grew up under the influence of his grandmother and aunts Viney, Mathilda, and Liz, who recounted stories about his African ancestor, Kunta Kinte. They planted in his imagination the seeds that would grow into in the novel *Roots*. Haley spent twelve years tracing his African family members to the Mandinka tribe in a tiny village in Juffure of the Gambia region of West Africa.

Uneventful School Days Lead to Service

As a boy, Haley was not an enthusiastic student. When he finished high school at age fifteen, he did so with a C average. Three years later, Haley joined the U.S. Coast Guard and began a twenty-year career in the service. Meanwhile, he married Nannie Branch in 1941 and they had two children, Lydia Ann and William Alexander. In the Coast Guard, Haley worked as a cook and made his first attempts at writing to fight the boredom aboard ship. Haley found himself penning love letters for his shipmates to send home to their wives and girlfriends. These letters would become practice for serious pieces that he submitted to various magazines. However, it took eight years and several hundred rejection notices before his first story was published in *This Week,* a syndicated Sunday supplement. Apparently impressed by this accomplishment, the Coast Guard created a new post especially for him. He became the service's chief—and only—journalist. Throughout his lifetime, Haley often returned to the sea to find peace and to write.

When Haley retired from the Coast Guard in 1959 he became a full-time writer and journalist. Times were lean at first. Moving into an apartment in New York's Greenwich Village, Haley told Morrow that all he had was "18 cents in my pocket. That's all I had in the world. There was nowhere to go but up." The day after that low point, Haley received a check for a piece he had written. Then he began getting assignments from *Reader's Digest* and *Playboy,* including an article on jazz trumpeter Miles Davis.

His first book, *The Autobiography of Malcolm X,* written with the controversial leader of the Na-

tion of Islam group, launched Haley's career in 1965. From 1963 until Malcolm X's assassination two years later, Haley saw the ex-convict, Black Muslim, and political activist for almost daily sessions. "Though Haley made extraordinary efforts to subordinate himself to his partner and subject, his more vital achievement was to get Malcolm X to *see, say* and *believe* the changes and continuities in his life and character which Haley had come to see," according to Albert E. Stone in *Revue Française d'Études Américaines.* The book quickly became required reading in many schools, eventually selling more than six million copies. "The power of Malcolm's book is that it speaks directly out of the totality of that life-history *and* the ingratiating openness of his own mind and recollection of it," according to Warner Berthoff in *New Literary History.* In 1964, while he was working on *The Autobiography of Malcolm X,* Haley divorced Branch and married Juliette Collins. They had one daughter, Cynthia Gertrude Haley. However, that marriage also ended in divorce in 1972.

Twelve-year Journey to Fame

Two weeks after finishing the *Malcolm X* manuscript, Haley started his twelve-year journey researching and writing *Roots.* He visited more than fifty libraries and archives on three continents. And in a dramatic effort to gain insight and authenticity, he sailed from West Africa to the United States and spent each night down in the hold in his underwear on a rough board between bales of raw rubber, trying to understand the filth, death, and deprivation that slaves had endured. While the book is based on facts he gathered in Africa, Europe, and the United States, the dialogue and other details are fictionalized. "*Roots* is all of our stories," Haley explained in an interview with William Marmon of *Time.* "When you start talking about family, about lineage and ancestry, you are talking about every person on earth. We all have it; it's a great equalizer." Haley, who was stocky and had freckled-brown skin, saw a commonality among the races. He said there were few black Americans who didn't have whites in their family background and many whites who, knowingly and unknowingly, had black ancestors.

Roots was adapted as a television miniseries that drew 130 million viewers. The television viewing spurred a rush for the 688-page book and even ignited some outbreaks of violence, mostly among

Levar Burton played Haley's ancestor Kunta Kinte in the 1977 television adaptation of *Roots,* **which garnered a record-breaking thirty-seven Emmy Awards.**

the long term, *Roots* would improve race relations, particularly because of the televised version's profound impact on whites." Within two years of first publication, Haley had won 271 awards, including special citations from the judges of the 1977 National Book Awards and the 1977 Pulitzer Prizes. The miniseries was so successful that ABC produced a sequel, *Roots: The Next Generation*, two years later. The overwhelming success of the book and miniseries transformed Haley's life. At one point he signed at least five hundred copies of *Roots* daily, spoke to an average of six thousand people a day, and traveled round trip coast-to-coast at least once a week. "It's like a kaleidoscope, a whirlpool into which I've fallen," he told *Time* magazine. "My feet are suspended above ground and I can't get a perch." The television adaptation of *Roots* was given a record-breaking thirty-seven Emmys. The book sold millions of copies worldwide and made Haley well more than a million dollars in royalties.

Haley used money from the sale of *Roots* to establish The Alex Haley Roots Foundation. In an interview with Jeffrey Elliot of the *Negro History Bulletin*, Haley explained: "The Foundation is a reflection of the responsibility I feel as a result of the success of *Roots*. I very much want to do something constructive with the profits from the book." Elliot observed that *Roots* brought Haley fame and fortune, but it placed him "in the role of major black leader." Haley's response was: "Well, I would quibble with the word, 'leader,' I just don't feel like a leader. I have become a prominent black voice on account of the tremendous media exposure I've received." The same interviewer asked Haley what Roots' greatest impact was. He answered that because Roots had been translated into more than twenty languages, "the *Tarzan* and *Jungle Jim* images, as pervasive world symbols of Africa and African people, will be replaced by Kunta Kinte and his brave people." However, the fame and attention did not seem to change Haley's personality, according to Howard Rosenberg of the *Los Angeles Times*. "Because of who he was, he had access to the highest circles. When you met him, however, he seemed to be such a natural guy. He was just folks."

Critics Find Weaknesses

Some critics argued that Roots was not an original work. In fact, two lawsuits were filed by au-

If you enjoy the works of Alex Haley, you may also want to check out the following books and films:

Walter Dean Myers, *The Glory Field*, 1994.
Gary Paulsen, *Nightjohn*, 1993.
Margaret Walker, *Jubilee*, 1966.
The Autobiography of Miss Jane Pittman, an Emmy Award-winning drama, 1974.

thors who claimed Haley had drawn upon their writings. Harold Courlander, a novelist and folklorist, claimed Haley plagiarized from his 1967 novel, *The African*. Margaret Walker, a poet, novelist, and literary biographer, claimed Haley had copied from her 1966 novel, *Jubilee*. Walker's claim was dismissed by a judge. "However, despite Haley's sworn testimony that he had never seen *The African* until after *Roots* was published, Courlander was offered and accepted a $650,000 settlement, and Haley admitted that 'various materials from *The African* found their way into *Roots*,'" Calvin Reid reported in *Publishers Weekly*. Nevertheless, Haley had addressed this issue in a 1979 *Time* interview, "There were three paragraphs from the book that appeared verbatim in my notes," Haley admitted, "and it was futile to try to defend myself. I honestly can't recall what was in my mind when I wrote something at 3 a.m. five years ago."

Courlander also pointed out ethnological errors in *Roots* and argued that Kunta Kinte is far from being an "authentic African." Writing in *Phylon*, Courlander commented, "One of the disturbing aspects of Kunta's character is Haley's concept of him as a primitive being, which actually derogates both the protagonist and the level of his tribal culture." Haley reacted to this and other similar criticism by pointing out that *Roots* was "faction"—a mixture of facts and fiction. He stressed that the novel is important not so much for its names and dates as for its reflection of human nature: "*Roots* is all of our stories. . . . It's just a matter of filling in the blanks," he once stated. "When you start talking about family, about lineage and ancestry, you are talking about every person on earth."

Haley went on to being researching his own paternal heritage, but he died from cardiac arrest

February 10, 1992, in Seattle, Washington, where he had been scheduled to speak. Haley was survived by his third wife, the former Myra Lewis, from whom he was separated. Haley, who had four grandchildren, was buried on the grounds of the Alex Haley Museum at his childhood hometown of Henning, Tennessee. Before his death, Haley had been working on a novel set in Appalachia that focused on the relationships among a mountain father, son, and grandson. He was also working on a series of interviews with black filmmakers, and the long-awaited story of the town of Henning. In 1993, a year after his death, CBS television aired a three-episode miniseries, *Queen*, about his great-grandmother, the daughter of a mulatto slave girl and a white slave owner.

In an obituary about Haley, *Los Angeles Times* reporter Garry Abrams quoted Eric Foner, a visiting professor at UCLA who had written extensively on slavery, the Civil War, and the Reconstruction period, as saying that historians tend to regard *Roots* as a work of fiction and doubt that Haley actually located his particular ancestor. "Having said that," Foner said, "Haley is very well respected (among historians) for having stimulated interest (in academia) in black genealogy and history and the heritage of African-Americans." Jacqueline Trescott, in a *Washington Post* obituary, noted that "[Haley] pulled us into the drawing rooms of living history and created characters that became part of the American lexicon." She concluded, "Our archives would have been sadly shortchanged without him. But those of us who were fortunate enough to hear him know he also represented a unique oral tradition. He could talk."

■ Works Cited

Abrams, Garry, "An Enduring Legacy," *Los Angeles Times*, February 12, 1992, pp. E1, E8.
Berthoff, Warner, *New Literary History*, Winter, 1971.
Courlander, Harold, "Kunta Kinte's Struggle to be African," *Phylon*, December, 1986, pp. 294-302.
Elliot, Jeffrey, interview with Alex Haley in *Negro History Bulletin*, January-February, 1978.
Marmon, William, *Time*, October 18, 1976.
Morrow, Lance, *Time*, February 14, 1977, pp. 69-77.
Reid, Calvin, "Fact or Fiction? Hoax Charges Still Dog 'Roots' 20 Years On," *Publishers Weekly*, October 6, 1997, pp. 16-17.
Rosenberg, Howard, "Alex Haley, a 'Groit' for Modern Times," *Los Angeles Times*, February 12, 1992, p. F9.
Stone, Albert E., "Collaboration in Contemporary American Autobiography," *Revue Française d'Études Américaines*, May, 1982, pp. 151-65.
Trescott, Jacqueline, "Alex Haley, Taking Us Back Home," *Washington Post*, February 11, 1992, pp. E1-E2.
"View from the Whirlpool," *Time*, February 19, 1979, p. 88.

■ For More Information See

BOOKS

Contemporary Literary Criticism, Gale, Volume 8, 1978, Volume 12, 1980, Volume 76, 1993.
Dictionary of Literary Biography, Volume 38: *Afro-American Writers after 1955: Dramatists and Prose Writers*, Gale, 1985, pp. 115-19.

PERIODICALS

Ebony, April, 1977.
Forbes, February 15, 1977.
Los Angeles Times Book Review, December 25, 1988, p. 1.
Ms., February, 1977.
National Review, March 4, 1977.
Negro History Bulletin, January, 1977.
New Republic, March 12, 1977.
Newsweek, September 27, 1976; February 14, 1977.
New Yorker, February 14, 1977.
New York Review of Books, November 11, 1976.
New York Times, October 14, 1976; February 12, 1993, p. C34; February 14, 1993, p. H1; March 3, 1993, p. C18.
New York Times Book Review, September 26, 1976; January 2, 1977; February 27, 1977.
People, March 28, 1977.
Publishers Weekly, September 6, 1976; March 2, 1992; October 12, 1992, p. 10.
Saturday Review, September 18, 1976.
Washington Post, September 26, 1976, pp. 1-2.

■ Obituaries

PERIODICALS

Chicago Tribune, February 11, 1992, section 1, pp. 1, 10; February 16, 1992, section 2, p. 10.

Essence, February, 1992, pp. 88-92.
New York Times, February 11, 1992, p. B8;
Times (London), February 11, 1992, p. 15.*

—Sketch by Diane Andreassi

Robert Jordan

Conan the Defender, Tor, 1982.
Conan the Triumphant, Tor, 1983.
Conan the Unconquered, Tor, 1983.
Conan the Destroyer (based on the motion picture of the same name), Tor, 1984.
Conan the Magnificent, Tor, 1984.
Conan the Victorious, Tor, 1985.
The Conan Chronicles (omnibus volume), Tor, 1995.

UNDER PSEUDONYM ROBERT JORDAN; "WHEEL OF TIME" FANTASY SERIES

The Eye of the World, Tor, 1990.
The Great Hunt, Tor, 1990.
The Dragon Reborn, Tor, 1991.
The Shadow Rising, Tor, 1992.
The Fires of Heaven, Tor, 1993.
Lord of Chaos, Tor, 1994.
The Wheel of Time (six-volume set; includes *The Eye of the World, The Great Hunt, The Dragon Reborn, The Shadow Rising, The Fires of Heaven,* and *Lord of Chaos*), Tor, 1995.
A Crown of Swords, Tor, 1996.
(With Teresa Patterson) *The World of Robert Jordan's The Wheel of Time,* Tor, 1997.
The Path of Daggers, Tor, 1998.

UNDER PSEUDONYM REAGAN O'NEAL; "FALLON" SERIES

The Fallon Blood, Forge, 1980.
The Fallon Pride, Forge, 1981.

Also author of *The Fallon Legacy,* published in 1982.

■ Personal

Born James Oliver Rigney, Jr., October 17, 1948, in Charleston, SC; son of James Oliver and Eva May (Grooms) Rigney; married Harriet Stoney Popham McDougal, March 28, 1981; children: William Popham McDougal. *Education:* The Citadel, B.S., 1974.

■ Addresses

Agent—c/o Sobel, Weber Associates, 146 E. 19th St., New York, NY 10003.

■ Career

U.S. Civil Service, nuclear engineer, 1974-78; freelance writer, 1978—. *Member:* Science Fiction Writers of America.

■ Writings

UNDER PSEUDONYM ROBERT JORDAN; "CONAN" FANTASY SERIES

Conan the Invincible, Tor, 1982.

OTHER

Author, under pseudonym Jackson O'Reilly, of *Cheyenne Raiders*, 1982. Contributor of articles and dance reviews, sometimes under pseudonym Chang Lung, to periodicals.

■ Adaptations

Lord of Chaos, A Crown of Swords, The Great Hunt, The Fires of Heaven, The Dragon Reborn, and *The Shadow Rising* have been adapted for audio cassette. A game based on the "Wheel of Time" series is being produced by Legend Entertainment.

■ Sidelights

Writing under several pseudonyms, James Oliver Rigney, Jr. is a prolific author of genre fiction. As Robert Jordan, he is the author of the popular fantasy series "The Wheel of Time," which he began in 1990 with his novel *The Eye of the World.* Using the Jordan pseudonym, he has also written a number of highly praised sword and sorcery novels that feature the heroic protagonist Conan the Barbarian, a muscle-bound free agent who roams a fantastic kingdom full of strange creatures and evildoers outfitted with magical powers in search of wealth and adventure. Originally created in the 1930s by Texas author Robert E. Howard (1906-1936), Conan is confronted with a number of seemingly impossible tasks in Jordan's continuation of this action-packed he-man saga.

Included among Jordan's "Conan" novels are *Conan the Invincible, Conan the Triumphant,* and *Conan the Unconquered,* all of which feature a bevy of beautiful women, wicked foes, and a series of obstacles, and all of which this champion of good against evil, well skilled in all forms of battle, overcomes with ease. In *Conan the Destroyer,* based on the motion picture of the same title that starred bodybuilder Arnold Schwarzenegger in one of his early acting roles, Conan teams up with the princess Jehnna to search for treasure. Unknown to the pair, Jehnna's aunt, the sorceress, plans to sacrifice the young woman upon her return, and Conan must foil the intended evil. Praising Jordan's style as "straightforward" and "uncomplicated," Frances Friedman wrote in *Voice of Youth Advocates* that *Conan the Destroyer* "is a pleasant, fast moving" adventure. Dragons and Amazons

Having tapped into the "Eye of the World," Rand becomes the defender of good against evil in this second installment in the "Wheel of Time" series.

enter the mythical mix of characters in *Conan the Magnificent,* while the superhero saga is partially collected in *The Conan Chronicles,* which includes *Conan the Invincible, Conan the Defender,* and *Conan the Unconquered.*

"Wheel of Time"

Jordan is probably most well known for his second series of books. The "Wheel of Time" fantasy series follows a classic struggle between good and evil set in a long-ago land of brutality and sorcery. The series opens with *The Eye of the World,* followed by such titles as *The Great Hunt* and *The Dragon Reborn*, which continue the high fantasy saga. In the first book readers are introduced to a fantasy kingdom and its history through the adventures of three young men. Rand al'Thorn, Matrim, and Perrin find their uneventful lives in their rural farming village disrupted after a stranger named Moiraine and her well-armed bodyguard stop in the local inn for the night. After dark, the three young locals are attacked for seemingly no reason by evil beast-men, servants of the Dark One, a powerful witch believed to have been eliminated. Moiraine, a witch herself, explains to Rand, Matrim, and Perrin that they have been singled out for death by the returning Dark One, and convinces them to accompany her to a place of sanctuary. On their journey they confront a series of events that cause the friends to realize that no sanctuary will shield them from evil; they will have to travel to the kingdom of the Dark One and confront the growing force of evil directly. Praising *The Eye of the World* in her review for *Voice of Youth Advocates* as containing "well-drawn, believable characters; an intelligent plot; and something significant to say about the range of good and evil and the effects of fear and obsession on the human character," Laura Staley added that Jordan "weaves his many strands into a memorable, highly enjoyable tale."

In an online interview, Jordan stated that the character of Rand is meant to be a messiah figure, incorporating "some elements" from the story of Jesus Christ, though he is not a true manifestation of Jesus. Rather, Rand can be seen as "an archetype such as [King] Arthur." Jordan also mentioned that although he does not incorporate any of his personal traits into his characters, "there is a touch of my wife in all of the major female characters, however, and a good many of the secondary female characters."

The Great Hunt features Rand, who has tapped into the power of the One Source, the "Eye of the World," in an effort to battle the Dark One, hailed as a witch ("dragon") in his own right. Now called the Dragon Reborn as one of the few males allowed to wield magic in his world, Rand grudgingly comes to terms with his new role as defender of good against evil, and helps his friends in the bargain. Continuing books in the series, including *The Dragon Reborn* and *The Shadow Rising*, follow Rand al'Thorn on his quest to obtain the sword Callandor, which may help

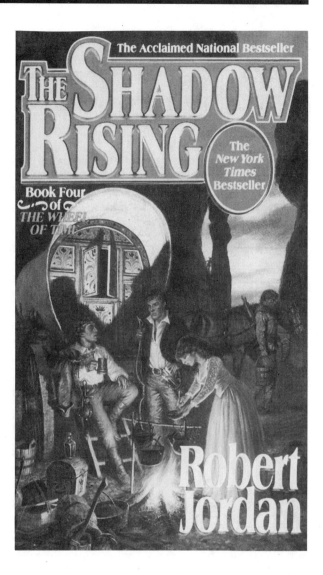

With the help of friends and magicians, Rand journeys to the home of the Dark One, hoping to stop this force from regaining power in this 1992 novel.

him keep the Dark One from regaining power. Helped by a group of female magicians and childhood friends Matrim and Perrin, the powerful young wizard continues on his trek toward the home of the Dark One, despite the threat of ancient prophecies of madness befalling any male who uses magic to fight the forces of evil. Against this heroic journey, Jordan paints a vibrant world filled with hundreds of unique characters, local wars, mythology, betrayals, and deep loyalties. While noting that "in each successive volume [the author] introduces more new elements than he resolves," a *Publishers Weekly* reviewer praised the

Rand journeys on to the lair of the Dark One in this 1993 work.

"sheer force" of the author's inventiveness for retaining fan appeal.

Characters Make the Story

Though his novels feature plenty of action, Jordan believes that the key to a good story is in the characters. He remarked in an online interview that "action is alway secondary. The main part of the story is the relationships between people. Those relationships sometimes lead to god-awful troubles, battles, . . . but it's the relationships that are the important things." Jordan added that he begins each book with a general idea of how the plot will develop, though certain aspects of the plot can change during the writing process: "Some parts are very close to what I intended in the beginning, some parts vary to a great degree. It all depends on how I feel things should weave together at the particular moment I'm writing them." The author acknowledged that he takes time to revise his work before publication, but "I always have to set myself a cut-off point. Otherwise I will keep rewriting and rewriting, and the period between the books will stretch out to . . . five or six years."

The "Wheel of Time" saga continues in *The Fires of Heaven, Lord of Chaos, A Crown of Swords,* and *The Path of Daggers,* as Rand proceeds on his jour-

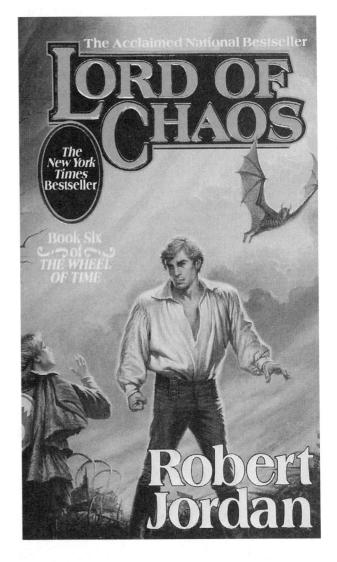

Jordan's sixth "Wheel of Time" novel continues his epic high-fantasy saga.

ney to the lair of the Dark One before that power of evil breaks his chains and is released into the world. Some critics have opined that the numerous twists and turns of the plot, the legions of characters, and the sheer bulk of the series—each volume is upwards of five hundred pages in length—made later books impenetrable by new or novice readers. (When asked how he manages to keep the complex story together in his mind, Jordan replied that it's "nothing that any genius

---

If you enjoy the works of Robert Jordan, you may also want to check out the following books and films:

Mercedes Lackey, *Arrow's Flight,* 1987.
Tamora Pierce, *Wild Magic,* 1992.
Tad Williams, *The Dragonbone Chair,* 1988.
Willow, a film by Ron Howard, 1988.

---

couldn't do.") Others, however, continued to find praise for the voluminous work. For example, Roland Green noted in *Booklist* that *The Fires of Heaven* "upholds the very high standards" of the series, "with battle scenes, comic interludes, and character development all reaching perhaps the highest point in a work that has lacked for none of these." As the series continued to wind its way toward a conclusion, a *Publishers Weekly* reviewer noted that Jordan's "narrative employs elements of realism rare in high fantasy," while Sally Estes commented in her *Booklist* review of series installment number seven, *A Crown of Swords,* that "Throughout the saga, the characters, . . . the world, and the source of powers have remained remarkably rich and consistent."

The "Wheel of Time" books enjoy a large and enthusiastic following, with dozens of sites on the Internet devoted to the series. Jordan has stated that he plans to write at least three more volumes; he doesn't feel he could finish the story in fewer than that. Though Jordan wouldn't mind seeing his books adapted for film (if they were done well), he believes that the complexity of the works would make it difficult, if not impossible, to adapt them successfully to the typical two-hour feature-length format.

In addition to spinning his intricate "Wheel of Time" books and "Conan" adventures, Jordan has employed several additional pseudonyms to produced other writings, including novels within the "Fallon" series and several journalistic pieces for national publications. When asked what he does to keep busy away from his work on the "Wheel of Time" books, Jordan replied, "I occasionally find time to go fishing. . . . I find time to read a little bit. . . . And I don't really have a great deal of time for anything else. When I'm doing anything else, I feel I should be writing." He jokingly added, "It's a sickness."

■ **Works Cited**

Review of *A Crown of Swords, Publishers Weekly,* June 10, 1996, p. 90.
Estes, Sally, review of *A Crown of Swords, Booklist,* June 1, 1996, p. 1630.
Friedman, Frances, review of *Conan the Destroyer, Voice of Youth Advocates,* February, 1985, p. 336.
Green, Roland, review of *The Fires of Heaven, Booklist,* October 15, 1993, p. 195.
Jordan, Robert, online interview at http://www.utw.com/~cluff/rjlog.html.
Review of *The Shadow Rising, Publishers Weekly,* October 19, 1992, p. 64.
Staley, Laura, review of *The Eye of the World, Voice of Youth Advocates,* June, 1990, p. 116.

■ **For More Information See**

PERIODICALS

Booklist, October 1, 1989, p. 218; September 1, 1990, p. 394; September 15, 1991, p. 99; October 15, 1994, p. 372.
Kirkus Reviews, December 15, 1989, p. 1791; October 1993, p. 1234; October 1, 1994, p. 1318; May 1, 1995, p. 596.
Publishers Weekly, September 20, 1991, p. 124; November 1, 1993, p. 71; July 3, 1995, p. 52; October 13, 1997, p. 61.
Voice of Youth Advocates, August, 1991, p. 181; February, 1992, p. 383; June, 1992, p. 144; April, 1993, p. 41; February, 1996, p. 384; April, 1997, p. 10.*

—*Sketch by Pamela L. Shelton*

Charles Keeping

■ Personal

Full name Charles William James Keeping; born September 22, 1924, in Lambeth, London, England; died May 16, 1988; son of Charles (a professional boxer, under name Charles Clark, and newspaperman) and Eliza Ann (Trodd) Keeping; married Renate Meyer (an artist and illustrator), September 20, 1952; children: Jonathan, Vicki, Sean, Frank. *Education:* Polytechnic of Central London, National Diploma in Design, 1952. *Politics:* "Individualist." *Religion:* None. *Hobbies and other interests:* Walking, good conversation over a pint of beer in a pub, modern jazz, folksinging.

■ Career

Illustrator and author. Apprenticed to printing trade, 1938; after war service, worked as engineer and rent collector before starting full-time art studies in 1949; also worked as a cartoonist and commercial artist. Polytechnic of Central London, London, England, visiting lecturer in lithography, 1956-63; Croydon College of Art, Croydon, England, visiting lecturer in lithography, 1963-78; Cam-

berwell School of Art and Crafts, London, visiting lecturer in print making, 1979-88. Lithographs exhibited in London, Italy, Australia, and United States, including International Exhibition of Lithography, Cincinnati, OH, 1958; prints in many collections, including the Victoria and Albert Museum, London. *Military service:* Royal Navy, 1942-46; served as telegraphist.

■ Awards, Honors

Carnegie Medal commendation, British Library Association, 1957, for *The Silver Branch,* 1958, for *Warrior Scarlet,* 1963, for *The Latchkey Children,* 1965, for *Elidor,* 1967, for *The Dream Time,* and 1978, for *A Kind of Wild Justice;* Carnegie Medal, British Library Association, 1959, for *The Lantern Bearers,* and 1970, for *The God Beneath the Sea;* Spring Book Festival older honor, *New York Herald Tribune,* 1958, for *The Silver Branch,* and 1962, for *Dawn Wind;* International Board on Books for Young People (IBBY) honour list, 1960, for *Warrior Scarlet;* Certificate of Merit, British Library Association, 1966, for *Shaun and the Cart-Horse,* and 1970, for *The God Beneath the Sea;* Certificate of Merit, Leipzig Book Fair, 1966, for *Black Dolly: The Story of A Junk Cart Pony;* Kate Greenaway Medal, British Library Association, 1967, for *Charley, Charlotte and the Golden Canary,* and 1981, for *The Highwayman;* Kate Greenaway honour, 1969, for *Joseph's Yard,* commendations, 1970, for *The God Beneath the Sea,* and 1974, for *The Railway Passage;* W. H.

Smith Illustration Award, Victoria and Albert Museum, 1972, for *Tinker, Tailor: Folk Song Tales*, and 1977, for *The Wildman*; Bratislava Biennale, honorable mention, 1973, for *The Spider's Web*; Golden Apple Award, 1976, for *The Railway Passage*; Hans Christian Andersen highly commended illustrator award, IBBY, 1974; Kurt Maschler Award runner-up, 1985, for *The Wedding Ghost*.

■ Writings

SELF-ILLUSTRATED CHILDREN'S BOOKS

Shaun and the Cart-Horse, F. Watts, 1966.

Molly o' the Moors: The Story of a Pony, World Publishing, 1966, published as *Black Dolly: The Story of a Junk Cart Pony*, Brockhampton Press, 1966.

Charley, Charlotte and the Golden Canary, F. Watts, 1967.

Alfie Finds "The Other Side of the World," F. Watts, 1968, published as *Alfie and the Ferryboat*, Oxford University Press, 1968.

(Compiler) *Tinker, Tailor: Folk Song Tales*, Brockhampton Press, 1968.

(Reteller) *The Christmas Story, as Told on "Play School,"* British Broadcasting Corporation, 1968, published as *The Christmas Story*, F. Watts, 1969.

Joseph's Yard (also see below), Oxford University Press, 1969, F. Watts, 1970.

Through the Window (also see below), F. Watts, 1970.

The Garden Shed, Oxford University Press, 1971.

The Spider's Web, Oxford University Press, 1972.

Richard, Oxford University Press, 1973.

The Nanny Goat and the Fierce Dog, Abelard, 1973, S. G. Phillips, 1974.

(Compiler of words and music) *Cockney Ding-Dong*, Kestrel Books, 1973.

The Railway Passage, Oxford University Press, 1974.

Wasteground Circus, Oxford University Press, 1975.

Inter-City, Oxford University Press, 1977.

Miss Emily and the Bird of Make-Believe, Hutchinson, 1978.

River, Oxford University Press, 1978.

Willie's Fire-Engine, Oxford University Press, 1980.

(With Kevin Crossley-Holland) *Beowulf*, Oxford University Press, 1982.

Sammy Streetsinger, Oxford University Press (England), 1984, Oxford University Press (United States), 1987.

(Compiler) *Charles Keeping's Book of Classic Ghost Stories*, Peter Bedrick, 1987.

(Compiler) *Charles Keeping's Classic Tales of the Macabre*, Peter Bedrick, 1987.

Adam and Paradise Island, Oxford University Press, 1989.

Also adapter of *Joseph's Yard* and *Through the Window* for television.

ILLUSTRATOR

Nicholas Stuart Gray, *Over the Hills to Babylon*, Oxford University Press, 1954, Hawthorn, 1970.

Rosemary Sutcliff, *The Silver Branch*, Oxford University Press, 1957, Walck, 1959.

Sutcliff, *Warrior Scarlet*, Walck, 1958, 2nd edition, 1966.

John Stewart Murphy, *Bridges*, Oxford University Press, 1958.

Murphy, *Ships*, Oxford University Press, 1959.

Sutcliff, *Knight's Fee*, Oxford University Press, 1960, Walck, 1961.

Murphy, *Roads*, Oxford University Press, 1960.

Ira Nesdale, *Riverbend Bricky*, Blackie, 1960.

Kathleen Fidler, *Tales of Pirates and Castaways*, Lutterworth, 1960.

Fidler, *Tales of the West Country*, Lutterworth, 1961.

Charles Kingsley, *The Heroes*, Hutchinson, 1961.

Mitchell Dawson, *The Queen of Trent*, Abelard, 1961.

Sir Henry Rider Haggard, *King Solomon's Mines*, Blackie, 1961.

Sutcliff, *Dawn Wind*, Oxford University Press, 1961, Walck, 1962.

Murphy, *Canals*, Oxford University Press, 1961.

Sutcliff, reteller, *Dragon Slayer*, Bodley Head, 1961, published as *Beowulf*, Dutton, 1962, published as *Dragon Slayer: The Story of Beowulf*, Macmillan, 1980.

Ruth Chandler, *Three Trumpets*, Abelard, 1962.

Kenneth Grahame, *The Golden Age* [and] *Dream Days*, Bodley Head, 1962, Dufour, 1965.

Barbara Leonie Picard, *Lost John*, Oxford University Press, 1962, Criterion, 1963.

Murphy, *Dams*, Oxford University Press, 1963.

Clare Compton, *Harriet and the Cherry Pie*, Bodley Head, 1963.

E. M. Almendingen, *The Knights of the Golden Table*, Bodley Head, 1963, Lippincott, 1964.

Philip Rush, *The Castle and the Harp*, Collins, 1963.

Paul Berna, *Flood Warning*, Pantheon, 1963.

Eric Allen, *The Latchkey Children*, Oxford University Press, 1963.

Wilkie Collins, *The Moonstone*, Oxford University Press, 1963.

Mollie Hunter, *Patrick Kentigern Keenan*, Blackie, 1963, published as *The Smartest Man in Ireland*, Funk, 1965.

James Holding, *The King's Contest and Other North African Tales*, Abelard, 1964.

Henry Treece, *The Children's Crusade*, Longmans, 1964.

Nesdale, *Bricky and the Hobo*, Blackie, 1964.

Murphy, *Railways*, Oxford University Press, 1964.

Treece, *The Last of the Vikings*, Brockhampton Press, 1964, published as *The Last Viking*, Pantheon, 1966.

Elizabeth Grove, *Whitsun Warpath*, Jonathan Cape, 1964.

Jacoba Tadema-Sporry, *The Story of Egypt*, translated by Elsa Hammond, Thomas Nelson, 1964.

Hunter, *The Kelpie's Pearls*, Blackie & Son, 1964, Funk, 1966.

Almedingen, *The Treasure of Siegfried*, Bodley Head, 1964, Lippincott, 1965.

Treece, *Horned Helmet*, Puffin, 1965.

Murphy, *Wells*, Oxford University Press, 1965.

Gray, *The Apple Stone*, Dobson, 1965, Hawthorn, 1969.

Alan Garner, *Elidor*, Collins, 1965.

Henry Daniel-Rops, *The Life of Our Lord*, Hawthorn, 1965.

Sutcliff, *The Mark of the Horse Lord*, Walck, 1965.

Sutcliff, *Heroes and History*, Putnam, 1965.

Treece, *Splintered Sword*, Brockhampton Press, 1965, Duell, Sloan & Pearce, 1966.

John Reginald Milsome, *Damien the Leper's Friend*, Burns & Oats, 1965.

Kevin Crossley-Holland, *King Horn*, Macmillan, 1965, Dutton, 1966.

Walter Macken, *Island of the Great Yellow Ox*, Macmillan, 1966.

Richard Potts, *An Owl for His Birthday*, Lutterworth, 1966.

Erich Maria Remarque, *All Quiet on the Western Front*, translated by A. W. Wheen, Folio Society, 1966.

Eric and Nancy Protter, editors and adapters, *Celtic Folk and Fairy Tales*, Duell, Sloan & Pearce, 1966.

Holding, *The Sky-Eater and Other South Sea Tales*, Abelard, 1966.

Edna Walker Chandler, *With Books on Her Head*, Meredith Press, 1967.

Geoffrey Trease, *Bent is the Bow*, Nelson, 1967.

Trease, *The Red Towers of Granada*, Vanguard Press, 1967.

James Reeves, *The Cold Flame*, Hamish Hamilton, 1967, Meredith, 1969.

Treece, *Swords from the North*, Pantheon, 1967.

Gray, *Mainly in the Moonlight: Ten Stories of Sorcery and the Supernatural*, Meredith, 1967.

Treece, *The Dream Time*, Brockhampton Press, 1967, Hawthorn, 1968.

Gray, *Grimbold's Other World*, Meredith Press, 1968.

W. Somerset Maugham, *The Mixture as Before*, Heron, 1968.

Kenneth McLeish, *The Story of Aeneas*, Longmans, 1968.

Potts, *The Haunted Mine*, Lutterworth, 1968.

Reeves, compiler, *An Anthology of Free Verse*, Basil Blackwell, 1968.

Macken, *The Flight of the Doves*, Macmillan, 1968.

Holding, *Poko and the Golden Demon*, Abelard, 1968.

(With Sweithlan Kraczyna) Kenneth Cavander, *The 'Iliad' and 'Odyssey' of Homer: Radio Plays*, British Broadcasting Company, 1969.

Aldous Huxley, *After Many a Summer*, Heron, 1969.

Nevil Shute, *Ruined City* [and] *Landfall: A Channel Story*, Heron, 1969.

Margaret Jessy Miller, editor, *Knights, Beasts and Wonders: Tales and Legends from Mediaeval Britain*, David White, 1969.

Roger Lancelyn Green, reteller, *The Tale of Ancient Israel*, Dent, 1969, Dutton, 1970.

Robert Elliot Rogerson, *Enjoy Reading!*, edited by Rogerson and C. M. Smith, W. & R. Chambers, Book 4, 1970, Book 5, 1971.

John Watts, *Early Encounters: an Introductory Stage*, Longmans, 1970.

Lee Cooper, *Five Fables from France*, Abelard, 1970.

Leon Garfield and Edward Blishen, *The God Beneath the Sea*, Kestrel books, 1970, Pantheon, 1971.

Nigel Grimshaw, *The Angry Valley*, Longman, 1970.

Pamela L. Travers, *Friend Monkey*, Harcourt, 1971.

William Cole, compiler, *The Poet's Tales: A New Book of Story Poems*, World Publishing, 1971.

Fedor Dostoyevski, *The Idiot*, Folio Society, 1971.

Mary Shura Craig, *The Valley of the Frost Giants*, Lothrop, 1971.

Treece, *The Invaders: Three Stories*, Crowell, 1972.

Robert Newman, *The Twelve Labors of Hercules*, Crowell, 1972.

Roger Squire, reteller, *Wizards and Wampum: Legends of the Iroquois*, Abelard, 1972.

Garfield and Blishen, *The Golden Shadow*, Kestrel Books, 1972, and Pantheon, 1973.

Ursula Synge, *Weland: Smith of the Gods*, Bodley Head, 1972, S. G. Phillips, 1973.

Montague Rhodes James, *Ghost Stories of M. R. James*, selected by Nigel Kneale, Folio Society, 1973.

Ian Seraillier, *I'll Tell You a Tale: A Collection of Poems and Ballads*, Longman, 1973.

Sutcliff, *The Capricorn Bracelet*, Oxford University Press, 1973.

Cooper, *The Strange Feathery Beast and Other French Fables*, Carousel, 1973.

Helen L. Hoke, *Weirdies: A Horrifying Concatenation of the Super-Sur-Real or Almost or Not-Quite Real*, Franklin Watts, 1973, published as *Weirdies, Weirdies, Weirdies: A Horrifying Concatenation of the Super-Sur-Real or Almost Not-Quite Real*, F. Watts, 1975.

Daphne du Maurier, *The Birds, and Other Stories*, abridge and simplified by Lewis Jones, Longman, 1973.

Hoke, *Monsters, Monsters, Monsters*, F. Watts, 1974.

Forbes Stuart, reteller, *The Magic Horns: Folk Tales from Africa*, Abelard, 1974, Addison-Wesley, 1976.

Travers, *About the Sleeping Beauty*, McGraw, 1975.

Marian Lines, *Tower Blocks: Poems of the City*, F. Watts, 1975.

Bernard Ashley, *Terry on the Fence*, Oxford University Press, 1975, S. G. Phillips, 1977.

Robert Swindells, *When Darkness Comes*, Morrow, 1975.

David Kossoff, *The Little Book of Sylvanus (died 41 A.D.)*, St. Martin's 1975.

Sutcliff, *Blood Feud*, Oxford University Press, 1976, Dutton, 1977.

Potts, *A Boy and His Bike*, Dobson, 1976.

Crossley-Holland, *The Wildman*, Deutsch, 1976.

Horace Walpole, *The Castle of Otranto: A Gothic Story*, Folio Society, 1976.

Victor Hugo, *Les Miserables*, translated by Norman Denny, Folio Press, 1976.

Rene Guillot, *Tipiti, The Robin*, translated by Gwen March, published with *Pascal and the Lioness*; illustrated by Barry Wilkinson, translated and adapted by Christina Holyoak, Bodley Head, 1976.

Hoke, compiler, *Haunts, Haunts, Haunts*, F. Watts, 1977, published as *Spectres, Spooks, and Shuddery Shades*, 1977.

Ashley *A Kind of Wild Justice*, S. G. Phillips, 1979.

Stuart, *The Mermaids' Revenge: Folk Tales from Britain and Ireland*, Abelard, 1979.

Leonard Clark, *The Tale of Prince Igor*, Dobson, 1979.

Nina Bawden, *The Robbers*, Gollancz, 1979.

Charles Causley, editor, *The Batsford Book of Stories in Verse for Children*, Batsford, 1979.

Tony Drake, *Breakback Alley*, Collins, 1979.

Ashley, *Break in the Sun: A Novel*, S. G. Phillips, 1980.

Alfred Noyes, *The Highwayman*, Oxford University Press, 1981.

(With Derek Collard and Jeroo Roy) John Bailey, McLeish, and David Spearman, retellers, *Gods and Men: Myths and Legends from the World's Religions*, Oxford University Press, 1981.

Charles Dickens, *The Posthumous Papers of the Pickwick Club*, Folio Society, 1981.

Dickens, *Great Expectations*, Folio Society, 1981.

Dickens, *Our Mutual Friend*, Folio Society, 1982.

Rudyard Kipling, *The Beginning of the Armadilloes*, Macmillan, 1982, Peter Bedrick, 1983.

Dickens, *The Mystery of Edwin Drood*, edited by Arthur J. Cox, Folio Society, 1983.

Dickens, *The Personal History of David Copperfield*, Folio Society, 1983.

Causley, compiler, *The Sun Dancing: Christian Verse*, Puffin, 1984.

Kipling, *Rikki-Tikki-Tavi and Other Animal Stories*, Macmillan, 1984.

Garfield, *The Wedding Ghost*, Oxford University Press, 1985.

Alfred Tennyson, *The Lady of Shalott*, Oxford University Press, 1985.

Dickens, *The Life and Adventures of Nicholas Nickelby*, Folio Society, 1986.

Edgar Allan Poe, *Two Tales*, Chimaera Press, 1986.

Neil Philip, reteller, *The Tale of Sir Gawain*, Philomel Books, 1987.

Crossley-Holland, reteller, *Beowulf*, Oxford University Press, 1988.

Bram Stoker, *Dracula*, Blackie, 1988.

Mary Shelley, *Frankenstein*, Blackie, 1988.

Anna Sewell, *Black Beauty*, Gollancz, 1989.

Also illustrator of Ted Kavanaugh's *Man Must Measure*, 1955; Martha Freudenberger and Magda Kelber's *Heute Morgen*, 2 and 3, 1956-57; Guthrie Foote's *Merrily on High*, 1959; Sutcliff's *The Lantern-Bearers*, 1959; Joseph Conrad's *The Shadow-Line* [and] *Within the tides*, 1962; Frank Knight's *They Told Mr. Hakluyt*, 1964; Emily Bronte's *Wuthering Heights*, 1964; Joan Tate's *Jenny*, 1964, *The Next-Doors*, 1964, and *Mrs. Jenny*, 1965; Lace Kendall's *The Rain Boat*, 1965; Denys Thompson and R.J. Harris's *Your English*, 1965; Harold Keith's *Komantcia*, 1966; Murphy's *Harbours and Docks*, 1967; Marie Butts's *Champion of Charlemagne*, 1967; Frederic Westcott's *Bach*, 1967; Hunter's *Thomas and the Warlock*, 1967; H. G. Wells's *Mr. Britling Sees It Through*, 1969; Huxley's *Time Must Have a Stop*, 1969; Shute's *On the Beach*, 1970; Potts's *The Story of Tod*; Maugham's *Of Human Bondage*; and Robert Louis Stevenson's *Stumpy, Dr. Jekyll and Mr.*

Hyde, The Wrecker, New Arabian Nights, and *More New Arabian Nights.*

■ Adaptations

Charley, Charlotte and the Golden Canary, Alfie Finds "The Other Side of the World," and *Through the Window* were adapted for filmstrips by Weston Woods.

■ Sidelights

In a speech published in *Children's Literature in Education* in 1970, artist, illustrator, and author Charles Keeping responded to those who found his picture books to be too mature for children: "How the devil I can disturb anybody I really don't know." He continued, "all these books that seem to be in a land of sugar puffs and cream— it doesn't exist, you know. Turn your television on any day and you will see that. Vietnam is happening and you can't dismiss it by living in a world of sugar puffs. Kids know it is happening, therefore violence and all these things are a part of their life."

The prolific Keeping, who illustrated mythological stories, monster stories, classics, poems, and works of nonfiction written by other authors as well as over twenty stories he wrote himself, was as controversial as he was hard-working. As Brian Alderson commented in *Illustrators of Children's Books: 1967-76,* Keeping was "without any doubt . . . the artist who has caused the most discussion." According to Frank Eyre, writing in *British Children's Books in the Twentieth Century,* Keeping's "strangely hypnotic style" was either "greatly liked or strongly detested." Eyre wrote that Keeping was "unusual among what are perhaps too loosely described as 'picture book artists'" because he was "passionately interested in ideas."

As Eyre noted, Keeping "originally made his name as an illustrator in black and white," but "first came into real prominence with a series of books in full colour which he produced as both artist and author." Keeping's color illustrations shocked readers and critics alike with their bright tones, odd combinations, abstract designs, and unexpected textures. Yet they were most sensational because they conveyed feeling. "Keeping is an emotional illustrator who can portray moods, noise and emotions in colour . . . vibrant three dimensional colour," wrote Jean Russell in *Books for Your Children.*

Despite their opinion of his style, many critics and fans appreciated Keeping's renderings of life—especially Cockney life—in London. Keeping, according to the *Junior Bookshelf's* M. S. Crouch, "was happiest in portraying the squalor and mystery of the streets and alleys he knew best." Elaine Moss of *Signal* praised Keeping, "arguably the greatest picture-book artist of our time," for "exploring the world of the underprivileged child so brilliantly." In *Growing Point* Margery Fisher said of Keeping: "he has left the most satisfying record of the real, abiding London."

Keeping received the 1970 Carnegie Medal for his drawings, like this one of Prometheus, in *The God Beneath the Sea,* Leon Garfield and Edward Blishen's collection of Greek myths.

Storytelling Excited Young Keeping

Keeping was born in Lambeth Walk, near the docks and market, in South London in 1924. He explained in a speech published in *Children's Literature Association Quarterly* in 1983 that his family was "comfortable working class." Although "there was much poverty around us," Keeping's large family was not poor. Keeping and his sister were "encouraged to create, to do everything: singing, reciting, talking," and telling stories. Storytelling was important to his grandmother, and his grandfather, a merchant seaman, who excited Keeping with his tales.

Keeping was a careful observer of his own neighborhood. Although he was not allowed to wander about the streets, he watched people from his own home and garden. He especially enjoyed watching the cart-horses walking through an adjoining yard past a blank black wall. Keeping began to draw these scenes when he was a child. He enjoyed drawing because by drawing a thing, "you had it again . . . and no one could take it from you." Keeping "spent so much time drawing," he recalled, that he "was very bad at most other things at school."

When Keeping's father, a professional boxer, died, the fourteen-year-old went to work as a printer's apprentice. Later, after serving for four years in the Royal Navy during World War II, he went to art school at the Regent Street Polytechnic School of Art. During his years as an art student, he lived in Paddington, worked as a rent collector, and "saw more real poverty" than he "had ever seen as a child." After earning a national diploma in art and design, Keeping worked for a newspaper as a cartoonist for three years. This work taught Keeping how to design and "how to attract people's attention, how to make them look at my work and not just miss over." He went on to work as a commercial artist, but found this work to be "absolutely soul destroying."

Keeping went to work as a visiting lecturer in lithography in London in 1956. Around this time, as he recalled in his 1983 speech, Keeping asked his agent to help him find work illustrating books. Oxford University Press gave him the opportunity to illustrate a book by Rosemary Sutcliff. Published in 1957, *The Silver Branch* won a Carnegie Medal commendation and a Spring Book Festival older honor from the *New York Herald Tribune*. The

next book he illustrated, Sutcliff's *Warrior Scarlet*, also did well; it won a Carnegie Medal commendation and was placed on the IBBY honour list. When Sutcliff retold *Beowulf*, Keeping illustrated it as well.

In the mid-1960s, as Keeping continued to lecture, he began to illustrate books by Henry Treece, who, according to Keeping in his 1983 speech, "was very into Vikings." Keeping did not know much about Vikings, so he "invented my own. . . . I took my Vikings from my own imagination." Keeping did such a good job illustrating those books, he became a sought after Viking book illustrator. He once commented, "I'd done so many of them I was beginning to look like one."

Begins Life As An Author

It was at this point that Keeping put together some of his own writings and illustrated them to create a picture book, *Shaun and the Cart-Horse*. The story is about a cockney boy whose friend becomes ill and must sell his cart-horse. Shaun comes up with a plan to save the horse from the knacker (a buyer of worn-out domestic animals) and return it to his friend; the street vendors help with contributions. A *Junior Bookshelf* critic found the story "a little thin" but judged the illustrations to be "extremely vigorous and disturbing." Della Thomas of *School Library Journal* described the illustrations as "distinctive and vital" and the story as "simple, but satisfying." In *Growing Point*, however, Fisher commented that children "may find the pictures ugly." The book was a runner-up for the Kate Greenaway Award, and Keeping's publisher asked for more.

The third book Keeping wrote and illustrated, *Charley, Charlotte and the Golden Canary*, won the Kate Greenaway Award. Colored in what a *Junior Bookshelf* critic called "brilliant yellows, blue-greens and oranges," this book tells the story of two children who are separated when one of them moves away. When Charley's pet canary escapes, it flies to Charlotte's high window and the children find one another again. Critics praised Keeping's illustrations for their ability to communicate emotions. John Rowe Townsend commented in *Written for Children* that this work is "stunning . . . to look at; the colours are so wild, glowing and vibrant that it is hard to take one's eyes off them. . . ." "This is a book for *feeling*," stated

Keeping illustrated *Beowulf*, Kevin Crossley-Holland's retelling of the classic eighth-century English poem about a brave young man who battles two ferocious monsters.

Fisher in *Growing Point*. Zena Sutherland wrote in *Saturday Review*, "the pages glow. . . ."

Alfie and the Ferryboat, known in the United States as *Alfie Finds "The Other Side of the World,"* is also set in London. Alfie loves to listen to Bunty the sailor's tales about the other side of the world. One day, when Bunty leaves Alfie and seemingly disappears in the fog, Alfie follows and wanders onto a ship. In a trip across the Thames, Alfie comes to believe that he is crossing to the other side of the world. There, lights and blurs of color

greet him, yet Bunty emerges from it all and helps Alfie find his way. As Joyce Baumholtz noted in *School Library Journal*, Keeping rendered Alfie's home near the docks in "dull browns, greens and blues" and colored the amusement park on the other side of the world with "psychedelic hue and intensity." "A fine, disturbing book," commented a *Junior Bookshelf* critic, "incomparably Keeping's best to date."

Another of Keeping's better-known picture books, *Joseph's Yard,* was originally created as a film. In the story, a young boy clears a cluttered yard and trades a piece of metal for a seedling. Joseph is so enchanted with its first rose that he picks it, killing the plant. The plant revives the next spring, but Joseph accidentally kills it again in an attempt to keep birds and insects away from it. As Muriel Whitaker observed in *Children's Literature in Education,* "[d]rab greys and browns" are used as the story opens: rain is green, "threatening cats" are blue. "Keeping has expressed the desire for beauty in a wholly effective and simple symbol," wrote Fisher in *Growing Point.* Margaret Meek of *School Librarian* exclaimed that the "subtle interplay of colour and texture combined with feeling tone are breathtaking."

Through the Window elicited debate from critics. Readers see London as a young boy does (and as Keeping did), through an opening in a curtained window. The boy watches people go by, as they do everyday, but then something happens. People begin running, horses began sprinting. An old woman's precious pet dog seems to be killed by the horses, and she grieves. The boy reacts by fogging up the window and drawing the woman, happy and holding her live dog. *Through the Window,* according to Elaine Moss in *Signal,* is "heart-rending and terrifying." "The pages explode with colour and yet the colour is carefully organised and disciplined," wrote Margery Fisher in *Growing Point.* A *Junior Bookshelf* critic called the book "brilliant, profound" and "disturbing." A critic in the *Times Literary Supplement* described the work as a "sombre little saga." Other critics took issue with *Through the Window.* Kevin Crossley-Holland wrote in the *Spectator* that the publication of the

Alfie was so excited he ran and joined the stream of people moving down an iron gangway and into the ship—and no one, not even the sailors, seemed to notice him.

Having never left his dingy factory neighborhood, a small boy finds himself on a ferryboat crossing the river in this self-illustrated work titled *Alfie Finds "The Other Side of the World."*

"arrogant" book by Oxford University Press was "irresponsible." "It is high time Mr. Keeping realised that he has a responsibility not only to his art but also to his audience."

Keeping maintained that his work could be appreciated by children, even if he did not write or illustrate with any specific audience in mind. He recalled the story of a young child who was so stimulated by one of his books, the child licked its pages. Some reviewers, like Aidan Chambers in *Booktalk*, defended his work by asserting the capacity of children to learn from sophisticated material.

Keeping illustrated *The God Beneath the Sea*, Greek myths collected by Leon Garfield and Edward Blishen. Keeping, who had never much liked Greek mythology, found the assignment difficult. He focused on "people, their emotions and their reactions to emotions. . . . I took a symbolic line" to visually project "cruelty and violence," he wrote in *Children's Literature in Education*. In *Illustrators of Children's Books, 1967-76* Treld Pelkey Bicknell in *Illustrators of Children's Books* praised Keeping's work in *The God Beneath the Sea*: "what drawings, what breaking of new ground. . . ." The myths are "treated with compassion, pathos, strength, horror, and intelligence." A critic in the *Times Literary Supplement* found Keeping's work "magnificent. Pain stares naked from the tortured figure of Prometheus. . . . Demeter's grief for the lost Persephone is audible to the ears of the imagination, so powerfully has Charles Keeping delineated her anguish." While Alan Garner criticized the book in the *New Statesman*, he lauded Keeping's work as "a singular vision of what Classical myths must have been. . . . Two drawings especially—Cronos and Prometheus—are more terrible and beautiful than Goya." He continued, "take Charles Keeping's drawings, and frame them." *The God Beneath the Sea* won several honors, including the Carnegie Medal.

Keeping Returns to London Streets

Critics who found Keeping's early 1970 works frightening or too sophisticated for children were cheered by the appearance of *Richard, The Railway Passage*, and *Cockney Ding-Dong*. In these works, Keeping returned to the streets of London. Richard is a police horse who is trained, groomed, and ridden during police duty. *The Railway Pas-*

If you enjoy the works of Charles Keeping, you may also want to check out the following:

The macabre cartoons of Charles Addams, who created "The Addams Family" of television and movie fame.
The works of award-winning author and illustrator Edward Ardizzone.

sage is about a family who wins a prize in the pools and becomes wealthy. The eight adults who share the winnings spend their money in different ways. According to Elaine Moss in *Children's Books of the Year: 1974*, Keeping explores his story "with a new-found joy in his heart." Clive Phillpot of *Children's Book Review* noted the use of color in the description of characters, while "a pervading sepiatone is shot through with passages of pure bright colour. . . ." "Charles Keeping has his best story to date," wrote M. Crouch for *Junior Bookshelf*.

Cockney Ding-Dong presents some of the songs Keeping's family sang during his childhood. Critics praised the collection of songs as well as Keeping's portrayal of characters. The book, "full of vitality and the sound of singing, will become a classic," wrote Meek in the *School Librarian*. Bicknell commented in *Illustrators of Children's Books* that the illustrations for *Cockney Ding-Dong* "would at any time stand alone as works of art."

By 1973, Edward Hudson of *Children's Book Review* could write that Keeping "has changed and extended the world of picture-story-book illustration . . . in the space of less than a decade." Keeping continued to innovate. In his 1978 book, *River*, he abandoned text altogether, and presented what Fisher described as a "sequence of pictures." A landscape is depicted over time. In the beginning, the scene is a river bank with a tree, but gradually development transforms the landscape into a view of a building. The building, at first ornate, is bombed and then destroyed. By the end of a book, an office building takes up the scene. Sarah Hayes, in the *Times Literary Supplement*, commented, "*River* is a book whose graphic sophistication is seductive, surprisingly, to children as well as adults." "*River* is an astonishing work, certainly the finest yet in Keeping's long line of brilliantly designed picture books," remarked a *School Librarian* critic.

Sammy Streetsinger marked another departure. Sammy the Streetsinger performs as a one-man band for subway passengers until he is discovered by a circus manager and then becomes a rock star. Jane Doonan wrote in *The Signal Selection of Children's Books 1984* that Keeping employed "screaming reds, harsh greens, electric blues, and shrieking purples" in this book. *Junior Bookshelf*'s M. Crouch commented that Keeping "never shows a sign of repeating himself or building on past successes." *Adam and Paradise Island,* the last book Keeping wrote and illustrated, was published posthumously. In colors from orange to pink, Keeping shows how a group of friends build a playground together after a neighborhood is destroyed by local officials. Keeping also collected and illustrated ghost stories in two books in the years before he died: *Charles Keeping's Book of Classic Ghost Stories* and *Charles Keeping's Classic Tales of the Macabre.* According to Crouch in *School Librarian,* Keeping's illustrations for the latter book are "terrifying in a most subtle way."

Keeping died on Monday, May 16th, 1988. His editor at Oxford University Press, Ron Heapy, remembered in *Books for Keeps* that Keeping loved to eat fish, and "always had a great passion for the sea." "The sense of loss I feel for this dear, warm man is appalling," he wrote. A commemorative plaque has been placed on the Keeping residence in Bromley, Kent, England.

■ Works Cited

Alderson, Brian, "A View from the Island: European Picture Books 1967-1976," *Illustrators of Children's Books: 1967-76,* edited by Lee Kingman, Grace Allen Hogarth, and Harriet Quimby, The Horn Book, Inc., 1978, pp. 20-43.

Review of *Alfie and the Ferryboat, Junior Bookshelf,* August, 1968, p. 222.

Baumholtz, Joyce, review of *Alfie Finds "The Other Side of the World," School Library Journal,* December, 1968, p. 38.

Chambers, Aidan, "Axes for Frozen Seas," *Booktalk: Occasional Writing on Literature and Children,* The Bodley Head, 1985, pp. 14-33.

Review of *Charley, Charlotte and the Golden Canary, Junior Bookshelf,* December, 1967, p. 372.

Crossley-Holland, Kevin, "Artistic Licence," *Spectator,* December 5, 1970, pp. xii-xiii.

Crouch, M., review of *The Railway Passage, Junior Bookshelf,* December, 1974, p. 336.

Crouch, M., review of *Sammy Streetsinger, Junior Bookshelf,* December, 1984, p. 245.

Crouch, M. S., review of *Charles Keeping's Classic Tales of the Macabre, School Librarian,* February, 1988, pp. 35-36.

Crouch, M. S., "Makers of Images," *Junior Bookshelf,* August, 1988, pp. 173-75.

Doonan, Jane, review of *Sammy Streetsinger, Signal Selection of Children's Books 1984,* Thimble Press, 1985, p. 12.

Eyre, Frank, "Books with Pictures," *British Children's Books in the Twentieth Century,* 1979, pp. 38-58.

Fisher, Margery, review of *Shaun and the Cart-Horse, Growing Point,* November, 1966, p. 802.

Fisher, Margery, review of *Charley, Charlotte and the Golden Canary, Growing Point,* October, 1967, pp. 973-74.

Fisher, Margery, review of *River, Growing Point,* July, 1978, p. 3370.

Fisher, Margery, review of *Joseph's Yard, Growing Point,* March, 1970, pp. 1482-83.

Fisher, Margery, review of *Through the Window, Growing Point,* September, 1970, p. 1578.

Fisher, Margery, review of *Adam and Paradise Island, Growing Point,* September, 1989, pp. 5205-6.

Garner, Alan, "The Death of Myth," *New Statesman,* November 6, 1970, pp. 606-7.

Review of *The God Beneath the Sea, Times Literary Supplement,* October 30, 1970, p. 1254.

Hayes, Sarah, "The Power of Pictures," *Times Literary Supplement,* July 7, 1978, p. 763.

Heapy, Ron, "Working with Charlie," *Books for Keeps,* July, 1988.

Hudson, Edward, review of *Richard, Children's Book Review,* October, 1973, p. 139.

Keeping, Charles, "Illustration in Children's Books," *Children's Literature in Education,* March, 1970, pp. 41-54.

Keeping, Charles, "Greek Myths and the Twentieth Century Reader," *Children's Literature in Education,* November, 1970, pp. 52-54.

Keeping, Charles, "My Work as a Children's Illustrator," *Children's Literature Association Quarterly,* Winter, 1983, pp. 14-19.

Meek, Margaret, review of *Joseph's Yard, School Librarian,* March, 1970, p. 126.

Meek, Margaret, review of *Cockney Ding-Dong: A Songbook, School Librarian,* March, 1976, p. 80.

Moss, Elaine, "Picture Books: 'The Railway Passage,'" *Children's Books of the Year: 1974*, Hamish Hamilton, 1975, pp. 19-20.

Moss, Elaine, "Them's for the Infants, Miss," *Signal*, September, 1978, pp. 144-49.

Pelkey Bicknell, Treld, "In the Beginning Was the Word: The Illustrated book 1967-1976," *Illustrators of Children's Books: 1967-76*, edited by Lee Kingman, Grace Allen Hogarth, and Harriet Quimby, The Horn Book, Inc, 1978, pp. 58-89.

Phillpot, Clive, review of *The Railway Passage*, *Children's Book Review*, Spring, 1975, pp. 12-13.

Review of *River*, *School Librarian*, September, 1978, p. 230.

Russell, Jean, "Charles Keeping," *Books for Your Children*, Autumn, 1970, pp. 2-3.

Review of *Shaun and the Cart-Horse*, *Junior Bookshelf*, October, 1966, p. 305.

Sutherland, Zena, review of *Charley, Charlotte and the Golden Canary*, *Saturday Review*, July 20, 1968, p. 30.

Thomas, Della, review of *Shaun and the Cart-Horse*, *School Library Journal*, February, 1967, p. 59.

Review of *Through the Window*, *Junior Bookshelf*, October, 1970, p. 278.

Review of *Through the Window*, *Times Literary Supplement*, October 30, 1970, p. 1260.

Townsend, John Rowe, "Picture Books in Bloom: British," *Written for Children: An Outline of English-Language Children's Literature*, J. B. Lippincott, 1987, pp. 317-25.

Whitaker, Muriel, review of *Joseph's Yard*, *Children's Literature in Education*, Number 16, Spring, 1975, pp. 10-20.

■ **For More Information See**

PERIODICALS

Booklist, June 1, 1984, p. 1396.
Books and Bookmen, November, 1972, pp. xi-xv.
Bulletin of the Center for Children's Books, April, 1981, p. 153.
Growing Point, November, 1973, p. 2270.
Horn Book, January-February, 1988, p. 78.
Kirkus Reviews, September 1, 1989, p. 1329.
Library Journal, October 15, 1989, p. 93.
Spectator, November 11, 1966, pp. 627-28.
Times Educational Supplement, June 9, 1989, p. B11.
Times Literary Supplement, October 30, 1970, p. 1254; December 8, 1972, p. 1495.
Voice of Youth Advocates, June, 1988, p. 84.

■ **Obituaries**

PERIODICALS

School Library Journal, August, 1988.
Times (London), May 20, 1988.*

—Sketch by R. Garcia-Johnson

David Klass

Wrestling with Honor, and 1997, for *Danger Zone;* Keystone State Reading Association Young Adult Award, Pennsylvania, 1996, for *California Blue.*

■ Writings

FOR YOUNG ADULTS

The Atami Dragons, Scribner, 1984.
Breakaway Run, E. P. Dutton, 1986.
A Different Season, E. P. Dutton, 1989.
Wrestling with Honor, E. P. Dutton, 1989.
California Blue, Scholastic, 1994.
Danger Zone, Scholastic, 1995.
Screen Test, Scholastic, 1997.

FOR ADULTS

Night of the Tyger, St. Martin's Press, 1990.
Samurai, Inc., Ballantine Books, 1992.

SCREENPLAYS

Kiss the Girls, Paramount, 1997.
Desperate Measures, TriStar, 1998.

OTHER

Also contributor of short stories to anthologies.

■ Work in Progress

A young adult novel and three screenplays: *In the Time of the Butterflies,* adapted, with sister Judy

■ Personal

Born March 8, 1960, in Vermont; son of Morton (an anthropology professor) and Sheila (a writer and English professor; maiden name, Solomon) Klass. *Education:* Yale University, B.A., 1982; University of Southern California, School of Cinema-Television, M.A., 1989.

■ Addresses

Agent—Aaron M. Priest Literary Agency, 708 Third Ave., 23rd floor, New York, NY 10017.

■ Career

Novelist and screenwriter. Worked in Japan as an English teacher and at various odd jobs in Los Angeles. *Member:* Writers Guild of America West, PEN Center USA West (former member of board of directors).

■ Awards, Honors

Outstanding Works of Fiction for Young Adults Award, Southern California Council, 1990, for

Klass, for a television movie from a novel by Julia Alvarez; *The Millennium Plague,* an original script for television written with sister, Perri Klass; and *Run for Your Life,* an original feature film script for Universal.

■ Sidelights

David Klass is a screenwriter and novelist whose work for young adults deals with contemporary themes from ecology to coping with loss. In books such as the award-winning *Wrestling with Honor, California Blue,* and *Danger Zone,* Klass also employs the microcosm of high school athletics as a matrix for teens who are in crisis or faced with difficult decisions. Baseball, soccer, wrestling, track, and basketball all form a backdrop for Klass's young, mostly male protagonists who must learn to deal with personal traumas and dislocations. Divorce or the death of a parent, as well as racial, gender, and environmental issues, all become part of the stew of a Klass novel.

"I'm not writing about sports so much as I am about character," Klass told *Authors and Artists for Young Adults (AAYA)* in an interview. "You write about what you know, and when I think back to my high school years, much of my self-esteem came on the athletic field. Sports were, and still are, one of the great pleasures of my life. It's not that I'm trying to make a statement about athletics, but it is what I know. Also, the young adult novel format, at about 200 pages, lends itself to a time span of about three months. And that is about the length of a sports season in high school. What I'm trying to do with my books is to marry the sports side with other issues and transcend genre."

A Writing Family

Klass was born in Vermont and grew up in Leonia, New Jersey, the son of Morton Klass, an anthropology professor, who also edited science fiction journals, and Sheila Solomon Klass, a well-known writer for young adults. "I came from a family of readers and writers," Klass told *AAYA.* "I can't imagine a family where more emphasis and love was given to literature. My family reads ferociously." Both Klass's younger and older sisters, Judy and Perri, are novelists, and an uncle writes science fiction novels. "Growing up in this

family, it was almost impossible not to become a writer," Klass noted.

A self-confessed reluctant reader, Klass was, as he described himself, "the least intellectual in the family," and the only one to focus on sports in school. His interest in reading was sparked by books which dealt with his athletic interests, and soon he too was hooked on books of all stripes, including Jack London's *White Fang, Call of the Wild,* and *Martin Eden,* Alexandre Dumas's *The Three Musketeers, The Count of Monte Cristo,* and *The Man in the Iron Mask,* and Robert Louis Stevenson's *Treasure Island.* "I still think *Treasure Island* is one of the greatest adventure books ever written and re-read it every few years," Klass told *AAYA.* Later, Klass was deeply influenced by the writings of John Le Carre, especially his *Tinker, Tailor, Soldier, Spy.* "Our father used to read to us every night for years," Klass recalled for *AAYA,* "and mom used to get up an hour or two before any of us in the morning to get her writing in. I remember waking up to the sound of her typewriter filtering down to us from the attic. For her, publishing a novel was the highest mission someone could achieve."

However, it wasn't a mission Klass immediately accepted. Sports still took priority for him throughout high school and into his first years at Yale, baseball and soccer being his strongest sports. But there were hints of what was to come: as a high school senior he was already writing short stories. "My older sister Perri had won *Seventeen*'s short story contest a couple of times in high school. A sort of sibling rivalry prompted me to enter in, and I took first place in their annual contest with a story about a carnival game on the New Jersey shore, 'Ring Toss'," Klass recalled.

At Yale, he was at first overwhelmed with the academic work, and ultimately decided that his future did not lay in professional sports. He developed a real love for poetry, and as a history major impressed the student body by winning the English department's poetry contest in his junior year, and then topped this his senior year by winning the award for the best imaginative writing by an undergraduate. Taking classes from author John Hersey and critic Gordon Lish introduced Klass to subtler depths of appreciation for the written word, yet he still did not think of writing as a possible career.

CALIFORNIA BLUE

a novel by David Klass

A teenager's discovery of a new species of butterfly threatens the existence of a California lumber town in this 1994 novel.

"Almost all my friends went to law school immediately upon graduation from Yale," Klass told *AAYA*. "I was leaning toward law, too, but decided to intern for a year before committing to law school." Klass took a job as clerk with a Washington, D.C., law firm specializing in entertainment, working for a year to get a feel for the profession. "By the end of the year," Klass said, "I knew two things: one, that I did not want to be a lawyer, and two, that I wanted to have an adventure."

From "Sensei" to Writer

To find adventure, Klass took a job with the Japanese Ministry of Education, which was recruiting native-English speakers to work in Japanese schools, providing conversational English to round out students' work in grammatical English. Klass was sent to Atami, a coastal resort and spa not far from Tokyo, where he became a "sensei" or teacher. "I had my own classroom where I taught conversational English, and I also helped out on the baseball team," Klass noted. "I was very fortunate to be sent to Atami, which is a beautiful town. They had never had an American teacher there before and I was treated with great respect. They gave me a three-bedroom apartment overlooking the bay."

Klass would stay there for two years, but within three days of arrival, he had come to a decision. "I told myself that if I ever had any thoughts of becoming a writer, then I would do it here." He set out to write a story that could incorporate the experiences he was having every day: his wonder at a new culture, all the sights and sounds of a Japanese town that were so unique and fresh for him. "The book just flew off my fingers," Klass told *AAYA*. "From the outset I determined to write a young adult title. It just seemed right for me. I was twenty-three at the time, and in many ways still had the maturity level of a seventeen-year-old. The voice of a high school kid came naturally to me—it still does. And I was not ready to tackle the length and complexity of an adult novel."

In the resulting book, *The Atami Dragons*, Klass transformed his own occasional feelings of homesickness into the loss young Jerry Sanders feels at the death of his mother. Jerry's father decides to take his family to Japan for the summer to help heal their emotional wound. At first Jerry, a star first baseman, is reluctant to leave his team in the States, but once in Japan—and bored in the seaside town where they are staying—he eagerly joins a local team, the eponymous Atami Dragons, who are badly in need of a slugger after an injury to one of their players. Playing on the team gives Jerry a chance to learn a little about this new culture, and the stay in Japan helps Jerry, his father, and his sister come to terms with the mother's death. At one point, they climb Mount Fuji and pile rocks as a shrine to her.

"The book was about three months in the writing," Klass recalled, "and when I finished I wrapped it up and sent it off to Scribner. Then I went off to Thailand for a little vacation, and when I returned to Japan, there was a letter from Scribner saying they wanted to buy my book." Reviews of the book were solid. Jean S. Bolley in *Voice of Youth Advocates* called the work an "effective story of a teen coming to terms with loss" and observed also that there was "enough baseball detail to keep the sports fan happy." A *School Library Journal* reviewer concluded that "the baseball action is sparse but good, the writing sprightly, and the cultural information is interesting," while *Booklist*'s Stephanie Zvirin noted that Klass "brings equal shares of humor, sports, and sentiment" to his story.

This was encouragement enough for Klass to turn his hand to other works of fiction, including an adult gothic horror thriller, *Night of the Tyger,* published in 1990, and another young adult novel set in Japan, *Breakaway Run.* "By the end of my two years in Japan, I was beginning to learn about the country more, to see beyond the tourist veneer," Klass explained. While Jerry Sanders's experiences in *The Atami Dragons* were those of an outsider, a visitor to a culture, those of the new protagonist, Tony Ross, would have more depth, more understanding. "I wanted to write about Japan from the inside of a Japanese family," Klass stated, "to talk about the differences between school in Japan and the United States, to describe the closeness of families in Japan, to describe the beauty of the country. I once visited Kyoto and was so taken with the place that I knew I would have to include a scene in my novel set there. So Tony takes a trip there in my book. And mostly, I wanted to talk about how traveling in a foreign country can help you grow up and find out who you are, like it did for me."

Tony Ross leaves for a five-month exchange program in Japan to attend a high school in Atami. In ways it is a relief to leave his quarreling parents, but he finds adjusting to his new environment and life with his Japanese host family difficult at first. While in Japan, he learns of his parents' separation, and his attempts at fitting in with Japanese culture are initially a failure. The Maeda family, with whom he lives, seem distant to him, and their daughter, Yukiko, is so shy she barely looks at him. His poor attitude on the school soccer team gets him sidelined. But when he runs a marathon, he begins to earn the respect of the captain of the soccer team, Tanaka, who helps Tony, as a *Publishers Weekly* critic observed, "understand the Japanese attitude toward discipline."

By the end of his stay, Tony finds his place in the society, and he even begins dating Yukiko, following the Japanese customs in such things. Back home in the United States, Tony sees how much he has learned from his experience, and how much he has grown as a result of it.

"While showing a young man's efforts at self-mastery, the story offers some telling observations about marriage, family life and divorce," concluded the *Publishers Weekly* critic. Writing in *Booklist,* Zvirin noted that Klass's "portrayal of Japanese culture and customs" demonstrated "obvious respect and knowledge," while Robert E. Unsworth in *School Library Journal* observed that the "writing is crisp, and [Klass] often comes up with a clever turn of phrase. . . . In addition to

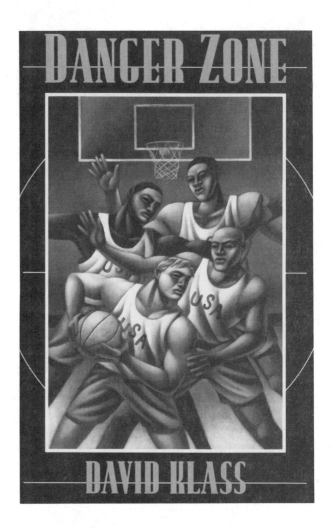

In this 1995 work, a "Teen Dream Team" encounters racism at a European basketball tournament.

the involving story, readers will find the candid descriptions of Japanese life both interesting and informative." A critic in the *New York Times Book Review* summed up the book as a "perceptive novel" with "details of place and custom" that were "particularly vivid."

Down and Out in Hollywood

While writing *Breakaway Run*, Klass received some exciting news. His first novel had been optioned by the movies, and a Hollywood producer came to Atami to visit Klass and view the possible location. At the time, Klass was still toying with the idea of going to law school once he was back in the United States, but this producer convinced him that his real future lay in Hollywood as a screenwriter. "So I went to Hollywood," Klass told *AAYA*, "and of course the movie deal fell through, as so many do. I found myself in Los Angeles, one of a million other young screenwriters, alone, broke, and with no sense of how to break through as a screenwriter."

For the next seven years, Klass lived close to the bone economically, working at various odd jobs, doing treatments for producers that earned a meager living, and also studying for a master's degree at the University of Southern California, putting himself through graduate school by working as a teacher's assistant in English composition sections. "During this time my work on YA novels was about the only thing that kept me sane, that made me believe I really was a writer," Klass recalled. "I didn't much like L.A., I missed the seasons, and I found the whole entertainment business and social life surrounding it slightly surreal." During his time in Hollywood, Klass published three more YA titles: *A Different Season*, *Wrestling with Honor*, and *California Blue*. He also published his two adult novels, *Night of the Tyger*, which he had begun in Japan, and *Samurai, Inc.*, an international thriller set partly in Japan. Sales on this last title were good, and the book found a place on several bestseller lists. Screenplays were also consuming much of his time, but work on the YA novels continued to sustain him emotionally.

With *A Different Season*, a baseball story with a twist, Klass moved his setting to the United States. Jim Roark, known as "Streak," is looking forward to another great season as a pitcher for his New

Jersey high school team, but when Jennifer Douglas breaks the gender barrier and joins the squad, Jim's pitching suffers. He is attracted to Jennifer but does not think it is right for girls to be on the team. Further plot complications come from Jim's father, who lost his chance to play for the New York Yankees after being hit by a drunk driver. Jennifer is finally accepted by the team, and the romance between her and Jim can continue when they agree to disagree about women playing on men's teams. A *Publishers Weekly* critic praised Klass for not resolving "the book's central conflict," allowing readers to "draw their own conclusions." A contributor in the *New York Times Book Review* called the novel "Nicely written," while *Booklist*'s Hazel Rochman concluded that "Klass writes with precision and grace about baseball—its skills, comradeship, and mystique. . . ." Writing in *Voice of Youth Advocates*, Myrna Feldman observed that "Baseball, romance, major league recruiters, problem drinking, and feelings of failure are all successfully dealt with in a novel as current as the daily news."

Wrestling with Honor is one of Klass's personal favorites, and deals with the issue of drug testing in sports. Ron Woods is not only captain of the wrestling team but also a star student. When he tests positive for marijuana in a mandatory drug test, he cannot believe the results. He knows there must be some mistake which another test could likely rectify, but he also feels his civil rights have been violated and refuses a further test. When the team turns against him for his stand, he takes out his anger on the memory of his father, who was killed in Vietnam. Eventually Ron comes to terms with this anger and is also allowed back on the team after it is discovered how his first drug test had been tampered with. Barred from the final tournament, in the end he is able to beat his rival in a post-tournament match. Shirley A. Bathgate, writing in *Voice of Youth Advocates*, noted that "The descriptions of wrestling drills and take-down moves indicates real familiarity with the sport," and also observed that the book "should appeal to a more mature audience than Klass' earlier *Atami Dragons*." A *Publishers Weekly* reviewer concluded that "Klass creates a moving, emotionally involving story; readers will be cheering all the way through its exciting—if manipulated—final scene."

One of Klass's more ambitious novels for young adults is *California Blue*, a story with a Northern

If you enjoy the works of David Klass, you may also want to check out the following books and films:

James W. Bennett, *A Different Season*, 1995.
Thomas J. Dygard, *The Rookie Arrives*, 1988.
Sarah Sargent, *Seeds of Change*, 1989.
Breaking Away, starring Dennis Christopher, Paul Dooley, Dennis Quaid, and Daniel Stern, 1979.

California setting that focuses on environmentalism. While most of Klass's books are written quickly, *California Blue* was several years in the making as he experimented with point of view and genre. Klass attempted the story variously as an adult novel, a screenplay, and a stage play before realizing that it was essentially a young adult novel and should be narrated from the point of view of a teenage boy, John Rodgers, whose father works in a lumber mill. Conflict comes when the boy discovers a rare butterfly in danger of extinction from the operation of the mill where his father works.

The residents of Kiowa, California, are completely dependent on the lumber industry, and when seventeen-year-old John discovers the new species of butterfly, their existence—as much as the butterfly's—is called into question. John becomes a target for the vindictiveness of the townspeople and runs off to San Francisco, but he eventually returns to Kiowa. Further complications arise from subplots involving a romantic attraction between John and his biology teacher, a disagreement between John and his father over the place of athletics, and a serious illness—leukemia—that is killing John's father. Todd Morning, writing in *School Library Journal*, observed that "In a touching final scene, [John] has a quiet talk with his dying father. John knows, however, that he will have to leave again." Morning went on to explain that the "novel's strength does not lie simply in its willingness to tackle big issues," but that the book had "texture and depth," was both "thoughtful and fair," and would "strike a chord with many YAs." Deborah Stevenson wrote in *Bulletin of the Center for Children's Books* that Klass's novel was about "manhood and the price of inclusion as well as ecology," while a *Publishers Weekly* critic dubbed the work "a beautifully rendered novel."

A Switch Hitter

Klass's screenwriting career was also taking off, with successes such as *Kiss the Girls,* a thriller starring Morgan Freeman and Ashley Judd, and *Desperate Measures,* featuring Michael Keaton. Klass was able to leave Hollywood for the East Coast, settling in Manhattan, where he could write for the movies at a distance and continue with his YA novels.

Klass finds a balance between writing screenplays and YA novels. "I love the freedom that YA novels provide me," Klass told *AAYA*. "Hollywood wants to know what they're going to get in a script. I present them with a detailed, ten-page, scene-by-scene outline, and then follow that closely as I write the screenplay. I am always aware of audience reaction when writing for Hollywood. It is a constant exercise in calculation. You can make your hero a drunkard, but never a coward, for example. Viewers wouldn't allow that. But with YA novels I try to avoid such calculation. I try to write from inside the characters, not separate enough to figure out what the audience wants or needs. I have a general idea where the story begins and where it ends up. Then I have to find the voice of the narrator—I generally write these novels in first person. Once I find the voice, I just let my character take me through the story and stay out of the way. It's wonderfully freeing not to have to work form a detailed outline for my YA novels."

Klass usually writes very quickly: two titles, *Danger Zone* and *Screen Test,* were written in an energetic three-month period after moving from Hollywood. With *Danger Zone*, Klass turned to basketball and a high school "Teen Dream Team" which competes in Europe in an international tournament. Jimmy Doyle, a star guard from Minnesota, finds that he is distrusted by much of the rest of the team, largely made up of inner-city African American players. Doyle must win their respect, battling against rivalry and racism to do so. But once in Europe, a new form of racism appears: German skinheads threaten the team, and in the final game, Jimmy takes a terrorist bullet just as he sinks the winning shot.

Critics found the novel both exciting and sobering. A *Kirkus Reviews* contributor thought that Klass embroidered the plot with "frank, thoughtful observations about fathers and sons, city versus small town values, race, friendship, and courage," while Tom S. Hurlburt noted in *School Library Journal* that "the racial tension throughout the book rings true, and readers seeking lots of hoop action will be thoroughly satisfied." Nancy Zachary, writing in *Voice of Youth Advocates*, called the book a "fast-paced adventure that deals realistically with pressure, racism, and terrorism."

Screen Test is Klass's take on Hollywood. "I don't think I've ever sat down to write a novel with a conscious message I wanted to impart—with the possible exception of *Screen Test*," Klass explained to *AAYA*. "Rather than impart a message, I try to create a difficult situation with lots of conflict and let any message grow out of the characters' response to the situation." The situation in *Screen Test* involves sixteen-year-old Liz, who is discovered by a big-shot Hollywood producer when she takes part in a student film. Offered a starring role in a feature film, Liz leaves her New Jersey home for a summer in Hollywood and a possible film career. But Liz soon learns painful truths about "Tinsel Town" and her seductive male co-star; she eventually learns to value her parents and the East Coast more than the flaky values of Hollywood.

A novel with a female protagonist and a non-sports background, *Screen Test* broke new ground for Klass. A contributor in *Kirkus Reviews* noted this, observing that "Klass demonstrates abilities to depart from his sports stories for which he is better known, and to do his homework." The reviewer went on to explain that Klass "offers eye-opening glimpses of the Southern California scene as well as workaday life on the set." Marilyn Heath concluded in *School Library Journal* that "Liz's summer makes for an interesting vicarious adventure."

Future plans for Klass include several screenplays, more sports adventures on the two soccer teams he plays on in New York—"I'm the grandpa out on the field at thirty-eight"—and of course, more YA novels. "Everybody tells you that it is very hard to publish books for boys between the ages of thirteen and eighteen. But my feeling is that if there are no books out there for them, that will become a self-fulfilling prophecy. If you write exciting, true, meaningful stories, they will read them. And reading is important. As someone who works in Hollywood, I know there is something unique and almost mystical about the experience of reading. It's an older form than the visual of movies, and despite all the money spent to make movies, I think that written words are an infinitely more powerful way to tell a story."

■ Works Cited

Review of *The Atami Dragons, School Library Journal,* December, 1984, p. 104.

Bathgate, Shirley A., review of *Wrestling with Honor, Voice of Youth Advocates,* December, 1988, pp. 239-40.

Bolley, Jean S., review of *The Atami Dragons, Voice of Youth Advocates,* August, 1985, p. 186.

Review of *Breakaway Run, New York Times Book Review,* July 26, 1987, p. 21.

Review of *Breakaway Run, Publishers Weekly,* April 24, 1987, p. 73.

Review of *California Blue, Publishers Weekly,* February 14, 1989, p. 90.

Review of *Danger Zone, Kirkus Reviews,* November 15, 1995.

Review of *A Different Season, New York Times Book Review,* February 28, 1988, p. 35.

Review of *A Different Season, Publishers Weekly,* November 27, 1987, p. 86.

Feldman, Myrna, review of *A Different Season, Voice of Youth Advocates,* August, 1988, p. 132.

Heath, Marilyn, review of *Screen Test, School Library Journal,* October, 1997.

Hurlburt, Tom S., review of *Danger Zone, School Library Journal,* March, 1996, p. 218.

Klass, David, interview with J. Sydney Jones for *Authors and Artists for Young Adults,* conducted April 21, 1998.

Morning, Todd, review of *California Blue, School Library Journal,* April, 1994, p. 152.

Rochman, Hazel, review of *A Different Season, Booklist,* January 1, 1988, p. 775.

Review of *Screen Test, Kirkus Reviews,* July 15, 1997.

Stevenson, Deborah, review of *California Blue, Bulletin of the Center for Children's Books,* April, 1994, p. 263.

Unsworth, Robert E., review of *Breakaway Run, School Library Journal,* August, 1987, p. 96.

Review of *Wrestling with Honor, Publishers Weekly,* September 30, 1988, p. 71.

Zachary, Nancy, review of *Danger Zone, Voice of Youth Advocates,* April, 1996, p. 27.

Zvirin, Stephanie, review of *The Atami Dragons, Booklist,* December 1, 1984, p. 518.

Zvirin, Stephanie, review of *Breakaway Run, Booklist,* August, 1987, pp. 1737-38.

■ For More Information See

BOOKS

Something about the Author, Volume 88, Gale, 1996, pp. 123-25.

PERIODICALS

Booklist, July, 1992, p. 1933; March 1, 1994, p. 1252; April 1, 1996, p. 1354.
Bulletin of the Center for Children's Books, December, 1984, p. 69; June, 1987, p. 191; December, 1987, p. 68; March, 1998, pp. 248-49.
Los Angeles Times Book Review, July 24, 1994, p. 9.
Publishers Weekly, September 29, 1997, p. 90.
School Library Journal, October, 1988, p. 162.

—Sketch by J. Sydney Jones

Mary E. Lyons

■ Personal

Born November 28, 1947, in Macon, GA; daughter of Joseph and Evelyn Lyons; married Paul Collinge (owner of a used and rare bookstore), 1982. *Education:* Appalachian State University, North Carolina, B.S., 1970, M.S., 1972; University of Virginia, doctoral studies. *Hobbies and other interests:* Playing Irish penny whistle and old-time banjo.

■ Addresses

Home—Charlottesville, VA. *Agent*—William Reiss, John Hawkins Associates, Suite 1600, 71 West 23rd St., New York, NY 10010.

■ Career

Writer. Has worked as a reading specialist at elementary and middle schools in North Carolina and Charlottesville, VA, and as a school librarian at elementary, middle, and high schools in Charlottesville.

■ Awards, Honors

Best Book for Young Adults, American Library Association (ALA), and Carter G. Woodson Book Award, National Council for the Social Studies (NCSS), 1991, master list, Virginia Young Readers' Award, *Horn Book* Fanfare Book, Best Book for the Teen Age Reader, New York Public Library, Teacher's Choice, International Reading Association, Recommended Books for Reluctant Young Readers, ALA, Outstanding Social Studies Book Award, Society of School Librarians International, Charlton W. Tebeau Award, Florida Historical Association, and honorable mention, Joan Sugarman Award, Washington Independent Writers, all for *Sorrow's Kitchen: The Life and Folklore of Zora Neale Hurston*; Notable Children's Trade Book for the Social Studies, National Council for the Social Studies and Children's Book Council (NCSS/CBC), 1992, for *Raw Head, Bloody Bones: African-American Tales of the Supernatural*; Best Book for Young Adults and Notable Book for Children, both ALA, Golden Kite Award for Fiction, Society of Children's Book Writers and Illustrators, 1992, Honor Book, Jane Addams Children's Book Award, 1993, Notable Book, Parents' Choice, 1996, and *Horn Book* Fanfare Book, all for *Letters from a Slave Girl: The Story of Harriet Jacobs*; Notable Children's Book, ALA, 1993, Notable Children's Trade Book for the Social Studies, NCSS/CBC, Carter G. Woodson Elementary Book Award, NCSS, 1994, all for *Starting Home: The Story of Horace Pippin, Painter*; Notable Children's Trade Book for the

Social Studies, NCSS/CBC, 1994, for *Stitching Stars: The Story Quilts of Harriet Powers*; Best Book for the Teen Age, New York Public Library, 1995, and Notable Children's Trade Book for the Social Studies, NCSS/CBC, for *Deep Blues: Bill Traylor, Self-Taught Artist*; Carter G. Woodson Elementary Merit Book, NCSS, 1995, Notable Children's Trade Book for the Social Studies, NCSS/CBC, and *Booklist* Editor's Choice, all for *Master of Mahogany: Tom Day, Free Black Cabinetmaker*; Notable Children's Trade Book for the Social Studies, NCSS/CBC, for *Keeping Secrets: The Girlhood Diaries of Seven Women Writers*; One Hundred Books for Reading and Sharing list, New York Public Library, and *Booklist* Editor's Choice, both for *Catching the Fire: Philip Simmons, Blacksmith*; One Hundred Books for Reading and Sharing list and Best Book for the Teen Age, both New York Public Library, both for *The Poison Place: A Novel*; Jefferson Cup Series Award, Virginia Library Association, 1996, for "African-American Artists and Artisans" series. Lyons's books have also been nominated for numerous state reading awards. Virginia Teacher/Scholar Award, National Endowment for the Humanities, 1991; Virginia Foundation for the Humanities, 1991, 1994, 1995, 1999; Writer-in-Residence, Sweet Briar College, Virginia, 1998.

■ Writings

FOR YOUNG PEOPLE

Sorrow's Kitchen: The Life and Folklore of Zora Neale Hurston, Scribner, 1990.
(Editor) *Raw Head, Bloody Bones: African-American Tales of the Supernatural*, Scribner, 1991.
Letters from a Slave Girl: The Story of Harriet Jacobs, Scribner, 1992.
(Reteller) *The Butter Tree: Tales of Bruh Rabbit*, illustrated by Mireille Vautier, Holt, 1995.
Keeping Secrets: The Girlhood Diaries of Seven Women Writers, Holt, 1995.
The Poison Place: A Novel, Atheneum, 1997.

"AFRICAN-AMERICAN ARTISTS AND ARTISANS" SERIES

Starting Home: The Story of Horace Pippin, Painter, Scribner, 1993.
Stitching Stars: The Story Quilts of Harriet Powers, Scribner, 1993.
Master of Mahogany: Tom Day, Free Black Cabinetmaker, Scribner, 1994.
Deep Blues: Bill Traylor, Self-Taught Artist, Scribner, 1994.

Painting Dreams: Minnie Evans, Visionary Artist, Houghton Mifflin, 1996.
Catching the Fire: Philip Simmons, Blacksmith, Houghton Mifflin, 1997.
Talking with Tebé: Clementine Hunter, Memory Artist, Houghton Mifflin, 1998.

FOR ADULTS

A Story of Her Own: A Resource Guide to Teaching Literature by Women, National Women's History Project, 1985.

■ Work in Progress

A collaboration on a historical novel, for Atheneum.

■ Sidelights

Mary E. Lyons has turned a search for personal roots into a literary exploration of the South. "My way of finding home" is how Lyons has explained her work. In award-winning fiction and nonfiction titles for middle readers and young adults, Lyons has explored the lives of historically marginalized members of our society, both African Americans and women. Her nonfiction works for middle readers include the highly praised series, "African-American Artists and Artisans," and her books for young adults include *Sorrow's Kitchen: The Life and Folklore of Zora Neale Hurston, Letters from a Slave Girl: The Story of Harriet Jacobs*, and *The Poison Place: A Novel*. Her books celebrate the "triumph of the human spirit," Lyons told *Authors and Artists for Young Adults (AAYA)* in an interview. "As corny as it might sound, that's what the subjects of my books have accomplished. As women and African Americans, they had to overcome neglect and prejudice to build creative and full lives." Lyons has thus far specialized in telling the stories of creative artists, as in her "African-American Artists and Artisans" series, and in her biographies and fictional works. Most important, however, most of her protagonists and subjects are of the South, and taken collectively, their tales fill in missing pieces of the social history of that part of the United States.

Growing up Southern

Lyons was born in Macon, Georgia, on November 28, 1947, the daughter of Joseph and Evelyn

In this 1990 work of nonfiction, Lyons documents the life of pioneering African American author Zora Neale Hurston.

breakfast, but we all had to obey the no-reading-at-the-dinner-table rule." Visits to the local library were considered a great treat, perhaps foreshadowing her later career as a school librarian. Lyons, her older brother, and her younger sister and brother were all avid consumers of the written word. "Katie Keene" comics provided light relief for her reading, while the Newbery Award-winning *Hitty, Her First Hundred Years* was one of her favorite books. Reading also stirred the beginnings of a social conscience in Lyons. "I remember that in the ninth grade," Lyons told *AAYA*, "I borrowed a book my brother was reading, *Hawaii* by James Michener. I burst into tears when I read how missionaries brought disease to the native islanders and that so many died as a result."

As a youth, Lyons liked the idea of being a writer, but aside from school assignments, she did not write much on her own. She and a friend spent lazy afternoons thinking up possible titles for romance novels, and as a ninth grader she began keeping a diary. "When researching *Keeping Secrets* [a book about girlhood diaries of writers], I went back and looked at my own journal," Lyons told *AAYA*. "I was moved by the pain I was in as an adolescent yet didn't understand at the time. I was also surprised to see that the fissures of my adult life started many years ago. Journals are so revealing." Lyons describes herself as "dreamy" as an adolescent. "In my history classes, I hid a historical novel behind the textbook." Throughout most of her education, Lyons attended Catholic schools, but in the eleventh grade in Charlotte, North Carolina, she transferred to a public high school.

Lyons. "We moved a lot when I was a child," Lyons told *AAYA*. "We followed my father in his work, and by the time I was eleven, I had already lived in five southern states and eight southern towns." It was this somewhat rootless childhood, Lyons contends, that later made her search for southern roots in her writing. "Moving around was hard for a little girl," Lyons commented. "I didn't know it at the time, but reading provided an instant escape. If I felt uncomfortable in a strange neighborhood or new school, I glued myself to a book and forgot it all."

Reading was definitely encouraged in Lyons's home. "Mom had a hard time getting us to put our books down long enough to eat real food. It was okay to prop a book against a cereal box at

"I was disgustingly boy crazy as a teen," Lyons recalled for *AAYA*, "though I actually led a pretty sheltered life then, especially compared to today's kids. I was always home by eleven, just as my parents asked. They trusted my judgment, so I had a fair amount of freedom." After high school graduation, Lyons attended Appalachian State University in North Carolina. This experience was a revelation for her in many regards. "Not until I was a freshman in college did I discover I had a talent with words that most of my classmates did not have. I was able to organize my thoughts and put them down on paper with fluency. I did well in my writing, so well that one professor once accused me of plagiarizing a paper. I was innocent; it was my work, but she just couldn't believe I hadn't copied it from a book."

Another revelation was of a more universal sort, but no less influential in her life. A pivotal experience during college was the assassination of Martin Luther King. "I was the only white working in a city employment agency that was created to deal with the aftermath of the assassination. The experience changed me. I saw first-hand the way blacks were treated." The Civil Rights movement in the South was more than a historical backdrop for Lyons's coming of age. She slowly began to identify with the dispossessed and "invisible" members of society. "I had gone to almost all-white schools, including college. But once for an education course in college, I tutored a black child who lived outside the town limits. She and her family had no access to water or sewage facilities. Apparently, the town boundaries were deliberately drawn so that African Americans were excluded from public services. This experience showed me one of the many ways that blacks were ignored by society."

After graduation, Lyons's first teaching job was in an all-black inner-city school. The school was situated in the middle of a housing project; the doors were locked most of the time for security. Lyons, who was a mediocre science student in college, was assigned science classes. Firsthand, she learned the difficulties of teaching under adverse circumstances. "The kids were great," she recalled for *AAYA*, "but teaching without books, without supplies, without materials for science experiments, was an incredibly challenging job." After this first year, Lyons returned to college to earn a master's degree in reading, a subject she taught in public schools for the next seventeen years.

Sorrow's Kitchen

After becoming burned out as a reading teacher, Lyons once again returned to college to become credentialed as a school librarian, a position she held for the last six years of her public school career. By 1988, another impulse began guiding her. "Life has a weird way of sending us what we need to complete ourselves," Lyons noted. "When I was a reading teacher, I discovered that my eighth-grade classes enjoyed stories by woman writers and African American writers. They especially loved the humorous folktales collected by Zora Neale Hurston. There was no biography of her in the school library for the students to read, so I wrote my first book, *Sorrow's Kitchen: The Life*

and Folklore of Zora Neale Hurston." There was also a resonance in Hurston's life with her own that piqued Lyons's interest in the black writer. "I found out that Hurston was the only southerner in the Harlem Renaissance, and I identified with that. I knew how it felt to be the only one with a southern accent, that you had to hide it sometimes because of southern stereotypes. Look at television, for example. If they want to depict an ignorant person, they often give him or her a southern accent." Hurston's forthrightness, her sincerity, and her need for honesty also appealed to Lyons.

What resulted is a book that is part biography, part introduction to the works of Hurston. Lyons's biographical sections trace Hurston's life from her childhood in Eatonville, Florida, at the turn of the century through her fight to become educated, her participation in the Harlem Renaissance, and finally to her collecting and preserving the folklore of both her native South and of the West Indies. Researching and writing the book was a challenge for Lyons, who stated that "history classes have always made me yawn." But now history took on a new meaning; not simply a list of dates and battles, but within the context of a person's life. "I had to relearn everything I had studied years before in high school and college," Lyons noted. "World War I, the Depression, World War II, the Civil Rights movement. This time I studied with Zora in mind. Now I like learning history, especially when it's told from a woman's point of view."

"I was very fortunate with this first book," Lyons recalled for *AAYA*. "Unknown to me, the timing was perfect. Interest in Hurston was growing at the time. There was an Off-Broadway show about her, a PBS production in the works, several adult biographies were underway, and all her books were being reprinted in new editions. I worked with one publisher on my manuscript for nine months, and when they rejected it, I quickly reworked it and sent it off to Scribner. The editor there bought it almost immediately." Critical reception was as positive as that of the publishing community. *Booklist*'s Hazel Rochman observed that the "strength of Lyons' book is that she includes long excerpts from Hurston's works, set off within each chapter by a handsome border design." Elizabeth S. Watson, writing in *Horn Book*, called the book "fascinating, enlightening, stimulating, and satisfying," and also noted Lyons's use of extended quotes from Hurston's writing. The biography was chosen as a Best Book for Young Adults by the American Library Association, among other honors that it garnered. Most importantly, as far as Lyons is concerned, is the fact that it made young readers, intrigued by the life of Hurston, search out the woman's writings.

From Book Lender to Book Writer

Lyons herself used Hurston's writings as a springboard for her second book, *Raw Head, Bloody Bones: African-American Tales of the Supernatural*. *Raw Head, Bloody Bones* incorporated some of the stories and tales that Hurston collected as well as others that were compiled by the Federal Writers' Project. Some of the fifteen stories of ghosts and demons that she retells are cast in the Gullah dia-

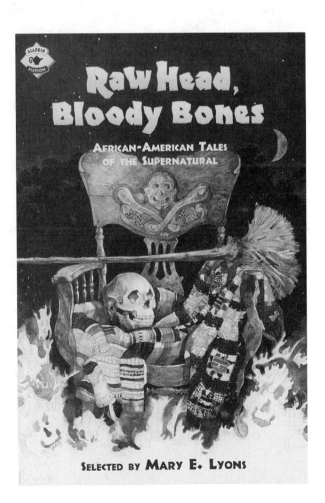

Lyons gathered fifteen spine-chilling tales for this 1991 collection.

lect spoken by African American inhabitants of the South Carolina and Georgia coasts, a region where Lyons lived as a child. A reviewer in *Horn Book Guide* called this book an "engaging collection" and concluded that it "will be hard to resist." *Booklist*'s Denia Hester warned that the "timid and fainthearted" should beware, as this "collection of African American tales is a bone chiller . . . a scary good read." A critic in *Publishers Weekly* observed that the tales "derive their bewitching quality from the rhythms of the spoken word and the dancelike quality of early African American speech" which "provide a quixotic contrast to the often gruesome subject matter."

The success of this second title, as well as encouragement from awards such as a National Endowment for the Humanities Teacher/Scholar sabbatical, prompted Lyons to leave behind her career as a school librarian for the world of professional writing. "I am fortunate that my husband operates a used and rare bookshop. He has been a great help in researching the books I've written and has been very supportive of my decision to become a full-time writer. It hasn't been easy financially, but I have successful women friends in the corporate world whose jobs are not as satisfying as mine." During her last year of full-time work in the schools, Lyons researched what would become her third title—one of her personal favorites and one of her best-selling books. *Letters from a Slave Girl* is an account of the early life of Harriet Ann Jacobs, a slave who later fled to the North and became, through her writings, an important voice in the abolitionist movement.

Lyons meticulously researched Jacobs's life, relying heavily on the woman's autobiography, and recreated her life from age twelve to twenty-nine in letters she might have written. A *Kirkus Reviews* critic deemed the book "a moving evocation of the tragedies inflicted by slavery." These letters reveal the story of one young girl who might stand as a voice for thousands of others who suffered under slavery. They detail the loss of her mother and the forced separation of her family after the death of one owner. There is a letter to her dead father after she is denied permission to attend his funeral; another letter to the man she loves describes how she has decided to accept the attentions of one relatively kind white man in order to escape those of her brutal master. Jacobs later ran away from her owners and hid for seven years in a crawl space under the eaves of her grandmother's cabin, eventually escaping to the North in 1842. The *Kirkus Reviews* critic went on to state that the "style Lyons creates for Harriet— a luminous character, gentle and resolute—is graceful and direct," while a *Horn Book* reviewer declared that the book was "Historical fiction at its best." A contributor in *Publishers Weekly* also found much to praise in the book, describing it as a "searing epistolary work" which "stirringly celebrates the strength of the human spirit." Award committees agreed, and *Letters from a Slave Girl* won a slew of honors.

"African-American Artists and Artisans"

Starting in 1993 Lyons initiated an impressive series detailing the lives of seven African American artists and artisans, some overlooked during their lifetimes. "I've always loved the decorative arts," Lyons told *AAYA*, "and in 1990, I found several scholarly books describing a group of African American artists and artisans—from blacksmiths to quilt-makers—whose works were highly respected by folklorists and art historians. But most people, including children, were not familiar with them. During my sabbatical year as NEH teacher-scholar, I began tracking down articles about the artists. I showed slides of their work to children, who loved the art. Even more, they liked the idea that a person can be artistic in many ways, that you don't have to have a degree from an art school to be creative." Lyons decided to honor the artists with books for middle readers that, as much as possible, would allow the artists to speak for themselves. She also wanted to show how their art tells the stories of their lives.

The first title in the series, *Starting Home*, features the self-taught black painter, Horace Pippin, many of whose works depict scenes from World War I where he fought in an all-black regiment, the first to fight overseas for the United States. Wounded in the war and unable to lift his right hand above shoulder level, he went on to become a highly renowned folk artist. Lyons's second subject was Harriet Powers, and in *Stitching the Stars* she profiles this former slave who "wrote" stories in quilts with needle and thread. (Slaves were forbidden to read or write but went on to tell their powerful stories—a mixture of Bible stories and folklore—by sewing them.) Her two story quilts are now on display at the Museum of American History and are considered priceless examples of

folk art. Reviewing both titles for *Booklist*, Rochman noted that "Lyons' sensitive commentary will draw middle-grade readers to look at the paintings and photographs." Reviewing *Stitching Stars* in the *Bulletin of the Center for Children's Books*, Deborah Stevenson remarked that "Lyons's lively writing stitches concepts together with smoothness and clarity. . . . [This] is both an unusual take on history and a reminder of the democratic possibilities of art."

Other titles in the series deal with more artisans. In *Master of Mahogany* and *Catching the Fire*, Lyons tells the stories of a cabinetmaker and a blacksmith, respectively. Born of free parents in 1801,

This 1992 work, based on a true story, describes a slave's ordeals as she attempts to win her freedom.

Thomas Day became one of the most successful cabinetmakers in pre-Civil War North Carolina, and his works have become collector's items today. In *Master of Mahogany*, "Lyons does an excellent job of piecing together the sketchy details of Day's life, of which little is known," wrote a *Horn Book* reviewer. In *Catching the Fire*, Lyons presents the life and work of Philip Simmons, a blacksmith whose gates, fences, and railings decorate the city of Charleston, South Carolina, where Simmons has lived most of his life. Based on personal interviews with Simmons and those who have worked with him, the book was dubbed "an engrossing biography" by a *Kirkus Reviews* critic and "engaging" by a reviewer in *Horn Book*. Stevenson concluded sthat *Catching the Fire* would be "useful not only as an introduction to a gifted professional craftsman, but also a reminder of how unexpected things can become art when executed with authority."

Further visual artists in the series include Bill Traylor in *Deep Blues*, Minnie Evans in *Painting Dreams*, and Clementine Hunter in *Talking with Tebé*. A personal favorite for Lyons in the series is *Deep Blues*, which details the life and works of Traylor, who was born into slavery in Alabama in 1856 and did not begin painting until he was eighty. His works are now acclaimed and exhibited throughout the United States. A critic in *Horn Book* noted that "Lyons' perceptive commentary . . . points out possible connections between Traylor's life as a farmer and the subject matter of his works." Minnie Evans was forty-three before she began to draw pictures that were based on dreams that had haunted her all her life. Born into poverty and untrained as an artist, Evans did not let this stop her, nor would she be stopped by her family and friends who thought she was crazy. "Lyons has brought us the life and work of an African American folk artist who succeeded despite community prejudice," commented Rochman. In the final book in the series, Lyons presents the art of Clementine Hunter, called Tebé, whose work portrays the life of a southern laborer. This story is told through Hunter's own words in magazine and newspaper articles and in tape-recorded interviews.

Toward Historical Fiction

Other books from Lyons include *Keeping Secrets, The Butter Tree: Tales of Bruh Rabbit*, and *The Poi-*

If you enjoy the works of Mary E. Lyons, you may also want to check out the following books and films:

Russell Freedman, *Lincoln: A Photobiography*, 1987.
Gary Paulsen, *Nightjohn*, 1993.
Mary Stolz, *Cezanne Pinto: A Memoir*, 1994.
The Autobiography of Miss Jane Pittman, an Emmy Award-winning film, 1974.

son Place. In the first of these titles, Lyons blends her own commentary with excerpts from the girlhood diaries of seven nineteenth-century women writers; Louisa May Alcott, Charlotte Forten, Sarah Jane Foster, Kate Chopin, Alice Dunbar-Nelson, Ida B. Wells, and Charlotte Perkins Gilman. Lyons demonstrates how keeping a diary helped each of these young writers eventually develop a public voice. A critic in *Kirkus Reviews* noted that "Lyons writes with style and feeling, creating a strong sense of each individual life story, even as she gives us a social history of what it was like to be a woman at that time." A *Horn Book* reviewer called the work "a fascinating look at the public and private lives" of these writers that explores "issues of femininity, social expectations, family, and racism." In a somewhat lighter vein, Lyons has also retold African American trickster tales in *The Butter Tree*. The six tales from South Carolina included here involve the usual scenario of a small animal tricking a much larger one, and as a critic in *Publishers Weekly* noted, "undoubtedly helped the enslaved originators of these tales endure their own oppression." "Bruh" as well as "brer" is a variant of "brother," an indication that the slaves held this wily rabbit close to their hearts. *Horn Book*'s Maeve Visser Knoth noted that "Lyons' skilled retellings are brief and uncluttered, recalling the oral tradition. She uses few adjectives, yet her language is colorful and evokes regional flavor."

In *The Poison Place* Lyons gives full vent to her fiction. It is by her accounts the most difficult of her books thus far—difficult in terms of researching and writing. Begun in 1989 as a scrap of an idea, Lyons finally got back to the work years later. The book uses historical fact as its background, detailing the lives of two men. One is Charles Willson Peale, the eighteenth-century portraitist and founder of the first museum of natural history in the United States, the Peale Museum in Philadelphia. The other is Moses Williams, Peale's former slave who became a silhouette cutter and the first black professional artist in post-revolutionary America. The novel is told through the voice of Williams on a night-time tour with his young daughter through the museum. Williams's own struggle for survival is contrasted to Peale's story and that of his museum. As Rachelle M. Bilz noted in *Voice of Youth Advocates*, "Moses' lifelong quest for freedom is intertwined with the Peale family's success and failure." Through the narrator's revelations, the reader is led to wonder how much responsibility Peale himself had in the eventual poisoning of his own son, a taxidermist in the museum who died from the arsenic he used in his work. Bilz concluded that the novel was "Fast paced and well written . . . sure to appeal to historical fiction fans." A contributor in *Kirkus Reviews* called the novel "a riveting work of historical fiction."

Lyons intends to continue with historical fiction in the future, and to write for young readers. "I can't imagine writing for anyone besides young people," Lyons told *AAYA*. "They like to be told the truth and can handle complexities that adults can't." She also maintains contact with her audience by frequent visits to schools. "Teachers often expect a black author to show up because so many of my books have dealt with African American issues. I'm always flattered that people assume I'm black; it means I'm doing my job as a writer. But now I consider myself not only a writer of black history or of women's history, but increasingly as a historian of the South." For Lyons this means giving a voice to those who have not been heard before. "Many people I write about have never had a chance to speak for themselves. In articles already written about them, you don't really hear their voices. I want to let my subjects tell their own stories in a form accessible to young readers."

■ Works Cited

Bilz, Rachelle M., review of *The Poison Place: A Novel, Voice of Youth Advocates*, December, 1997, p. 318.

Review of *The Butter Tree: Tales of Bruh Rabbit, Publishers Weekly*, February 20, 1995, p. 206.

Review of *Catching the Fire: Philip Simmons, Blacksmith, Horn Book*, September-October, 1997, p. 592.

Review of *Catching the Fire: Philip Simmons, Blacksmith, Kirkus Reviews*, July 1, 1997.

Review of *Deep Blues: Bill Traylor, Self-Taught Artist, Horn Book*, March, 1995, p. 221.

Hester, Denia, review of *Raw Head, Bloody Bones: African-American Tales of the Supernatural, Booklist*, January 1, 1992, pp. 830-31.

Review of *Keeping Secrets: The Girlhood Diaries of Seven Women Writers, Horn Book*, September, 1995, p. 614.

Review of *Keeping Secrets: The Girlhood Diaries of Seven Women Writers, Kirkus Reviews*, June 1, 1995.

Knoth, Maeve Visser, review of *The Butter Tree: Tales of Bruh Rabbit, Horn Book*, September-October, 1995, p. 614.

Review of *Letters from a Slave Girl: The Story of Harriet Jacobs, Horn Book*, November, 1992, p. 729.

Review of *Letters from a Slave Girl: The Story of Harriet Jacobs, Kirkus Reviews*, November 1, 1992, p. 1380.

Review of *Letters from a Slave Girl: The Story of Harriet Jacobs, Publishers Weekly*, October 26, 1992, pp. 72-73.

Lyons, Mary E., interview with J. Sydney Jones for *Authors and Artists for Young Adults*, conducted June 29, 1998.

Review of *Master of Mahogany: Tom Day, Free Black Cabinetmaker, Horn Book*, November, 1994, p. 750.

Review of *The Poison Place: A Novel, Kirkus Reviews*, October 1, 1997.

Review of *Raw Head, Bloody Bones: African-American Tales of the Supernatural, Horn Book Guide*, Spring, 1992, p. 91.

Review of *Raw Head, Bloody Bones: African-American Tales of the Supernatural, Publishers Weekly*, October 25, 1991, p. 69.

Rochman, Hazel, review of *Sorrow's Kitchen: The Life and Folklore of Zora Neale Hurston, Booklist*, December 15, 1990, p. 866.

Rochman, Hazel, review of *Starting Home: The Story of Horace Pippin, Painter* and *Stitching Stars: The Story Quilts of Harriet Powers, Booklist*, November 15, 1993, pp. 618-19.

Rochman, Hazel, review of *Painting Dreams: Minnie Evans, Visionary Artist, Booklist*, July, 1996, pp. 1825-26.

Stevenson, Deborah, review of *Stitching Stars: The Story Quilts of Harriet Powers, Bulletin of the Center for Children's Books*, December, 1993, p. 128.

Stevenson, Deborah, review of *Catching the Fire: Philip Simmons, Blacksmith, Bulletin of the Center for Children's Books,* October, 1997, p. 57.

Watson, Elizabeth S., review of *Sorrow's Kitchen: The Life and Folklore of Zora Neale Hurston, Horn Book,* March-April, 1991, p. 216.

■ For More Information See

BOOKS

Seventh Book of Junior Authors and Illustrators, edited by Sally Holmes Holtze, H. W. Wilson, 1996.

Twentieth-Century Children's Writers, 4th edition, edited by Laura Standley Berger, St. James Press, 1995.

PERIODICALS

Bulletin of the Center for Children's Books, January, 1991, p. 124; February, 1992, p. 162; November, 1992, p. 79; December, 1994, p. 136; September, 1996, p. 21.

Horn Book Guide, Spring, 1993, p. 82; Spring, 1994, p. 140; Spring, 1995, p. 134; Fall, 1995, pp. 332, 387; Fall, 1996, p. 356.

Kirkus Reviews, July 1, 1998, p. 968.

School Library Journal, January, 1991, p. 119; December, 1992, p. 113; February, 1994, p. 113; January, 1995, p. 127; July, 1995, p. 100; July, 1996, p. 93.

Voice of Youth Advocates, February, 1991, p. 378; December, 1992, p. 282; October, 1995, p. 252.

—Sketch by J. Sydney Jones

Michael Moorcock

■ Personal

Born December 18, 1939, in Mitcham, Surrey, England; son of Arthur and June (Taylor) Moorcock; married Hilary Bailey (a writer), September, 1962 (divorced, April, 1978); married Jill Riches, 1978 (divorced); married Linda Mullens Steele, September, 1983; children: (first marriage) Sophie, Katherine, Max. *Education:* Attended ten schools, including Michael Hall School, Sussex, and Pitman's College. *Hobbies and other interests:* Songwriting, performing in rock and roll bands.

■ Addresses

c/o Howard Moreham, HML, 841 Broadway, New York, NY 10003.

■ Career

Writer and editor; has also worked as a singer/guitarist. Editor, *Tarzan Adventures* (juvenile magazine), 1956-58; Amalgamated Press, London, England, writer and editor for the Sexton Blake Library and for comic strips and children's annuals, 1959-61; pamphleteer and editor, Liberal Party, 1962; *New Worlds* (science fiction magazine), London, England, editor and publisher, 1964-70; leads rock band Michael Moorcock and the Deep Fix; also works with bands Hawkwind and Blue Oyster Cult. *Military service:* Served in the Air Training Corps. *Member:* Authors Guild, Fawcett Society, National Socialist Party for the Prevention of Cruelty to Children (NSPCC; council member), Royal Overseas League, SPLC (leadership council), Shelter.

■ Awards, Honors

Nebula Award, Science Fiction Writers of America, 1967, for *Behold the Man;* British Science Fiction Association Award and Arts Council of Great Britain Award, both 1967, both for *New Worlds;* August Derleth Award, British Fantasy Society, 1972, for *The Knight of the Swords,* 1973, for *The King of the Swords,* 1974, for *The Jade Man's Eyes,* 1975, for *The Sword and the Stallion,* and 1976, for *The Hollow Lands;* International Fantasy Award, 1972 and 1973, for fantasy novels; Guardian Fiction Prize, 1977, for *The Condition of Muzak;* John W. Campbell Memorial Award, 1978, and World Fantasy Award, World Fantasy Convention, 1979, both for *Gloriana; or, The Unfulfilled Queen.*

■ Writings

(With James Cawthorn, under house pseudonym Desmond Reid) *Caribbean Crisis*, Sexton Blake Library, 1962.

The Sundered Worlds, Compact Books, 1965, Paperback Library, 1966, published as *The Blood Red Game*, Sphere Books, 1970.

The Fireclown, Compact Books, 1965, Paperback Library, 1966, published as *The Winds of Limbo*, Sphere Books, 1970.

(Under pseudonym James Colvin) *The Deep Fix*, Compact Books, 1966.

The Wrecks of Time (bound with *Tramontane* by Emil Petaja), Ace Books, 1966 (revised edition published separately in England as *The Rituals of Infinity*, Arrow Books, 1971).

The Twilight Man, Compact Books, 1966, Berkley Publishing, 1970 (published in England as *The Shores of Death*, Sphere Books, 1970).

(Under pseudonym Bill Barclay) *Printer's Devil*, Compact Books, 1966, published under name Michael Moorcock as *The Russian Intelligence*, Savoy Books, 1980.

(Under pseudonym Bill Barclay) *Somewhere in the Night*, Compact Books, 1966, revised edition published under name Michael Moorcock as *The Chinese Agent*, Macmillan, 1970.

(Ghostwriter) Roger Harris, *The LSD Dossier*, Compact Books, 1966.

The Ice Schooner, Sphere Books, 1968, Berkley Publishing, 1969, revised edition, Harrap, 1985.

(With wife, Hilary Bailey) *The Black Corridor*, Ace Books, 1969.

The Time Dweller, Hart-Davis, 1969, Berkley Publishing, 1971.

(With James Cawthorn under joint pseudonym Philip James) *The Distant Suns*, Unicorn Bookshop, 1975.

Moorcock's Book of Martyrs, Quartet Books, 1976, published as *Dying for Tomorrow*, DAW Books, 1978.

(With Michael Butterworth) *The Time of the Hawklords*, A. Ellis, 1976.

Sojan (juvenile), Savoy Books, 1977.

Epic Pooh, British Fantasy Society, 1978.

Gloriana; or, The Unfulfilled Queen, Allison & Busby, 1978, Avon, 1979.

The Real Life Mr. Newman, A. J. Callow, 1979.

The Golden Barge, DAW Books, 1980.

My Experiences in the Third World War, Savoy Books, 1980.

The Retreat from Liberty: The Erosion of Democracy in Today's Britain, Zomba Books, 1983.

(With others) *Exploring Fantasy Worlds: Essays on Fantastic Literature*, edited by Darrell Schweitzer, Borgo, 1985.

Letters from Hollywood, Harrap, 1986.

(With James Cawthorn) *Fantasy: The One Hundred Best Books*, Carroll & Graf, 1988.

Mother London, Crown, 1989.

Wizardry and Wild Romance: A Study of Heroic Fantasy, Gollancz, 1989.

Casablanca, Gollancz, 1989.

Blood: A Southern Fantasy, Morrow, 1994.

Hawkmoon, White Wolf (Stone Mountain, GA), 1995.

Fabulous Harbors: A Sequel to Blood, Avon, 1996.

The War Amongst the Angels, Avon, 1997.

"ELRIC" SERIES; "ETERNAL CHAMPION" BOOKS

The Stealer of Souls, and Other Stories (also see below), Neville Spearman, 1963, Lancer Books, 1967.

Stormbringer, Jenkins, 1965, Lancer Books, 1967.

The Singing Citadel (also see below), Berkley Publishing, 1970.

The Sleeping Sorceress, New English Library, 1971, Lancer Books, 1972, published as *The Vanishing Tower*, DAW Books, 1977.

The Dreaming City, Lancer Books, 1972 (revised edition published in England as *Elric of Melnibone*, Hutchinson, 1972).

The Jade Man's Eyes, Unicorn Bookshop, 1973.

Elric: The Return to Melnibone, Unicorn Bookshop, 1973.

The Sailor on the Seas of Fate, DAW Books, 1976.

The Bane of the Black Sword, DAW Books, 1977.

The Weird of the White Wolf (contains some material from *The Stealer of Souls, and Other Stories* and *The Singing Citadel*), DAW Books, 1977.

Elric at the End of Time, DAW Books, 1985.

The Fortress of the Pearl, Ace Books, 1989.

The Revenge of the Rose, Ace Books, 1991.

"MICHAEL KANE" SERIES; UNDER PSEUDONYM EDWARD P. BRADBURY

Warriors of Mars (also see below), Compact Books, 1965, published under name Michael Moorcock as *The City of the Beast*, Lancer Books, 1970.

Blades of Mars (also see below), Compact Books, 1965, published under name Michael Moorcock as *The Lord of the Spiders*, Lancer Books, 1971.

The Barbarians of Mars (also see below), Compact Books, 1965, published under name Michael Moorcock as *The Masters of the Pit*, Lancer Books, 1971.

Warrior of Mars (contains *Warriors of Mars, Blades of Mars,* and *The Barbarians of Mars*), New English Library, 1981.

"THE HISTORY OF THE RUNESTAFF" SERIES

The Jewel in the Skull (also see below), Lancer Books, 1967.
Sorcerer's Amulet (also see below), Lancer Books, 1968 (published in England as *The Mad God's Amulet*, Mayflower Books, 1969).
Sword of the Dawn (also see below), Lancer Books, 1968.
The Secret of the Runestaff (also see below), Lancer Books, 1969 (published in England as *The Runestaff*, Mayflower Books, 1969).
The History of the Runestaff (contains *The Jewel in the Skull, Sorcerer's Amulet, Sword of the Dawn,* and *The Secret of the Runestaff*), Granada, 1979.

"JERRY CORNELIUS" SERIES

The Final Programme (also see below), Avon, 1968, revised edition, Allison & Busby, 1969.
A Cure for Cancer (also see below), Holt, 1971.
The English Assassin (also see below), Allison & Busby, 1972.
The Lives and Times of Jerry Cornelius (also see below), Allison & Busby, 1976.
The Adventures of Una Persson and Catherine Cornelius in the Twentieth Century (also see below), Quartet Books, 1976.
The Condition of Muzak (also see below), Allison & Busby, 1977, Gregg, 1978.
The Cornelius Chronicles (contains *The Final Programme, A Cure for Cancer, The English Assassin,* and *The Condition of Muzak*), Avon, 1977.
The Great Rock n' Roll Swindle, Virgin Books, 1980.
The Entropy Tango (also see below), New English Library, 1981.
The Opium General (also see below), Harrap, 1985.
The Cornelius Chronicles, Volume 2 (contains *The Lives and Times of Jerry Cornelius* and *The Entropy Tango*), Avon, 1986.
The Cornelius Chronicles, Volume 3 (contains *The Adventures of Una Persson and Catherine Cornelius in the Twentieth Century* and *The Opium General*), Avon, 1987.
A Cornelius Calendar, Phoenix House, 1993.
The Cornelius Quartet (contains *The Final Programme, A Cure for Cancer, The English Assassin,* and *The Condition of Muzak*), Phoenix Books, 1993.

"KARL GLOGAUER" SERIES

Behold the Man, Allison & Busby, 1969, Avon, 1970.
Breakfast in the Ruins: A Novel of Inhumanity, New English Library, 1972, Random House, 1974.

"CORUM" SERIES; "ETERNAL CHAMPION" BOOKS

The Knight of the Swords (also see below), Mayflower Books, 1970, Berkley Publishing, 1971.
The Queen of the Swords (also see below), Berkley Publishing, 1971.
The King of the Swords (also see below), Berkley Publishing, 1971.
The Bull and the Spear (also see below), Berkley Publishing, 1973.
The Oak and the Ram (also see below), Berkley Publishing, 1973.
The Sword and the Stallion (also see below), Berkley Publishing, 1974.
The Swords Trilogy (contains *The Knight of the Swords, The Queen of the Swords,* and *The King of the Swords*), Berkley Publishing, 1977.
The Chronicles of Corum (contains *The Bull and the Spear, The Oak and the Ram,* and *The Sword and the Stallion*), Berkley Publishing, 1978.

"JOHN DAKER" SERIES; "ETERNAL CHAMPION" BOOKS

The Eternal Champion, Dell, 1970, revised edition, Harper, 1978.
Phoenix in Obsidian, Mayflower Books, 1970, published as *The Silver Warriors*, Dell, 1973.
The Dragon in the Sword, Granada, 1986.

"OSWALD BASTABLE" SERIES

The Warlord of the Air (also see below), Ace Books, 1971.
The Land Leviathan (also see below), Quartet Books, 1974.
The Steel Tsar (also see below), DAW Books, 1983.
The Nomad of Time (contains *The Warlord of the Air, The Land Leviathan,* and *The Steel Tsar*), Granada, 1984.

"THE DANCERS AT THE END OF TIME" SERIES

An Alien Heat (also see below), Harper, 1972.
The Hollow Lands (also see below), Harper, 1974.
The End of All Songs (also see below), Harper, 1976.
Legends from the End of Time, Harper, 1976.

The Transformations of Miss Mavis Ming, W. H. Allen, 1977, published as *A Messiah at the End of Time*, DAW Books, 1978.

The Dancers at the End of Time (contains *An Alien Heat, The Hollow Lands*, and *The End of All Songs*), Granada, 1981.

"CASTLE BRASS" SERIES; "ETERNAL CHAMPION" BOOKS

Count Brass (also see below), Mayflower Books, 1973.

The Champion of Garathorm (also see below), Mayflower Books, 1973.

The Quest for Tanelorn (also see below), Mayflower Books, 1975, Dell, 1976.

The Chronicles of Castle Brass (contains *Castle Brass, The Champion of Garathorm*, and *The Quest for Tanelorn*), Granada, 1985.

"VON BEK FAMILY" SERIES

The War Hound and the World's Pain, Timescape, 1981.

The Brothel in Rosenstrasse, New English Library, 1982, Tigerseye Press, 1986.

The City in the Autumn Stars, Ace Books, 1986.

Lunching with the Antichrist: A Family History: 1925-2015 (omnibus), Mark V. Ziesing (Shingleton, CA), 1995.

Von Beck (contains *The War Hound and the World's Pain, The City and the Autumn Stars, The Dragon in the Sword*, and *The Pleasure Garden of Felipe Sagittarius*), White Wolf, 1996.

"COLONEL PYAT" SERIES

Byzantium Endures, Secker & Warburg, 1981, Random House, 1982.

The Laughter of Carthage, Random House, 1984.

Jerusalem Commands, Secker and Warburg, 1992.

SCREENPLAYS

The Final Programme (based on his novel of the same title; removed name from credits after dispute with director), EMI, 1973.

The Land That Time Forgot, British Lion, 1975.

EDITOR

(And contributor under name Michael Moorcock and under pseudonym James Colvin) *The Best of "New Worlds,"* Compact Books, 1965.

Best SF Stories from "New Worlds," Panther Books, 1967, Berkley Publishing, 1968.

The Traps of Time, Rapp & Whiting, 1968.

(And contributor under pseudonym James Colvin) *The Best SF Stories from "New Worlds"* 2, Panther Books, 1968, Berkley Publishing, 1969.

(And contributor under pseudonym James Colvin) *The Best SF Stories from "New Worlds"* 3, Panther Books, 1968, Berkley Publishing, 1969.

The Best SF Stories from "New Worlds" 4, Panther Books, 1969, Berkley Publishing, 1971.

The Best SF Stories from "New Worlds" 5, Panther Books, 1969, Berkley Publishing, 1971.

(And contributor) *The Best SF Stories from "New Worlds"* 6, Panther Books, 1970, Berkley Publishing, 1971.

The Best SF Stories from "New Worlds" 7, Panther Books, 1971.

New Worlds Quarterly 1, Berkley Publishing, 1971.

New Worlds Quarterly 2, Berkley Publishing, 1971.

New Worlds Quarterly 3, Sphere Books, 1971.

(With Langdon Jones and contributor) *The Nature of the Catastrophe*, Hutchinson, 1971.

New Worlds Quarterly 4, Berkley Publishing, 1972.

New Worlds Quarterly 5, Sphere Books, 1973.

New Worlds Quarterly 6, Avon, 1973.

Before Armageddon: An Anthology of Victorian and Edwardian Imaginative Fiction Published before 1914, W. H. Allen, 1975.

England Invaded: A Collection of Fantasy Fiction, Ultramarine, 1977.

New Worlds: An Anthology, Fontana, 1983.

(With David Garnett) *New Worlds 1* (also called V. 62, no. 217 in continuation of the numbering of *New Worlds*), VGSF (London), 1991.

(With David Garnett and consultant editor) *New Worlds 2*, VGSF, 1992.

RECORDINGS; UNDER NAME "MICHAEL MOORCOCK AND THE DEEP FIX"

The New Worlds Fair, United Artists, 1975.

Dodgem Dude/Starcruiser (single), Flicknife, 1980.

The Brothel in Rosenstrasse/Time Centre (single), Flicknife, 1982.

(With others) *Hawkwind Friends and Relations*, Flicknife, 1982.

(With others) *Hawkwind & Co.*, Flicknife, 1983.

Also composer of songs recorded by others, including "Sonic Attack," "The Black Corridor," "The Wizard Blew His Horn," "Standing at the Edge," "Warriors," "Kings of Speed," "Warrior at the End of Time," "Psychosonia," "Coded Languages," "Lost Chances," "Choose Your Masks," and "Arrival in Utopia," all recorded by Hawkwind; "The Great Sun Jester," "Black Blade," and "Veteran of the Psychic Wars," all recorded by Blue Oyster Cult.

OTHER

Has also written as William Ewert Barclay and Michael Barrington. Contributor, sometimes under pseudonyms, to *Punch*, *Ambit*, the London *Times*, the *Guardian*, the *New Statesman*, the *Daily Telegraph*, and other publications. Writer of comic strips in 1957-64 (DC Comics and Dark Horse Comics) and in 1997 with *Michael Moorcock's Multiverse* (DC Comics). Writer of introduction to *The Time Machine* by H. G. Wells, J. M. Dent (London), 1993. Also credited with providing ideas for two books by Michael Butterworth, *Queens of Deliria* and *The Time of the Hawklords*, both published by Collectors Guides in 1995.

The Bodleian Library, Oxford, and Texas A&M University hold collections of Moorcock's papers.

■ Adaptations

The character Elric is featured in role-playing games from the Avalon Hill Game Company and from Chaosium, in comic books published by Pacific Comics and by Star Reach Productions, and in miniature figures marketed by Citadel Miniatures; the characters Elric and Oswald Bastable are featured in computer games.

■ Sidelights

Michael Moorcock is considered among the most original and influential writers to have emerged from the New Wave of science fiction, an international movement of the 1960s that brought a wide range of subjects and experimental literary styles to the genre. A prolific author with twelve series and many individual works to his credit, Moorcock has written comic novels, satires, high fantasy in the sword and sorcery vein, historical allegory, and nonfiction as well as science fiction; he has also written short stories and screenplays and has edited several science fiction collections. As editor of the British science fiction magazine *New Worlds*, Moorcock is credited with helping to create the New Wave movement and for providing a showcase for some of its most talented practitioners. As a writer, Moorcock is acknowledged

by most observers as a gifted storyteller who is, in the words of *Booklist* reviewer Algis Budrys, one of "fantasy/sf's most uninhibited experimenters." Commentators praise his books, which characteristically combine imaginative narratives with experimental literary structures, humor, and joyous wordplay, as thoughtful, inventive, literate, entertaining, and, on occasion, profound; several of his works, in fact, are considered tour de forces. Some critics are less enthralled with Moorcock's books, calling them obscure, self-indulgent, and disturbing. Moorcock is well regarded, however, both for the quality of his writing and the sincerity of his approach. In his entry on Moorcock in *Dictionary of Literary Biography*, Colin Greenland writes, "His editorial work and his own fiction together represent a titanic effort, often against great resistance from the establishments of magazine and book publishing, to reunite the highest literary values with the forms and vitality of popular culture." *Washington Post Book World* critic Gregory Feeley adds that Moorcock "has long been Britain's quintessential novelist of urban life" and concludes that he is "one of our very best novelists and a national treasure."

Although he is the author of only one book for children, the heroic fantasy *Sojan* (1977), Moorcock has been a popular figure among young people for the last thirty years. Writing in *Science Fiction Studies*, Ralph Willett claims that during the 1960s and early 1970s Moorcock became "that rare phenomenon, the popular novelist whose work has also become a cult among the young and avant-garde"; *Spectator* critic Paul Ableman called the author "the thinking hippy's bard." Several of Moorcock's books feature youthful protagonists who search for their identities. He has commented, "All the characters in a Fantasy have to be childish or adolescent in order to function. Because they're larger than life their emotions are huge, their ambitions and their destinies are vast." In one of his most prominent series, Moorcock describes the adventures of Elric of Melnibone, a young hero who differs vastly from the macho figures who often appear in fantasy stories. A fey albino who is dependent on his vampiric broadsword Stormbringer, Elric battles for his soul with the Lords of Order and Chaos; in *Dictionary of Literary Biography*, Colin Greenland notes that Elric's "problems of identity and meaning, purpose and desire, battled out in a crude and violent universe ruled by ambiguous powers indifferent to his values, are essentially problems of adolescent frustration." The Elric books are among the most popular of Moorcock's titles among the young, inspiring comic books and games as well as a line of miniature figures. Young people may also be aware of Moorcock through his work as a recording artist and performer. Working with his own band, the Deep Fix, Moorcock recorded an album and two singles and contributed to recordings by the English progressive/psychedelic group Hawkwind, who took their name from a character in one of his novels and have recorded several of his songs; Moorcock has also written three songs for the American hard rock band Blue Oyster Cult. His official fan club is the Nomads of the Time Streams; both the Bodleian Library, Oxford, and Texas A&M University hold collections of his papers.

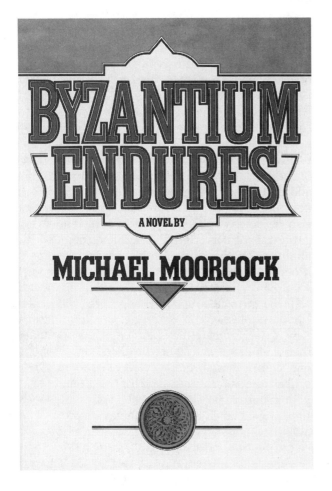

Born on the first of January 1900, in Russia, international traveler Maxim Arturovitch Pyatnitski traces the course of the twentieth century as he careens from one major event to another in this 1981 novel.

Childhood Influences

Born in Surrey, England, Moorcock has related that his earliest memories are of "air-raid shelters, dogfights, searchlights, barrage balloons, collecting shrapnel and bits of planes on the Common, . . . of ruined buildings, of endless landscapes where bombs had cleared eccentric spaces amongst shops and houses." Critics note that, like his friend and fellow writer J. G. Ballard, Moorcock's imaginary worlds are strongly influenced by his wartime background. Although he was deserted by his father in 1945, Moorcock claims that he had a happy childhood. An only child, he read a great deal, and was familiar with the works of such authors as Charles Dickens, George Bernard Shaw, T. S. Eliot, and Edgar Rice Burroughs by the age of eight. He also enjoyed the books of such writers as Rudyard Kipling, H. G. Wells—whose novel *The Time Machine* includes an introduction by Moorcock in an edition published in 1993—and E. Nesbit, the English fantasist and writer of realistic fiction for children; Moorcock later published a series of fantasies featuring the time-traveller Oswald Bastable, who takes his name from the young narrator of Nesbit's children's books *The Story of the Treasure Seekers, The Wouldbegoods, The New Treasure Seekers,* and *Oswald Bastable and Others.* As a boy, Moorcock was inspired by his affection for Richmal Crompton's "William" books to create the first of his magazines; called *Outlaws Own,* it contained mainly self-penned material.

"Effectively self-educated," writes Colin Greenland, "[Moorcock] developed broad tastes and unorthodox literary principles that have sustained his determinedly unconventional career." He was formally educated at a total of ten schools, some of which asked him to leave. For example, while a primary grader at Michael Hall school in Sussex, Moorcock led a group of students on several nocturnal adventures and kept his friends up at night telling them stories; these activities, among others, caused his expulsion from the school, the first in the history of the institution. After failing his exams at fifteen, he went to Pitman's College for a clerical education after deciding to become a writer. Before he left school, Moorcock joined the Air Training Corps, hoping that the experience would help him when he was drafted into the Royal Air Force; ironically, the draft was abolished a few days before he turned eighteen. Meanwhile, Moorcock had worked in a series of office jobs;

in his last assignment of this type, he was encouraged by a group of management consultants to produce magazines on the firm's copying machines. Moorcock created several science fiction fanzines as well as one on jazz and one on Edgar Rice Burroughs; the success of the latter led him to be asked to write for the juvenile magazine *Tarzan Adventures*, where he wrote articles and stories in the style of Burroughs, including an early version of "Sojan," the fantasy that would later become his sole contribution to children's literature. At seventeen, Moorcock became editor of the magazine. He also gigged semi-professionally as a singer and guitarist throughout the early 1960s, became involved with the anarchist movement, corresponded with songwriters Woody Guthrie and Pete Seeger, and was active in the National Union of Journalists while still too young for full membership.

Interest in Sci-Fi Begins

While writing and editing *Tarzan Adventures*, Moorcock began creating realistic short stories for adults. Attracted by both the freedom and the marketability of science fiction, Moorcock began contributing stories to magazines, including "The Stealer of Souls," which introduced his character Elric. Encouraged by E. J. (Ted) Carnell, the editor of *New Worlds* magazine whom Moorcock calls "the single most influential figure in British sf," he wrote more Elric stories and began producing novellas and novelettes for Carnell's magazines *New Worlds*, *Science Fantasy*, and *Science Fiction Adventures*. After leaving *Tarzan Adventures*, Moorcock joined the Sexton Blake Library and Amalgamated Press, considered the longest-running detective series in the world, and wrote the Sexton Blake novel *Caribbean Crisis* (1962) with James Cawthorn under the house pseudonym Desmond Reid; he also worked for several children's annuals and wrote comic strips featuring both real and imaginary heroes before becoming employed by the British Liberal Party. During this period, Moorcock published his first two solo books, *The Stealer of Souls, and Other Stories* (1963) and *Stormbringer* (1965), before becoming editor of *New Worlds* after Ted Carnell's retirement. Moorcock began to implement a new policy in *New Worlds*, adding, as he says, "more social and political engagement, better writing, better characterization, more experimental prose, more urgent subject matter. . . . I felt sf could become a genu-

ine literary form whilst retaining its popular audience." *New Worlds* became a keystone of the New Wave movement, featuring the experimental stories of such writers as Jorge Luis Borges, William S. Burroughs, and J. G. Ballard and publishing the work of Brian Aldiss, Samuel R. Delany, and Thomas M. Disch. among others.

In an interview with Ian Covell of *Science Fiction Review*, Moorcock says of the New Wave: "We were a generation of writers who had no nostalgic view of the pulp magazines, who had come to SF as a possible alternative to mainstream literature and had taken SF seriously. . . . We were trying to find a viable literature for our time. A literature which took account of science, of modern social trends, and which was written . . . according to the personal requirements of the individuals who produced it." Although *New Worlds* was an influential magazine in its field, it was never a financial success and was attacked for its inclusion of explicit sex and violence. As editor and publisher, Moorcock was often forced to write a quick novel to pay the bills. In his *Dream Makers: The Uncommon People Who Write Science Fiction*, Charles Platt recounts, "It was not unusual for the magazine's staff to be found cowering on the floor with the lights out, pretending not to be home, while some creditor rang the bell and called hopefully through the mail slot in the front door—to no avail." Ignored by British publishing distributors, *New Worlds* ceased publication in 1970; since then, Moorcock has edited several original anthologies of *New Worlds*, both individually and with David Garnett.

As he did with *New Worlds*, Moorcock attempted to liberate his own writing from the traditional forms of fantasy and science fiction. *The Final Programme* (1968), the ironic thriller that introduces popular protagonist Jerry Cornelius, is the first of Moorcock's books that he feels accomplishes this goal. Jerry Cornelius, a physicist turned adventurer, is the antihero of a multivolume series of darkly comic contemporary novels that are often considered Dickensian in their scope. Combining fantastic elements with James Bond-style adventures, the series marks Jerry as a symbol of 1960s values while lampooning his excesses. Described by his creator as "something of a modern Candide" and by Colin Greenland as "an entirely new kind of fictional character," Jerry has no consistent gender, personality, or appearance, changing sex and color and morphing into different characters in every volume. The landscape he inhabits is just as flexible, containing a multitude of alternative histories—all contradictory and peopled with characters who die and resurrect as a matter of course. Jerry travels from one inconclusive adventure to another, trapped in an endless existence. Throughout this series, as with others in his oeuvre, Moorcock creates a "multiverse," or parallel universes with their own realities, and underscores his imaginative landscapes with the theme of how society's emphasis on power and war has led to its deterioration. The Jerry Cornelius novels *The Condition of Muzak* (1977) and *The Great Rock and Roll Swindle* (1980) may be of special interest to young people: *Muzak* casts Jerry as a working-class lad who dreams of becoming a rock star, while *Swindle* is a novel written at the same time as the film that shares its name about seminal punk band the Sex Pistols. Moorcock considers four Jerry Cornelius novels—*The Final Programme, A Cure for Cancer* (1971), *The English Assassin* (1972), and *The Condition of Muzak*—to be a single work; these books, which were collected as *The Cornelius Chronicles* (1977), are considered by Angus Wilson in the *Washington Post Book World* to form "one of the most ambitious, illuminating, and enjoyable works of fiction published in English since the last war."

Like the Jerry Cornelius books, several of Moorcock's other works comment on contemporary society; "in short," notes John Clute in *New Statesman*, the author has written "the history of the modern world." For example, *Behold the Man* (1969), a novel expanded from a novella of the same title for which Moorcock received a Nebula Award in 1967, describes how Karl Glogauer, a modern Jewish man, time-travels to ancient Palestine to search for the truth about the Crucifixion and discovers Jesus Christ, in the words of Janice Elliott in *New Statesman*, as "a hunchbacked congenital imbecile." Assuming Christ's identity, Karl is finally crucified as Jesus—"leaving" as Colin Greenland notes, "no opportunity for a second coming." The publication of *Behold the Man* is usually accepted as the point at which critics began to recognize Moorcock as a serious writer. In the second Karl Glogauer novel, *Breakfast in the Ruins* (1972), Moorcock resurrects the character and presents accounts of his incarnations during times of catastrophe and torture—past, present, and future—in such cities as Capetown, Kiev, Shanghai, and Saigon. Moorcock's literary reputation has also been enhanced by the publication

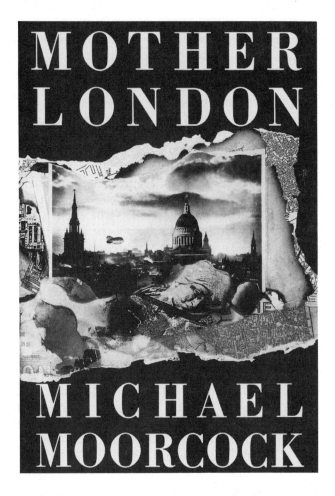

Three former patients of a mental health clinic who are survivors of German bombings in World War II narrate this tribute to the city of London.

of *Byzantium Endures* (1981) and *The Laughter of Carthage* (1984), novels that are often considered among his finest contributions to more conventional fiction. Together, the books describe the autobiography of Russian emigre Colonel Maxim Arturovitch Pyatnitski (shortened to Pyat), born 1 January 1900, whose life mirrors the history of the twentieth century. A figure who first appeared peripherally in the Jerry Cornelius tetralogy, Pyat survives the Russian Revolution, travels throughout America and Europe, meets figures ranging from Dylan Thomas to Tom Mix, and participates in several important historical events. He is, however, a self-aggrandizing megalomaniac and cocaine addict who imagines himself to be a great engineer and inventor—the equal of Thomas Edison—and a major figure on the stage of world history. The illegitimate son of a Jewish father,

Pyat is an anti-Semite who sees the truest form of Christianity, as embodied in the Russian Orthodox Church, in opposing the Jews, Asians, Bolsheviks, and other groups whom he considers destroyers of order; he likens Western Christianity to Byzantium, his enemies to Carthage. In his review in the *Chicago Tribune Book World*, Robert Onopa calls *Byzantium Endures* "utterly engrossing as narrative, historically pertinent, and told through characters so alive and detail so dense that it puts to shame all but a few writers who have been doing this kind of work all along." *Times Literary Supplement* reviewer Valentine Cunningham says of *The Laughter of Carthage*, "This is epic writing," while Gregory Sandow observes in the *Village Voice*, "It's wonderful to see Moorcock grow from a genre writer into, simply, a writer. . . . [He] has had to come the long way to literary recognition. But now, with *The Laughter of Carthage*, he can surely no longer be denied his due; this enormous book—with its forerunner, *Byzantium Endures*—must establish him in the front rank of practising English novelists."

Prodigious and Inventive

Evaluations of Moorcock's career often emphasize the sheer volume and variety of his work. "It is like trying to evaluate an industry," as Philip Oakes explains in the London *Sunday Times Magazine*. Throughout his career, Moorcock has been credited for his impressive ability to write consistently well within a wide range of genres and styles. "I have read about half his prodigious output . . . ," Oakes writes, "and on the strength of that sample Moorcock strikes me as the most prolific, probably the most inventive and without doubt the most egalitarian writer practising today." In the *Washington Post Book World*, Angus Wilson calls Moorcock "one of the most exciting discoveries that I have been able to make in the contemporary English novel during the 40 or so years that I have been publishing my own novels and reviewing those of my contemporaries. Exciting for myself and, as is becoming increasingly clear with the appearance of each Moorcock book, for a legion of other readers."

In an interview with Ian Covell for *Science Fiction Review*, Moorcock spoke about his literary philosophy: "I'm attempting all the time to find equilibrium between unchecked Romanticism ("Chaos") and stifling Classicism ("Law"). Pinocchio and

---

If you enjoy the works of Michael Moorcock, you may also want to check out the following books and films:

Douglas Adams, *The Hitchhiker's Guide to the Galaxy*, 1979.
Samuel R. Delany, *The Einstein Intersection*, 1967.
Thomas M. Disch, *On Wings of Song*, 1979.
Nancy Kress, *Beggars in Spain*, 1993.
Orlando, a film based on a novel by Virginia Woolf, 1992.

Jiminy Cricket, Pierrot and Columbine, Ego and Superego. Make your own choice. And in form I'm always looking for a combination (that will work) of the epic and the novel—or the romance and the novel. You will notice that I call very few of my books 'novels' because they are not, classically speaking, novels. They are romances. Scene and idea (allegorical concerns) in general take precedence over characters. . . . The same moral arguments are debated again and again from my earliest (*The Golden Barge*) to my latest (*Gloriana*). The trick is to look at them from as many different ways as possible." Moorcock has written that most of his work "recently has been in terms of a moral and psychological investigation of Imperialism (Western and Eastern) seen in terms of fiction. Even my fantasy novels are inclined to deal with moral problems rather than magical ones. I'm turning more and more away from SF and fantasy and more towards a form of realism used in the context of what you might call an imaginative framework. Late Dickens would be the model I'd most like to emulate." In *Contemporary Authors Autobiography Series*, Moorcock speaks of the writing life: "The job of a novelist has its own momentum, its own demands, its own horrible power over the practitioner. When I look back I wonder what I got myself into all those years ago when I realised I had a facility to put words down on paper and have people give me money in return. For ages the whole business seemed ludicrous. I couldn't believe my luck. Frequently, I still can't but it seems an unnatural way of earning a living. Of course, it's no longer easy. It's often a struggle. It spoils my health. . . . I suppose it must be an addiction. I'm pretty sure, though I deny it heartily, that I could now no longer give it up. I'm as possessed as any fool I used to mock."

■ Works Cited

Ableman, Paul, "Unagonising Saga," *Spectator*, June 27, 1981, pp. 24-25.

Budrys, Algis, review of *Gloriana: ar, The Unfulfilled Queen*, *Booklist*, September 1, 1979, p. 29.

Clute, John, "No Escape," *New Statesman*, September 7, 1984, pp. 31-32.

Contemporary Authors Autobiography Series, Volume 5, Gale, 1987.

Cunningham, Valentine, "Incontinent Continents-Full," *Times Literary Supplement*, September, 7, 1984, p. 1005.

Elliott, Janice, "Present & Past," *New Statesman*, April 4, 1969, p. 486.

Feeley, Gregory, "In the Heart of the Heart of the City," *Washington Post Book World*, May 14, 1989, p. 8.

Greenland, Colin, "Michael Moorcock," *Dictionary of Literary Biography*, Volume 14: *British Novelists since 1960*, Gale, 1983.

Moorcock, Michael, and Ian Covell, in an interview, *Science Fiction Review*, January, 1979, pp. 18-25.

Oakes, Philip, "Michael Moorcock," *Sunday Times Magazine*, November 5, 1978, p. 100.

Onopa, Robert, review of *Byzantium Endures*, *Chicago Tribune Book World*, March 21, 1982, p. 10.

Platt, Charles, *Dream Makers: The Uncommon People Who Write Science Fiction*, Berkley Publishing, 1980.

Sandow, Gregory, review of *Byzantium Endures*, *Village Voice*, March 2, 1982, pp. 42-43.

Willett, Ralph, "Moorcock's Achievement and Promise in the Jerry Cornelius Books," *Science Fiction Studies*, March, 1976, pp. 75-79.

Wilson, Angus, "The Picaresque Imagination of Michael Moorcock," *Washington Post Book World*, December 23, 1984, pp. 1, 13.

■ For More Information See

BOOKS

Bilyeu, R., *Tanelorn Archives*, Pandora's Books, 1979.

Callow, A. J., compiler, *The Chronicles of Moorcock*, A. J. Callow, 1978.

Carter, Lin, *Imaginary Worlds*, Ballantine, 1973.

Contemporary Literary Criticism, Gale, Volume 27, 1984, Volume 58, 1990.

Greenland, Colin, *The Entropy Exhibition: Michael Moorcock and the British "New Wave" in Science Fiction*, Routledge & Kegan Paul, 1983.

Harper, Andrew and George McAulay, *Michael Moorcock: A Bibliography*, T-K Graphics, 1976.

Moorcock, Michael, *Death Is No Obstacle* (interview by Colin Greenland), Savoy Books, 1992.

Walker, Paul, editor, *Speaking of Science Fiction: The Paul Walker Interviews*, Luna Publications, 1978.

Wollheim, Donald A., *The Universe Makers*, Harper, 1971.

PERIODICALS

Analog, February, 1970; March, 1990.

Booklist, February 15, 1995, p. 1064.

Books and Bookmen, June, 1971, p. 44; October, 1972, p. 72; May, 1974, p. 86; August, 1978, p. 44.

Chicago Tribune Book World, January 31, 1982.

Commonweal, August 1, 1975.

Encounter, November, 1981, p. 81.

Extrapolation, winter, 1989, p. 412.

Guardian Weekly, April 10, 1969, p. 15.

Kirkus Reviews, October 1, 1995, p. 1387.

Listener, June 23, 1988, p. 31; January 18, 1990, p. 33.

Locus, November, 1989, p. 57; February, 1990, p. 15.

New Republic, June 15, 1974.

New Statesman, June 18, 1976, p. 821.

New York Times Book Review, April 5, 1970, p. 43; April 25, 1976, p. 46; February 21, 1982, p. 12; February 10, 1985, p. 24; November 23, 1986, p. 31.

Observer, April 4, 1976, p. 27; April 3, 1977, p. 26.

Publishers Weekly, January 16, 1995, p. 442; October 30, 1995; September 29, 1997, p. 67

Punch, January 16, 1985, p. 82.

Saturday Review, April 25, 1970. p. 61.

Spectator, August 10, 1974, p. 182; April 9, 1977, p. 21; June 27, 1981, p. 24; February 9, 1985, p. 24.

Time, January 28, 1985, p. 82.

Times Literary Supplement, May 31, 1974, p. 577; May 7, 1976, p. 561; June 30, 1978, p. 742; July 3, 1981, p. 747; July 1, 1988, p. 731; February 23, 1990, p. 202.

Tribune Books (Chicago), March 26, 1989.

—Sketch by Gerard J. Senick

Alan Paton

marizburg, Natal, president of the Convocation, 1951-55 and 1957-59; founder and president, Liberal Party of South Africa (originally the Liberal Association of South Africa before emergence as a political party; declared an illegal organization, 1968), 1958-68. Non-European Boys' Clubs, president of Transvaal association, 1935-48.

■ Personal

Full name Alan Stewart Paton; surname rhymes with "Dayton"; born January 11, 1903, in Pietermaritzburg, South Africa; died of throat cancer, April 12, 1988, in Botha's Hill (near Durban), Natal, South Africa; son of James (a civil servant) and Eunice Warder (James) Paton; married Doris Olive Francis, July 2, 1928 (died October 23, 1967); married Anne Hopkins, 1969, children: (first marriage) David Francis, Jonathan Stewart. *Education:* University of Natal, B.Sc., 1923. *Religion:* Anglican.

■ Career

Writer. Ixopo High School, Ixopo, Natal, South Africa, teacher of mathematics and physics, 1925-28; Maritzburg College, Pietermaritzburg, Natal, teacher of mathematics, physics, and English, 1928-35; Diepkloof Reformatory, near Johannesburg, South Africa, principal, 1935-48; Toc H Southern Africa, Botha's Hill, Natal, honorary commissioner, 1949-58; University of Natal, Durban and Pieter-

■ Awards, Honors

Anisfeld-Wolf *Saturday Review* Award, 1948, Newspaper Guild of New York Page One Award, 1949, and London *Sunday Times* Special Award for Literature, 1949, all for *Cry, the Beloved Country*; Benjamin Franklin Award, 1955; Freedom House Award (U.S.), 1960; Medal for Literature, Free Academy of Arts, 1961; National Conference of Christians and Jews Brotherhood Award, 1962, for *Tales from a Troubled Land*; C.N.A. Literary Award for the year's best book in English in South Africa, 1965, for *Hofmeyr*, and 1973, for *Apartheid and the Archbishop: The Life and Times of Geoffrey Clayton, Archbishop of Cape Town*; L.H.D., Yale University, 1954, Kenyon College, 1962, La Salle University, Philadelphia, 1986; D. Litt., University of Natal, 1968, Trent University, 1971, Harvard University, 1971, Rhodes University, 1972, Williamette University, 1974, University of Michigan—Flint, 1977, University of Durban/Westville, 1986; D.D., University of Edinburgh, 1971; LL.D., Witwatersrand University, 1975.

■ **Writings**

NOVELS AND SHORT STORIES

Cry, the Beloved Country, Scribner, 1948, Macmillan, 1987.

Too Late the Phalarope, Scribner, 1953, reprinted, Penguin, 1971.

Tales from a Troubled Land (stories), Scribner, 1961, published in England as *Debbie Go Home*, J. Cape, 1961, new edition, Penguin, 1965.

Knocking on the Door: Alan Paton/Shorter Writings, edited by Colin Gardner, Scribner, 1975.

Ah, But Your Land Is Beautiful (novel; first in an unfinished trilogy), Scribner, 1981.

OTHER

Meditation for a Young Boy Confirmed (poem), S.P.C.K., 1944, Forward Movement, 1954.

Cry, the Beloved Country (screenplay based on novel of the same title), United Artists, 1951.

The Land and the People of South Africa, Lippincott, 1955 (published in England as *South Africa and Her People*, Lutterworth, 1957), revised edition published under original title, Lippincott, 1972.

South Africa in Transition, Scribner, 1956.

Hope for South Africa, Praeger, 1959.

Hofmeyr (biography), Oxford University Press, 1964, abridged edition published as *South African Tragedy: The Life and Times of Jan Hofmeyr*, Scribner, 1965, new edition, Oxford University Press, 1971.

(With Krishna Shah) *Sponono* (play; based on three stories from *Tales from a Troubled Land*; first produced on Broadway at the Cort Theatre, April 2, 1964), Scribner, 1965.

Instrument of Thy Peace: The Prayer of St. Francis, Seabury, 1968, revised edition, 1982.

The Long View, edited by Edward Callan, Praeger, 1968.

For You Departed, Scribner, 1969 (published in England as *Kontakion for You Departed*, J. Cape, 1969).

(With others) *Creative Suffering: The Ripple of Hope*, Pilgrim, 1970.

Apartheid and the Archbishop: The Life and Times of Geoffrey Clayton, Archbishop of Cape Town, David Phillip (Cape Town, South Africa), 1973, Scribner, 1974.

Towards the Mountain: An Autobiography, Scribner, 1980.

(Author of forward) Elsa Joubert, *Poppie Nongena*, Norton, 1985.

Journey Continued: An Autobiography, Scribner, 1988.

■ **Adaptations**

Lost in the Stars, a musical, was adapted from *Cry, the Beloved Country* by Maxwell Anderson and produced on Broadway at the Music Box, October 30, 1949; the motion picture based on the musical *Lost in the Stars* was produced by American Film Theatre in 1974; *Too Late the Phalarope* was adapted as a play by Robert Yale Libott and produced on Broadway at the Belasco Theatre, October 11, 1956; the stage and screen rights to *For You Departed* have been sold; *Cry, the Beloved Country* was adapted as a motion picture in 1951, and by Ronald Harwood through Miramax Films in 1995.

■ **Sidelights**

In a cathedral in Norway in 1946, Alan Paton sat looking at a rose window. "There was still enough light in the sky to see its magnificent design and colors," wrote Paton in *Towards the Mountain*, his autobiography. "I was in the grip of powerful emotion, not directly to do with the cathedral and the rose window, but certainly occasioned by them. I was filled with an intense homesickness, for home and wife and sons, and for my far off country." Paton went back to his hotel and wrote the following sentences: "There is a lovely road that runs from Ixopo into the hills. These hills are grass-covered and rolling, and they are lovely beyond any singing of it." Paton kept writing, and the sentences stretched out into what would become a classic South African novel, *Cry, the Beloved Country*. According to William Minter, writing in *New York Times Book Review*, the 1948 publication of the book "transformed" Paton "overnight into South Africa's most celebrated writer." Carol Iannone of *American Scholar* explained, "Within a few years of its publication in 1948, it had become a worldwide best-seller and was eventually translated into twenty, languages." In 1988, "it had sold over fifteen million copies and was still selling at the rate of one hundred thousand copies a year."

Iannone wrote that the novel takes up a particular moment in South African history: "The depression and war had passed. Industrialization and urbanization were breaking down tribal customs, even as the increasing population of blacks and whites in the cities was worsening the tensions under separatism. The novel strips away the surface assurances of white supremacy to reveal what has in some respects become a wasteland—a literal wasteland in the case of the sordid slums and the dying tribal lands, but also a spiritual wasteland, characterized by alienation and mistrust among races and peoples and families and generations."

Paton, who had worked as a teacher and reform school principal, began a serious career as a writer after the publication of *Cry, the Beloved Country.* He also became a public figure and a founder of the Liberal Party of South Africa. In his essays, poems, novels, biographies, and autobiographies, as well as in his political activities, the religious and liberal author promoted racial equality and freedom for all South Africans. Paton's writings were well known outside South Africa and did much to focus international attention on the political situation there. Paton's *Cry, the Beloved Country,* especially, became a work of historical as well as literary importance.

Paton was born in 1903, at the end of the Boer War. Paton's father, originally from Scotland, worked as a shorthand court recorder. A Christadelphian, he professed Christian values (including kindness and tolerance), appreciated literature, and ran his home in what Paton described as an authoritarian fashion in *Towards the Mountain.* James Paton's use of physical force "never achieved anything but a useless obedience," explained Paton. "But . . . I grew up with an abhorrence of authoritarianism, especially the authoritarianism of the State, and a love of liberty, especially liberty within the State."

Paton was an excellent student, and he was busy with extracurricular activities. He won a scholarship to attend Maritzburg College, and went on to win a bursary at Natal University College. Upon his graduation he married a widow, Doris (Dorrie) Francis Lusted, and worked as a teacher of physics at Ixopo High School. During his years in Ixopo Paton became an Anglican and learned to speak Afrikaans.

On July 1, 1935, Paton began work as the principal of a boys' reformatory, Diepkloof. The reformatory, more like a prison than school, kept four hundred African boys in squalor: they were cramped into small rooms with buckets instead of toilets. The offenses of the hundred children at the

reformatory, wrote Paton in *Towards the Mountain,* "were trivial. They should never have been there at all. They had pilfered from shops and fruit stalls and at the markets. . . . Most of them were in need of care, but what was to be done with them?" Three hundred older children had committed a variety of offenses: "Some had committed murder, for reasons of passion or after a quarrel. . . . Some had committed rape. . . . Some had stolen or killed cattle or sheep. . . ."

During the thirteen years he spent there, Paton transformed Diepkloof. He opened the living quarters, set rules to allow the boys to win respect and freedom, and created an environment suitable for learning. In the process of managing Diepkloof, Paton himself thought a great deal about punishment, individual responsibility, the human spirit, and his country. He hoped, as Anthony Delius of the *Times Literary Supplement* noted, to become "the country's Director of Prisons," and to transform the prison system in South Africa as well.

As Paton worked at Diepkloof, he became friends with Afrikaners and Africans. "Drawn some way towards Afrikaner nationalism in his search for a deeper South African patriotism, he grew a beard like a Boer," related Delius. Yet he found the racism demonstrated by those celebrating the centenary of the Great Trek deplorable, and shaved off his beard. As Thomas Pakenham of the *New York Times Book Review* noted, Paton's "second great spiritual jolt came in 1941 when he served on the Anglican Diocesan Commission in Johannesburg. . . . He saw that white supremacy and apartheid could not be reconciled with his own Christianity."

Cry, the Beloved Country

Paton was on leave from the reformatory researching prison systems when he wrote *Cry, the Beloved Country."* "Paton had always shown a literary bent and had been writing poetry and attempting novels since his college days," explained Iannone in *American Scholar.* While traveling in Norway Paton wrote the first chapter, and he wrote the rest of the book as he traveled in Europe and the United States. "I do not even remember if I knew what the story was to be. . . . It became clear that the story was to be not so much about the beauties of the land, but about its men and women, and about the gross inequalities that so disfigured our national life," Paton recalled in *Towards the Mountain*. The first two readers of the manuscript gathered with Paton to choose a title for the novel, and each chose "Cry, the Beloved Country." The title, explained Paton, "came from the book itself," which contains the lines "Cry, the beloved country, for the unborn child that is the inheritor of our fear. . . ."

Paton's *Cry, the Beloved Country* begins with a description of the countryside surrounding Ixopo. Despite its beauty, in the "valleys women scratch the soil that is left, and the maize hardly reaches the height of a man. They are valleys of old men and old women, of mothers and children. The men are away, the young men and the girls are away. The soil cannot keep them any more." In the next chapter, Paton introduces the black protagonist in the novel: Reverend Stephen Kumalo receives a letter regarding his sister, Gertrude, in Johannesburg. Kumalo's son Absalom has already gone to look for Gertrude, but now Kumalo must leave his wife, home, and church to seek out both of them.

When he arrives in Johannesburg, he finds that Gertrude is a prostitute, and that his son Absalom has just killed a white young man, Arthur, who served as the African Boys Club president. Kumalo's grief at his son's actions is paralleled by that of Jarvis, the father of Arthur. Jarvis learns a great deal about his son and his work for racial equality as he looks through his papers and belongings. Although defenders of Absalom argue that he did not mean to shoot Arthur during the robbery Absalom and two others were committing, Kumalo's son is sentenced to death. Kumalo leaves Johannesburg with Absalom's pregnant wife and Gertrude's young son. By the end of the novel, Jarvis and Kumalo reach a sympathetic understanding; Jarvis helps Kumalo get a new church.

Cry, the Beloved Country won enthusiastic reviews from critics and elicited tears from readers. "I have just finished a magnificent story," wrote Harold C. Gardiner in a 1948 review. As the novel took up complicated issues, and "reduced to these simple, almost fabular, terms, it was intelligible and it made an impact," wrote Dennis Brutus in *Protest and Conflict in African Literature*. "The emotional impact of *Cry, the Beloved Country* is achieved, first of all and most consistently, by Paton's stylistic understatement, by his use and

This 1948 novel about blacks living under white supremacy in South Africa became an instant classic and a worldwide bestseller.

reuse of a few simple, almost stilted, formal phrases," explained Myron Matlaw in *Arcadia*. Edmund Fuller, writing in *Man and Modern Fiction*, lauded Paton's message that environmental conditions, as well as individual choice, affect human action. Martin Tucker commented in *Africa in Modern Literature* that "Paton is the most important force in the literature of forgiveness and adjustment." Yet as Iannone noted in *American Scholar*, "[a]fter initial widespread adulation, critics began to find fault with *Cry, the Beloved Country*, seeing it as sentimental and propagandistic, more a treatise than a work of art. The novel tends to survive these objections, however, because the whole is greater than the sum of its parts."

After *Cry, the Beloved Country* made him famous, Paton resigned from his post at the reformatory and began to act upon and speak about his beliefs. (As Iannone pointed out, "all reports portray him as an electrifyingly gifted orator.") Paton helped found the Liberal Party and served as its president in 1953; the party promoted racial equality and worked in nonviolent ways against the Nationalist government's policy of apartheid. Paton was never imprisoned for his work, but his passport, as Herbert Mitgang noted in the *New York Times*, was temporarily taken away in 1960. The organization disbanded itself in 1968 to avoid a forced disorganization by the government, which prohibited multiracial parties.

Too Late the Phalarope and Other Works

It was not until 1971 that Paton's next novel, *Too Late the Phalarope*, was published. The story is narrated by a woman, Tante Sophie, whose brother Pieter van Vlanderen was once a rugby star and a respected policeman in the Afrikaner community. Pieter and his family seem to be doing well until he begins brooding over his relationship with his wife and stops a white young man from pursuing a woman of color, Stephanie. (By law, sexual relations among the two races are forbidden). Then Pieter engages in an affair with Stephanie. The scandal ruins Pieter and his family who withdraw from the community. Pieter is sent to jail, and his father, a powerful landowner, dies of shame. According to Edmund Fuller, writing in *Books with Men behind Them*, Pieter's story is a tragic one. Pieter's act was not a primarily sexual one, but one of "destruction and revenge. This is the one sure and deadly blow against his father, against Nell and his children, against Tante Sophie, and against the Afrikaner community . . . and against himself." In *English Studies in Africa*, Sheridan Baker found Paton's second novel less genuine than his first: "the literary qualities of the first book . . . seem in the second imported." Baker argues, for example, that "Sophie is too clearly, for all her substance, a literary device, and a rather old-fashioned one at that."

Sidney Poitier and Canada Lee starred in the 1951 film adaptation of *Cry, the Beloved Country*.

Tales from a Troubled Land includes ten stories, most of them, as John Barkham of the *New York Times Book Review* found, "drawn" from Paton's days at the reformatory. Barkham stated that "Life for a Life," a story involving the murder of an Afrikaner, was the best among them. D. D. Chambers of *Canadian Forum* commented that none of the stories "really approaches the tenor and almost 'fey' quality" of his first two novels; still, he spotted Paton's "intangible genius" at work in "Debbie Go Home" and "A Drink the Passage."

By the early 1960s Paton had produced a body of work that critics used to judge him as a writer. F. Charles Rooney in *Catholic World*, for one, lauded Paton's skill as a writer, and his unwillingness to moralize in his first books. *Cry, the Beloved Country* "is a great novel, but not because it speaks out against racial intolerance and its bitter effects. Rather, the haunting milieu of a civilization choking out its own vitality is evoked naturally and summons our compassion. . . . It is a great compliment to Paton's genius that he communicates both a story and a lasting impression without bristling, bitter anger." In *Too Late the Phalarope* "Tante Sophie . . . becomes such a real person to the reader that there is never a question of sermonizing." In *Tales from a Troubled Land*, however, asserted Rooney, "Paton has unfortunately abandoned his story to profess his heart."

Between 1964 and 1974, Paton published two biographies. The first, *Hofmeyr*, is about Paton's friend Jan Hofmeyr, a deputy prime minister and liberal. According to Edward Callan in *Alan Paton*, Paton wrote this biography because he "was convinced that the story of Hofmeyr's life could reveal the true spirit of South Africa in our times more clearly than the biography of any other public figure." Callan asserted that the "judgment of the future may rank his . . . biography of Jan Hofmeyr as a literary achievement equal to the novels and possibly surpassing them." *Apartheid and the Archbishop*, wrote Callan, "is a portrait of a spiritual man reluctantly forced by his Christian perspective to act in the political sphere."

Ah, But Your Land Is Beautiful appeared in 1981, as the first in a trilogy Paton envisioned. The story contains both real and fictional characters, and real and fictional events. According to Graham Hough in *London Review of Books*, it "unrolls in a series of short episodes," all of which feature "characters covering a wide spectrum of South African

life." "Paton is relentless in his faith in the moral meaning of individual human experience . . .," wrote John Romano in the *New York Times Book Review*. "Paton's technique [of using voices] remains the same, but his viewpoint has changed from sorrowful compassion to irony," wrote *New Republic*'s Nadine Gordimer. Praising the result of this stylistic shift, Gordimer noted its "shining intelligence and acerbity."

Paton Tells His Own Story

Paton postponed the trilogy project begun with *Ah, But Your Land Is Beautiful* to write about his own life. Paton's autobiography, *Towards the Mountain*, tells of his life up until the publication of *Cry, the Beloved Country* in 1948. "He writes in a

Paton's 1953 novel deals with illegal interracial relations in South Africa.

rigorously unmannered prose, lightened by gentle irony, sometimes breaking into comedy—to my mind this is his best writing yet," commented Delius in the *Times Literary Supplement*. "Candor and moral courage are the qualities that shine from these memoirs," wrote a *Publishers Weekly* critic.

Journey Continued, the second half of Paton's autobiography, relates the events of his life after 1948; it was published the year of his death. The "core" of the book, wrote Martin Rubin in the *Los Angeles Times Book Review*, "is surely the story of Paton's relationship with the short-lived political party he helped found." Paton wrote about the party's "travails and . . . achievements," "genuinely multiracial character" and "internal dissensions." "It is a story of police harassment, torture, murder and banishment—of incredible insensitivity and cruelty. He believed at the end of his life that somehow there would be no bloody revolution, with its subsequent and inevitable totalitarianism," commented Thomas Williams in the *Chicago Tribune*.

During the last decade of his life, Paton was criticized for his stance on sanctions and disinvestment. He disagreed with other liberals, saying that such actions would do more harm than good. He elaborated in *Journey Continued*, "You cannot change a society for the better by damaging or destroying its economy. Sanctions are intended to be punitive, and punishment is not the way to make people behave better. I learned that fifty-two years ago at Diepkloof Reformatory." "Paton stuck by his moderate stance, advocating a cautious but steady course of change in South Africa," explained William Claiborne in the *Washington Post*.

When Paton died in 1988 of throat cancer, South Africa had yet to abolish apartheid, or to establish democracy. Still, critics pointed out the effects of his work on South African politics, or rather, on the way people outside South Africa viewed the country. Tom McGurk wrote in *New Statesman* after Paton's death, "Perhaps more than anything else it [*Cry, the Beloved Country*] succeeded in opening the first window on life in South Africa. . . . The enchanting power of Paton's tale gave generations a commitment towards justice" in that country. A *Commonweal* critic pointed out that while Paton's "moderate position ultimately excluded him from political life" in South Africa,

If you enjoy the works of Alan Paton, you may also want to check out the following books and films:

Sheila Gordon, *Waiting for the Rain*, 1987.
Beverly Naidoo, *Chain of Fire*, 1989.
Hazel Rochman, *Somehow Tenderness Survives: Stories of Southern Africa*, 1988.
Bopha!, starring Danny Glover and directed by Morgan Freeman, 1993.

Cry the Beloved Country helped people in the United States deal with "our race problem." "In the end . . . he will be remembered . . . for his cry for justice that continues to echo today," wrote Minter in the *New York Times Book Review*.

■ Works Cited

"Alan Paton," *Commonweal*, May 20, 1988, pp. 292-93.

Baker, Sheridan, "Paton's Late Phalarope," *English Studies in Africa*, September, 1960, pp. 152-59.

Barkham, John, "Meekness and Brutality," *New York Times Book Review*, April 16, 1961, p. 4.

Brutus, Dennis, "Protest against Apartheid," *Protest and Conflict in African Literature*, edited by Cosmo Pieterse and Donald Munro, Africana Publishing, 1969, pp. 93-100.

Callan, Edward, *Alan Paton*, Twayne, 1968.

Chambers, D. D., "Books Reviewed: 'Tales from a Troubled Land'," *Canadian Forum*, September, 1961, p. 144.

Claiborne, William, "S. African Author Alan Paton Dies," *Washington Post*, April 12, 1988, p. A8.

Delius, Anthony, "Seeds on Stony Ground," *Times Literary Supplement*, March 6, 1981, p. 250.

Fuller, Edmund, *Man in Modern Fiction: Some Minority Opinions on Contemporary American Writing*, Random House, 1958, p. 40.

Fuller, Edmund, "Alan Paton: Tragedy and Beyond," *Books with Men behind Them*, Random House, 1962, pp. 83-101.

Gardiner, Harold C., "Chapter Three: On Saying 'Boo!' to Geese," and "Chapter Three: Alan Paton's Second Masterpiece," *In All Conscience: Reflections on Books and Culture*, Hanover House, 1959, pp. 108-12, 112-16.

Gordimer, Nadine, "Unconfessed History," *New Republic*, March 24, 1982, pp. 35-37.

Hough, Graham, "Doomed," *London Review of Books*, December 3-16, 1981, pp. 16-17.

Iannone, Carol, "Alan Paton's Tragic Liberalism," *American Scholar*, Summer, 1997, p. 442-52.

Matlaw, Myron, *Arcadia*, Walter de Gruyter & Co., 1975.

McGurk, Tom, "Paton's Nightmare Came True," *New Statesman*, April 15, 1988, pp. 7-8.

Minter, William, "Moderate to a Fault?" *New York Times Book Review*, November 20, 1988, p. 36.

Mitgang, Herbert, "Alan Paton, Author and Apartheid Foe, Dies of Cancer at 85," *New York Times*, April 12, 1988, pp. A1, D35.

Pakenham, Thomas, "The Beginning of Alan Paton," *New York Times Book Review*, December 14, 1980, p. 8.

Paton, Alan, *Towards the Mountain: An Autobiography*, Scribner, 1980.

Paton, Alan, *Journey Continued: An Autobiography*, Scribner, 1988.

Paton, Alan, *Cry, the Beloved Country*, Scribner, 1948.

Romano, John, "A Novel of Hope and Realism," *New York Times Book Review*, April 4, 1982, pp. 7, 22.

Rooney, F. Charles, "The 'Message' of Alan Paton," *Catholic World*, November, 1961, pp. 92-8.

Rubin, Martin, "South Africa since World War II," *Los Angeles Times Book Review*, October 30, 1988, pp. 2, 11.

Review of *Towards the Mountain*, *Publishers Weekly*, September 19, 1980, p. 152.

Tucker, Martin, *Africa in Modern Literature: A Survey of Contemporary Writing in English*, Ungar, 1967.

Williams, Thomas, "Generous Spirit," *Chicago Tribune*, November 27, 1988, pp. 5, 9.

■ For More Information See

BOOKS

Contemporary Literary Criticism, Gale, Volume 4, 1975, Volume 10, 1979, Volume 25, 1983, Volume 55, 1989.
Major Twentieth-Century Writers, Gale, 1991.

PERIODICALS

Booklist, February 1, 1982, p. 682.
Economist, March 7, 1981, p. 91.
Esquire, March, 1966, p. 44.
Horn Book, April, 1965, p. 180.
Kirkus Reviews, November 1, 1975, p. 1274.
New York Times, April 2, 1988, p. 11.
New York Times Book Review, August 4, 1974, p. 7.
Times Literary Supplement, April 29, 1965, p. 328.
Variety, August 2, 1993, p. 45.

■ Obituaries

PERIODICALS

Chicago Tribune, April 13, 1988.
Los Angeles Times, April 12, 1988.
New York Times, April 13, 1988.
Spectator, April 16, 1988, pp. 18-19.
Times (London), April 13, 1988.*

—Sketch by R. Garcia-Johnson

Tamora Pierce

89; freelance writer, 1990—. Former instructor, Free Woman's University, University of Pennsylvania. *Member:* Authors Guild, Science Fiction and Fantasy Writers of America.

■ Personal

Born December 13, 1954, in Connellsville, PA; daughter of Wayne Franklin and Jacqueline S. Pierce; married to Tim Liebe. *Education:* University of Pennsylvania, B.A., 1977.

■ Addresses

Agent—Craig R. Tenney, Harold Ober Associates, 425 Madison Ave., New York, NY 10017.

■ Career

City of Kingston, NY, tax data collector, 1977-78; towns of Hardenburgh and Denning, NY, tax clerk, 1978; McAuley Home for Girls, Buhl, ID, social worker and housemother, 1978-79; Harold Ober Associates, New York City, assistant to literary agent, 1979-82; creative director of ZPPR Productions, Inc. (radio producers), 1982-86; Chase Investment Bank, New York City, secretary, 1985-

■ Awards, Honors

Author's Citation, Alumni Association of the New Jersey Institute of Technology, 1984, for *Alanna: The First Adventure;* Schuler-Express ZDF Preis (Germany), 1985, and South Carolina Children's Book Award nomination, 1985-86, both for *In the Hand of the Goddess;* Children's Paperbacks Bestseller, *Australian Bookseller and Publisher,* 1995, for *Wolf-Speaker;* Best Books for Young Adults list, Hawaii State Library, Best Science Fiction, Fantasy and Horror list, *Voice of Youth Advocates,* both 1995, and Best Books for Young Adults list, American Library Association, 1996, all for *The Emperor Mage;* Best Science Fiction, Fantasy and Horror list, *Voice of Youth Advocates,* 1996, and Best Books for the Teen Age list, New York Public Library, 1997, both for *The Realms of the Gods.*

■ Writings

"SONG OF THE LIONESS" SERIES

Alanna: The First Adventure, Atheneum, 1983.
In the Hand of the Goddess, Atheneum, 1984.

The Woman Who Rides like a Man, Atheneum, 1986.
Lioness Rampant, Atheneum, 1988.

"THE IMMORTALS" SERIES

Wild Magic, Atheneum, 1992.
Wolf-Speaker, Atheneum, 1994.
The Emperor Mage, Atheneum, 1995.
The Realms of the Gods, Atheneum, 1996.

"CIRCLE OF MAGIC" SERIES

Sandry's Book, Scholastic, 1996.
Tris's Book, Scholastic, 1998.
Daja's Book, Scholastic, 1998.
Briar's Book, Scholastic, in press.

OTHER

(Contributor) Steve Ditlea, editor, *Digital Deli*, Workman, 1984.
(Contributor) Douglas Hill, editor, *Planetfall*, Oxford University Press, 1985.

Author of radio scripts aired on National Public Radio, 1987-89. Contributor to periodicals, including *Christian Century* and *School Library Journal*.

Pierce's works have been translated into German, Danish, and Spanish.

■ Sidelights

As a youngster, Tamora Pierce often turned to books for comfort. She now hopes that young readers will do the same with her works—fantasy novels featuring strong female protagonists. "I enjoy writing for teenagers," Pierce once explained to *Something about the Author (SATA)*, "because I feel I help to make life easier for kids who are like I was." Pierce told *Twentieth-Century Young Adult Writers* that readers sometimes send her the kind of letters that she might have written as a teenager to the writers who inspired her and helped her to get through rough times; the author said that she find this particularly rewarding.

Pierce was born December 13, 1954, to Wayne and Jacqueline Pierce, who divorced when she was twelve. Pierce had attended eleven schools by the time she graduated from high school. She sought solace and friendship in books. "Books were my constant friends," she recalled in the *Seventh Book of Junior Authors and Illustrators*. Her father had inspired her to start writing when she was in the sixth grade, but Pierce stopped after four years. She attended the University of Pennsylvania to study psychology, and didn't return to writing until her junior year in college, when she penned a five-page short story.

After selling another story a year later, she enrolled in a fiction writing course. "I owe my career as a writer and my approach to writing to people like my writing mentor, David Bradley (a college fiction writing teacher), who taught me that writing is not an arcane and mystical process, administered by the initiate and fraught with

The sequel to *Wild Magic* finds Daine expanding her powers as she and her animal friends struggle to save their land.

obstacles, but an enjoyable pastime that gives other people as much pleasure as it does me," Pierce once told *SATA*. "I enjoy telling stories, and, although some of my topics are grim, people get caught up in them."

On the advice of Bradley, Pierce began writing a novel. Putting her psychology degree on hold, she tried to get the 732-page work published: *The Song of the Lioness*, about an adventurous young woman named Alanna. During this time, Pierce took a number of "rent-paying" jobs, which included measuring and drawing scales of houses, reviewing martial arts movies for a magazine, reading manuscripts for Silhouette romances, tutoring high school students, and working as a tobacco farm laborer. She eventually moved in with her father and stepmother in Idaho and landed a job as a housemother in a group home for teen girls. In pursuit of her literary career, Pierce then moved to Manhattan, and on the advice of her agent she turned her novel into four books for teenagers.

A turning point in her life came when she worked as a secretary and helped to start a radio comedy and production company while she was rewriting Alanna's story. It was there that she met her husband, Tim Liebe, an actor, video maker, and writer. Working at the radio company also exposed her to an array of talent among the actors, writers, singers, dancers, and artists. It taught her that all creativity "springs from the same place, and that, to keep the mind limber, a wide variety of input, from as many sources as possible, is necessary," as Pierce explained in the *Seventh Book of Junior Authors and Illustrators*.

In this first of four books in the "Circle of Magic" series, four young people with strange powers are taken to a community where they are taught to make use of their unique gifts.

Secret Identity Revealed

Before Pierce began writing her fantasy works, she studied the ancient cultures and arts that often wind themselves through her imaginative plots for young readers. The first novel in Pierce's "Song of the Lioness" quartet, the 1983 work *Alanna: The First Adventure*, features Alanna, a young woman who disguises herself as a man in order to train as a knight. She then uses her physical strength and her capabilities as a healer to serve Prince Jonathan and engage in numerous medieval adventures.

The book focuses on the character's determination to avoid the traditional fate of young women her age: life in a secluded convent. Instead, she cuts her hair, binds her breasts, and, as "Alan," changes identities with her brother and begins training to become a knight in the service of her country's king. During her grueling education, she becomes close friends with Prince Jonathan, who does not know that his favorite knight-in-training is, in fact, a young woman. Only during a battle in the forbidding Black City does the prince discover Alanna's true gender; on the pair's return to the palace he makes her his squire regardless.

In Pierce's second novel, the highly praised *In the Hand of the Goddess*, Alanna, now a squire, struggles to master the skills she will need to survive her test for knighthood in the Chamber of the Ordeal. She goes to war against a neighboring country and clashes repeatedly with Duke Roger, an urbane and devious man who is determined to usurp the throne from his cousin, Prince Jonathan. Successful in her efforts to protect Jonathan despite the duke's attempts to get rid of her, she eventually decides to leave royal service and journey out into the world in search of further adventures. In a *School Library Journal* review, Isabel Soffer praised Pierce's Alanna series as "sprightly, filled with adventure and marvelously satisfying." Barbara Evans, in *Voice of Youth Advocates*, stated that the book "will appeal to a wide range of readers because of the combination of mystical fantasy and science fiction."

In *The Woman Who Rides like a Man,* the third installment of "Song of the Lioness," Alanna is on her own. With her servant Coram Smythesson and Faithful, her cat, she encounters a tribe of desert warriors called the Bazhir. Proving her worth in physical combat, she is accepted by the Bazhir and ultimately becomes their shaman, or wizard. Alanna broadens the outlook of these desert people, raising a few women of the tribe to an equal level with the men before moving on to other adventures. And in the final volume of the quartet, *Lioness Rampant,* the stubborn heroine has become legendary for her skills in battle and for her magical powers; now she goes on a quest for the King of Tortall. Ascending to the Roof of the World after encountering numerous trials and challenges, she attempts to claim the Dominion Jewel, a precious stone said to give its bearer the power to do good. In addition to adventure, she also encounters love in the person of Liam, a warrior known far and wide as the Shang Dragon; however, his dislike of her magical powers makes their relationship a fragile one. A critic in *Kirkus Reviews* referred to the story as an "extended superheroes comic, full of slam-bam action interposed with musings about the meaning of life." Calling Pierce a "great storyteller," a *Junior Bookshelf* reviewer praised the series' inventive characters in particular.

Magic Abounds

Magic and mystics always interested Pierce, who once worked as an instructor in the history of witchcraft at the University of Pennsylvania's Free Woman's University. Pierce's second series, "The Immortals," began in 1992 with the novel *Wild*

If you enjoy the works of Tamora Pierce, you may also want to check out the following books and films:

Robert Jordan's "Wheel of Time" series, 1990—.
Tanith Lee, *The Black Unicorn*, 1991.
Shirley Rousseau Murphy, *The Catsworld Portal*, 1992.
Ladyhawke, an adventure fantasy starring Michelle Pfeiffer, 1985.

Magic. Although Alanna makes an appearance in the novel, the new protagonist is a thirteen-year-old orphan named Daine, who has an unexplained empathy with wild creatures and a second sense that allows her to foresee danger. In fact, she is in danger of reverting to a wild creature herself until the wizard Numair teaches her to control and channel her "wild magic." Daine then uses her magical powers to stop evil humans from coercing the newly arrived Immortals—dragons, griffins, spidrens, and Stormwings—to help them accomplish destructive purposes. Called "a dynamic story sure to engross fantasy fans" by Sally Estes in *Booklist, Wild Magic* was praised by Anne A. Flowers, who maintained in her *Horn Book* review that readers will "find in Daine a strong heroine whose humble beginning makes her well-deserved rewards even more gratifying."

Wolf-Speaker continues the adventures of Daine as the fourteen year old and her mentor, the mage Numair, join a wolf pack that is at odds with humans. Men, working for an evil wizard named Tristan, have discovered opals in the wolves' hunting lands in Dunlath Valley. They scramble for the precious gems, polluting the mine and destroying the ecosystem. Hunted by Stormwings controlled by Tristan, Daine and her companions must use all their powers, including shape changing, to stop the impending ecological catastrophe. "Daine is a super new heroine who makes this action-packed fantasy a joy to read," Mary L. Adams wrote in *Voice of Youth Advocates.* Mary Harris Veeder, in *Booklist,* was more critical when she wrote that "Suspense is stronger than characterization here, but the exploration of diverse animal personalities will intrigue readers." Bonnie Kunzel stated in her *School Library Journal* review that *Wolf-*

Speaker "is a compulsively readable novel that YAs won't be able to put down until the final battle is over and good triumphs. Pierce's faithful readers as well as any action-adventure or animal fantasy fans will be delighted with this new series."

Daine's adventures continue in other "Immortals" novels, which include *The Emperor Mage*. Patricia A. Dollisch in *School Library Journal* said Pierce "skillfully creates a sense of time and place that enhances the plot and transforms a good read into a page turner." That book was followed by *The Realms of the Gods*, the concluding novel of the series in which Pierce's young female protagonist convinces dragons and other Immortal creatures to fight on her side against the powers of evil. Mary Jo Drungil in *School Library Journal* concluded that fans of Pierce's earlier titles "will appreciate this satisfying conclusion."

Magic also plays an important role in Pierce's fantasy series, "Circle of Magic." In *Sandry's Book*, "a rich and satisfying read," according to a *Kirkus Reviews* critic, Sandry, Daja, Briar, and Trisana—four young people from various walks of life—meet and become friends while living in a temple community. As the four protagonists overcome the negative aspects of their lives, they learn a variety of crafts as well as the use of their unique powers, including magic. While Susan Dunn in *Voice of Youth Advocates* found weaknesses in the work, she declared, "Pierce can do no wrong." The "Circle of Magic" series also includes *Tris's Book* and *Daja's Book*; *Briar's Book* is expected to be published in 1999.

Pierce has strong feelings about series books. She wrote in an autobiographical sketch that appears on her Web site, "In life we know people over years or even decades. Series books enable writers to get some of that feel to the reader's acquaintance with characters: as in life, we follow their doings over time and through periods where they behave better than during others. Some critics argue that sticking to the same characters over several books is "safe": it is just about as safe as real life, when people you know change, growing away from you or closer."

A Tamer Existence

Pierce's personal life is somewhat more mundane than those of the characters she writes about.

"Occasionally I rescue hurt or homeless animals in a local park . . . [I] visit schools as often as I can, and read, read, read," Pierce told *SATA*. A woman with wide-ranging interests, she focuses her research in specific areas, many of which eventually become incorporated into her fantasy novels for teens. "I am interested in medieval customs, life, and chivalry," she told *SATA*. Pierce also studies such diverse topics as Japanese, Central Asian, and Arabic history and culture, wildlife and nature, crime, the American Civil War, the conflicts between Islam and Christianity in the Middle Ages, the Renaissance, martial arts cinema, film writing and production, history of the 1960s and 1970s, and the history of Hungary, Wallachia, and the Ottoman Empire in the 1400s and 1500s.

Pierce lives in Manhattan with her husband, Liebe, their cats and budgies, and "a floating population of rescued wildlife," Pierce said in her Web site. (She also has an online fan club.) "Having stumbled into writing for teenagers, I've learned that I love it, and I plan to keep doing it. When a kid tells you that your books have made a difference in her or his life, you truly have something to be proud of."

■ Works Cited

Adams, Mary L., review of *Wolf-Speaker, Voice of Youth Advocates,* August, 1994, p. 159.

Dollisch, Patricia, review of *Emperor Mage, School Library Journal,* July, 1995, p. 80.

Drungil, Mary Jo, review of *The Realms of the Gods, School Library Journal,* November, 1996, p. 124.

Dunn, Susan, review of *Sandry's Book, Voice of Youth Advocates,* December, 1997, p. 327.

Estes, Sally, review of *Wild Magic, Booklist,* October 15, 1992, p. 419.

Evans, Barbara, review of *In the Hand of the Goddess, Voice of Youth Advocates,* April, 1985, p. 56.

Flowers, Anne A., review of *Wild Magic, Horn Book,* January-February, 1993, p. 93.

Kunzel, Bonnie, "The Call of the Wild: YAs Running with the Wolves," *School Library Journal,* August, 1995, pp. 37-38.

Review of *Lioness Rampant, Kirkus Reviews,* August 1, 1988, pp. 1154-55.

Pierce, Tamora, comments in *Seventh Book of Junior Authors and Illustrators,* edited by Sally Holmes Holtze, H. W. Wilson, 1996, pp. 248-50.

Pierce, Tamora, comments in *Something about the Author,* Volume 96, Gale, 1997, p. 149.

Pierce, Tamora, comments in *Twentieth-Century Young Adult Writers*, 1st edition, St. James Press, 1994, pp. 534-35.

Pierce, Tamora, autobiographical sketch posted on Web site at http://www.sff.net/people/Tamora.pierce/.

Review of *Sandry's Book, Kirkus Reviews,* July 15, 1997, p. 1115.

Soffer, Isabel, review of *In the Hand of the Goddess, School Library Journal,* December, 1984.

Veeder, Mary Harris, review of *Wolf-Speaker, Booklist,* March 15, 1994, p. 1344.

Review of *The Woman Who Rides like a Man, Junior Bookshelf,* October, 1989, p. 243.

■ For More Information See

BOOKS

The Encyclopedia of Fantasy, St. Martin's Press, 1997.

Speaking for Ourselves II: More Autobiographical Sketches by Notable Authors of Books for Young Adults, National Council of Teachers of English, 1993.

PERIODICALS

Booklist, June 1-15, 1995, p. 1757; October 15, 1996, p. 414.

Bulletin of the Center for Children's Books, November, 1984, p. 53; April, 1986, p. 156; April, 1998, p. 292.

Horn Book, May-June, 1986, pp. 333-34; March-April, 1989, p. 234; September-October, 1994, p. 613; July-August, 1995, p. 485.

Kirkus Reviews, October 15, 1992, p. 1314.

Voice of Youth Advocates, April, 1985, p. 56; December, 1988, p. 248; April, 1995, p. 14.*

—*Sketch by Diane Andreassi*

Kim Stanley Robinson

■ Personal

Born March 23, 1952, in Waukegan, IL; married Lisa Howland Nowell, 1982; two children. *Education:* University of California, San Diego, B.A. (literature), 1974, Ph.D. (literature), 1982; Boston University, M.A. (English), 1975.

■ Addresses

Agent—Ralph Vicinanza, 111 Eighth Ave., New York, NY 10011.

■ Career

Writer; visiting lecturer at University of California, San Diego, 1982 and 1985, and University of California, Davis, 1982-84 and 1985.

■ Awards, Honors

Nebula Award nomination, Science Fiction Writers of America, 1981, for "Venice Drowned," 1983, for "Black Air," 1984, for *The Wild Shore* and "Lucky Strike," 1986, for "Escape from Kathmandu," 1990, for "Before I Wake," 1992, for "Vinland the Dream," and 1994, for *Green Mars;* Hugo Award nomination, World Science Fiction Society, 1983, for "To Leave A Mark," 1984, for "Black Air," 1985, for "Lucky Strike" and "Ridge Running," 1986, for "Green Mars," 1987, for "Escape from Kathmandu," 1988, for "The Blind Geometer" and "Mother Goddess of the World," 1991, for "A Short, Sharp Shock," and 1993, for *Red Mars;* World Fantasy Award for best novella, World Fantasy Convention, 1983, for "Black Air"; Locus Award for best first novel, *Locus* magazine, 1985, for *The Wild Shore;* Nebula Award for best novella, 1987, for "The Blind Geometer," and for best novel, 1993, for *Red Mars;* John W. Campbell Award, 1991; British Science Fiction Award, 1992; Hugo Award for best novel, 1994, for *Green Mars,* and 1997, for *Blue Mars;* National Science Foundation grant for study in Antarctica, 1995.

■ Writings

NOVELS

The Wild Shore, Ace, 1984.
Icehenge, Ace, 1984.
The Memory of Whiteness: A Scientific Romance, Tor, 1985.
The Gold Coast, Tor, 1988.
Pacific Edge, Tor, 1990.

A Short, Sharp Shock, illustrations by Arnie Fenner, M. V. Ziesing, 1990.
Red Mars, Bantam, 1993.
Green Mars, Bantam, 1994.
Blue Mars, Bantam, 1996.
Antarctica, Bantam, 1998.

SHORT STORIES

The Blind Geometer, illustrated by Judy King-Rieniets, Cheap Street, 1986.
The Planet on the Table, Tor, 1986.
Black Air, Pulphouse, 1991.
Remaking History, Tor, 1991.
A Sensitive Dependence on Initial Conditions, Pulphouse, 1991.
Escape from Kathmandu, Orb, 1994.
Remaking History and Other Stories, Orb, 1994.

Stories represented in anthologies, including *Orbit 18* and *Orbit 19,* both edited by Damon Knight, Harper, 1975 and 1977; *Clarion SF,* edited by Kate Wilhelm, Berkley, 1977; *Universe 11, Universe 12, Universe 13, Universe 14,* and *Universe 15,* all edited by Terry Carr, Doubleday, 1981-85; and *The Year's Best Science Fiction 1,* edited by Gardner Dozois and Jim Frenkel, Bluejay Books, 1984. Contributor of stories to science fiction magazines, including *Isaac Asimov's Science Fiction Magazine.*

OTHER

The Novels of Philip K. Dick, UMI Research Press, 1984.
Editor, *Future Primitive: The New Ectopias,* Tor, 1994.

■ Work in Progress

A Martian Romance, a collection of stories and essays.

■ Sidelights

"The colored sands in their patterns, the fluted and scalloped canyon walls, the volcanoes rising right through the sky, the rubbled rock of the chaotic terrain, the infinity of craters, ringed emblems of the planet's beginning. . . . The visible language of nature's mineral existence.

"Mineral; not animal, nor vegetable, nor viral. It could have happened but it didn't. There was never any spontaneous generation out of the clays or the sulphuric hot springs; no spore falling out of space, no touch of a god; whatever starts life (for we do not know), it did not happen on Mars. Mars rolled, proof of the otherness of the world, of its stony vitality."

(Kim Stanley Robinson, *Red Mars*)

There are no little green men on the Mars of science fiction writer Kim Stanley Robinson. His is the Mars of the satellite photos and geologic surveys of NASA's Mariner and Viking missions. It is the Mars of hard science brought to life through human endeavors and pulsed by human history, culture, politics, and ethics, all of which Robinson explores in his epic trilogy about the twenty-first-century colonization of Mars. That trilogy, according to Edward James in the *Times Literary Supplement,* has established Robinson "as the pre-eminent contemporary practitioner of science fiction. He has earned that position by taking the central tenet of science fiction—the extrapolation of current trends and beliefs into the construction of a future history—to greater lengths than any of his predecessors, and the Mars books are likely to be the touchstone of what is possible in the genre for a long time to come."

Before setting out for the red planet, Robinson had already blazed his own trail into science fiction with consistently well-received short stories, novellas, and novels, including a trilogy depicting three near-future versions of southern California. Notable throughout his work is a narrative style informed by history and literature, one which relies heavily on setting and which bypasses science fiction's typical action-plotting devices in favor of telling stories through thematic extrapolation, character study, and multiple, often conflicting, points of view. The scientific and technical detail, interdisciplinary themes, and adult relationships depicted in Robinson's work both require and reward reader maturity. "The novels and short stories of Kim Stanley Robinson constitute one of the most impressive bodies of work in modern science fiction," hailed Gerald Jonas in the *New York Times Book Review,* adding in a later critique, "If I had to choose one writer whose work will set the standard for science fiction in the future, it would be Kim Stanley Robinson."

Given the rigorous scientific detail built into his best known work, it may be surprising to learn that Robinson is not a scientist. Instead, his credentials are decidedly literary. Born in Waukegan, Illinois, in 1952, Robinson grew up in Orange County, California and graduated from the University of California, San Diego in 1974 with a degree in literature. He went on to earn a master's degree in English from Boston University the following year, and then returned to the University of California, San Diego to earn a doctorate in literature in 1982, writing his dissertation on the novels of Philip K. Dick. (Dick, who died in 1982, is best known for his 1968 novel *Do Androids Dream of Electric Sheep?*, on which the 1982 movie *Bladerunner* was based, and for his

1962 Hugo Award-winner, *The Man in the High Castle*. Dick's science fiction is characterized by metaphysical concerns and psychological intensity; the changing points of view in Robinson's narrative hearken those used by Dick.)

Many of Robinson's short stories were first published in the 1970s and early 1980s in the science fiction journals *Orbit* and *Universe*, garnering him major award nominations. Some of Robinson's best short stories have been incorporated into longer works, notably *Icehenge* (based on his stories "On the North Pole of Pluto" and "To Leave a Mark") and *The Memory of Whiteness: A Scientific Romance* (based on the story "In Pierson's Orchestra"). Other best-known shorter works by Robinson are *Escape from Kathmandu*, four novella-length stories which tell of the Himalayan adventures of two American expatriates, and *A Short, Sharp Shock*, a fantasy novella in which a man wakes up in a strange world surrounded by water and can remember nothing but a vanished woman with whom he washed up on the beach. His becomes a dream-like quest through a society of peaceful tree people and brutal "spine kings" as he seeks out answers, identity, and his unknown companion. Robinson's first novel, *The Wild Shore*, was published in 1984, and the following year, he left his university teaching job in order to devote himself to world travel and a full-time writing career.

WINNER OF THE 1993 NEBULA AWARD FOR BEST NOVEL

RED MARS

"A STAGGERING BOOK... THE BEST NOVEL ON THE COLONIZATION OF MARS THAT HAS EVER BEEN WRITTEN. IT SHOULD BE REQUIRED READING FOR THE COLONISTS OF THE NEXT CENTURY." —Arthur C. Clarke

KIM STANLEY ROBINSON

BESTSELLING AUTHOR OF *BLUE MARS*

One hundred settlers are sent to Mars to give the planet an Earth-like atmosphere in Robinson's Nebula Award-winning story.

Before Mars, Three Californias

The Wild Shore was chosen to relaunch the discontinued Ace Specials, a line of cutting-edge science fiction novels first published in the 1960s by Ace Books. It and Robinson's subsequent *The Gold Coast* (1988) and *Pacific Edge* (1990) comprise the "Orange County" trilogy, which, according to David P. Snider in *Voice of Youth Advocates*, is in its entirety "an excellent exercise in what speculative fiction is all about: 'What if?'"

What if there were a nuclear disaster? Described by numerous reviewers as a Huckleberry Finn-like frontier novel, *The Wild Shore* features a seventeen-year-old narrator named Henry who is making his way into adulthood in an America destroyed decades ago by a nuclear holocaust. Since the country is under a United Nations quarantine and barred from redeveloping its technology, Henry and his friend Steve know little about

America than what they can see from their isolated coastal village and what they hear in the past-glorifying stories of old-timers. As Henry strikes out to pursue his own adventures and discoveries in a dangerous new world, a novel that appears on the surface to be yet another post-nuclear disaster tale becomes a character-rich coming-of-age story. "By the novel's end, Henry's family and friends have been brought to life with a vivid depth rarely encountered in science fiction," remarked Stephen P. Brown in the *Washington Post Book World.* "Robinson's approach to storytelling is the traditional literary one, in its best sense, rather than the unique tone science fiction has developed in years of trying to translate commercial values into literature," wrote Algis Budrys in the *Magazine of Fantasy and Science Fiction.* Budrys called *The Wild Shore* "a remarkably powerful piece of work."

Its follow-up, *The Gold Coast,* also depicts a dystopian Orange County, but one that tries to answer a different question: What might America be like in the next century if current trends continue? Robinson's answer is a freeway-tracked, polluted, overdeveloped, overpopulated, defense-industry-dependent society. Wandering through it is a disconnected young poet named Jim McPherson, who, with his zoned-out friends, seeks to dull his idealistic pangs with designer drugs and casual sex. At last trying to take meaningful action in his life, he rebels against the establishment beliefs of his parents—his father is an aerospace engineer and his mother a devout Christian—by joining a revolutionary group that targets weapons manufacturers, including his father's employer. "*The Gold Coast* is ambitious, angry, eccentric," wrote T. Jefferson Parker in the *Los Angeles Times Book Review.* Though he called Robinson's dialogue writing weak, he concluded that "Robinson has succeeded at a novelist's toughest challenge: He's made us look at the world around us. This isn't escapist stuff—it sends you straight into a confrontation with yourself."

In the trilogy's concluding book, *Pacific Edge,* Robinson creates his version of utopia, a place that is not yet perfect but moving in that direction. This novel's El Modena, California, is part of a new society brought about by peaceful revolution, where multinational corporations no longer rule and technology serves people's simpler, ecology-friendly lifestyles. Newly elected town councilman Kevin finds himself in the midst of conflict, how-

The author received the 1994 Hugo Award for this sequel to *Red Mars,* in which members of the next generation of settlers fight to preserve Mars in its natural state.

ever, when water-rights issues and the potential commercial development of a pristine hillside threaten to split the community. The political troubles are further complicated by personal relationships between allies and opponents. Wrote Jonas in the *New York Times Book Review,* "through a blend of dirt-under-the fingernails naturalism and lyrical magical realism, [Robinson] invites us to share his characters' intensely personal, intensely local attachment to what they have. The result is a bittersweet utopia that may shame you into entertaining new hope for the future."

Robinson is an avid mountain trekker who loves wilderness landscapes, and much in his fiction seeks to shed light on the disconnection he sees between urban life and nature. "I spend as much time as I can in the wilderness," he told Sebastian Cooke in an *Eidolon* interview. "It's got me thinking about the environmental catastrophe we're sitting on the edge of and solutions to that. It doesn't make any sense just to throw up your hands in despair and say, 'The world is doomed!'" Robinson does not see environmental movements like those suggested in *Pacific Edge* as utopian. "There will always be competing interests that will be viciously fought over . . . to pretend otherwise is what makes people uninterested," Robinson told Cooke.

In Living Color: Red, Green, Blue

Just such conflicting human interests drive Robinson's award-winning and best-selling "Mars" trilogy, described by a critic in *Science Fiction Weekly* as "what might be one of the grandest literary science fiction epics to date." Totaling some 1,600 pages and taking six years to write, *Red Mars*, *Green Mars*, and *Blue Mars* chronicle human efforts over a period of several hundred years to colonize and "terraform" Mars.

The term terraforming was coined in 1938 by science fiction writer Jack Williamson, and refers to the process of creating an Earth-like biosphere on a dead planet, so that life can be introduced and sustained there. "I got interested in the whole idea because Mars is one of the best candidates for terraformation that you can possibly imagine: its conditions are close to those of Earth in terms of gravity, it's got water and it also contains all the various volatile chemicals to create an atmosphere," Robinson explained in an on-line interview for HarperCollins, adding that "It has now become clear that this isn't just science fiction, or pie in the sky, it's something that could be done with the science and technology that we have now."

The colors in the books' titles represent the stages of Martian transformation: red for its original state, green for the successful introduction of plant life there, and blue for eventual creation of oceans and an oxygen-enriched atmosphere. "Having decided to write a novel about the terraforming of Mars, I was committed to a long novel. The long novel, or the Really Long Novel, is another subgenre slightly different from the novel, like the novella in the other direction," Robinson explained in an on-line question and answer session for *Science Fiction Weekly.*

Robinson began the "Mars" trilogy with just twenty or so pages of notes—ideas and dialogue out of which he hoped to create a book. "Then, as I went along, the story as written began to require that other things happen later in it. This is the great interest of novel writing; 20 pages of image fragments have to be worked out into 1,600 pages of narrative. A lot of it necessarily gets worked out en route, and some of what appears late in the game is very surprising to me," he said in *Science Fiction Weekly.* Once you've mastered the science, colonizing Mars sounds straightforward enough, until you delve, as Robinson so thoroughly does, into another of its key components: humanity. As Faren Miller wrote in *Locus* magazine, the central question behind Robinson's "Mars" trilogy is as social and cultural as it is scientific: "As planets are transformed, human societies change as well—but are the social transformations entirely controlled, rational, and to the good?"

A Great Human Project?

"December 21st, 2026: they were moving faster than anyone in history. They were on their way. It was the beginning of a nine-month voyage—or of a voyage that would last the rest of their lives. They were on their own." Thus, in *Red Mars*, the first colonists—100 carefully selected scientists who hold a diversity of views about the political and ethical aspects of their mission—journey to Earth's frigid, lifeless neighbor to create settlements and begin a terraforming process that will take hundreds of years to complete. "The science of *Red Mars* is impeccably researched, convincing, and often thrilling in its moments of peril and grand implications," observed Miller in *Locus.* Liaisons and clashes soon emerge between strong personalities like those of team leaders Frank Chalmers and Maya Toitova, early Mars pioneer John Boone, political renegade Arkady Bogdanov, and subversive ecologist Hiroko Ao, among others.

Perhaps most fierce and divisive is the argument that persists throughout the trilogy: whether Mars should be terraformed as quickly and fully as possible, a position advocated by the "Green" character Sax Russell and strongly supported by Earth governments, or whether its natural environment and evolution should be studied and preserved, a less popular position held by geologist Ann Clayborne and her "Red" followers. By the end, initial visions for Mars's future are nearly subsumed by the multicultural complexities and mixed motives of an influx of new settlers, which lead to acts of sabotage and ultimately, a violent revolt. "In the debate over terraforming and its consequences, Mr. Robinson has all the makings of a philosophical novel of suspense. The stakes are high, the sides are shrewdly drawn, the players on both sides range from politically naive idealists to ambitious manipulators without discernible scruples," wrote Jonas in the *New York Times Book Review.*

Robinson's own views on the terraforming issue "are almost perfectly split down the middle, which I think is one of the driving emotional forces in me for writing" the "Mars" trilogy, he told Cooke in *Eidolon.* "There's a part of me that thinks that terraforming is a beautiful spiritual, almost religious project and that to be able to walk around on Mars in the open air . . . is absolutely one of the great human projects and ought to be done." He added, however, that he also thought this was a desecration of a unique, beautiful landscape. The different views give energy to the characters and the argument.

Red Mars begins with a murder in an established Martian settlement, then backtracks to the beginning of the colonization story so that readers may trace the motive, a plot device that some reviewers found faulty. Many note, however, that plot is less important to Robinson than point of view: Each chapter is told from the perspective of a different character, allowing Robinson to put forth a society of views that is in keeping with the scale of the terraforming effort. "His point is the reshaping of a world; people are hardly more than footnotes, and if their motives ultimately seem a little thin and their actions futile, never mind," concluded Tom Easton in *Analog: Science Fiction/ Science Fact.*

The colonists are ultimately upstaged, many conclude, by Mars itself, through Robinson's descriptive landscaping and the science and technology he uses to bring Mars to life. "On one level, the planet itself becomes a major character," observed Jonas in the *New York Times Book Review.* The reader feels the changes in the atmosphere and the "beauty of this fundamentally inhuman setting and its effect on its all-too-human inhabitants," Jonas continued.

Green Mars begins about twenty years later and it chronicles the next forty years of life on Mars. Due to anti-aging treatments, many of the "first 100" characters are still around, though driven underground by the failed rebellion that closes *Red Mars.* Focusing on the coming-of-age journey of a

BLUE MARS

"A LANDMARK IN THE HISTORY OF THE GENRE."
—The New York Times Book Review

KIM STANLEY ROBINSON

HUGO AND NEBULA AWARD-WINNING AUTHOR OF *GREEN MARS*

Robinson completes his "Mars" trilogy with the planet divided into warring factions and facing overpopulation as Earth becomes flooded and increasingly polluted.

new young character, Nirgal, who has grown up in a southern colony established by rebel Hiroko Ao, the plot recalls some of the pioneering spirit of *Red Mars*. For the most part, however, *Green Mars* is devoted to the process of creating a central Martian government out of its numerous colonies. It concludes with revolutionary war and an environmental disaster on Earth.

Some critics found that *Green Mars* suffers from "the middle book problem," meaning the way in which second books in trilogies often struggle to keep up the established pace while at the same time trying to become more than just a bridge between the first and final books. "There are enough kidnappings, murders, rescues, disasters, and acts of sabotage to keep it all exciting, but the tale is driven by the problems of gaining independence from both earthly governments and the giant corporations who continually seek ways of exploiting the Martian colony. This leads to long passages of political and economic debate that slow down Robinson's momentum," remarked Gary K. Wolfe in *Locus*.

"The breadth of Robinson's interests makes for a dense and intellectually ambitious book: psychology, political-economic theory, history, the planetary sciences and ecology, and the interactions of all these," wrote Russell Letson, also in *Locus*. "Robinson often shows a reluctance to depend on plot as the driving force of a narrative," he added. With most of the action taking place off stage, so to speak, "It's as if Robinson were avoiding as much of the vulgarity of action as he could and still have a narrative in which crucial events occur. What we get instead is a book tied together by thematics and character," wrote Letson.

Having successfully gained independence from Earth, Martian society's biggest threat in *Blue Mars* is the ongoing battling between the Reds, who want to sever ties with Earth and protect what's left of untouched Mars, and the Greens who want to continue altering the planet for human use. At the risk of setting an ice age in motion, Green leader Sax Russell attempts to make peace with Red leader Ann Clayborne by removing from orbit the mirrors that create the atmospheric heat necessary for terraforming. As a result, the rival factions must together begin hammering out an appropriate government for themselves. Meanwhile, Earth faces a population crisis and impending planetary flooding, as its polar cap melts and

If you enjoy the works of Kim Stanley Robinson, you may also want to check out the following books and films:

Greg Bear, *Moving Mars*, 1993.
Ray Bradbury, *The Martian Chronicles*, 1950.
Frederik Pohl, *Mars Plus*, 1994.
Total Recall, starring Arnold Schwarzenegger, 1990.

ocean levels rise due to global warming. The crisis puts pressure on Mars to allow for the immigration of Terran refugees and leads to further Martian conflict. Describing *Blue Mars* in a Bantam Double Day on-line feature, Robinson said, "Events branch out as in a genealogical chart, and the problem is to keep a handle on them all. . . . And on a personal level, the characters we began with in *Red Mars* are getting very, very old, with interesting results."

"Robinson is as meticulous with his details as ever, whether he's describing the mechanisms of memory, the political and economic theories behind the new Martian constitution, or his characters' internal emotional and mental struggles," wrote Clinton Lawrence in *Science Fiction Weekly*, adding, "In *Blue Mars* it becomes clear that Robinson is writing about humanity's next great cultural leap as much as he is writing about the colonization of Mars."

Not a Bolt Hole

As vivid a reality as Robinson makes Martian colonization seem, he does not in the end believe Mars is a means of escaping Earth's current and impending environmental and population problems. "The only solutions are going to be right here on Earth. Mars can help as experiment in planetary engineering—what we learn there will be applicable here—but it cannot help us as a new physical space, because the problems will be severe in the next hundred years, and Mars cannot be made inhabitable in less than 300 years; probably more like 3,000. . . . Mars is a mirror, not a bolt hole," Robinson said in *Science Fiction Weekly*.

As a follow-up to his trilogy, Robinson is compiling *A Martian Romance*, a volume of stories and essays about Mars resulting from his trilogy-writing experiences. "I noticed rereading the Mars books, which I'd never done before, that there are a lot of opportunities for interweaving short stories that will describe interesting moments along the way that the novel itself didn't talk about," Robinson told Elisabeth Sherwin in the *Davis Enterprise,* adding, "I don't want to leave Mars, that's why I'm doing this companion book."

Then, he is on to another novel project, *Antarctica,* new territory that is closer to home but no less harsh or complex. In 1995, Robinson won a National Science Foundation grant—the first science fiction writer to do so—and spent six weeks in Antarctica, accompanying a glacier research team on field work and visiting the McMurdo American base camp there. With Antarctica's oil riches at stake, the potential environmental, political, and territorial conflicts of the twenty-first century set the stage for his *Antarctica.*

"The issues that Robinson explores in his fiction reflect a world view that is initially dark but ultimately hopeful," Sherwin wrote in an *Enterprise* column, in which Robinson told her, "I'm not cheerful about the future. Historically, the world has not responded well to crises but I want to remain hopeful. We have the spiritual and technical abilities to pull through . . . we could get in balance with the environment and manage the population."

Science fiction, Robinson believes, has a role to play in political discourse, by using the future as a way to view the present. "It's some kind of funhouse mirror where you exaggerate some parts and minimize others depending on what you're talking about at the time," Robinson explained in the HarperCollins interview. "Future fictions are not truly about the future which will always be different to what any science fiction novel talks about. So these novels are not predictions, but ways of talking about the situation now and what it might become. Novels about the future deal with what we might work towards and what we might try to guard against."

■ Works Cited

Brown, Stephen P., review of *The Wild Shore, Washington Post Book World,* April 22, 1984, p. 11.

Budrys, Algis, review of *The Wild Shore, Magazine of Fantasy and Science Fiction,* May, 1984, pp. 38, 40.

Cooke, Sebastian, "An Earth-Man With a Mission," *Eidolon,* July, 1993.

Easton, Tom, review of *Red Mars, Analog: Science Fiction/Science Fact,* August, 1993, p. 249.

James, Edward, "The Landscape of Mars," *Times Literary Supplement,* May 3, 1996, p. 23.

Jonas, Gerald, review of *Pacific Edge, New York Times Book Review,* December 9, 1990, p. 32.

Jonas, Gerald, review of *Red Mars, New York Times Book Review,* January 31, 1993, p. 25.

Jonas, Gerald, review of *Blue Mars, New York Times Book Review,* June 30, 1996, p. 28.

"Kim Stanley Robinson: The Man from Mars," from HarperCollins on-line feature at http://www.harpercollins.co.uk/voyager/intervws.

Lawrence, Clinton, review of *Blue Mars, Science Fiction Weekly,* June 17, 1996.

Letson, Russell, review of *Green Mars, Locus,* November, 1993, p. 19.

Miller, Faren, review of *Red Mars, Locus,* October, 1992, pp. 19, 21.

Parker, T. Jefferson, "Orange County, Thus Will You Live," *Los Angeles Times Book Review,* March 13, 1988, p. 6.

Robinson, Kim Stanley, online interview from Bantam Doubleday Dell Online at http://www.bdd.com.

Robinson, Kim Stanley, *Red Mars,* Bantam, 1993.

Robinson, Kim Stanley, interview in *Science Fiction Weekly,* June 17, 1996.

Sherwin, Elisabeth, "Robinson Completes Mars Trilogy, Turns to Antarctica," *Davis Enterprise,* January 21, 1996.

Sherwin, Elisabeth, "Next Stop for Mars Junkies? How About 'Antarctica'," *Davis Enterprise,* November 2, 1997.

Snider, David P., review of *Pacific Edge, Voice of Youth Advocates,* June, 1991, p. 113.

Wolfe, Gary K., review of *Green Mars, Locus,* November, 1993, p. 55.

■ For More Information See

BOOKS

Contemporary Literary Criticism, Volume 34, Gale, 1985.

St. James Guide to Science Fiction Writers, Fourth Edition, St. James Press, 1996.

PERIODICALS

Analog: Science Fiction/Science Fact, September, 1988; April, 1990; August, 1990.

Los Angeles Times Book Review, February 3, 1991.

New York Times Book Review, October 20, 1985; September 21, 1986; May 8, 1994; July 12, 1998, p. 26.

Publishers Weekly, December 14, 1992; February 21, 1994; May 13, 1996; June 22, 1998, pp. 72-73.

School Library Journal, May, 1994; February, 1995.

Voice of Youth Advocates, October, 1994; April 1, 1997.

Washington Post Book World, August 25, 1985; February 28, 1988.

Wilson Library Bulletin, February, 1993.

—Sketch by Tracy J. Sukraw

Graham Salisbury

of Children's Book Writers and Illustrators, Women's National Book Association, American Library Association, Hawaiian Mission Children's Society.

■ Personal

Born April 11, 1944, in Philadelphia, PA; son of Henry Forester Graham (an officer in the U.S. Navy) and Barbara Twigg-Smith; married second wife, Robyn Kay Cowan, October 26, 1988; children: Sandi Weston, Miles, Ashley, Melanie, Alex, Keenan, Zachary. *Education:* California State University at Northridge, B.A. (magna cum laude), 1974; Vermont College of Norwich University, M.F.A., 1990. *Politics:* "Middle of the road."

■ Addresses

Office—319 Southwest Washington, No. 320, Portland, OR 97204. *Agent*—Emilie Jacobson, Curtis Brown Ltd., 10 Astor Pl., New York, NY 10003.

■ Career

Writer. Worked variously as a deckhand, glassbottom boat skipper, singer-songwriter, graphic artist, and teacher; manager of historic office buildings in downtown Portland, OR. *Member:* Society

■ Awards, Honors

Parents Choice Award, Bank Street College Child Study Children's Book Award, Judy Lopez Memorial Award for Children's Literature, Women's National Book Association, Best Books for Young Adults citation, American Library Association, and best books of the year citation, *School Library Journal*, all 1992, all for *Blue Skin of the Sea*; PEN/ Norma Klein Award, 1992; John Unterecker Award for Fiction, Chaminade University and Hawaii Literary Arts Council; Scott O'Dell Award for Historic Fiction, 1994, for *Under the Blood-Red Sun*.

■ Writings

Blue Skin of the Sea, Delacorte (New York City), 1992.
Under the Blood-Red Sun, Bantam (New York City), 1994.
Shark Bait, Delacorte, 1997.
Jungle Dogs, Delacorte, 1998.

Contributor to periodicals, including *Bamboo Ridge*, *Chaminade Literary Review*, *Hawaii Pacific Review*, *Journal of Youth Services in Libraries*, *Manoa: A Journal of Pacific and International Writing*, and *Northwest*.

■ Sidelights

Characterizing himself as an author who writes for and about teenage boys, Graham Salisbury has published four books: *Blue Skin of the Sea, Under the Blood-Red Sun, Shark Bait,* and *Jungle Dogs,* all of which are set on the Hawaiian islands where Salisbury was raised. In addition to an exotic island setting, his fictional coming-of-age novels feature intricate interpersonal relationships that sometimes make the task of growing up more difficult that it otherwise would be. "I've thought a lot about what my job is now, or should be, as an author of books for young readers," Salisbury

Salisbury received numerous awards for his series of interrelated stories following two young cousins growing up on the Hawaiian islands during the 1950s and 1960s.

noted in the *ALAN Review.* "I don't write to teach, preach, lecture, or criticize, but to explore. I write to make good use of the amazing English language. And if my stories show boys choosing certain life options, and the possible consequences of having chosen those options, then maybe I will have finally done something worthwhile."

While Salisbury entered the world in the city of Philadelphia, Pennsylvania—the date was April 11, 1944—generations of his family had lived far from the U.S. mainland, on the islands of Hawaii. Salisbury's ancestors were missionaries who went to the big island of Hawaii in the early nineteenth century. Salisbury's father, a young ensign in the U.S. Navy, was at Pearl Harbor during the Japanese attack on December 7, 1941; although he survived that ordeal, he would die when he was shot down with his fighter plane on April 11, 1945—his son's first birthday.

Island Upbringing

Given his family history, it is not surprising that Salisbury spent little time in Pennsylvania; he and his mother made their home in the Hawaiian islands. In turn, he has set his books on the islands as he remembers them from his childhood. "I can *feel,* even now, the rocking of my stepfather's deep-sea charter fishing boat, the hot sun on my shoulders, salt itching under my T-shirt after swimming," Salisbury once told *Something About the Author (SATA).* "I can hear the constant rumble of waves and smell the sweet aroma of steaks cooking at the hotels in the village of Kailua-Kona. I can even make myself shudder when I remember the time I got caught in quicksand in Kanehoe, Oahu, and had to wait, sinking slowly, while my friend ran for help."

Unlike many writers, Salisbury was not interested in books as a child. Because of his father's untimely death, Salisbury was raised without a solid male role model to provide guidance, and he was left with a lot of time on his hands in which to wander the islands with his friends. His mother, whom Salisbury has described as "wonderful but needy," was immersed in her own problems and was often absent from the home, both emotionally and physically. Salisbury was left to search for guidance and approval from other adults in his life: friends, relatives, teachers, and family friends.

Salisbury attended boarding school from grades seven through twelve, and this experience provided him with the structure and guidance that he had missed earlier in life. However, it wouldn't be until Salisbury's college days at California State University at Northridge, where he graduated with a bachelor's degree in 1974, that the idea of being a writer even occurred to him. "I didn't read until I was a little past thirty," Salisbury confided to *SATA*. "Sure, I escaped with Edgar Rice Burroughs and Louis L'Amour a couple of times, and I read the required *Iliad* and *Odyssey* in high school, but I didn't read of my own choice until my first son was born. Then I read Alex Haley's *Roots*, which changed my life forever." It was *Roots* that inspired Salisbury to become a voracious reader and then to write books of his own. He also went on to obtain his master in fine arts

degree at Vermont College of Norwich University in 1990.

Salisbury began by writing what he calls "memory pieces": autobiographical vignettes that eventually got stretched and shaped into fiction. The pieces retained the island setting and the themes of relationships that informed his memories—most markedly the relationship that Salisbury had always desired but never had as a boy: that between father and son. But it was the medium of fiction that would allow him full reign to use his imagination. And it was fiction writing that Salisbury enjoyed the most.

Publishes Debut Novel

Salisbury's first novel, *Blue Skin of the Sea*, was published in 1992. Composed of a series of eleven interlinking short stories, the book tells the story of two boys, Sonny Mendoza and his cousin Keo, who are growing up in Hawaii during the 1950s and 1960s, at a time when the old island ways were beginning to be lost due to the increasing influx of tourists. Keo is fearless, while Sonny, whose mother died when he was very young, is more thoughtful and introspective. But as friends the two cousins balance one another. Throughout the book, the boys learn to deal with the school bully, try to cope with their growing attraction to girls, figure out ways to earn spending money, and jump other hurdles of everyday teen life. Along the way they meet up with a Hollywood film crew, sent out to the Mendoza's corner of Hilo to film actor Spencer Tracy in *The Old Man and the Sea*. The boys, thinking that the props make the action look unrealistic, decide to educate the veteran actor in how to deal with real, rather than fake sharks. A *New York Times Book Review* critic termed *Blue Skin of the Sea* an "impressive debut," while *Five Owls* contributor Gary D. Schmidt deemed it "entertaining, moving, and poignant," adding praise for the novelist's realistic depiction of island life, with all its "pressures and tensions and loves and fears." *Blue Skin of the Sea* won several awards, including being chosen as one of the American Library Association's Best Books for Young Adults.

Salisbury took four years to write *Blue Skin of the Sea*; in fact, he claimed in an interview with Janet Benton in the *ALAN Review* that he actually "taught" himself to write while working on the

After the Japanese attack on Pearl Harbor, Tomi's father and grandfather are arrested, leaving him to help his mother and sister survive.

book: "I wrote all the stories . . . as individual stand-alone stories, then wove them together with the 'dream memory' thread which, luckily, seems to have worked. . . . As far as I am concerned, [all the characters in that book] actually lived on this earth and I, for a while, knew them and learned from them. Writing fiction is like that for me. It's one of the great glories of reveling in this art form."

Painful World War II Reminiscence Results in Second Novel

Sparked by reflecting upon his own father's experiences during and after the bombing raid at Pearl Harbor, a new novel began to grow when Salisbury imagined what it would be like to be there, as a boy, during the bombing and its aftermath. *Under the Blood-Red Sun*, published in 1992, is the story of a Japanese American eighth-grader named Tomikazu "Tomi" Nakaji, whose parents had left Japan to find a better life in the United States, settling on the island of Hawaii. Set during World War II, the novel shows how Tomi's life is suddenly, radically altered after the Japanese attack on Pearl Harbor. Where baseball, school assignments, and a local bully once occupied his thoughts, young Tomi now must worry about battling the increased tensions between Japanese immigrants and native islanders. Of real difficulty is toning down his elderly grandfather's proud display of his Japanese heritage, a heritage which is now viewed with suspicion by the Nakaji's American neighbors. Praising Salisbury for "subtly reveal[ing] the natural suspicions of the Americans and the equally natural bewilderment of the Japanese immigrants," *Booklist* contributor Frances Bradburn stated that "It is a tribute to the writer's craft that, though there are no easy answers in the story, there is empathy for both cultures." *Voice of Youth Advocates* reviewer John R. Lord also praised the work, noting that "In a time when positive co-existence is being touted in our schools, this novel is an outstanding example of thought-provoking—and at the same time eerily entertaining—prose for the YA reader."

The world of boyhood is central to Salisbury's writing, and it is a world that he well remembers, particularly what he calls the "Silent Code of Conduct." In his *ALAN Review* interview, he recalled a scene from his youth, when he and friends were surfing. While sitting on their surf-

In this 1997 novel, Moke's friends urge him to help them get revenge on the sailors docked nearby, but his police chief father tries to protect him from their violent actions.

boards, legs dangling knee-deep in the salt water, one of the boys pointed out to a nearby reef and stated, simply, "'Got one shark surfing with us,' as if it were a mullet, or one of those fat hotel-pond carps," Salisbury recalled. "The strength in my arms suddenly felt like jelly," he continued, and stories of the infrequent shark attacks around the island of Oahu reeled through his mind. "None of us moved. None of us started paddling in to shore. We just kept sitting there with our legs, from the knee down, dangling underwater," he recalled. "I sat there with the rest of them, keeping an eye on the shark . . . trying not to look nervous, which I was." Salisbury believes the actions of his friends and him was due to the desire to be accepted as "'one of the boys'. . . .

If you enjoy the works of Graham Salisbury, you may also want to check out the following books and films:

S. E. Hinton, *The Outsiders*, 1967.
Craig Lesley, *The Sky Fisherman*, 1995.
Yoshiko Uchida, *Journey Home*, 1978.
The 400 Blows, the classic French film directed by Francois Truffaut, 1959.

It's that unspoken 'code,' lurking in the corner of [my] mind."

In Salisbury's 1997 novel, *Shark Bait*, that silent code of male conduct weighs heavily on fourteen-year-old protagonist Eric Chock, nicknamed "Mokes" or "tough guy." Mokes finds himself unsure where his loyalties lie when he and his school friends hear through the grapevine that tensions between Navy sailors from a destroyer docked nearby and native kids are about to spark a showdown. Mokes's father, the police chief in their small Hawaiian town, working to uphold the law and keep the peace, imposes a six o'clock evening curfew, but Mokes's best friend, seventeen-year-old Booley, plans to go to the fight and vows to kill one of the white sailors if he has the chance during the brawl. Wanting to obey his father, Mokes also feels he should stand by his friend in battle. Things take a sharp turn for the worse when it is discovered that one of the island kids is going to the fight with a loaded gun. Praising Salisbury's "surefooted" portrayal of "the teen milieu of fast cars, faster girls, rivalries, and swagger," a reviewer for the *Bulletin of the Center for Children's Books* complimented the novel as "a lot more diverting than luaus and ukuleles." While somewhat concerned about Salisbury's casual treatment of alcohol and drug use among his teen protagonists, reviewer Coop Renner of *School Library Journal* deemed *Shark Bait* "a consistently engaging, well-written problem novel in a well-realized setting," in a review for *School Library Journal*.

In *Shark Bait* Salisbury's characters speak in Pidgin English, a dialect spoken by many people native to the islands, which required the novelist to make several editorial passes through the manuscript to tone down the dialect so that readers could get the flavor of the language without having to struggle to understand each word. *Booklist* contributor Helen Rosenberg praised Salisbury's use of dialect for adding to his "colorful picture of island life, complete with love interests and local superstitions. Along with the local color, there's some riveting action and a [powerful] climax." Commenting on the novel on the Bantam Doubleday Dell Web site, Salisbury noted, "My desire for *Shark Bait* readers is for them to feel the experience, live the experience as if they were there, and yet come away with the thought that life and things that happen just may not be wheat they think they are. . . . Each decision you make has to be made carefully." He also weaves together stories of strong relationships—those between Mokes and his friends, and that between a father and son.

A 1998 work, *Jungle Dogs*, is also set in Hawaii. Twelve-year-old Boy Regis has taken over the paper route that belonged to his tough older brother Damon, but he fears the wild dogs that live along the route. To make matters worse, Boy must also contend with a bully at his school. When Damon and his gang step in to help Boy, they merely succeed in escalating the violence, which leads to a showdown. Paula Rohrlick, reviewing the work in *Kliatt*, called *Jungle Dogs* a "taut and compelling" work with "believable characters." A *Publishers Weekly* critic praised the "sharp characterizations and inventive, subtle plot twists."

Advice to Aspiring Writers

"There are so many things to learn about writing—about thought, about feelings and passions, about storytelling, about craft, about commitment, and about one's own personality and habits," Salisbury told *SATA*. "But in my mind, one element is most important. Without it a writer will struggle endlessly. That element is discipline. Someone once said that a published writer is an amateur who didn't give up. There's so much truth in that. Discipline, to me, means consistent—almost habitual—writerly thinking, writing, rewriting, revising, and submitting."

Salisbury went on to say that he feels it is important for a children's writer to understand that the world today is very different than that the writer experienced during his or her own childhood. But, he adds, "the basic needs of young people haven't [changed]. There are many, many kids out there with holes in their lives that they desperately want to fill. I can write about those holes. I can do this because I am human and have suffered and soared myself. Strange as it sounds to say, I—as a writer—consider myself lucky, indeed, to have all the holes I have in my own life. Because when I write, I remember, I understand, I empathize, and I feel a need to explore those holes and maybe even fill a couple of them—for myself and for any reader with a similar need who happens to stumble onto my work."

Although he still has many relatives in Hawaii, Salisbury—who goes by the nickname "Sandy"—has returned to the mainland. He lives in Portland, Oregon, with his family. His hobbies include boating and fishing, biking, and running, and he also enjoys researching his family history in Hawaii, both the positive and negative aspects of his Anglo-Saxon missionary past and its role in the colonization of the native Hawaiian people. While identifying with native Hawaiians' concern that their traditional culture is being destroyed, Salisbury maintains that looking back and apportioning blame is not constructive. As he told Benton, "We are all new people. The people of the past are dust."

■ Works Cited

Benton, Janet, "Writing My Way Home": An interview with Graham Salisbury," *ALAN Review,* winter, 1997.

Review of *Blue Skin of the Sea, New York Times Book Review,* May 2, 1993, p. 24.

Bradburn, Frances, review of *Under the Blood-Red Sun, Booklist,* October 15, 1994, p. 425.

Review of *Jungle Dogs, Publishers Weekly,* July 13, 1998, p. 78.

Lord, John R., review of *Under the Blood-Red Sun, Voice of Youth Advocates,* October, 1994, p. 216.

Renner, Coop, review of *Shark Bait, School Library Journal,* September, 1997, p. 225.

Rohrlick, Paula, review of *Jungle Dogs, Kliatt,* July, 1998, p. 8.

Rosenberg, Helen, review of *Shark Bait, Booklist,* September 1, 1997, p. 107.

Salisbury, Graham, comments in *Something About the Author,* Volume 76, Gale, 1992, pp. 200-1.

Salisbury, Graham, "A Leaf on the Sea," *ALAN Review,* fall, 1994, pp. 11-14.

Salisbury, Graham, comments on Bantam/Doubleday web page, http://www.bdd.com/bin/forums/teachers/sals.html (March 18, 1998).

Schmidt, Gary D., review of *Blue Skin of the Sea, Five Owls,* May/June, 1992.

Review of *Shark Bait, Bulletin of the Center for Children's Books,* December, 1997, pp. 138-39.

■ For More Information See

PERIODICALS

ALAN Review, winter, 1996, pp. 35-45; spring, 1998, p. 9.

Bulletin of the Center for Children's Books, November, 1994, p. 102.

Horn Book, September/October, 1995, pp. 634-39.

Kirkus Reviews, October 15, 1994, p. 1415; July 1, 1997, p. 1035.

Publishers Weekly, June 15, 1992, p. 104; July 13, 1992, p. 22; October 31, 1994, p. 64.

School Library Journal, July, 1995, p. 50.

Voice of Youth Advocates, June, 1998, p. 124.*

—*Sketch by Pamela L. Shelton*

Barry Sonnenfeld

cinematographer for a single episode of a regular or limited series or special, 1984, for *Out of Step*.

■ Credits

CINEMATOGRAPHER

In Our Water, Foresight Films, 1982.
Blood Simple, Circle Releasing Corp., 1984.
Compromising Positions, Paramount, 1985.
Three O'Clock High, Universal, 1987.
Raising Arizona, Twentieth Century-Fox, 1987.
Throw Momma from the Train, Orion, 1987.
Big, Twentieth Century-Fox, 1988.
When Harry Met Sally . . ., Columbia, 1989.
Miller's Crossing, Twentieth Century-Fox, 1990.
Misery, Columbia, 1990.

FILM DIRECTOR

The Addams Family, Paramount, 1991.
(And co-producer) *For Love or Money*, Universal, 1993.
Addams Family Values, Paramount, 1993.
(And executive producer) *Get Shorty*, MGM, 1995.
Men in Black, Columbia, 1997.

TELEVISION CINEMATOGRAPHER

Out of Step, ABC, 1984.

■ Personal

Born in 1953, in New York, NY; son of a lighting salesman father and an art teacher mother. *Education:* Attended New York University; Hampshire College, B.A.

■ Addresses

Agent—Creative Artists Agency, 9830 Wilshire Blvd., Beverly Hills, CA 90212; United Talent Agency, 9560 Wilshire Blvd., Beverly Hills, CA 90212.

■ Career

Cinematographer and director.

■ Awards, Honors

Received two Clio Awards for directing television commercials; Academy Award nomination, 1982, for documentary *In Our Water*; Emmy Award, best

Also cinematographer for *Doubletake*, 1985, *Welcome Home, Bobby*, 1986, and *Classified Love*, 1986.

TELEVISION PRODUCER

(And director of pilot episode) *Maximum Bob*, ABC, 1998.
(With Barry Josephson) *Fantasy Island*, ABC-TV, 1998.

FILM APPEARANCES

Mr. Glicker, *Addams Family Values*, Paramount, 1993.
Doorman (uncredited cameo), *Get Shorty*, MGM, 1995.

■ Work in Progress

Directing *The Wild Wild West*, expected 1998; *Chippendales*, expected 1999; *Men in Black 2*, expected 1999.

■ Sidelights

Before finding celebrity and success directing movies, Barry Sonnenfeld toiled for eight years as a cinematographer, quietly building a reputation as one of Hollywood's quirkiest and most inventive behind-the-scenes talents. Sonnenfeld enjoyed an auspicious directorial debut with the hit 1991 black comedy *The Addams Family*, which he followed with a successful 1993 sequel called *Addams Family Values*. Two years later, Sonnenfeld established his position as one of Hollywood's hottest and hippest young directors when he made *Get Shorty*, a hilarious satire about the movie industry and its glib, fast-talking hustlers and would-be starlets. However, it was *Men in Black*, a stylish, action-packed 1997 comedy about space aliens and the secret agents who battle them, that really put Sonnenfeld on top of the entertainment world. *Men in Black* became the year's top-grossing film and redefined the word "cool," touching off the summer of 1997's hottest fashion craze: a 1960s retro-look that features dark Ray-Ban sunglasses and jet-black clothing.

Not a lot of information about Sonnenfeld's early life is public; he jealously guards his privacy. What Sonnenfeld has revealed in media interviews is that he was born in 1953 and raised in New York

City, the son of a lighting salesman and a mother who worked as an art teacher. As a boy, he displayed an early interest in the performing arts. Sonnenfeld attended the High School of Music and Art in Manhattan, where he played the French horn. Upon graduating, he enrolled in a Bachelor of Arts program at New York University (NYU), majoring in political science. Sonnenfeld later transferred to Hampshire College in Amherst, Massachusetts, where he completed his senior year. Uncertain about what he wanted to do in life, Sonnenfeld then traveled across the country, but when he returned home to New York City he was still without career plans. "I liked to take still photographs, and my mother suggested that film school might be something I might enjoy," Sonnenfeld recalled in an interview with Nancy Harrison in the *New York Times*. "For lack of anything better to do, I applied to the NYU [Graduate Institute of Film and Television]."

Exploring Different Avenues

Sonnenfeld earned his living during the next few years by making short promotional films for industrial clients. He also directed commercials (at least two of which won the advertising industry's Clio Award), music videos, and occasionally even pornographic movies; in the process, Sonnenfeld learned to work quickly and efficiently, and with a sense a humor. In a *Newsweek* panel interview that also involved fellow directors Gus Van Sant (*Good Will Hunting*), Curtis Hanson (*L.A. Confidential*), and Paul Thomas Anderson (*Boogie Nights*), Sonnenfeld remarked, "Directing isn't a passion for me, and it's not who I am. I didn't grow up wanting to be a filmmaker. I'm a plumber that happens to make his living as a director."

Sonnenfeld's first taste of fame occurred when he filmed a 1982 movie called *In Our Water*, which earned an Academy Award nomination in the Best Documentary category. Surprisingly, it was not this accomplishment that gave him a chance to move on to bigger and better things. That happened when Sonnenfeld attended a party given by the daughter of the chairman of the Young & Rubican advertising agency; there Sonnenfeld met another young NYU film school grad. Joel Coen, who was scratching out a living by working as an assistant film editor, dreamed of directing in Hollywood. "We were the only Jews in the room. We gravitated to each other," Sonnenfeld recalled in

In 1990 Sonnenfeld was the cinematographer for *Miller's Crossing*, starring Gabriel Byrne and Albert Finney.

an America Online chat. When the two men became friends, Sonnenfeld offered Coen some work, and later he helped Coen and his producer brother, Ethan, raise money to make their first feature-length movie.

Blood Simple, cowritten by the Coens, is a grisly *film noir* murder mystery. Sonnenfeld worked as the cinematographer, while Joel Coen directed. In the film, veteran character actor M. Emmet Walsh plays a sleazy private detective who's hired by a strip bar owner in a small Texas town to kill his wife (played by Frances McDormand) and her lover (played by John Getz). When the murderous scheme goes awry, the consequences are violent and bloody.

Being a low-budget, independent production, *Blood Simple* was initially a problem for the Coens to distribute. Their solution was to enter the film in

the prestigious New York Film Festival. When it was screened there in the summer of 1984, *Blood Simple* was an instant hit. Festival audiences delighted in the film's offbeat humor, clever plot, and raw energy. A large part of *Blood Simple*'s success was also its evocative and imaginative photography; a critic for the online *TV Guide Movie Database* wrote that Sonnenfeld's cinematography made the Coen brothers' first feature film look "like it cost 10 times as much [as its $1.5 million budget]." Critic Janet Maslin of the *New York Times* pronounced *Blood Simple* to be "a directorial debut of extraordinary promise," and she noted that Sonnenfeld's camera work "is especially dazzling." Maslin's assessment was echoed by other New York critics, and *Blood Simple* was hailed as the best independent film of the year. When the film was released nationally, audiences and critics alike agreed with that assessment. Roger Ebert of the *Chicago Sun-Times* gave a quali-

Sonnenfeld made his directorial debut with the successful *Addams Family*, starring Anjelica Huston and Raul Julia, followed by the hit sequel, *Addams Family Values*.

fied "thumbs up" to *Blood Simple,* writing, "Is [it] fun? Well, that depends on you. It is violent, unrelenting, absurd, and fiendishly clever." Cinematographers aren't normally singled out for critical praise, and so people noticed when Ebert went on to mention, "The movie has been shot with a lot of style. . . . One of the pleasures in a movie like this is enjoying the low-angle and tilt shots that draw attention to themselves, that declare themselves as being part of the movie." Even those critics who disliked *Blood Simple* acknowledged its powerful visual style. For example, the *New Yorker*'s Pauline Kael remarked on what she described as the "grimy, lurid cinematography [of] Barry Sonnenfeld."

Highest Television Honor Bestowed

Hard on the heels of his initial feature films, in 1985 Sonnenfeld won an Emmy Award (the tele-

vision industry's top creative honor) for his cinematography on an ABC television special titled *Out of Step.* As a result, Sonnenfeld found he had entered the mainstream, and his talents were much in demand. From 1985 to 1987 Sonnenfeld worked on three made-for-television films and several theatrical features. One of these was the Coen brother's second feature film: a dark, surreal comedy called *Raising Arizona,* which starred a young Nicholas Cage and Holly Hunter. Critics were sharply divided on that film's overall merits; Roger Ebert felt it was unfocused and "all over the map," while Rita Kempley of the *Washington Post* wrote that *Raising Arizona* was "a wacky, happy, daring darkly comic tale [that's] . . . a bundle of joy." Nonetheless, Sonnenfeld was singled out for his imaginative cinematography, which Kempley described as "funny and telling."

Sonnenfeld also filmed the offbeat 1987 comedy *Throw Momma from the Train.* That movie is memorable mainly because it marked the directorial debut of the diminutive character actor Danny DeVito, who became one of Sonnenfeld's close friends. Again, even those critics who turned thumbs down on *Throw Momma from the Train* had praise for Sonnenfeld's cinematography, which syndicated movie reviewer Leonard Maltin wrote left "a distinctive stamp on this film."

By now, Sonnenfeld had risen to the top of his field, and he was regularly working with Hollywood's major stars and directors—the so-called "A-list" of talent. Sonnenfeld continued to win kudos for his work on a string of successful movies. He filmed director Penny Marshall's comedy *Big* (1988), which starred Tom Hanks; Rob Reiner's hit comedy *When Harry Met Sally . . .* (1989); and Reiner's version of the Stephen King thriller *Misery* (1990). Sonnenfeld also teamed again with his friends the Coen brothers to make the Prohibition Era gangster film *Miller's Crossing* (1990). Not long afterward, Sonnenfeld's career moved into a new phase when he was hired to direct his first feature-length movie, a $30-million update of the campy 1960s television sitcom *The Addams Family* (which had been inspired by the cartoons of the late *New Yorker* artist Charles Addams), starring Raul Julia, Anjelica Huston, and Christopher Lloyd.

Sonnenfeld, who was reportedly so excited on his first day on the set that he fainted, later admitted to having had serious misgivings about his new role. "It took me a long time to figure out what the film was about," he told Nancy Harrison of the *New York Times*. "I used to get depressed because I didn't think [*The Addams Family*] was about anything. But it slowly dawned on me that it was about family and romance and nonconformity." What Sonnenfeld decided was that the characters really have a strong sense of moral values, although those values are unorthodox. "[Morticia

John Travolta (shown with Rene Russo) received a 1995 Golden Globe Award for *Get Shorty*, Sonnenfeld's satire about the movie business, based on a novel by Elmore Leonard.

and Gomez, the parents] let their kids be anything they want," Sonnenfeld explained. "They set up rules, and as long as you obey those rules, you can try to kill your brother or your sister."

Despite mixed reviews, *The Addams Family* was a huge hit when it was released in the fall of 1991, earning more than $110-million. Joe Brown of the *Washington Post* praised Sonnenfeld's "stylish visual sensibility" and his attention to comic detail. *The Addams Family* was "creepy, kooky, even altogether ooky enough to satisfy any Addams addict," Brown wrote. However, he also pointed out that a "novelty like this is only as good as its gimmicks, and first-time director Sonnenfeld loads them generously into a storyline that resembles two hastily stitched-together circa-'66 TV scripts." Leonard Maltin joined in the praise for Sonnenfeld, terming *The Addams Family* an "impressive directorial debut."

Sonnenfeld's next film was a modest 1993 comedy called *For Love or Money*. Not surprisingly, the film was quickly forgotten amidst all of the hoopla surrounding the release that same fall of *Addams Family Values*, a lavish sequel to *The Addams Family*. Raul Julia, Anjelica Huston, Christopher Lloyd, and the rest of the original cast reprised their roles under Sonnenfeld's direction. Like the first Addams Family film, the picture scored big at the box office but received mixed reviews. Desson Howe of the *Washington Post* wrote that it was "a thinner, airier reunion," but Ebert felt that *Addams Family Values* was "a rare sequel" in that it "is better than its original."

The Hits Keep Coming

Next, Sonnenfeld was offered the chance to direct Tom Hanks in the 1994 film *Forrest Gump* (for

Sonnenfeld directed Tommy Lee Jones and Will Smith in the sci-fi action comedy *Men in Black*, the top-grossing film of 1997.

which Robert Zemeckis of *Back to the Future* would win an Academy Award), but he turned it down. Yet even this error in judgment did not slow Sonnenfeld's career. His next two films were major hits. *Get Shorty* is a hilarious satire about the glib, fast-talking moguls, hustlers, and assorted hangers-on who inhabit the Hollywood dream world. The film starred Sonnenfeld's old pal Danny DeVito, as well as Gene Hackman, Rene Russo, and John Travolta, who had resurrected his troubled career with a *tour de force* performance in director Quentin Tarantino's 1994 hit film *Pulp Fiction*. Critics adored *Get Shorty*, which earned a host of accolades, including the 1995 Golden Globe Award for Best Actor for Travolta. Hal Hinson of the *Washington Post* wrote that *Get Shorty* was an "irresistibly charming lampoon of Hollywood."

Men in Black, (or *MIB*, as it became known) Sonnenfeld's 1997 blockbuster, is a much different film from *Get Shorty*. That earlier production was based on a literate novel by the celebrated crime writer Elmore Leonard. *MIB* was inspired by an obscure, campy comic book series created by Lowell Cunningham. Leonard's humor is mostly understated and situational, while the laughs in *MIB* are akin to visual dynamite; in fact, big-budget special effects by Industrial Light and Magic (the creative wizards who brought to life the dinosaurs for Steven Spielberg's *Jurassic Park* films) were key to the film's success. Audiences loved *MIB*; it was hip, fast-paced, and very funny. And it became the runaway hit of the lucrative summer season, ending 1997 as Hollywood's top money-maker.

MIB stars Tommy Lee Jones and Will Smith as a couple of cynical, black-suited U.S. government secret agents whose job it is to protect the earth from scummy aliens that routinely adopt human forms. Reviewer Andy Jones of the online *Rough Cut* review service wrote, "Sonnenfeld has mastered the trickiest part of making a stand-out feature among the latest round of special effects-laden flicks: mating the pyrotechnics with a smart buddy flick and letting the real actors win." Susan Wloszczyna in *USA Today* admired Sonnenfeld's "lively deadpan direction," while Roger Ebert praised his irreverence and "cheerful willingness in the movie's first hour or so to completely cut loose from all conventions of dreary storytelling and simply let the story follow the laughs and absurdities."

If you enjoy the works of Barry Sonnenfeld, you may also want to check out the following films:

Fargo, written and directed by the Coen Brothers, 1996.
Starman, starring Jeff Bridges, 1984.
Who Framed Roger Rabbit?, an animated film by Robert Zemeckis, 1988.

The success of *Get Shorty* and *MIB* solidified Sonnenfeld's reputation as one of Hollywood's hottest and busiest young directors. In early 1998 he began work on three new big-budget films. The first is a feature-length version of *The Wild Wild West*, based on the 1960s television series of the same name, and stars Kevin Kline, Kenneth Branagh, and *MIB*'s Will Smith. The other two films are *Chippendales* and a sequel to *MIB* tentatively titled *Men in Black 2*. Based on Sonnenfeld's track record, fans and critics alike can bank on more cinematic magic.

■ Works Cited

Ansen, David, and Corrie Brown, "Lights, Camera, Oscars!," *Newsweek*, January 26, 1998, pp. 59-60, 62-63.

Review of *Blood Simple, TV Guide Internet Movie Database* at http://www.tvguide.com/movies.

Brown, Joe, review of *The Addams Family*, *Washington Post*, November 22, 1991.

Ebert, Roger, review of *Addams Family Values*, *Chicago Sun-Times*, November 19, 1993.

Ebert, Roger, review of *Blood Simple*, *Microsoft Cinemania '94*.

Ebert, Roger, review of *Men in Black*, *Chicago Sun-Times*, July, 1997.

Ebert, Roger, review of *Raising Arizona*, *Chicago Sun-Times*, March 20, 1987.

Harrison, Nancy, "Weird Addams Family at it Again," *New York Times*, November 17, 1991.

Hinson, Hal, review of *Get Shorty*, *Washington Post*, October 20, 1995.

Howe, Desson, review of *Addams Family Values*, *Washington Post*, November 19, 1993.

Jones, Andy, online review of *Men in Black*, *Rough Cut* at http://www.roughcut.com.

Kael, Pauline, review of *Blood Simple*, *Microsoft Cinemania '94*.

Kempley, Rita, review of *Raising Arizona, Washington Post,* March 20, 1987.

Maltin, Leonard, *Leonard Maltin's Movie and Video Guide,* Signet Books, 1994.

Maslin, Janet, "Two Brothers," review of *Blood Simple, New York Times,* October 12, 1984, p. C-10.

Sonnenfeld, Barry, America Online interview, July 28, 1997.

Wloszczyna, Susan, review of *Men in Black, USA Today,* October 29, 1997.

■ For More Information See

BOOKS

Katz, Ephraim, *The Film Encyclopedia,* 2nd edition, HarperCollins, 1994, p. 1269.

PERIODICALS

American Cinematographer, June, 1997.
USA Today, August 4, 1998, p. 3D.*

—Sketch by Ken Cuthbertson

Suzanne Fisher Staples

foreign desk, 1983-85; consultant, U.S. Agency for International Development, 1986-87; fiction writer, 1988—. Lecturer on the status of women in the Islamic Republic of Pakistan. Citizens for a Better Eastern Shore, board member. *Member:* Asia Society, Authors Guild, Authors League of America.

■ Personal

Born August 27, 1945, in Philadelphia, PA; daughter of Robert Charles (an engineer) and Helen Brittain (a manager) Fisher; married Nicholas Green, September 2, 1967 (divorced August, 1976); married Eugene Staples (a teacher and writer), January 25, 1980. *Education:* Cedar Crest College, B.A., 1967. *Politics:* Independent. *Religion:* Episcopalian. *Hobbies and other interests:* Running, tennis, music, theater.

■ Addresses

Home—New York, NY. *Agent*—Jeanne Drewsen, 250 Mercer, New York, NY 10012.

■ Career

Asian marketing director, Business International Corp., 1974-76; United Press International, Washington, DC, news editor and correspondent in New York, Washington, DC, Hong Kong, and India, 1975-83; *Washington Post*, part-time editor for

■ Awards, Honors

Newbery Honor book selection, 1990, Best Books for Young Adults citation, and Notable Books for Children citation, all American Library Association, Notable Book of the Year selection, *New York Times*, and 1992 IBBY Honor List selection, all for *Shabanu: Daughter of the Wind*; Best Books for Young Adults citation, American Library Association, 1994, for *Haveli*, and 1997, for *Dangerous Skies*.

■ Writings

Shabanu: Daughter of the Wind, Knopf, 1989.
Haveli, Knopf, 1993.
Dangerous Skies, Farrar, Straus, 1996.

Contributor, sometimes under name Suzanne Fisher, to periodicals, including *Smithsonian*.

■ Work in Progress

A book titled *Shiva's Fire.*

■ Sidelights

Suzanne Fisher Staples led an adventurous life as a foreign correspondent before she began writing fiction for young adults in 1989. She worked for the United Press International (UPI) news agency's New Delhi bureau, covering the war in Afghanistan and other major news stories during the eight years she was overseas (1975-83). Staples became frustrated by what she felt was a lack of interest in events in Asia by editors back home. "I began to believe the news was not necessarily a good medium for fostering cultural understanding in America—at least news from parts of the world where the way of life is very different from the American one," she recalled in an article for *Bookbird.* "I also grew increasingly interested in writing fiction." That interest has led Staples to publish three well-received young adult novels, including the Newbery Honor book, *Shabanu: Daughter of the Wind.*

Staples was born August 27, 1945, in Philadelphia, Pennsylvania, the daughter of Robert Charles and Helen Brittain Fisher. Her family moved to a northeastern rural part of the state when she was a girl. Young Suzanne was a tomboy who loved playing in the fields with the animals and listening to stories read by her grandmother. Robert Fisher was an engineer and Helen Fisher a manager, and so Suzanne grew up in a goal-oriented atmosphere. This made her love of daydreaming problematic. "So I figured out that fishing gave me the appearance of doing something and I could just daydream," Staples told Ellen A. Greever and Patricia Austin in an interview in *Teaching and Learning Literature.* Staples developed an interest in writing early in life. "I've always written—journals and letters and diaries and later papers for school and ultimately, I thought, newspaper reports when I grew up," she recalled in her interview with Greever and Austin. Staples was eight when she launched her literary career with a neighborhood newspaper started with her sister and two friends. Staples went on to graduate from Cedar Crest College in Allentown, Pennsylvania, with a bachelor's degree in literature and then pursued a journalism career by starting out at a small newspaper in Evergreen, Colorado. In 1967 she married Nicholas Green, an American who worked for the Ford Foundation in Asia. Their wedding was far from traditional in that it included including elephants, jugglers, and puppeteers, and it was catered by street vendors.

In 1974 Staples decided to see the world. She moved to Hong Kong and went to work for a company called Business International. The following year, she found a job with UPI's New Delhi Bureau as head of the South Asia edition. "I have never looked back," Staples told Greever and Austin. "I think my heart went to live in Asia at that point." Around this same time, Staples and her husband divorced, and she was on her own.

A Tapestry of People and Places

All the time that she was in India and Pakistan, Staples took scrupulous mental and written notes, and she dreamed of doing other kinds of writing. Later, she would weave her experiences and insights into her fiction. However, at the time, any ideas she had about writing books were still in the future. In 1983 she returned to the United States and took a part-time editor's job on the foreign desk of the *Washington Post.* However, her wanderlust returned, and just two years later she returned to Pakistan as a consultant on an United States Agency for International Development (USAID) project in the Cholistan Desert of the Punjab province. Her focus was on improving the health, nutrition, and housing of poor women and their families in rural areas. "The first step, we decided, should be to teach the women to read," Staples wrote in the *ALAN Review.* By doing so, USAID felt that the locals would better understand their own problems and how to deal with them. "Teaching people to read makes hope a reality, for many for the first time in their lives," Staples noted.

Determined not to depend on interpreters, who often distorted the meaning of comments, Staples studied the national language of Urdu for six months. She also decided it was important for her to wear native clothing. Staples told Greever and Austin that she was surprised to discover that the garb worn by local women was highly practical. The *shalwar kameez,* the baggy trousers and loose-fitting tunic on top, were comfortable when climbing on and off camels or hauling water from wells. And the head covering, the *chadr,* was extremely useful. Before living in the country, Staples had regarded this traditional clothing as a symbol of the repression of women. She changed her mind after watching the woman string the material between branches of trees to be used as a cradle for babies, as knapsacks for firewood, as bed sheets, bandages, washcloths, and as a drape for dressing and bathing.

While living in the desert, Staples spent many evenings sitting around the cooking fires and listening to the stories that served as lessons to the children, who heard about "the legends, the poetry, and the entire history of their people, a very rich and beautiful oral tradition," the author told Greever and Austin. In this way, not only did Staples live in and around the desert, she absorbed the ancient culture. Doing so, she decided there was a compelling story there that needed to be told. Upon her return to the United States in 1987, Staples began writing about what that she had seen and heard in Pakistan. The resulting novel was an auspicious literary debut. *Shabanu: Daughter of the Wind*, which was published in 1989, earned critical praise and was named a 1990 Newbery Honor book.

Shabanu, a story about a thirteen-year-old daughter of Pakistani desert nomads, is narrated by the title character. Since she has no brothers to tend the family's livestock, Shabanu is responsible for their care. The story recounts the events of the year leading up to the marriage of her older sister Phulan. It had been arranged that the sisters will marry two brothers. However, when the man Phulan is to marry dies, she instead marries Shabanu's fiance; Shabanu is then matched with a man named Rahim, a rich, old landowner who already has three wives. The novel shows the strength and courage of Shabanu, who is appalled by the marriage but comes to terms with her lot in life and comes to understand that she must listen to her parents and follow her culture. She rises to the challenges and becomes a stronger person in doing so. Staples herself felt that she had come to a similar realization. Writing in the *ALAN Review*, she pleaded for Westerners to understand that Islam "is more than terrorism and fundamentalism and suppression of women—that it's a religion of compassion and justice and poetry not at all dissimilar from Christianity and Judaism in its prescriptions for how we should behave toward each other."

Maurya Simon, writing in the *New York Times Book Review*, proclaimed that Staples had accomplished "a small miracle in the unfolding of her touching and powerful story." A reviewer in the *Bulletin of the Center for Children's Books* echoed that praise in commenting, "This first novel is, on several counts, one of the most exciting YA books to appear recently." In *Quill & Quire*, Susan Perren hailed the work as being "exceptionally vivid and compelling." Marijo Grimes, in *Voice of Youth Advocates*, wrote, "Staples' novel, set in modern day Pakistan, is a beautiful and moving story of a young girl caught between her culture and her heart." However, Barbara Bottner of the *Los Angeles Times Book Review* felt the sheer weight of the background detail sometimes "overwhelms the narrative." Yet, she also pointed out that Staples succeeds in making the reader understand the strict customs of the desert nomads about whom she was writing.

Shabanu Endures Challenges

While Staples originally planned to write a nonfiction book about Pakistan before going back to work as a journalist, she found that she had not said all she had to say about life in the Cholistan Desert. Staples' second novel was published in 1993. *Haveli*, which is written in the third-person to enable Staples to explain more of the details of Pakistani culture, picks up Shabanu's story when she is eighteen. By now, she has borne a daughter. But Shabanu's life is miserable because the three other wives and the children of Rahim are more cultured and look down on Shabanu. They are also jealous of the attention that Rahim pays to his newest bride. They play dirty tricks on Shabanu, leaving a scorpion in her bed, killing her daughter's puppy, and placing a bat in her cupboard.

Knowing that after Rahim dies she won't be safe in his house, Shabanu plots to make sure her future is secure. She is also determined to provide an education for her daughter since she knows that having a profession will ensure the girl has financial independence; this is one of the few ways a Pakistani women can control her own destiny. Shabanu also sets out to protect her only friend from having to marry Rahim's mentally deficient son. Facing another challenge, Shabanu resists an attraction to her husband's betrothed nephew.

In *Voices of Youth Advocates* Jane Chandra wrote that "High school girls—and adults—will quickly become immersed in this exciting story of a young married woman in love with another man and struggling to live within the confines of her or-

This 1996 murder mystery centers on the friendship between a young white man and a black girl whose family works on his farm.

thodox culture." Ellen Fader, critiquing the work in *Horn Book*, felt that "Staples shows considerable talent in crafting a taut, suspenseful narrative with strong female characters and a terrific sense of place."

While novel writing is different from nonfiction, Staples told Greever and Austin that when she wrote *Shabanu* and *Haveli* she put her journalism skills to use by trying to give the reader as much detail as possible. In fact, Staples even gives her readers a map, a list of characters, and a glossary to help them navigate through the story that blends "heart-pounding adventure and significant social issues," according to a reviewer in *Publishers Weekly*. The reviewer went on to say that Staples' description of Pakistan is fair: "she ac-

knowledges the society's inequities while celebrating its beauty and warmth." Daniyal Mueenuddin, a critic in the *New York Times Book Review* whose own childhood was spent in Pakistan, praised Staples for her smooth prose and her ability to create strong characters. Nevertheless, as a native of the country that Staples was writing about, Mueenuddin also pointed out flaws. *Haveli* both "exaggerates and naively caricatures the people and the society," Mueenuddin said. For one thing, Staples uses her own Western values to describe Shabanu's rebellion against her chauvinistic society, Mueenuddin noted, while adding that most readers would not pick up on the subtle distortions.

Mueenuddin was not Staples' only critic. *Shabanu* and *Haveli* came under fire from some Muslims living in the United States. Staples defended her work in a *Bookbird* article, explaining that she was deeply concerned about accuracy, authenticity, and cultural nuances. In fact, before she submitted *Shabanu*, she passed her manuscript by thirteen experts who knew the area she was writing about. "Each of them remarked that I had captured the place, the people, and their lives with a remarkable sense of realism," she wrote. Staples added that her sensitivity to outsiders' perspectives of other peoples' lives and society had been heightened by having lived in Asia and seeing how the local media reported on life in the United States. Some of the Asian journalists based there provided a skewed view of life by focusing on social problems in "the world's richest nation." Likewise, Staples said she saw a common thread in the complaints some Muslims voiced about her work: "The question of authenticity seems to arise when a group of people feels that someone who has no right to do so 'speaks' for them," Staples wrote.

A Sharp Change of Pace

Staples' third novel, *Dangerous Skies*, was a sharp change of pace. The book, a murder mystery that is set on the eastern shore of the Chesapeake Bay, deals with a variety of themes: friendship, coming of age, racial prejudice, sexual abuse, and power. The book does not have a happy ending, but according to a critic in the *New York Times Book Review*, "it offers much to think about." The narrator is a young man named Buck Smith, who, as he prepares to go away to college, recalls the defining moment in his life, when he was twelve

If you enjoy the works of Suzanne Fisher Staples, you may also want to check out the following books:

Lesley Beake, *Song of Be*, 1993.
Sheila Gordon, *Waiting for the Rain*, 1987.
Indi Rana, *The Roller Birds of Rampur*, 1993.

years old. Buck has grown up with Tunes, the daughter of a black family that has worked on the Smith family farm for generations. Buck and Tunes are best friends, yet in the outside world they lead separate lives. The friendship between the two is severely tested when the body of a murdered Hispanic farm labor manager is found floating in a creek. A bullet in his head has come from Tunes' gun. As the mystery surrounding the man's death is solved, Buck is forced to confront some terrible truths about his life in the community. A reviewer in *Publishers Weekly* compared *Dangerous Skies* to *To Kill a Mockingbird*, the famous 1960 novel by Harper Lee, because it "boldly expresses uncomfortable truths about society while upholding the innocence of childhood." M. Jerry Weiss, in the *ALAN Review*, wrote: "Some people believe only what they want to believe; how can there be justice in a society filled with such people?"

Societal change has long been at the forefront of Staples' agenda, both personally and professionally. In addition to having worked for the USAID, she has lectured on the status of women in the Islamic Republic of Pakistan, has served as a board member of the Citizens for a Better Eastern Shore, and has spoken out against censorship in school libraries. On a personal level, Staples remarried in 1980 to her college sweetheart. Staples and her second husband, teacher and writer Eugene Staples, make their home in Mount Dora, thirty-five miles northwest of Orlando, Florida. Even so, she has never forgotten her time in the Cholistan Desert; living among "the People of the Wind" was an experience that "transcends everything that's happened to me before or since" Staples told Greever and Austin. In the *ALAN Review*, Staples recalled how much she had grown personally by being forced to expand her understandings and to be understood. "My hope for *Shabanu* and Haveli and all good books about people who are different from us is that they will

inspire us to grow beyond our limits to learn understanding," she wrote. "And that this understanding will foster peace in the world by teaching us not to fear differences but to become more compassionate people."

■ **Works Cited**

Bottner, Barbara, review of *Shabanu: Daughter of the Wind, Los Angeles Times Book Review*, December 10, 1989, p. 8.

Chandra, Jane, review of *Haveli, Voices of Youth Advocates*, December, 1993, p. 302.

Review of *Dangerous Skies, New York Times Book Review*, February 16, 1997, p. 28.

Review of *Dangerous Skies, Publishers Weekly*, November 4, 1996, p. 49.

Fader, Ellen, review of *Haveli, Horn Book*, January-February, 1994, p. 75.

Greever, Ellen A., and Patricia Austin, "Suzanne Fisher Staples: From Journalist to Novelist," *Teaching and Learning Literature*, November/December, 1997, pp. 43-55.

Grimes, Marijo, review of *Shabanu: Daughter of the Wind, Voice of Youth Advocates*, April, 1990, pp. 34-35.

Review of *Haveli, Publishers Weekly*, July 19, 1993, p. 255.

Mueenuddin, Daniyal, review of *Haveli, New York Times Book Review*, November 14, 1993, p. 59.

Perren, Susan, review of *Shabanu: Daughter of the Wind, Quill & Quire*, February, 1990, p. 16.

Review of *Shabanu: Daughter of the Wind, Bulletin of the Center for Children's Books*, October, 1989, p. 45.

Simon, Maurya, review of *Shabanu: Daughter of the Wind, New York Times Book Review*, November 12, 1989, p. 32.

Staples, Suzanne Fisher, "Different Is Just Different," *ALAN Review*, Winter, 1995.

Staples, Suzanne Fisher, "Writing about the Islamic World: An American Author's Thoughts on Authenticity," *Bookbird*, Fall, 1997, pp. 17-20.

Weiss, M. Jerry, review of *Dangerous Skies, ALAN Review*, Winter, 1998, p. 50.

■ **For More Information See**

BOOKS

Children's Books and Their Creators, edited by Anita Silvey, Houghton Mifflin, 1995, p. 624.

PERIODICALS

ALAN Review, Winter, 1996, pp. 49-50.
Christian Science Monitor, July 6, 1990, p. 10.
New Yorker, November 27, 1989, p. 144.*

—*Sketch by Diane Andreassi*

Joyce Sweeney

■ Personal

Born November 9, 1955, in Dayton, OH; daughter of Paul (an engineer) and Catharine (a bookkeeper; maiden name, Spoon) Hegenbarth; married Jay Sweeney (a marketing director), September 20, 1979. *Education:* Wright State University, B.A. (summa cum laude), 1977; graduate study in creative writing at Ohio University, 1977-78. *Politics:* Democrat. *Religion:* Unity. *Hobbies and other interests:* Native American religions, hiking, basketball.

■ Addresses

Home—Coral Springs, FL. *Agent*—George Nicholson, Sterling Lord Literistic, Inc., 65 Bleecker St., New York, NY 10012.

■ Career

Philip Office Associates, Dayton, OH, advertising copywriter, 1978; Rike's Department Store, Dayton, advertising copywriter, 1979-81, legal secretary, 1980-81; freelance advertising copywriter in Day-

ton, 1981-82; full-time writer, 1982—. Leader of creative writing workshops in Ormond Beach and Ft. Lauderdale, FL. *Member:* Florida Council for Libraries, Mystery Writers of America.

■ Awards, Honors

Delacorte Press First Young Adult Novel Prize, and Best Books for Young Adult citation, American Library Association (ALA), both 1984, both for *Center Line;* Best Books for Reluctant Readers, ALA, 1988, for *The Dream Collector; The Dream Collector* and *Face the Dragon* were named among the Best Books for the Teen Age by the New York Public Library, 1991; Best Books for Young Adults citation, ALA, 1994, for *The Tiger Orchard;* Best Books for Young Adults citation, ALA, and Best Book for the Teenage list, New York Public Library, both 1995, and Nevada Young Readers' Award, young adult category, and Evergreen Young Adult Book Award, Washington Library Association, both 1997, all for *Shadows;* Best Book for Reluctant Readers citation, ALA, Best Book for the Teenage list, New York Public Library, Nevada Young Readers' Award list, all 1997, all for *Free Fall.*

■ Writings

YOUNG ADULT NOVELS

Center Line, Delacorte, 1984.

Right behind the Rain, Delacorte, 1985.
The Dream Collector, Delacorte, 1989.
Face the Dragon, Delacorte, 1990.
Piano Man, Delacorte, 1992.
The Tiger Orchard, Delacorte, 1993.
Shadow, Delacorte, 1994.
Free Fall, Delacorte, 1996.
The Spirit Window, Delacorte, 1998.

Sweeney wrote a monthly column on local books and authors for the Fort Lauderdale *News/Sun-Sentinel* and contributed book reviews to periodicals. Contributor of short stories and articles to periodicals, including *New Writers, Playgirl, CO-ED, Green's Magazine,* and *Writer*. Contributor of poetry to reviews, including *Blue Violin* and *Painting Daisies Yellow*. Sweeney's young adult titles have been translated in Danish, Dutch, Hebrew, and Italian.

■ Adaptations

Free Fall was adapted for audio cassette by Recorded Books Inc., 1997.

■ Work in Progress

Young adult thrillers, including one about high school basketball.

■ Sidelights

Simply put, Joyce Sweeney is a "master at depicting the inner working of families," according to *Horn Book* reviewer Patty Campbell. Sweeney writes realistic fiction, much of it focused on male protagonists, which deals heavily with family issues and friendship. In her first novel, *Center Line*, Sweeney announced an intention of putting the family under the magnifying lens and probing its structure, its dysfunctions, and its strengths. The winner of the Delacorte Prize for Outstanding First Young Adult Novel, *Center Line* traces the adventures and misadventures of five young brothers on their own in the world, escaping an abusive father. Subsequent novels have dealt with teen suicide, divorce, homosexuality, fantasized love, the supernatural, and environmental concerns—all against the backdrop of family relations. "Perhaps it's because I didn't have one in the traditional sense that I am always writing about families,"

Sweeney told *Authors and Artists for Young Adults* (*AAYA*) in an interview.

"My father died when I was very young," Sweeney noted, "and I was an only child, so it was just me and Mom." Sweeney's first five years were spent in a rural town near Dayton, Ohio, where she developed a lifelong love for the outdoors and nature. It was a rude awakening for her to move to Dayton just before beginning school. "I may not have realized it at the time," Sweeney told *AAYA*, "but I missed the country and didn't really like the city. When I went to school I was doubly an outsider—a country kid and one who was already bookish. I just had no idea how to relate to the other kids."

Books were an important part of Sweeney's childhood: *Heidi, The Wizard of Oz, Peter Pan*. "Any book where you could fly away and create your own reality. I can say I was literally surrounded by books as a kid. By age eight, I was already talking about becoming a writer." By the fourth grade Sweeney had moved on to the novels of Steinbeck and was also attempting to sell her own work—mostly poetry—in magazines. During her elementary school years, Sweeney was withdrawn. "I kept my own counsel," she recalled. But with the advent of adolescence, this changed. High school presented a new beginning to her, and she took advantage of it, inspired in part by the writings of Norman Vincent Peale. As a freshman in high school she met the boy who would later become her husband. These were also years of intense experimentation with things religious. "I bounced everywhere from spiritualism to fundamentalism," Sweeney noted. "At heart I was an anthropologist; I just didn't have the word for it then." In high school she also continued writing, branching out to fiction, influenced by a teacher who had actually published short stories and who could show her the ropes of publishing.

For reasons of economy, Sweeney lived at home during college, studying English and creative writing at Wright State University. As a college freshman, she sold her first piece of fiction to *New Writers,* and in her junior year she sold another story, this time to *Playgirl*. "That second sale was an affirmation for me," Sweeney said. "It told me that I could actually build a career as a writer." After graduation, Sweeney took more creative writing courses in a master's program at Ohio University. Though she did not complete the de-

There are happy results as well as unexpected surprises when Becky gives everyone in her family a book about how to make wishes come true.

gree, the experience was a positive one for her. "You're not taught how to write fiction in English classes. No one talks about how to stay in point of view, for example. For this you have to take creative writing courses. And I had some great teachers like Daniel Keyes who taught me valuable lessons. Also just being around professional writers was an inspiration. Here is this person who writes books for a living, and he goes to the dentist. He does shopping. He's a human like me. This made it seem possible for me to become a writer, too."

Sweeney married in 1979, and there followed several years of working in advertising and as a le-

gal secretary, which left her little time to work on her writing. Finally, however, Sweeney's husband, who had known her since she was fourteen, and knew of her dreams of becoming a writer, convinced her that the only way to become a writer was to do it full time. In 1980 she started the long process that led to her first publication. Not long thereafter, Sweeney and her husband moved to Florida, where they still reside.

Finding the *Center Line*

"Like most YA writers, I never really considered myself one," Sweeney told *AAYA*. "I never realized I was writing YA novels with my first two books. When I was growing up I was deeply influenced by J. D. Salinger and John Knowles. They wrote novels that happened to have young protagonists. But these were novels first. At that time there was no such thing as a YA novel. When I finished my first novel, my agent told me I had a YA book and I almost felt insulted. I had no idea what sorts of books were being published as YA, but when I read some of the titles, I realized that they were good literature."

Sweeney's first publication, *Center Line,* written as an adult novel with youthful protagonists, does indeed have some mature scenes, but its premise—five brothers escaping an abusive father to learn about family responsibilities on their own—was a natural winner with young readers. A year in the writing, this first published novel was inspired by some reading Sweeney was doing at the time about the Beatles as very young men in Hamburg, Germany. "Here were these irresponsible, overgrown kids in Hamburg," Sweeney explained to *AAYA*, "and they had to learn to look out for each other. Something similar was happening with me, too. In my marriage I was having to learn about responsibilities by caring for another human, my husband. I thought this would make a great centerpiece for a story about real coming of age." The writing was the easy part. Then came selling it. Sweeney's agent submitted the manuscript to almost thirty publishers before putting it in the pool of first-book contestants for the Delacorte YA prize. Winning that prize secured publication for *Center Line* as well as a healthy advertising budget for the book.

Center Line tells the story of the Cunnigan brothers: oldest brother Shawn, Steve, Chris, Rick, and

Mark. Their mother has been dead for a number of years, and their alcoholic father regularly beats one or the other of the boys. To escape this intolerable situation, Shawn cashes out his college account. The brothers steal their father's car and hit the road, determined to live on their own until they grow up. What follows is a classic road adventure, as the quintet travel from one little town to the other.

The skills of each brother come into play: Chris proves to be the Romeo of the group and scores so well in that domain that he even shares his

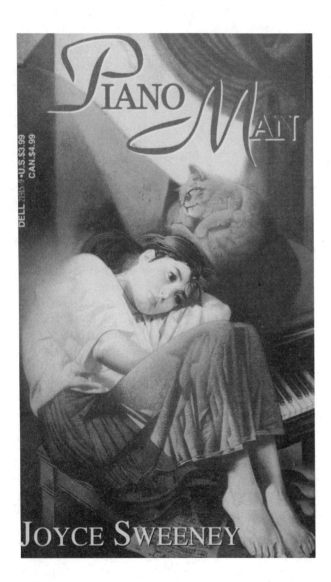

When a piano player in his twenties moves into the apartment next door, an infatuated fourteen-year-old girl becomes determined to win his heart.

surplus with his brothers. Young Mark earns money during difficult times as a "blind" guitarist in a shopping mall. Along the way, Steve drops out to marry an older woman, and the remaining four end up in Florida working on a fishing pier. Things are fine for a time until discontented Rick and Shawn get into a fight, and Rick blows the whistle on his brothers. An understanding judge, however, remands the others to Shawn's custody—their father has since disappeared—all neatly wrapped into a happy but cautionary ending.

Reviewers and readers alike reacted as positively as the Delacorte prize committee. Sue Estes, writing in *Booklist*, concluded that *Center Line* was a "powerful novel for mature teenagers," while a reviewer in *Bulletin of the Center for Children's Books* commented that "this is a strong first novel . . . with fast-moving adventure, a gritty sense of place, and controlled scenes of comedy, drama, and pathos." In a lengthy *Wilson Library Bulletin* review, Patty Campbell compared Sweeney's first novel to *The Outsiders* by S. E. Hinton, noting however that "*Center Line* has a plot twist that makes it a much more subtle and interesting work than *The Outsiders*." That plot twist is the enemy within, Rick, who turns against his brothers. A critic in *Publishers Weekly* noted that "the author writes engagingly and her young readers are more than likely to put her book on the bestseller lists." Such was the case; *Center Line* was also optioned for a movie.

Sweeney followed up this initial success by reworking a novella she had written before *Center Line*. Again, she was not consciously writing a YA novel but exploring a difficult time in her own life through a brother and sister in *Right behind the Rain*. Kevin is twenty-one, handsome, and a talented dancer with a part in an upcoming movie. He goes home to Ohio for the summer where his younger sister, Carla, is dazzled by his success. But she soon sees that he is deeply unhappy. His success has become a burden to him, perfection a prison. Others see only the golden boy; Carla is the only one to see possible danger ahead, and when Kevin buys a gun one day, it is left to her to talk him out of killing himself.

"The book was inspired by feelings I personally had during college," Sweeney explained to *AAYA*. "I felt I had to be perfect: the four-point student. I also took care of our home when mom was working. And I had to be the perfect girlfriend as well as future great writer. I finally worked things out, but I definitely had suicidal feelings for a time. And it is amazing how many kids respond to this when I visit at schools. Invariably there is at least one student in the crowd who says 'How did you know I was feeling like this?'"

Reviewers again reacted positively. A *Publishers Weekly* contributor noted that the "simple, sensitive writing conveys all the emotions of a memorable summer," while a critic in *Kirkus Reviews* emphasized the "close, caring relationship between brother and sister" which "is easy to believe," and concluded that this relationship "[is] the novel's strongest asset and one readers will appreciate." Sweeney commented to *AAYA* that "one of the obvious weird things about my life is that I was an only child and have devoted my whole career to writing about sibling relations."

A Self-Confessed YA Novelist

Since her third novel, Sweeney has consciously been writing for the YA market. "It's where I feel at home," she told *AAYA*. "In fact now the only time I get inspired is when it's a book for kids. I used to think that I would somehow graduate to adult fiction from YA, but no longer. This is where I can make a difference; this is my audience. And the teen years are where the important decisions are made, ones that effect the rest of a lifetime." Her third book, *The Dream Collector*, was a reworking of important lessons she herself learned as a teenager entering high school. "If you make a wish, you can work it out," Sweeney said in her interview. "It's important kids understand that. It's not so much magic as willing something to happen. But then of course you have to watch out what you wish for. That's what makes the dramatic tension in *The Dream Collector*."

Becky is fifteen and faced with a quandary—what to get the members of her family for Christmas with her limited funds and their sometimes extravagant lists. She opts to buy everyone a self-help book that describes how an individual can make his or her wishes become reality. Like a genie released from the bottle, the gift books unleash conflicts in the family as well as joyful surprises. Brother Tim gets the kitten he wanted; Scott manipulates family finances to get a fancy racing bike; the mother, who wanted lots of money, leaves their father for the boss; the bud-

The strange images Sarah sees of her dead cat Shadow seem to predict the future in this award-winning novel.

ding poet, Julia, finally gets published; and Becky herself goes out with the neighbor only to discover she likes his friend Tom more. A reviewer in *Publishers Weekly* commented that "Sweeney ably delineates family relationships as she explores the nature of dreams and the pitfalls of ambition," adding that "her affecting and tender novel presents a perfect blend of humor and dramatic tension." Susan Rosenkoetter, writing in *Voice of Youth Advocates*, commented that while *The Dream Collector* "doesn't have the lingering emotional impact of *Center Line* . . . [it] will have wider appeal."

Challenges to friendship, the agony of teen love, and dreams from the past inform the next three

Sweeney titles, *Face the Dragon, Piano Man,* and *The Tiger Orchard.* In *Face the Dragon,* Eric and Paul are best friends, and they join four other teens in an accelerated class at high school. *Beowulf* not only becomes the subject matter for the class, but the theme of the book, as well, as each of the characters has to confront his or her own personal dragon. Eric has always felt under the shadow cast by the more confident Paul, and determines not only to tackle the demon of public speaking, but also to battle Paul for the attentions of another student, Melanie. Though Eric has always considered him supremely confident, Paul is in fact racked by fears that he may be homosexual. When their teacher exposes these fears, Eric comes to Paul's defense, much like Beowulf's comrade, Wiglaf. Barbara Chatton noted in *School Library Journal* that the "frank language of adolescents is aptly depicted and flows naturally," and *Booklist*'s Stephanie Zvirin concluded her review by stating that "Sweeney says a lot about jealousy, pride, and embarrassment, and about what friendship really is."

Jeff, twenty-six, is the *Piano Man,* a talented young musician who lives next to fourteen-year-old Deidre, who is a budding chef in her own right. Falling in love with this older man, Deidre decides that the way to Jeff's heart is through his stomach, but in fact Jeff's heart belongs to another—gourmet cooking or no—and Deidre's love affair is destined for the garbage bin before it can get to the cooker. Subplots involve other wrong choices by women: Deidre's widowed mom is dating again, but not happily, and her cousin Suzie is going out with an abused teen who keeps her at arm's length. "This is far from a formula treatment of the not-smooth course of true love," observed Zena Sutherland in *Bulletin of the Center for Children's Books.* "The plots are smoothly integrated, the characters are well-defined and consistent, and the writing has, in both dialogue and exposition, a natural flow." Susan R. Farber commented in *Voice of Youth Advocates* that "Sweeney is expert at portraying the highs and lows, the dreams and expectations of young women in love (lust? like?)," while a *Kirkus Reviews* contributor noted in particular the "deft dialogue, willing players, and plausible events" that constitute this novel.

The Tiger Orchard was yet another well-regarded YA book, telling the story of Zack, who is haunted by strange nightmares. In therapy he tries to un-

cover the secrets these dreams might hold for him, and discovers that his father—who his mother always said was dead—is actually living. "The past is uncovered, secrets are revealed, and Zack finds his father as he finds the truth," noted Claire Rosser in *Kliatt*. Rosser added that "the real story here is the revelation of long-held, destructive secrets, and in the healing power of the revelation." A *Publishers Weekly* reviewer observed that Sweeney displayed "remarkable insights into family relationships and human nature."

Shadow and Beyond

For her seventh YA title, Sweeney again turned to her own experiences for inspiration. "When my husband was a kid, his family had no pets," Sweeney told *AAYA*. "And when I was growing up, we had lots of them. So his dream was to have pets galore. We adopted cats all over the place it seemed, and then feline leukemia struck. Over the course of several years we lost five cats. That loss touched me profoundly. I knew I wanted to use the material somehow in a book, but not a dead-pet story. Something more. Then I decided I wanted to write a supernatural story. I enjoy those tales myself and wanted to try my hand at one. It came to me that this might be the perfect way to use the grief I felt for the loss of those cats. Grief can alter your perceptions, so this would open up the whole question of whether the supernatural event in this case—the return of a cat—was indeed supernatural or if it was the result of emotions at work."

The eponymous cat in *Shadow* has been dead for a year, but still thirteen-year-old Sarah grieves its passing. Add this to the continual feuding between her older brothers, Brian and Patrick, a father who dotes on Brian and a mother who picks on him, and a girlfriend who nearly cuckolds one brother with the other, and a recipe for domestic disaster is set in place. Soon Sarah begins seeing her dead cat, and after confiding this to the housekeeper, Cissy, who has a natural proclivity for things supernatural, she is informed that her cat is probably returning in the spirit to warn her of impending danger. Further complications ensue when Sarah realizes she is in love with her childhood friend, Julian. When she confides her experiences with Shadow to Julian, his skepticism nearly destroys their newfound relationship. The impending danger becomes all too real when

Brian discovers his girlfriend about to make love with his brother Patrick. An enraged Brian nearly strangles Patrick; they are stopped only by what appears to be the ghost of Shadow.

"This page-turner is a psychic novel built around realistic feelings, emotions, hates, fears, and love," noted Bonnie Kunzel in *Voice of Youth Advocates.* Kunzel deemed the work "well-written and bound to be a teen pleaser with its mixture of sibling rivalry, romance, and psychic revelations." Bruce Anne Shook, writing in *School Library Journal*, observed that "Characters are realistically drawn, and the plot is riveting," and noted that the conclusion, "as Shadow withdraws and Sarah finds

Four boys against a cave.
They may never see the sun again.

FREE FALL
JOYCE SWEENEY

Trapped in a cave, four teenage boys learn about each other as they struggle to survive.

a new kitten suspiciously like him, is nicely done." A *Publishers Weekly* reviewer felt that Sweeney "offers believably complex characters" and "challenges conventional views of reality."

Sweeney's books are equally as popular with young male readers as with females. She writes about male protagonists with enough reality to elicit letters from these fans asking for more—more adventure, more sports. "I was definitely a tomboy, but I wasn't allowed to really act out the adventure and athletics that boys did at that time," Sweeny explained to *AAYA.* "There was a sense of frustration at that double standard. That is one reason I seem to be able to write male characters well. I'm doing now what I couldn't do myself as a kid. Also, I seem to be more in touch with the male psyche than the female. It may be my upbringing, raised by a single mom, and taught to be tough, resilient, in control, not dependent on anyone else. It's easy for me to be macho."

Sweeney spread her tomboy wings with *Free Fall,* the story of four young boys—two antagonistic brothers and their friends—who get trapped in an underground cave. Neil and Randy are high school athletes and best friends. Together with Neil's younger brother David and his friend Terry, they explore a cave in Florida's Ocala National Forest. There is tension between the boys from the outset, but it reaches a climax when they realize they are lost. No spelunkers, these four have come ill-prepared. Neil tries to climb out but falls and breaks a leg. David ultimately comes to the rescue by finding an underwater passage out of the cave, but not before the quartet have shed their macho facades and share their darkest secrets. *Booklist*'s Ann O'Malley commented that "Sweeney mixes excitement with finely crafted characters and credible psychological underpinnings to deliver a powerful punch." A reviewer in *Horn Book* called *Free Fall* a "taut survival story" and noted also that "the book features gritty, realistic dialogue and insightful characterizations," while Pam Carlson concluded in *Voice of Youth Advocates* that the novel was "a gripping, sometimes scary tale of survival and brotherhood." And a *Publishers Weekly* contributor felt *Free Fall* "goes beyond the action genre. . . . Lean and skillfully wrought, this novel hooks the reader and doesn't let go."

Environmental matters combine with another dysfunctional family in *The Spirit Window,* the story

If you enjoy the works of Joyce Sweeney, you may also want to check out the following books and films:

Lynn Hall, *Flyaway*, 1987.
Joan Lowery Nixon, *Whispers from the Dead*, 1989.
Neal Shusterman, *What Daddy Did*, 1991.
This Boy's Life, starring Leonardo DiCaprio, 1993.

of Miranda and her summer visit to her dying grandmother on a Florida island. Miranda is accompanied by her psychiatrist father, Richard, and his new, young, and spoiled wife, Ariel. Grandmother Lila and her son do not see eye to eye on the property that she will leave behind at her death: he intends to develop it but she wants it preserved. To this end, she leaves it to her young, part-Cherokee assistant, Adam, who shares her beliefs in preservation and to whom Miranda is strongly attracted. Miranda soon finds herself torn between loyalty to family and her feelings for Adam in this "gentle story about two adolescents far wiser and more mature than the adults in their lives," according to Beth Anderson, writing in *Voice of Youth Advocates*. A reviewer in *Bulletin of the Center for Children's Books* noted that "Sweeney has a strong sense of place that contributes to an overall setting of mood that is very effective," while Angela J. Reynolds concluded in *School Library Journal* that a "love story, a mystery, and a spiritual journey combine to make this a satisfying read."

A "satisfying read" is not necessarily what Sweeney sets out to do in her fiction, but if that is part of the result so much the better. "I try not to think of my audience a lot," Sweeney told *AAYA*. "Mostly I try to work through some experiences in my own life, thoroughly disguising myself, by the way, usually in the guise of one of the male characters. I don't think of message. My unconscious knows what the message is, but I don't want to be thinking about that. Instead, I want to put issues out there, to open things up for discussion. I certainly want to be a force for good, but that has to come naturally through the story. It can't be forced and planned."

Sweeney, who in the future plans to write thrillers for YA readers as well as sports books, feels there is a real mission in writing for the teen audience. "I hope parents understand that people who write YAs care very deeply about kids and are trying to address issues that effect them and help them work through such issues. In the end, we believe that information is better than ignorance."

■ **Works Cited**

Anderson, Beth, review of *The Spirit Window, Voice of Youth Advocates*, April, 1998, pp. 50-51.

Campbell, Patty, "The Young Adult Complex," *Wilson Library Bulletin*, March, 1984, pp. 502-3.

Campbell, Patty, "The Sand in the Oyster," *Horn Book*, November-December, 1994, pp. 756-59.

Carlson, Pam, review of *Free Fall, Voice of Youth Advocates*, June, 1996, p. 102.

Review of *Center Line, Bulletin of the Center for Children's Books*, June, 1984, pp. 194-95.

Review of *Center Line, Publishers Weekly*, February 10, 1984, p. 194.

Chatton, Barbara, review of *Face the Dragon, School Library Journal*, October, 1990, p. 145.

Review of *The Dream Collector, Publishers Weekly*, November 24, 1989, p. 72.

Estes, Sue, review of *Center Line, Booklist*, April 1, 1984, p. 1110.

Farber, Susan R., review of *Piano Man, Voice of Youth Advocates*, April, 1992, p. 37.

Review of *Free Fall, Horn Book*, Spring, 1997, p. 84.

Review of *Free Fall, Publishers Weekly*, June 24, 1996, p. 62.

Kunzel, Bonnie, review of *Shadow, Voice of Youth Advocates*, October, 1994, pp. 218-19.

O'Malley, Ann, review of *Free Fall, Booklist*, July, 1996, p. 1819.

Review of *Piano Man, Kirkus Reviews*, May 15, 1992, p. 676.

Reynolds, Angela J., review of *The Spirit Window, School Library Journal*, March, 1998, p. 224.

Review of *Right behind the Rain, Kirkus Reviews*, May 1, 1987, p. 726.

Review of *Right behind the Rain, Publishers Weekly*, May 8, 1987, p. 72.

Rosenkoetter, Susan, review of *The Dream Collector, Voice of Youth Advocates*, February, 1990, p. 348.

Rosser, Claire, review of *The Tiger Orchard, Kliatt*, March, 1995, p. 12.

Review of *Shadow, Publishers Weekly*, May 27, 1996, p. 81.

Shook, Bruce Anne, review of *Shadow, School Library Journal,* September, 1994, pp. 242-43.

Review of *The Spirit Window, Bulletin of the Center for Children's Books,* May, 1998, p. 341.

Sutherland, Zena, review of *Piano Man, Bulletin of the Center for Children's Books,* June, 1992, p. 281.

Sweeney, Joyce, interview with J. Sydney Jones for *Authors and Artists for Young Adults,* conducted June 1, 1998.

Review of *The Tiger Orchard, Publishers Weekly,* January 30, 1995, p. 101.

Zvirin, Stephanie, review of *Face the Dragon, Booklist,* September 15, 1990, p. 157.

■ **For More Information See**

PERIODICALS

Booklist, December 15, 1989, p. 827; July, 1994, p. 1936; April 1, 1995, pp. 1404, 1416; April 1, 1997, p. 1310.

Kirkus Reviews, May 1, 1984, p. 153; October 1, 1990, p. 1398; May 1, 1996, p. 694.

School Library Journal, April, 1984, p. 127; June, 1987, p. 114; November, 1989, p. 129; April, 1992, p. 150; November, 1996, p. 126.

Wilson Library Bulletin, January, 1990, p. 7; September, 1994, p. 127.

—Sketch by J. Sydney Jones

Laura Ingalls Wilder

Mansfield Farm Loan Association, secretary-treasurer, 1919-27; writer, 1932-43. *Member:* Athenian Club, Justamere Club, Interesting Hour Club, Wednesday Study Club, and Eastern Star.

■ Personal

Born February 7, 1867, in Pepin, WI; died February 10, 1957, in Mansfield, MO; buried in Mansfield Cemetery; daughter of Charles Philip and Caroline Lake (maiden name, Quiner) Ingalls; married Almanzo James Wilder, August 25, 1885 (died October 23, 1949); children: Rose (Mrs. Gillette Lane), a son (deceased). *Education:* Attended schools in Wisconsin, Iowa, Minnesota, and the Dakota Territory.

■ Addresses

Home—Rocky Ridge Farm, Mansfield, MO.

■ Career

Teacher in schools near De Smet, Dakota Territory (now South Dakota), 1882-85; farmer in De Smet, 1885-94, and Mansfield, MO, beginning in 1894; worked with Missouri Home Development Association, beginning in 1910; *Missouri Ruralist,* household editor and contributing editor, 1911-24;

■ Awards, Honors

Newbery Honor Book, 1938, for *On the Banks of Plum Creek,* 1940, for *By the Shores of Silver Lake,* 1941, for *The Long Winter,* 1942, for *Little Town on the Prairie,* and 1944, for *Those Happy Golden Years;* Pacific Northwest Library Association Young Readers' Choice Award, 1942, for *By the Shores of Silver Lake; Book World* Children's Spring Book Festival Award, 1943, for *These Happy Golden Years;* Laura Ingalls Wilder Award, American Library Association, 1954, for her autobiographical novels (since 1960 this award in her honor is made every five years to an outstanding author or illustrator of children's books); elected to Ozark Hall of Fame, 1977; inducted into South Dakota Cowboy and Western Hall of Fame, 1978.

■ Writings

NOVELS

Little House in the Big Woods, illustrated by Helen Sewell, Harper, 1932, illustrated by Garth Williams, Harper, 1953.
Farmer Boy, illustrated by Helen Sewell, Harper, 1933, illustrated by Garth Williams, Harper, 1953.

Little House on the Prairie, illustrated by Helen Sewell, Harper, 1935, illustrated by Garth Williams, Harper, 1953.

On the Banks of Plum Creek, illustrated by Helen Sewell and Mildred Boyle, Harper, 1937, illustrated by Garth Williams, Harper, 1953.

By the Shores of Silver Lake, illustrated by Helen Sewell and Mildred Boyle, Harper, 1939, illustrated by Garth Williams, Harper, 1953, special edition, E. M. Hale, 1956.

The Long Winter, illustrated by Helen Sewell and Mildred Boyle, Harper, 1940, illustrated by Garth Williams, Harper, 1953.

Little Town on the Prairie, illustrated by Helen Sewell and Mildred Boyle, Harper, 1941, illustrated by Garth Williams, Harper, 1953.

These Happy Golden Years, illustrated by Helen Sewell and Mildred Boyle, Harper, 1943, illustrated by Garth Williams, Harper, 1953.

The First Four Years, edited by Roger Lea MacBride, illustrated by Garth Williams, Harper, 1971.

OTHER

On the Way Home: The Diary of a Trip from South Dakota to Mansfield, Missouri, in 1894, edited by daughter, Rose Wilder Lane, Harper, 1962.

West from Home: Letters of Laura Ingalls Wilder, San Francisco, 1915, edited by Roger Lea MacBride, Harper, 1974.

(With daughter, Rose Wilder Lane) *A Little House Sampler*, edited by William Anderson, University of Nebraska Press, 1988.

Little House in the Ozarks (nonfiction), edited by Stephen W. Hines, Nelson, 1991.

Laura Ingalls Wilder's Fairy Poems, edited by Stephen Hines, and illustrated by Richard Hull, Doubleday, 1998.

A Little House Reader: A Collection of Writings by Laura Ingalls Wilder, edited by William Anderson, HarperCollins, 1998.

Contributor of articles to magazines and newspapers, including *Country Gentleman, McCall's Youth Companion, St. Nicholas, Child Life, San Francisco Bulletin, St. Louis Star, Missouri Ruralist, De Smet News*, and *Christian Science Monitor*. Wilder's books have been translated into more than twenty languages. Her manuscripts and letters are housed at the Laura Ingalls Wilder Home and Museum, Mansfield, MO, the Detroit Public Library, Detroit, MI, and the Pomona Public Library, Pomona, CA.

■ Adaptations

Little House on the Prairie was adapted for a television series of the same name, NBC, 1974-82, and for *Little House: A New Beginning*, NBC, 1982-83; *Little House in the Big Woods* was adapted for a sound recording, Pathways of Sound, 1976; Wilder's autobiographical novels were adapted for the musical *Prairie*, produced on Broadway, 1982.

■ Sidelights

Laura Ingalls Wilder has become an icon of family values and honest, simple living, creating in her eight "Little House" books an American myth of the frontier. Hailed by readers in the United States and around the world as one of the greatest children's writers of the century, Wilder still reaches readers, both young and old, some seventy years after publication of her first "Little House" title. Conservative estimates of printings of her books tally at over forty million, making her one of the most successful of children's authors, as well. Wilder's immense popularity is in no small part the result of her living what she wrote: her books featuring young Laura and her adventures, trials, and hard work on the American frontier have a strong ring of authenticity. They are rich not only in their evocation of the intricacies of survival on the American frontier, but also valuable as a socio-historical chronicle of the country's final westward expansion following passage of the Homestead Act of 1862.

Though not purely autobiographical, the "Little House" books recreate a lost world of simplicity and family courage. In fact, Wilder had little time for the writing of these experiences until she was in her sixties and had, of necessity, slowed down somewhat from her daily round of farm work. Dubbed the "Grandma Moses of fiction" by Isabelle Jan in her *On Children's Literature*, Wilder has also been called "the quintessential American pioneer" by William Anderson in *Children's Books and their Creators*. Simply put, Laura Ingalls Wilder "is one of the best-known and most widely respected authors who ever wrote for children," according to Kathy Piehl in *Dictionary of Literary Biography*.

Wilder was twenty-eight by the time she and her husband, Almanzo Wilder, left the South Dakota prairie for the verdant Ozarks of Missouri and set up farming there. In the nearly three decades of her life that preceded this move, she had already packed enough experience for several lifetimes, and the rhythmic, season-driven life of the farm in Missouri made her grow reflective. As Donald Zochert quoted in his biography, *Laura: The Life of Laura Ingalls Wilder,* the future author saw life around her as much too harried: "Notice the faces of the people who rush by on the streets or on our country roads. They nearly always have a strained, harassed look and any one you meet will tell you there is no time for anything anymore. . . . I believe we would be happier to have a personal revolution in our individual lives and go back to simpler living and more direct thinking. It is the simple things of life that make living worth while, the sweet fundamental things such as love and duty, work and rest and living close to nature. . . ." These sentiments from a century ago make Wilder sound very contemporary; a child of the flower generation, perhaps. Wilder spent the last years of her long life celebrating the "sweet fundamental things" in her writings.

A Little House in the Big Woods

Wilder was born on February 7, 1867, in the Big Woods near Pepin, Wisconsin. Even at the time of her birth, Wilder's father, Charles Ingalls, was infected with a fever that would keep his family in almost perpetual flux for the next decade: the desire to head out for less populated territory, to push westward. The descendant, according to Wilder, of *Mayflower* pioneers to America, Charles Ingalls was inclined toward adventure, a restless sort of man not unlike thousands of others who had pushed the U.S. frontier ever westward. He was born in Cuba, New York, in 1836, but had grown up largely on the frontier. His parents, Landsford and Laura Ingalls, are the Grandpa and Grandma of Wilder's later fiction. Charles Ingalls had a particular fondness for his fiddle, and his music would prove a joy and solace to his family in the coming years. An inveterate storyteller, he liked to refer to himself as a carpenter, but he also worked at various times as a farmer, hunter, trapper, hotel manager, butcher, storekeeper, and even Justice of the Peace. Wilder's mother, Caroline, was of Scottish ancestry, and though raised on the frontier, she was educated, teaching school for five years before her marriage. She loved books, especially *Millbank* by Mary Jane Holmes. As Ann Romines noted in her *Construct-*

ing the Little House, "Ma read aloud from this book so frequently that Laura memorized the first sentences before she learned to read." Caroline Ingalls instilled the need for education and culture in her children, including older sister Mary.

Not long after Laura's first birthday, the family set off westward, accompanied by the Quiners, an aunt and uncle on the mother's side. Initially they settled for a year in Chariton County, Missouri. Soon the Quiners decided to return to the forest near Pepin, but the Ingalls family headed farther west by covered wagon, into Kansas and Indian Territory. Settling in southeastern Kansas, some twelve miles from the town of Independence, they built a house on the prairie where Charles could both farm and hunt without feeling neighbors encroaching. Unwittingly, however, *they* had encroached on Native American lands. In the summer of 1870 the entire family came down with malaria and nearly died; later that same summer a third child was born, Caroline, known as Carrie. In 1871 the family had to leave their land, which in fact belonged to the Osage Indians. That summer they made their way back though Missouri and Iowa to Wisconsin, to their house in the Big Woods.

Wilder's family lived in a log cabin her father painstakingly built by hand, as seen in this illustration by Garth Williams from *Little House on the Prairie.*

Back in the relative civilization of Wisconsin, the Ingalls children attended their first public school, and with family nearby, there were many opportunities for get-togethers, social occasions that would later figure into the works of young Laura Ingalls. This hiatus from the frontier ended in 1874, however, when Charles sold the land near Pepin and moved the family to Minnesota where they settled initially in a dugout on Plum Creek, a mile from the town of Walnut Grove in the southwestern part of the state. With timber scarce on the prairie, the best building material was the earth itself. After the initial plowing of prairie land, a thick strata of grass roots and earth was available to be hacked by axe into smaller, brick-size lengths of sod. These could be used to build the walls of primitive dwellings, but settlers would usually dig down about four feet into the ground so that the walls did not have to stand so high and support too much weight—hence the name "dugout." The interior walls of such sod houses could be whitewashed and though damp at first, would provide excellent insulation from extreme heat and cold.

At Plum Creek the Ingalls took up wheat farming, joined in the activities of the local church, and soon constructed a wood-frame house. Laura and Mary attended school, making friends with the Kennedy children and an enemy of the snobby Nellie Owens. Things were looking up for the family when a plague of grasshoppers—millions of them that turned the sky dark—destroyed their wheat crop and forced Charles to leave the farm to seek work on farms further east. Returning to his family in the fall of 1875, he moved them into town where he could find work. That November, a fourth child was born, a son, Charles Frederick. The family made it through the winter, planting again, but when the grasshoppers returned for a second time, they had to sell up and leave. Departure was not made any easier by the death of the baby Freddie.

Next, the Ingalls family tried Iowa, where Charles and his wife helped to run a hotel in Burr Oak. Here Laura and Mary continued their education, and after school would help wait on tables and wash dishes. When the hotel was to be sold, Charles found other work around town and the family moved to a little brick house on the outskirts where a fourth daughter, Grace, was born. In the summer of 1877, with Laura just ten, the family moved back to Walnut Grove, Minnesota,

where the father found work in another hotel. He managed to save up enough money with other work as a butcher and carpenter to build the family a house. Laura and Mary again attended school in Walnut Grove, and by now Nellie Owens had a rival in Genny Masters. Both these girls would later form the composite character of Nellie Oleson in Wilder's "Little House" books. Things were looking up again when Mary contracted a fever that almost killed her. Though she survived, she was left blind for the rest of her life.

A Dakota Family

Life in Minnesota came to an end when Charles's sister Docia stopped by on her own way west. Her husband had been employed by the Chicago and North Western Railroad, and she was on her way to join him. She also informed Charles of a possible job for the company as storekeeper, book-

Wilder with her husband, Almanzo.

keeper, and timekeeper. It took little cajoling for Charles to set out for Dakota Territory and his new job. The family followed and spent the first winter at Silver Lake, where they were almost the only settlers. But by the spring, many newcomers arrived, and the town of De Smet quickly sprouted out of the prairie. Ingalls took a claim on 160 acres three miles from De Smet, near Silver Lake. Terms of the Homestead Act allowed a person to own the acreage outright after building some kind of home on the land, cultivating the land, and living on it for at least six months each year for five years. This was, Charles Ingalls promised his wife, the last move they would make.

After building a rough shanty on the claim for the summer, the family moved into town for the winter. It was fortunate they did, for they barely survived the harsh winter of 1880-81, isolated from the rest of the world from the first of the blizzards in December until May. Snow piled up forty feet high on the tracks and the handful of citizens had to count on each other for survival. When the spring thaws finally came, Laura began working in town to help the family save money to send sister Mary to a school for the blind in Iowa. Thereafter, the family alternated between living in town during the winters and on their claim in the summers.

As a teenager, Laura had turned shy and found it difficult to mix socially. She was a good student, especially in English, but for a time her haven at school was ruined when Genny Masters arrived from Walnut Grove along with a new teacher, Eliza Jane Wilder, who did not much like Laura. Soon, however, the new teacher left and Laura was once again top of her class. Though only fifteen, Laura was offered a teaching position at a small school about fifteen miles from De Smet. She stayed with the Bouchie family who ran the school, and if the students did not prove challenge enough, Mrs. Bouchie's depressions did. Soon Laura was courted by Almanzo Wilder, ten years her senior, who took to driving her between the school and De Smet for weekends. Wilder, originally from Minnesota, had been in the De Smet region since 1879 with a claim to the north of town, and it was his older sister who had been Laura's teacher for a time. Her first teaching experience over, Laura herself returned to school, though she never graduated from high school. In the summer of 1884 she and Almanzo Wilder

$1.50 J8
$1.70 in Canada

A Harper Trophy Book

THESE HAPPY GOLDEN YEARS
Laura Ingalls Wilder

pictures by Garth Williams

The author's fifth Newbery Honor Book describes her coming of age and her courtship and marriage to Almanzo Wilder.

were engaged; they married a year later, on August 25, 1885.

The first years of her marriage were not easy. Settling on Almanzo's land, they worked toward creating a real farm. Crop failures, however, sent the Wilders into debt. Their daughter Rose was born in 1886, but two years later she had to be sent to her grandparents when both Laura and Almanzo came down with diphtheria. Returning to work too soon after the illness, Almanzo suffered a stroke from which he never fully recovered. The next year a baby boy was born, only to die twelve days later, and shortly thereafter their house was destroyed by fire. These were enough setbacks to make the average person despair, and when the crops failed again in 1890, the Wilders migrated to Florida where it was thought the climate would make things easier for Almanzo. Two years later, however, they were back in what was now South Dakota, saving money for a move to Missouri. With $100 in savings, the family headed for the Ozarks, eventually buying forty acres of rocky farmland near Mansfield, Missouri.

Rocky Ridge Farm and the Birth of a Writer

The Wilders worked together clearing their land, spending the first years in a simple cabin on the property of Rocky Ridge Farm. Slowly they built up their holdings, increasing their acreage to 200 and building a ten-room house. They raised hogs, sheep, goats, and cows, and Laura Wilder became renowned for her poultry, selling eggs in addition to produce. The farm prospered. However, the years "were not all filled with work," as Wilder is quoted as saying in an *American Ideals* article by William Anderson. "Rose walked three-quarters of a mile to school the second year and after and her schoolmates visited her on Saturdays. She and I played along the little creek near the house. We tamed the wild birds and squirrels; picked wild flowers and berries. Almanzo and I went horseback riding over the hills and through the woods. And always we had our papers and books from the school library for reading in the evenings and on Sunday afternoon."

Their life together on the farm bred an independence of thought, as well. "We who lived in quiet places have the opportunity to become acquainted with ourselves, to think our own thoughts and live our own lives," she noted in *American Ideals*. Wilder could not understand women who were dissatisfied with the role of a farm wife, who wanted a modern life of a career woman. For Wilder, farm women had always been businesswomen.

After her daughter set out on her own in 1904, Wilder began to write for local periodicals, eventually doing a regular column for the *Missouri Ruralist* between 1911 and 1924. She also became an officer of the Missouri Home Development Association and took a lively interest in improving the lot of farm women, appearing as a speaker at various farmer's institutes and meetings and talking about her poultry methods and general improvements for country living. A 1915 trip to

San Francisco to visit her recently separated daughter was a turning point for Wilder. Her daughter Rose had become a writer, and while in San Francisco she worked with her mother on technique and style. By the time Wilder returned to Missouri, she was filled with plans for articles. It would take over another decade, however, for her to turn her hand to stories about her own youth.

Meanwhile, back at Rocky Ridge Farm, Wilder helped to found the Mansfield Farm Loan Association which offered low-interest federal loans to Ozark farmers. She served as secretary-treasurer of the company for eight years, using a small study of the farm house as her office. Beginning in 1924, Wilder's daughter Rose spent a good deal of time in Mansfield, and it was then that Wilder began to work on stories from her childhood. Rose Wilder Lane had by this time made a name for herself as a writer and journalist, and had spent time abroad, living in Albania primarily. Planning to live and work at Rocky Ridge Farm, Rose had a new cottage built for her parents while she took over the farm house.

It was during these years that a collaborative effort took place: Rose greatly influenced her mother to write about her own experiences, and later would also help with rewriting and editing. Recent critical debate has focused on the extent of Rose Lane's contribution to Wilder's novels. As Piehl observed in *Dictionary of Literary Biography*, "Probably Lane's contributions to the writing of the "Little House" books can never be determined exactly, but on the basis of the fiction she did write, it seems safe to say that she could not have written the children's books alone. . . . The books lose none of their value if we acknowledge that Lane contributed to their writing in many ways." By the late 1920s, Wilder had completed *Pioneer Girl*, an unpublished autobiography which was the skeleton of the eight books that would form the "Little House" series. *Pioneer Girl*, however, was a bare recital of facts as compared to what would be Wilder's first published works.

The "Little House" Books

Between 1932 and 1943, then in her sixties, Laura Ingalls Wilder produced her series of eight books chronicling, in the third person, her life as a child and a young woman. Written for middle-grade readers, the books can be appreciated, as a critic in the *Times Literary Supplement* noted, "on two levels": understandable to children who can participate in "the troubles and joys of Laura's daily life," and appreciated by adults who would be aware of what the parents were going through. The characters in the novels are the Ingalls family themselves, and later books include Almanzo, as well. The cycle takes the reader through the early years in Wisconsin to Laura's marriage in De Smet, and with the passage of time the books "show a decidedly more complex plot structure and character development," according to Anderson in *Children's Books and Their Creators*. Though largely autobiographical, the books do sometimes telescope time and experience for fictional ends. As Janet Spaeth observed in her critical study, *Laura Ingalls Wilder*, these ends sometimes "demanded a refashioning of the events of her life to retain the larger truth that she wanted to convey—the pioneer experience in America."

With the aid of her daughter Rose, Wilder offered the first book in the series, with a working title of "When Grandma Was a Little Girl," to Alfred A. Knopf, but it was finally published by Harper as *Little House in the Big Woods*. The children's editor at Harper was, as Piehl pointed out in *Dictionary of Literary Biography*, Virginia Kirkus, who would later found *Kirkus Reviews*. At first skeptical about this simple story of life in the Wisconsin woods, Kirkus soon grew enthusiastic about its potential to transcend the doldrums into which the Depression had thrown all U.S. industry, including publishing.

Little House in the Big Woods is set in the home near Pepin, Wisconsin, where Laura was born, though events chronicle a year in the life of the family during their second sojourn there, from 1870 to 1874. This book is full of the stories that Pa, as he is called, told the real Laura when she was a little girl. Isolated from other people, the family must learn to do things for themselves: smoke meat, gather provisions, make bullets and cheese, harvest grain, and cook maple syrup. Laura is five in the book and plays with her sister Mary and the baby Carrie. Introduced in this first story is the fact that Laura, despite her best efforts, can not always be good, unlike her older sister Mary. The timeless rhythm and routine of this simple life is captured in one scene, where Pa is playing his fiddle and Ma is knitting. Laura is in bed thinking of the safety of family: "She

thought to herself, 'This is now.'" With publication of the first title, Kirkus's intuition was proven correct. Readers responded favorably to the book, as did critics. A reviewer in the *Junior Bookshelf* noted that the novel was "an extremely good book, with an excellence which is so unobtrusive that it may well go unnoticed."

Wilder next wrote about her husband's boyhood, growing up on a farm in New York State. *Farmer Boy* looks at Almanzo, one of four children, at nine years old and goes into the same sort of loving detail about his farm childhood that she conjured up for her own youth. There is sheep-shearing and shingle-cutting, chores and county fairs. As Piehl noted in *Dictionary of Literary Biography*, "Rich detail about many aspects of farm life help the reader participate in Almanzo's experiences." But readers and editors wanted more of the Ingalls family, and Wilder's third book mined her own unpublished "Pioneer Girl" for further stories.

Little House on the Prairie relates a year in the life of the family after they leave the Big Woods for Kansas and settle in Indian Territory. Home-building is described in detail—from cutting the logs to making the pegs that substitute for nails on the frontier. Indeed, some critics have observed that Wilder's books are survival manuals, so detailed are her descriptions. There are high times and low: the family is stricken with malaria; Christmas is saved for the girls when a neighbor, Mr. Edwards, crosses a swollen creek to deliver presents. And there are the local Indians, most of whom scare Ma into giving them anything they set their eyes on in her home. As Piehl pointed out, "in this book Ma and Pa start to emerge as distinct characters rather than simply parents." Ma places the china figurine of a shepherdess—which she carries with them wherever they go—on the mantel of their new home to signify that they have arrived. And Laura herself continues to grow. She is not simply the naughty little girl of the first volume, but now displays real fortitude and courage, as when she saves Ma and Carrie from a chimney fire. The book ends with the family moving on once again, informed by the government that they can not stay in Indian Territory. This third title proved as popular as the earlier ones. A *Times Literary Supplement* reviewer noted especially that "Prairie wild life is vividly described . . . so too is the quiet everyday life of the pioneer and his family."

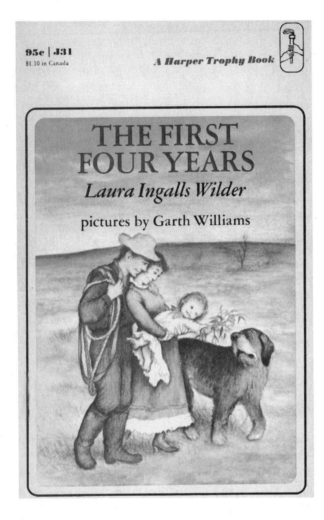

95¢ | J31
$1.10 in Canada

A Harper Trophy Book

THE FIRST
FOUR YEARS
Laura Ingalls Wilder

pictures by Garth Williams

This 1971 addition to the "Little House" series chronicles the joys and struggles the author encountered as she started a family of her own.

The family's experiences near Walnut Grove, Minnesota, form the core of Wilder's fourth title, *On the Banks of Plum Creek*. Here is the sod house they lived in the first year, the school Mary and Laura attend, and the snobby storekeeper's daughter, Nellie Oleson, a composite of real-life girls who plagued Wilder's youth. The grasshoppers ruin their crops two years running and Pa is forced to walk 300 miles east to find farm work. Laura and Mary grow closer as Laura begins to see that maybe her older sister is not so purely good as she thought, for they are both disappointed that their first Christmas at Plum Creek brings them only horses that Pa can use for plowing. But the book ends again on a positive note when their second Christmas brings the safe return of Pa through a blizzard. *On the Banks of*

Plum Creek was the first of Wilder's works to be named a Newbery Honor Book. Though none of her titles won the Newbery Medal, four more were named Honor Books.

Wilder picks up the family story two years later in *By the Shores of Silver Lake*. They are still in Minnesota, but things have gone from bad to worse. The family has scarlet fever, Mary is blind, and there have been more crop failures. Pa's sister comes for a visit, and he is offered a job with the railroad that will ultimately take the family to the Dakota Territory. They spend the first winter in the surveyor's house by Silver Lake, and in the spring Pa files a claim on land. The hours of work are long, but again present in the book are the simple rewards to be had from reliance upon family and honest labor. Laura loses her dog, Jack, before leaving Minnesota, and learns to take more responsibility, especially for her blind sister. At thirteen, she is growing into a young adult.

With these first five titles, Wilder had taken her family to De Smet, where the final three titles would take place. She had already gained fans around the world for her works. Anne Thaxter Eaton, in *Reading with Children*, observed that in these first five titles Wilder "has caught the very essence of pioneer life: the feeling of satisfaction brought by hard work, the thrill of accomplishment, and of safety and comfort made possible by resourcefulness and exertion." It was the perfect message for a country plagued by the despair of the Great Depression.

Wilder took some time out in 1939 after this fifth title to travel back to De Smet, South Dakota with her husband for Old Settlers' Day. Almanzo was eighty-two and Wilder seventy-three, but the couple drove all the way, re-establishing contact with the old friends who were still living. Wilder's father had died in 1902; her mother in 1924; her sister Mary in 1928. Carrie and Grace were still living, though they would both die in the next decade, leaving Laura the last living member of the family. Returning by car through Wyoming, Colorado, and Kansas, Wilder soon got to work on her sixth title in the series, *The Long Winter*. May Hill Arbuthnot noted in her *Children's Reading in the Home* that "No child in the United States should miss the Wilder *Little House* series. . . . Here in these books, children will find security of the heart and of the emotions, the kind

If you enjoy the works of Laura Ingalls Wilder, you may also want to check out the following books and films:

Patricia Beatty, *Bonanza Girl*, 1993.
Belinda Hurmence, *Dixie in the Big Pasture*, 1994.
Theodore Taylor, *Walking Up a Rainbow*, 1986.
Sarah, Plain and Tall, starring Glenn Close, 1991.

of security that weathers every storm." Arbuthnot also noted that if only one book of the series could be read, "don't let a child miss *The Long Winter*. It is the summation of the quiet, unsung heroism of thousands of nameless people who ventured into the wilderness and took and held the land."

As the title suggests, *The Long Winter* chronicles the harsh winter of 1880-81, when blizzards cut off De Smet from the outside world and starvation was a constant threat. In the book, Pa recognizes signs that a hard winter is to come, and an Indian who appears in town also prophesies a long winter. Pa moves his family into town from their claim shanty, but nothing prepares them for the blizzards that isolate them from the rest of the world from October through April. Even Pa's fiddle playing loses its therapeutic powers, and the family spends most of each day braiding prairie grass to burn in lieu of other fuel. Near starvation, the town is saved by Almanzo and another man who brave the snow to find a settler who has a surplus supply of wheat.

"In the book Wilder shows herself to be a master of using description to create a mood," observed Piehl in *Dictionary of Literary Biography*. "The endless succession of storms and wearing effect they have on people are created by repetition of words." A reviewer in the *Junior Bookshelf* noted that "Every detail shines clearly, so that the pages almost crackle with frost as one reads," and concluded that the series of Wilder novels "may well prove some of the best books describing real life on the prairies that have been written for this generation." A *Times Literary Supplement* critic thought that "*The Long Winter* [is] perhaps,

through its concentrated theme, the most impressive of [Wilder's] vivid and memorable narratives," while John Rowe Townsend remarked in his *Written for Children* that this novel "is about family solidarity, the warmth of love opposed to the hostile elements. The story intensifies until at last there is the one enemy, winter; the one issue, survival. The writing is clear, plain, and as good as bread."

The final two books in the series, *Little Town on the Prairie* and *These Happy Golden Years*, also take place in De Smet and depict both a town and Laura growing toward maturity. Nellie Oleson from Plum Creek shows up to give Laura a hard time, as well as Almanzo's sister, Eliza Jane Wilder, who treats Laura and Carrie unfairly. Laura is fifteen and soon will become a teacher in her own right. And Almanzo becomes more and more a part of Laura's fictional life, just as he did in real life. The settlers begin to lose some of the independence that sent them scrambling for the frontier: they begin to depend more and more on others not only for goods and services, but also for entertainment. By the completion of the eighth book, not only is the town of De Smet established, but Laura has also grown up, married Almanzo, and become a farmer's wife.

Reviewers and critics have posited many reasons for the popularity of the "Little House" books: their theme of optimistic resourcefulness that was so well received in the helpless, hopeless Depression years; their value as a historical record; the unswerving devotion of Wilder's daughter, Rose Lane, to the project, becoming editor (some would say co-author), agent and publicist for the books. Perhaps most important, however, is that the books live. Readers care about the characters, and the characters evolve and grow throughout the books. The "Little House" series has been compared to the books of Louisa May Alcott as being something of an American original. Eileen H. Colwell, writing in the *Junior Bookshelf*, noted that Laura "has something of the vitality, honesty and independence of Jo in *Little Women*, and she is brave and quick-witted." Colwell also noted that the story that runs through all eight books "is an absorbing one, full of humour, drama and warmth, and set against constantly changing background. The end of each book holds the promise of new adventures in the next. . . . There is no lack of adventure in these books, for it rises naturally from the environment and is never exaggerated for effect. . . . Surely the charm of these books lies in their warm humanity and faithfulness to life."

Colwell hits on many of the aspects of the "Little House" series that have made them an enduring classic: warmth, adventure, and sincerity. The children's novelist and essayist E. B. White also remarked on Wilder's sincerity and forthrightness of style. Writing in *Horn Book*, White observed that Wilder's prose "has a natural simplicity and goodness that [sets] it apart from the studied simplicity that often infects writing for children. In her books there are no traces of condescension—no patronage, no guile, and no cuteness. She speaks to us directly and brings her affectionate memories alive by the power of overwhelming detail and with a dramatic force that derives from honesty and accuracy. . . ." Susan Bagg, writing in *Atlantic Monthly*, echoed these comments, noting that "the adult voice behind the child's never condescends: she simplifies, omits what may be too difficult for a young listener to understand, but never shirks an experience. The result is a prose that is always dignified and restrained, often eloquent, a rarity in children's literature." Bagg concluded that in the "Little House" books "you are reading something that promised to be entertainment and that turns out to be art."

The Final Years

Wilder became a legend in her own lifetime, and the earnings from her books made her wealthy, but she and Almanzo never deviated from the simple farm routine they had established in the first years of their marriage. They sold off much of the land, but did move back into their original farm house when Rose once again moved on. Much of Wilder's time was taken up with answering fan mail from around the world. In 1949 Almanzo died, and Wilder stayed on the family farm, going to local events in Mansfield, but otherwise staying close to home. Late in life, Wilder suffered from several heart attacks, and died on February 10, 1957, just three days after her ninetieth birthday. She was buried in the Mansfield Cemetery next to her beloved husband.

Wilder's reputation continued to grow after her death, and her writings were added to by several books edited and prepared for publication in part by her daughter. The "Little House" series saw a new addition with *The First Four Years*, a chronicle of the initial difficult years of Wilder's marriage. Many reviewers felt this would have been better unpublished, as it did not have the usual Wilder finish to it, taken as it was from first-draft material. Piehl, in *Dictionary of Literary Biography*, noted that "Readers of Laura's earlier books will quickly notice the difference in style between this manuscript, taken directly from the orange-covered school tablets on which she always wrote, and the finished books that had been reworked." But avid fans of the "Little House" works met this new title with eager anticipation.

Unpublished letters and diary materials are included in two further titles published posthumously: *On the Way Home: The Diary of a Trip from South Dakota to Mansfield Missouri in 1894* and *West from Home: Letters of Laura Ingalls Wilder, San Francisco, 1915*. Yet Wilder's lasting achievement rests with the "Little House" books themselves which hold a message for the modern reader just as they did for those who read the first editions during the Great Depression. As Wilder noted in *American Ideals*, "The 'Little House' books are stories of long ago. Today our way of living and our schools are much different; so many things have made living and learning easier. But the real things haven't changed. It is still best to be honest and truthful; to make the most of what we have; to be happy with simple pleasures and have courage when things go wrong." In her life as in her writings, Wilder practiced what she preached.

■ Works Cited

Anderson, William, "Stories That Had to Be Told," *American Ideals*, 1981.

Anderson, William, "Wilder, Laura Ingalls," *Children's Books and Their Creators*, edited by Anita Silvey, Houghton Mifflin, 1995.

Arbuthnot, May Hill, *Children's Reading in the Home*, Scott, Foresman, 1969, pp. 132-33.

Bagg, Susan, *Atlantic Monthly*, February, 1975, pp. 117-18.

Colwell, Eileen H., "Laura Ingalls Wilder," *Junior Bookshelf*, November, 1962, pp. 237-43.

Eaton, Anne Thaxter, *Reading with Children*, Viking, 1940, p. 176.

Jan, Isabelle, *On Children's Literature*, Schocken, 1974, p. 119.

Review of *Little House in the Big Woods*, *Junior Bookshelf*, October, 1956, p. 221.

Review of *Little House on the Prairie, Times Literary Supplement*, November 15, 1957, p. xvi.

Review of *The Long Winter, Junior Bookshelf*, October, 1962, pp. 207-8.

Review of *The Long Winter, Times Literary Supplement*, November 23, 1962, p. 901.

Piehl, Kathy, "Laura Ingalls Wilder," *Dictionary of Literary Biography*, Volume 22: *American Writers for Children, 1900-1960*, Gale, 1983, pp. 352-66.

Romines, Ann, *Constructing the Little House*, University of Massachusetts Press, 1997, p. 14.

Spaeth, Janet, *Laura Ingalls Wilder*, Twayne, 1987.

Times Literary Supplement, June 1, 1962, p. 412.

Townsend, John Rowe, *Written for Children: An Outline of English-Language Children's Literature*, Lippincott, 1974, pp. 180-81.

White, E. B., *Horn Book*, August, 1970, pp. 349-50.

Wilder, Laura Ingalls, *Little House in the Big Woods*, Harper, 1953.

Zochert, Donald, *Laura: The Life of Laura Ingalls Wilder*, Regnery, 1976.

■ For More Information See

BOOKS

Anderson, William, *Laura Ingalls Wilder: A Biography*, HarperCollins, 1992.

Blair, Gwenda, *Laura Ingalls Wilder*, Putnam, 1983.

Children's Literature Review, Volume 2, Gale, 1976.

Dear Laura: Letters from Children to Laura Ingalls Wilder, HarperCollins, 1996.

Giff, Patricia Reilly, *Laura Ingalls Wilder: Growing up in the Little House*, Viking, 1987.

Hines, Stephen W., *I Remember Laura: Laura Ingalls Wilder*, Nelson, 1994.

Miller, John E., *Becoming Laura Ingalls Wilder: The Woman behind the Legend*, University of Missouri, 1998.

Twentieth-Century Children's Writers, 4th edition, St. James Press, 1995.

PERIODICALS

American West, Volume 21, 1984, pp. 35-42.

Children's Literature, Number 4, 1975, pp. 105-19; Number 7, 1978, pp. 7-16; Number 11, 1983, pp. 49-63.

Children's Literature in Education, Volume 8, 1977, pp. 63-70; Volume 11, 1980, pp. 101-19; Volume 20, number 3, 1989.

Elementary English, April, 1957, May, 1964; May, 1968; October, 1973.

Horn Book, October, 1943, pp. 293-306; December, 1953, pp. 411-39; October, 1965, pp. 465-73.

The Lion and the Unicorn, Volume 3, 1979, pp. 74-88.

New York Times Book Review, March 28, 1971, p. 28.

Time, March 15, 1971.

Top of the News, April, 1967, pp. 265-82.

Wilson Library Bulletin, April, 1948.

■ Obituaries

BOOKS

Current Biography, H. W. Wilson, 1957.

PERIODICALS

New York Times, February 12, 1957.

Publishers Weekly, February 25, 1957.

Wilson Library Bulletin, April, 1957.*

—Sketch by J. Sydney Jones

Virginia Euwer Wolff

■ Personal

Born August 25, 1937, in Portland, OR; daughter of Eugene Courtney (a lawyer and rancher) and Florence (a teacher and rancher; maiden name, Craven) Euwer; married Art Wolff, July 19, 1959 (divorced, June 1976); children: Anthony, Juliet. *Education:* Smith College, B.A., 1959. *Hobbies and other interests:* Playing the violin, swimming, hiking, gardening.

■ Career

The Miquon School, Philadelphia, PA, elementary school teacher, 1968-72; The Fiedel School, Glen Cove, NY, elementary school teacher, 1972-74; Hood River Valley High School, Hood River, OR, English teacher, 1976-86; Mt. Hood Academy, Government Camp, OR, English teacher, 1986—. Frequent speaker at children's book conferences. *Member:* Society of Children's Book Writers and Illustrators (national member and Northwest chapter member), Chamber Music Society of Oregon.

■ Awards, Honors

International Reading Association Award, young adult division, and PEN-West Book Award, both 1989, and Best Book for Young Adults selection, American Library Association (ALA), all for *Probably Still Nick Swansen;* award from Child Study Children's Book Committee at Bank Street College, and Golden Kite Award, Society of Children's Book Writers and Illustrators, both 1993, Oregon Book Award, Young Reader's category, 1994, Young Reader's Choice Award nominee, Canadian Library Association, 1996, Notable Book selection, and Best Book for Young Adults selection, both ALA, *Booklist* Editor's Choice and Top of the List winner, *School Library Journal* Best Books List, and *Parents Magazine*'s Reluctant Young Adult Readers list, all for *Make Lemonade;* Notable Book and a Best Book for Young Adults, ALA, Sixth Janusz Korczak Literary Competition honorable mention citation, Anti-Defamation League Braun Center for Holocaust Studies, all for *The Mozart Season.*

■ Writings

Rated PG (adult novel), St. Martin's, 1980.
Probably Still Nick Swansen, Holt, 1988.
The Mozart Season, Holt, 1991.
Make Lemonade, Holt, 1993.
Bat 6, Scholastic, 1998.

Wolff has also published poems and short stories in magazines, including *Ladies' Home Journal* and *Seventeen,* and was anthologized in the 1995 collection, *Ultimate Sports: Short Stories by Outstanding Writers for Young Adults,* edited by Donald R. Gallo.

■ Sidelights

Virginia Euwer Wolff came to young adult literature relatively late in life—approaching age fifty—but in a very short time and with four novels has created her own niche in the genre. "I major in disappointment," Wolff told *Booklist*'s Stephanie Zvirin in an interview, and indeed she is known for her incisive takes on outsiders, for kids who face and deal with disappointment, who confront confusing and disorienting experiences. From special education student Nick in *Probably Still Nick Swansen,* to Jolly, the single teenage mom in *Make Lemonade,* Wolff's protagonists face an uphill battle in life. And even when the way seems relatively smooth, as for the young violinist Allegra in *The Mozart Season,* the outsider status still pertains—in this case a gifted individual set apart from the quotidian.

Language is paramount in a Wolff novel. "We live by language," Wolff observed in a 1997 speech delivered at a children's literature conference and reprinted in *Horn Book.* "Incendiary and insightful. The language of the In-group, the Out-group—and always the potential for hostile fire between them." For Wolff, the type of language used either separates or includes: the language of education, of poverty, of music, of inchoate longing. The use of a particular form of speech or code sets a person in his or her world as firmly as does their economic or physical condition. "Insider and Outsider language are always a fragile, trembling balance," Wolff noted in her 1997 address. It is not surprising then that she has also declared that "Words have probably guided my life."

The Language of Oregon

Wolff was born in Portland, Oregon, on August 25, 1937, the second of two children. Her father, Eugene Courtney Euwer, was a lawyer in Pennsylvania before abandoning the rat race to move to the Pacific Northwest and grow fruit. Her mother, Florence, was a teacher. Though the Euwers lived in a hand-built log house without electricity, theirs was not a simple back-to-nature life; it was not a rejection of civilization but an enlargement on it. "I was born into a loved and loving home," Wolff recalled in *Horn Book.* "From our backyard we had a towering view of Mt. Hood, 11,235 feet high, with snow on it all year round. From our front lawn on a clear day we could see three more of the Cascades, including Mt. St. Helens." Surrounding the house were orchards and old growth Douglas fir, and inside "we had a grand piano, a huge stone fireplace, and a house full of books and paintings." Wolff grew up listening to Chopin and Beethoven, and learned early the pleasure of books, with Winnie the Pooh a constant companion.

In this 1988 work, a learning-disabled teen is forced to come to terms with himself and his past when he has a traumatic experience at the school prom.

This idyllic childhood was drastically altered with the death of her father when Wolff was five. "Suddenly the world that had just the day before made sense to us went kerplooey," she noted in *Horn Book*. In an autobiographical essay for *Seventh Book of Junior Authors and Illustrators*, Wolff observed that "this loss may have been the chief shaping event of my life." Wolff's mother determined to continue working the farm, a gutsy decision for a single woman in 1942. The life of music and art continued for both Wolff and her older brother. Going to school was a shock for the young Wolff, for here she came into contact with peers who spoke another sort of language—the direct speech of the playground. And trips to New York introduced her to still another reality—the world of museums and theater. Under the influence of a New York cousin, Wolff requested to learn the violin and her passion for music won her another vocabulary, one that she has continued to enlarge upon all her life.

At sixteen, Wolff was sent to boarding school far from the forests of Oregon, and from there she went on to study English at Smith College. During these years she fell under the influence of language masters such as the poets Gerard Manley Hopkins and Dylan Thomas, novelists like James Joyce and Nikolai Gogol, and of course Shakespeare. "I am in love with the English sentence," Wolff told Zvirin in her *Booklist* interview. The works of these writers helped to foster that love.

Family Years

Wolff married directly out of college and was introduced to the world of the theater, the world of her husband. For the next seventeen years she was a wife and mother of two children. Off-Broadway, regional, and repertory theaters on the Atlantic seaboard became her new reality, and the family moved twelve times in these years, living in Philadelphia, New York City, Long Island, Washington, D.C., Ohio, and Connecticut. She also taught English at both public and private schools. When her son and daughter were teenagers, she began to try to write. An M.F.A. program in writing put her on track for the long-distance job of novel writing, but she left two-thirds of the way through without finishing the degree.

Divorced in 1976, Wolff returned to her native Oregon, more an Easterner than a member of the Pacific Northwest community. Language differences were symbolic of how she had become an outsider to her own roots: "I said *ahpricot*, but had not gone as far as *tomahto*," she recalled in *Horn Book*. She taught at a public high school in Hood River, Oregon for ten years. During that time she published her first and only adult novel, *Rated PG*. "I don't admire the book," Wolff told *Booklist*'s Zvirin. "I guess first novels are always embarrassing." It was another seven years until she turned her hand to novel writing again, and this time she had in mind a story dealing with the young people whom she worked with daily as a teacher.

Early Successes

Wolff's first YA title, *Probably Still Nick Swansen*, deals with a learning-disabled student, a sixteen-year-old boy who is ridiculed by other students and also haunted by the death of his beloved sister who drowned seven years earlier. Room 19, the special education room, is the center of his school universe, but there are other challenges as well: learning to drive and learning to deal with emotional pain. Stood up by a former special education student, Shana, whom he has asked to the prom, he comes to understand the complexities of the world. Though Shana has mainstreamed from Room 19, she is still considered stupid by the others and still lives in turmoil and self-doubt.

Over the several weeks in Nick's life that the novel covers, "the reader becomes immersed . . . in Nick's world," according to Barbara A. Lynn, writing in *Voice of Youth Advocates*. Lynn concluded that this "is an exceptional novel for junior and senior high teens." Wolff also manages, through her close and detailed writing of character, to make Nick's problems not just those of a special education student. As Constance A. Mellon noted in *School Library Journal*, the book "stresses the similarities between Nick and other teens rather than highlighting the differences."

Wolff next turned to music and a twelve-year-old protagonist for her second title, *The Mozart Season*. Instead of an outsider, she chose someone very much on the inside of her chosen specialty. Allegra Shapiro is preparing for a music competition in which she will play Mozart's Fourth Violin Concerto in D. The way in which this young girl spends the summer mastering the work of a nineteen-year-old composer who wrote two cen-

Wolff received numerous awards for her 1993 portrayal of the friendship between a seventeen-year-old single mother and her poor but ambitious fourteen-year-old babysitter.

turies before her "is the basis of a sturdy, engrossing novel," according to a critic in the *New York Times Book Review*. Along the way, Allegra wrestles with what it means to be herself versus what her parents—both concert musicians—want her to be, as well as trying to come to terms with her Jewish identity.

Friends and relatives help Allegra: she learns of love from a singer friend of her mother; a homeless man, Mr. Trouble, seeks her help in assuaging the wounds of his past; her friends Jessica and

Sarah not only challenge her but also make her have fun; and her parents and brother lend their support. Rachel Gonsenhauser, writing in *Voice of Youth Advocates,* felt that "Wolff's story is mesmerizing" and went on to note that the author "conveys eloquently the fragility of life, and the importance of heritage." A reviewer for *Publishers Weekly*, while commenting on parts that seemed "slightly flawed," concluded that "it is a pleasure to have a novel of ideas for young adults that describes the delicate dance between honoring traditions of the past and being your own person in the present."

Make Lemonade

Wolff noted in her 1997 speech that after this second book "I needed to go in a different direction. I thought I could do something more dangerous." In *Make Lemonade,* partly inspired by a television series about the poor who fall into the cracks of the system and remain there for generations, Wolff decided to focus on several such individuals and most emphatically not make them victims. LaVaughn is fourteen and a bright student, saving money for college. Her mom is widowed and hard-working, but LaVaughn knows that if she wants an education, she is going to have to pay for it herself. To this end, she takes a job babysitting two young children, Jeremy and Jilly, offspring of a seventeen-year-old single parent, Jolly. When Jolly loses her job after rebuffing the sexual advances of her supervisor, LaVaughn is drawn more closely into Jolly's world, ultimately prompting the older girl to go back to school.

A critic in *Publishers Weekly* noted that this story, "radiant with hope" and told in a "meltingly lyric blank verse," was a "stellar addition to YA literature." Barbara Gorman, writing in *Kliatt*, noted in particular the format of the book, divided into sixty-six brief chapters "set up like a blank verse poem." A *Kirkus Reviews* contributor observed that *Make Lemonade* provided a "spare, beautifully crafted depiction of a 14-year-old whose goal of escaping poverty is challenged by friendship with a single teenage mother," and went on to remark that while the protagonists could be from almost any ethnic group or inner city, "their troubles—explored in exquisite specificity—are universal. Hopeful—and powerfully moving." Writing in *School Library Journal,* Carolyn Noah called the

If you enjoy the works of Virginia Euwer Woolf, you may also want to check out the following books and films:

Brock Cole, *The Goats*, 1987.
James Lincoln Collier, *The Jazz Kid*, 1994.
Cynthia Voight, *Izzy, Willy-Nilly*, 1986.
Jacqueline Woodson, *The Dear One*, 1991.
What's Eating Gilbert Grape, starring Johnny Depp and Leonardo DiCaprio, 1993.

book "a triumphant, outstanding story." Many other critics and awards committees agreed with that opinion.

Less Is More

Wolff is a self-confessed procrastinator. As she told *Booklist*'s Zvirin, "I'm able to delay and delay and delay, and even sabotage a book." Indeed, Wolff's books are slow in coming. Her fourth title, *Bat 6*, appeared in 1998, five years after *Make Lemonade*. *Bat 6* once again is a complete departure from Wolff's previous work. The book uses a softball game in 1949 between the sixth grade girls of two small Oregon towns to explore the meanings and echoes of prejudice. Told as a series of flashbacks by various players, the central conflict develops between Aki, a Japanese American, and Shazam, whose father was killed at Pearl Harbor.

Once again, Wolff employed the rhythms and vernacular of actual everyday speech to build her narrative. A *Kirkus Reviews* critic remarked that "Through the first-person narrations of the 21 girls of the two teams, the story emerges . . . their emotions and perspectives ring true." Bill Mollineaux, writing in *Voice of Youth Advocates*, stated that the author "paints a picture of small-town America in the Forties that shows its beliefs, attitudes, and values. . . ." *School Library Journal* contributor Luann Toth observed that "Wolff delves into the irreversible consequences of war and the necessity to cultivate peace and speaks volumes about courage, responsibility, and reconciliation—all in a book about softball."

Wolff is untroubled by the fact that her books take years to complete, for writing is not her only

work. She still teaches English, but now only during the ski season at Mt. Hood Academy, a school for competitive skiers, many of whom are preparing for the Olympics. She also takes pleasure in her children—her son, a jazz guitarist with a degree in religious studies, and her daughter, a psychotherapist and a mother in her own right—and in her grandchild. Life, in many ways, has come full circle for Wolff, for she is once again living in the shadow of Mt. Hood, just as she did as a child. Language is still paramount for her, but in the final analysis, as she concluded to Zvirin, "I guess I'd rather write fewer books and have them be unusual . . . than write quantity."

■ Works Cited

Review of *Bat 6, Kirkus Reviews*, May 1, 1998, p. 666.

Gonsenhauser, Rachel, review of *The Mozart Season, Voice of Youth Advocates*, December, 1991, p. 320.

Gorman, Barbara, review of *Make Lemonade, Kliatt*, November, 1994, p. 16.

Lynn, Barbara A., review of *Probably Still Nick Swansen, Voice of Youth Advocates*, June, 1989, p. 109.

Review of *Make Lemonade, Kirkus Reviews*, May 15, 1993, p. 670.

Review of *Make Lemonade, Publishers Weekly*, May 31, 1993, p. 56.

Mellon, Constance A., review of *Probably Still Nick Swansen, School Library Journal*, December, 1988, p. 124.

Mollineaux, Bill, review of *Bat 6, Voice of Youth Advocates*, June, 1998, pp. 126-27.

Review of *The Mozart Season, New York Times Book Review*, August 4, 1991, p. 21.

Review of *The Mozart Season, Publishers Weekly*, May 24, 1991, p. 59.

Noah, Carolyn, review of *Make Lemonade, School Library Journal*, July, 1993, p. 103.

Seventh Book of Junior Authors and Illustrators, edited by Sally Holmes Holtze, H. W. Wilson, 1996, pp. 348-50.

Toth, Luann, review of *Bat 6, School Library Journal*, May, 1998, p. 150.

Wolff, Virginia Euwer, "If I Was Doing It Proper, What Was You Laughing At?," *Horn Book*, May-June, 1998, pp. 297-308.

Zvirin, Stephanie, "The *Booklist* Interview," *Booklist*, March 1, 1994, pp. 1250-51.

■ For More Information See

BOOKS

Twentieth-Century Young Adult Writers, St. James Press, 1994, pp. 713-14.

PERIODICALS

Books for Keeps, July, 1995, p. 28; November, 1996, p. 11.
Bulletin of the Center for Children's Books, July-August, 1991, p. 279; July-August, 1993, p. 361; June, 1998, pp. 378-79.

Horn Book, September-October, 1991, p. 599; September-October, 1993, p. 606; July-August, 1998, pp. 500-1.
New York Times Book Review, October 17, 1993, p. 33.
Publishers Weekly, July 11, 1994, p. 80; April 20, 1998, p. 67.
School Library Journal, November, 1989, pp. 42-43; December, 1993, p. 28.
Times Educational Supplement, September 1, 1995, p. 24.
Voice of Youth Advocates, October, 1993, p. 220.
Wilson Library Bulletin, June, 1989, p. 101; November, 1989, p. 11.*

—Sketch by J. Sydney Jones

Acknowledgments

Acknowledgments

Grateful acknowledgment is made to the following publishers, authors,
and artists for their kind permission to reproduce copyrighted material.

JAMES BENNETT. Hillenbrand, William, illustrator. From a jacket of *I Can Hear the Mourning Dove,* by James Bennett. Houghton Mifflin, 1990. Jacket art © 1990 by William Hillenbrand. All rights reserved. Reproduced by permission of Houghton Mifflin Company. / O'Brien, Tim, illustrator. From a jacket of *The Squared Circle,* by James Bennett. Scholastic Inc., 1995. Jacket illustration © 1995 by Tim O'Brien. Reproduced by permission of Scholastic Inc. / Bennett, James, photograph. Reproduced by permission of James Bennett.

JUDY BLUME. Cover of *Forever,* by Judy Blume. Pocket Books, 1976. Copyright © 1975 by Judy Blume. Reproduced by permission of Simon & Schuster Books for Young Readers, an imprint of Simon & Schuster Children's Publishing Division. / Earley, Lori, illustrator. From a cover of *Are You There God? It's Me, Margaret,* by Judy Blume. Bantam Books, 1986. Reproduced by permission of Bantam Doubleday Dell Books for Young Readers. / Cover of *Deenie,* by Judy Blume. Bantam Books, 1991. Reproduced by permission of Bantam Doubleday Dell Books for Young Readers. / Cover of *Tiger Eyes,* by Judy Blume. Bantam Books, 1991. Reproduced by permission of Bantam Doubleday Dell Books for Young Readers. / Blume, Judy, photograph. AP/Wide World Photos. Reproduced by permission.

JORGE LUIS BORGES. Kuhlman, Gilda, illustrator. From a cover of *Labyrinths: Selected Stories & Other Writings,* by Jorge Luis Borges. Translated by James E. Irby. New Directions, 1964. Copyright © 1962, 1964, renewed 1992 by New Directions Publishing Corporation. Reproduced by permission of New Directions Publishing Corporation. In the British Commonwealth by Laurence Pollinger Ltd. / Braren, Ken, illustrator. From a jacket of *Selected Poems, 1923-1967,* by Jorge Luis Borges. Edited and translated by Norman Thomas di Giovanni. Delacorte Press/Seymour Lawrence, 1972. Reproduced by permission of Bantam Books, a division of Bantam Doubleday Dell Publishing Group, Inc. / McMullan, James, illustrator. From a cover of *The Aleph and Other Stories, 1933-1969,* by Jorge Luis Borges. Edited and translated by Norman Thomas di Giovanni. E. P. Dutton, 1978. Translation copyright © 1968, 1969, 1970 by Emece Editores, S. A. and Norman Thomas di Giovanni. Used by permission of Dutton, a division of Penguin Putnam Inc. / McMullan, James, illustrator. From a jacket of *Six Problems for Don Isidro Parodi,* by Jorge Luis Borges and Adolfo Bioy-Casares. Translated by Norman Thomas di Giovanni. E. P. Dutton, 1981. Translation copyright © 1980, 1981 by Jorge Luis Borges, Adolfo Bioy-Casares, and Norman Thomas di Giovanni. Used by permission of Dutton, a division of Penguin Putnam Inc. / Borges, Jorge Luis, photograph by Harold Mantell. Reproduced by permission of Harold Mantell.

BEBE MOORE CAMPBELL. Jacket of *Brothers and Sisters,* by Bebe Moore Campbell. Berkley Books, 1995. Copyright © 1994 by Bebe Moore Campbell. Reproduced by arrangement with The Berkley Publishing Group, a division of Penguin Putnam Inc. All rights reserved. / Campbell, Bebe Moore, photograph by Gene Golden. G. P. Putnam's Sons.

JOSEPH CONRAD. Detail from "Istana from the Slanting Bridge, Sarawak," painting by Marianne North. From a cover of *Almayer's Folly,* by Joseph Conrad. Penguin Books, 1976. Reproduced by permission of the Director of the Royal Botanic Gardens, Kew. / Detail from "The Congo," painting by Fritz Klingelhofer. From a cover of *The Heart of Darkness,* by Joseph Conrad. J. M. Dent, 1996. Reproduced by permission of Christie's Images, London. / Brando, Marlon, and Martin Sheen in the film *Apocalypse Now,* photograph. Archive Photos, Inc. Reproduced by permission. / Conrad, Joseph, photograph. Archive Photos, Inc. Reproduced by permission.

CARL DEUKER. Cover of *On the Devil's Court,* by Carl Deuker. Avon Flare Books, 1991. Reproduced by permission. / Cover of *Heart of a Champion,* by Carl Deuker. Avon Flare Books, 1994. Reproduced by permission. / deBarros, Jim, illustrator. From a jacket of *Painting the Black,* by Carl Deuker. Houghton Mifflin, 1997. Jacket art © 1997 by Jim deBarros. Reproduced by permission of the illustrator. / Deuker, Carl (with Marian Mitchell Deuker), photograph by Anne Mitchell. Courtesy of Houghton Mifflin Company.

NANCY FARMER. Farmer, Nancy, photograph. Reproduced by permission of Nancy Farmer.

IAN FLEMING. Blumrich, Christoph, illustrator. From a jacket of *Diamonds Are Forever,* by Ian Fleming. MJF Books, 1994. Reproduced by permission of Fine Communications. / Blumrich, Christoph, illustrator. From a jacket of *Live and Let Die,* by Ian Fleming. MJF Books, 1994. Reproduced by permission of Fine Communications. / Blumrich, Christoph, illustrator. From a jacket of *Moonraker,* by Ian Fleming. MJF Books, 1994. Reproduced by permission of Fine Communications. / Connery, Sean, with Shirley Eaton in a scene from *Goldfinger,* photograph. Archive Photos, Inc. Reproduced by permission. / Dalton, Timothy, holding gun in a scene from *License to Kill,* photograph. Archive Photos, Inc. Reproduced by permission. / Moore, Roger, with Richard Kiel in a scene from *The Spy Who Loved Me,* photograph. Archive Photos, Inc. Reproduced by permission. / Fleming, Ian, photograph. © Jerry Bauer. Reproduced by permission.

GRAHAM SALISBURY. Cover of *Blue Skin of the Sea,* by Graham Salisbury. Delacorte Press, 1994. Reproduced by permission of Bantam Doubleday Dell Books for Young Readers. / Sano, Kazu, illustrator. From a cover of *Under the Blood-Red Sun,* by Graham Salisbury. Dell Books, 1995. Reproduced by permission of Bantam Doubleday Dell Books for Young Readers. / Lieder, Rick, illustrator. From a jacket of *Shark Bait,* by Graham Salisbury. Delacorte Press, 1997. Jacket illustration © 1997 by Rick Lieder. All rights reserved. Reproduced by permission of Delacorte Press, a division of Bantam Doubleday Dell Publishing Group, Inc. / Salisbury, Graham, photograph. Reproduced by permission of Graham Salisbury.

BARRY SONNENFELD. Huston, Angelica with Raul Julia in a scene from *Addams Family Values,* photograph. Archive Photos, Inc. Reproduced by permission. / Travolta, John, with Rene Russo in a table scene from *Get Shorty,* photograph. Archive Photos, Inc. Reproduced by permission. / Smith, Will with Tommy Lee Jones in a scene from *Men in Black,* photograph. Archive Photos, Inc. Reproduced by permission. / Finney, Albert with Gabriel Byrne in a scene from *Miller's Crossing,* photograph. Archive Photos, Inc. Reproduced by permission. / Sonnenfeld, Barry, photograph. Archive Photos, Inc. Reproduced by permission.

SUZANNE FISHER STAPLES. Lee, Paul, illustrator. From a jacket of *Dangerous Skies,* by Suzanne Fisher Staples. Frances Foster Books, 1996. Copyright © 1996 by Suzanne Fisher Staples. Jacket art © 1996 by Paul Lee. All rights reserved. Reproduced by permission of Farrar, Straus & Giroux, Inc. / Staples, Suzanne Fisher, photograph. Reproduced by permission of Suzanne Fisher Staples.

JOYCE SWEENEY. Kaufman, Stuart, illustrator. From a jacket of *The Dream Collector,* by Joyce Sweeney. Delacorte Press, 1989. Copyright © 1989 by Joyce Sweeney. Jacket illustration copyright © 1989 by Stuart Kaufman. All rights reserved. Reproduced by permission of Delacorte Press, a division of Bantam Doubleday Dell Publishing Group, Inc. / Cover of *Piano Man,* by Joyce Sweeney. Laurel Leaf Books, 1994. Reproduced by permission of Bantam Doubleday Dell Books for Young Readers. / Cover of *Shadow,* by Joyce Sweeney. Laurel-Leaf Books, 1996. Reproduced by permission of Bantam Doubleday Dell Books for Young Readers. / Ducak, Danilo, illustrator. From a cover of *Free Fall,* by Joyce Sweeney. Laurel-Leaf Books, 1997. Cover illustration copyright © 1996 by Danilo Ducak. All rights reserved. Reproduced by permission of Bantam Doubleday Dell Books for Young Readers. / Sweeney, Joyce, photograph. Reproduced by permission of Joyce Sweeney.

LAURA INGALLS WILDER. Williams, Garth, illustrator. From a cover of *The First Four Years,* by Laura Ingalls Wilder. Harper Trophy Books, 1971. Illustrations copyright © 1970 by Garth Williams. All rights reserved. Reproduced by permission of HarperCollins Publishers, Inc. / Williams, Garth, illustrator. From an illustration in *Little House on the Prairie,* by Laura Ingalls Wilder. Harper Trophy Books, 1971. Pictures copyright 1953 by Garth Williams. Copyright © renewed 1981 by Garth Williams. All rights reserved. Reproduced by permission of HarperCollins Publishers, Inc. / Williams, Garth, illustrator. From a cover of *These Happy Golden Years,* by Laura Ingalls Wilder. Harper Trophy Books, 1971. Illustrations copyright 1953 by Garth Williams. Copyright © renewed 1981 by Garth Williams. All rights reserved. Reproduced by permission of HarperCollins Publishers, Inc.

VIRGINIA EUWER WOLFF. Nones, Eric Jon, illustrator. From a jacket of *Probably Still Nick Swansen,* by Virginia Euwer Wolff. Henry Holt and Company, Inc., 1988. Jacket illustration copyright © 1988 by Eric Jon Nones. / Crawford, Denise, illustrator. From a cover of *Make Lemonade,* by Virginia Euwer Wolff. Scholastic Inc., 1994. Cover illustration copyright © 1994 by Scholastic Inc. Reproduced by permission. / Wolff, Virginia Euwer, photograph. Reproduced by permission of Curtis Brown, Ltd.

Cumulative Index

Author/Artist Index

The following index gives the number of the volume in which an author/artist's biographical sketch appears.